THE DESIRE AND PURSUIT
OF THE WHOLE

THE
DESIRE
AND
PURSUIT
OF THE
WHOLE

A Romance of Modern Venice

BY

FREDERICK ROLFE
BARON CORVO

Author of 'Hadrian the Seventh'

With an Introduction by
A. J. A. SYMONS
and
Foreword by
W. H. AUDEN

GREENWOOD PRESS, PUBLISHERS
WESTPORT, CONNECTICUT

Library of Congress Cataloging in Publication Data

Rolfe, Frederick William, 1860-1913.
  The desire and pursuit of the whole.

  Reprint of the ed. published in New York as a New
Directions book.
  I. Title.
[PZ3.R644De 1977] [PR5236.R27] 823'.8   77-10836
ISBN 0-8371-9808-9

Copyright 1953 by New Directions

Originally published in 1953 by New Directions, New York

Reprinted with the permission of New Directions Publishing
Corporation

Reprinted in 1977 by Greenwood Press, Inc.

Library of Congress Catalog Card Number 77-10836

ISBN 0-8371-9808-9

Printed in the United States of America

FOREWORD

by W. H. AUDEN

A GIFT for literary expression can embarrass its owner for it is always revealing his nature to others without his consent or even his knowledge. Banalities and platitudes are effective masks which can be worn by any face and it is impossible to guess the character of the wearer through them; but a genuine style, however 'artificial' or 'impersonal', however intended to conceal, is the creation of the unique face behind it and its 'unlikeness' to the latter is never arbitrary. *The Desire and Pursuit of the Whole* is as striking a proof of this as I know. In writing it, Rolfe certainly expected that his readers would see life as Crabbe sees it, that they would take his side, agree that he was the innocent genius victim of a gang of malicious boobies, 'bullocks stamping on the fallen', and share his indignation. Thanks to Rolfe's remarkable talent, however, the reader has the very different and, for him, much more interesting experience of knowing that he is looking at the world through the eyes of a homosexual paranoid: indeed, so brilliantly does the author draw his own portrait that one is more likely to be unjust to him and dismiss all his grievances as imaginary which, in one instance at least, the behaviour of Bonsen (Benson), was not the case.

I would strongly advise anyone who has not read A. J. A. Symons' fascinating biography *The Quest For Corvo* to postpone that pleasure until he has read both of Rolfe's fictionalised autobiographies, *Hadrian the Seventh* and this book. He will then be surprised, I think, when he comes to the historical facts, to discover how much he has already inferred from the literary fictions.

The Desire and Pursuit of The Whole interweaves a nightmare and a day-dream. The figures in the nightmare really existed in Venice or England but appear distorted into sinister shapes by Crabbe's rage and suspicion: Zildo never was on land or sea but is as accurate, as 'realistic' a revelation as one could find anywhere of what, in all its enormity, every human ego secretly demands of life. One of the triumphs of the book, one which Rolfe certainly did not consciously intend, is that, though Zildo and the 'enemies' never meet, the relation between the two worlds is made so clear: a person who surrenders himself so completely to such a day-dream without acknowledging its absurdity is bound to make his daily life in the world a nightmare.

I cannot agree with Mr. Symons that the Zildo story is 'exquisite' and 'romantic'; to me it is quite terrifying. Crabbe begins by telling us, blandly, that for a long time he could not make up his mind whether his Other Half was a person or a position, a statement which is surely as brutal as anything in Rochefoucauld. Granted that Half-Two is a person, what properties must 'It' possess? Well, physically, of course, It must be a seventeen-year-old boy because that is Crabbe's physical type; but a boy, unfortunately, is not capable of an absolute and life-long devotion to a middle-aged man with no money, a boy will grow up and become hirsute and coarse-featured and, furthermore, neither Church nor State will permit you to marry one; consequently, Zildo, the boy, is declared Zilda, the girl, by fiat: It throws snowballs overarm but knows when to stop because Half-One is getting bored. It must be a poor orphan because it must owe its life, livelihood and education to Half-One; but, since It must be worthy of such a union, It must be descended from a Doge. Lastly, It must be, like the Miltonic Eve, a servant but by choice not fate, finding in the service of Its master Its 'perfect freedom'.

The characteristics of this day-dream which are abnormal and peculiar to Crabbe should not conceal its generic likeness to the reader's; on the contrary, they should help to prevent the latter from thinking of his own as 'romantic'.

A paranoid goes through life with the assumption: 'I am so extraordinary a person that others are bound to treat me as a unique end, never as a means'. Accordingly, when others treat him as a means or are just indifferent, he cannot believe this and has to interpret their conduct as malignant; they are treating him as an end, but in a negative way; they are trying to destroy him.

The 'normal' person knows that, as a matter of fact, in most of our relations most of the time, we are doing no more than make use of each other, as a rule with mutual consent, as a means to pleasure, intellectual stimulus, etc., but keeps up the convention, both with himself and others, that we love and are loved for 'ourselves alone', a fiction which is probably wise for, not only would social life be unbearable without it, but also the possibilities of genuine agape which, rare and delicate as they may be, do exist, would wither without its protective encouragement.

But it is a salutary experience also that, every now and then, we should have it stripped from us and that is what the paranoid does.

His inordinate demand that we love him very much and his accusation when we do not that we hate him very much compel us to realise that we very rarely love or hate anybody; on the contrary, we can only stand each other in small doses without getting bored. The paranoid is the epitome of the bore. Crabbe was mistaken in thinking that the British colony in Venice hated him, but he was quite correct in thinking that they would be highly relieved to hear that he was dead.

Any paranoid is a nuisance, but a penniless one is a torment. The average person, if he has enough money in his pockets to be comfortable, will feel an obligation to help an acquaintance in a financial jam such as being unable to pay a hotel bill, but he hopes that will be the end of the matter and he certainly does not expect it to be taken too personally. Personally, however, is just how the paranoid takes it; he will never leave a benefactor alone because, to him, the important thing is not his hotel bill but the interest another has shown in him by paying it; consequently, he will soon create another crisis as a test and continue until the wretched benefactor can bear no more and the inevitable explosion occurs.

Anyone who has had personal experience of a paranoid, will sympathise with the Thiasarkh's final remark to Crabbe when, out of sheer despair, he reveals himself as a Pharisee:

'Oooh, my dear person, what are you going to do?'
'Leave, when you leave. I suppose you won't be long'.
'But—look at the rain. Where will you go?'
'I haven't quite made up my mind'.

The Warden emitted a noise like 'Oooooeughph', which was a sort of mixture of a snarl and a growl and a screech strangulated in twisted guts.

'Dear me!' said Crabbe, eyeing him fastidiously.

'Of course, you know, I'm not really bound to help you, seeing that you're not a co-religionist', screamed the infuriated self-condemner.

'Comfort yourself, o blessed of God, with that beautiful thought', said Crabbe—and went out.

Rolfe-Crabbe had every right to be proud of his verbal claws. Like most suspicious people, he had a sharp eye; more than most he knew how to describe what he saw. For instance, the 'blubber-lipped Professor of Greek with a voice like a strangled Punch' happens to be a friend of mine and I can vouch for the remarkable accuracy, within its unkind limits, of the description. A large vocabulary is essential to the invective style, and Rolfe by study and constant practice became one of the great masters of vituperation; when he uses a rare word or a neologism such as 'banausic' or 'bestemmiating' it is never out of place, and he is equally at home in ornate abuse.

> Some coarse, raucous, short-legged hockey—or hunting—female hideous in hairy felt-some bulgy kallipyg with swung skirts and cardboard waist and glass-balled hatpins and fat open-work stockings and isosceles shoes—some pink-nosed and round-eyed and frisky, as inane and selfish and snappy-mannered as a lapdog—some leek-shaped latest thing, heaving herself up from long tight lambrequins to her own bursting bosom and bonneted with a hearse-plumed jungle-crowned bath;

and in the plainest of 'plain-speaking'.

> As for your letter, let me congratulate you (from a literary point of view) on having produced a masterpiece of hypocrisy. Thank you very much, but I firmly refuse to oblige by going and dying on someone else's doorstep, even with my clothes washed. You don't seem to understand that I take a fierce (but purely academic) interest in you, for I really did not believe that such dreadful people existed outside Ouida's *Friendship* and *In a Winter City*. Erastians one knows, metoikoi one has heard of, but what the devil you are will be my pleasing pastime to determine. And, as perhaps it will suit you (as well as me) if I make the breach between us as inviable as possible, kindly note that you are prohibited from mentioning my name or work in the preface of your book. I'm going to choose my company, for future; and I don't choose to appear in connection with a character like yours.

Safely inside a novel, such letters are fun to read—if the series to Caliban are a bit wearisome to us, it is because The Order of Sanctissima Sophia is not the sort of private world that is now in fashion—but in real life it is said that the recipients trembled when they saw an envelope or 'a severe postcard' addressed in Rolfe's handwriting.

If there were nothing in *The Desire and Pursuit of The Whole* but Rolfe's nightmare and his daydream, it might be too depressing to read except as a clinical study; luckily there is a third story behind both which is a real love story, the story of Rolfe's love for Venice. Just when we are beginning to think that we cannot take any more clapper-clawing and megalomania, Crabbe suddenly notices where he is and becomes quiet, self-forgetful, truthful and happy.

> He slowly paced along cypress-avenues, between the graves

of little children with blue or white standards and the graves of
adults marked by more sombre memorials.   All around him
were patricians bringing sheaves of painted candles and gorgeous
garlands of orchids and everlastings, or plebeians on their knees
grubbing up weeds and tracing pathetic designs with cheap
chrysanthemums and farthing night-lights.   Here, were a
baker's boy and a telegraph messenger, repainting their father's
grave-post with a tin of black and a bottle of gold.   There,
were half a dozen ribald venal dishonest licentious young
gondolieri, quiet and alone on their wicked knees round the
grave of a comrade.

Rolfe arrived in Venice in the summer of 1908 and never left it
again till his death in October, 1913.   The only money he earned
during those five years was an odd guinea here and there from a
magazine; his friends in England were willing to help if he returned
but he absolutely refused to budge; he would sponge, he would
starve, but he would not leave Venice.

Whatever else about him was distorted or sham, his passion for the
city was genuine.   Sex had something, no doubt, to do with it.
After years of chastity—if Crabbe's vow is autobiographical, as it
very well may be—Rolfe let go with a vengeance and was leading a
life which he could neither have dared nor afforded to lead in
England.   But this was not the only nor, I think, the most important
attraction.   Venice was for him The Great Good Place, a city built
by strong and passionate men in the image of their mother, the
perfect embodiment of everything he most craved and admired,
beauty, tradition, grace and ease.

As we read the extraordinary and magnificent twenty-fifth and
twenty-sixth chapters of this book, in which Crabbe, friendless,
homeless, penniless, delirious for lack of food, wanders day and night
through the streets, we cease to laugh at or pity him and begin to
admire.   Faced with the choice of going home or dying in the place
that he loves, he will choose to die, and behind all his suffering there
is a note of exaltation.   Like his author, Crabbe is more than a little
crazy, more than a bit of a scoundrel, and a most dreadful nuisance,
but he is neither a wet-leg nor ignoble.

INTRODUCTION

THE extraordinary Romance that follows is the last work of an even more extraordinary man. Elsewhere [1] I have told as much as is known of the life of the fantastic, talented, distorted 'Fr. Rolfe.' Those who have read my biography know already how *The Desire and Pursuit of the Whole* came to be written; for those who have not, an outline of Rolfe's life, and a few clues to his character, are essential to an understanding of the present book.

No detailed record of Frederick William Rolfe's childhood life is available, but it is known that after being sent to a sound school in Camden Town at the usual age, his schooldays were cut short by his waywardness and discontent. Young Rolfe left home in 1875, being then fifteen, and succeeded in earning his living as a schoolmaster for ten difficult years, which brought him a deep but narrow knowledge of life and literature. The religious principles of his family had been in the narrowest form of Protestantism, but suddenly, in a day, Rolfe became a convert to the Roman Catholic faith, and, a year later, offered himself as a candidate for priesthood. He was then twenty-five.

Both this and a later attempt to secure ordination were, however, unsuccessful. Already the eccentricity of his temperament had made itself seen by the fantastic quality of his artistic bent. His superiors could discern little sanctity in the queer student who painted a picture of St William of Norwich in which the hundred and forty-nine bearers of the sacred body, and even the saint himself, were marked as self-portraits by sharing the Rolfian nose. But to be a priest became the abiding dream of this unprosperous son of a prim Anglican piano-maker. Throughout his stormy life the fashion of his dress suggested holy orders; sometimes he even referred to himself as a priest; and he contracted his first name 'Frederick' to 'Fr.' in the hope that it might be read as 'Father.'

The reason for this persistence is not difficult to trace. Rolfe felt himself not as other men; he was repelled by women; and he strove to gain admittance to the ranks of those who by the condition of

[1] *The Quest for Corvo: an Experiment in Biography.* Penguin Books.

their calling are necessarily celibate. His failure threw him back into the world of ordinary men, and left him a conscious misfit. To console himself he adopted the style of 'Baron Corvo,' but though the title brought him the attention of some who might otherwise have ignored the unsuccessful candidate for priesthood (now turned painter) it was not a source of income.

For six years 'Corvo' was driven by fate from pillar to post, and his life of bizarre misadventure has probably no equal among those of modern authors. He claimed to have invented a new instrument for submarine photography, and to have discovered a process by which photographs could be reproduced in natural colours, but he failed to find finance for them, and was reduced to accepting a pittance as a photographer's 'learner.' He designed furniture, acted as special correspondent, reverted to the thankless task of tutor, and painted a set of banners for Holywell shrine. But throughout all these occupations he remained penniless and on the verge of starvation: in Scotland he suffered ignominious ejection in pyjamas from his lodgings, in Wales he sought the refuge of the workhouse. And then, suddenly, he won minor fame as the author of half a dozen stories published in the *Yellow Book*. Henry Harland, Kenneth Grahame, John Lane and others applauded and encouraged the would-be priest into the paths of literature. He returned to start a new career in London at the age of thirty-seven.

Ten years of desultory suffering followed upon Rolfe's adoption of literature as a profession. His work was widely applauded, but brought him little money; for not only circumstances, but his own nature, fought against him. The rejection of his clerical ambitions, and his consciousness of being a man apart, had combined to produce a chronic sense of persecution and injustice which made him bitterly suspicious of all men, and resentfully ungrateful to those who befriended him. Henry Harland, Trevor Haddon, Sholto Douglas and a dozen others who put themselves out to assist the struggling author found themselves, after a time, treated as enemies instead of friends, for, like those credulous believers who see an omen in every chance event, Rolfe saw the hand of an enemy in every misfortune, and where he saw an enemy, he struck. He wasted time and temper in unnecessary quarrels, and began to be shunned as a malevolent ingrate.

Yet during that decade of his London career he wrote some remarkable books, only now beginning to find their mead of praise and appreciation: *Chronicles of the House of Borgia*, an historical study shot with tart epigrams and curious knowledge; *Don Tarquinio*, an account of twenty-four hours in the life of a young nobleman in the company of the Borgia, A.D. 1495; *In His Own Image*, described as 'the most amazing, fantastical, whimsical, bizarre, erratic and hare-brained of books'; a translation of Omar into 'diaphotick verse'; and, above all, *Hadrian the Seventh*. Elsewhere I have paid full tribute to Rolfe's masterpiece, one of the most remarkable books in the English language. Those who have not read it are fortunate, in that their first reading is still to come. It is autobiography dramatized, and portrays 'Fr. Rolfe's' early life as he wished it to be remembered, and his future years as he would have liked them to be. *Hadrian* was too excellent to be disregarded; it was, indeed, widely praised, but brought no money to its harassed writer, who retired to Oxford to act as secretary to the one friend with whom he never quarrelled, Dr Hardy, the late principal of Jesus College, Oxford.

It was at this point in Rolfe's life (1905, 1906) that he began the friendships with Mgr. Robert Hugh Benson and Mr C. H. C. Pirie-Gordon, which led to his last work, the present book. Collaborations in literary projects were started with both the new-found friends, but, like all Rolfe's friendships, these were not made to last; and the break came when 'Fr. Rolfe,' after being taken by another friend to Italy for a month's holiday, fell so much in love with Venice and Venetian life that he flatly refused to return to England. Instead, he settled down in a Venetian hotel, ignored his mounting bill, and appealed for help to his friends at home. Help was offered on condition that he returned to England, a condition with which he flatly refused to comply. His letters became more frequent and more abusive, till at last they were destroyed unopened by Benson. Even his relations with his solicitors, whom he had persuaded into making him an allowance pending the decision of a lawsuit and the expected success of one of his books, came to an end in a shower of comically bitter correspondence, and Rolfe was left penniless in Venice.

After a time he was turned out of his hotel; later he managed to secure fresh credit; later still he was turned out again. He became a byword among the English residents, both for his ingratitude, his poverty, and a suspicion of his perversion. In 1910 he was admitted to the British Infirmary, suffering from pneumonia induced by exposure. But it was not till three years later that, retiring to bed after dinner, he was struck by death while removing his boots.

The Desire and Pursuit of the Whole is Rolfe's own account of his last years, and his revenge against the friends who, in his view, should have done more to help him. The most notable, the Rev. Bobugo

Bonsen, and C. H. C. Peary-Buthlaw, are obviously taken from Mgr. Benson and Mr Pirie-Gordon. As to his quarrel with Benson, the story is too long to be retold here; undoubtedly there were faults on both sides. In his quarrel with Mr Pirie-Gordon, who is happily still alive, Rolfe reached his highest point of sheer ingratitude. For more than a year he had lived entirely at the expense of the Pirie-Gordons'; it was due to their introduction that he was given the holiday in Venice; they had made much of him in a hundred ways, and given him affection as well as financial help; and when they refused to support Rolfe in Italy their reward was to be denounced to themselves and to their county neighbours in a series of vitriolic though highly entertaining letters, and to be caricatured in *The Desire and Pursuit of the Whole*.

The Desire and Pursuit was written with extreme care. There are in existence four manuscripts, each showing variations of text, each rejoicing in the elaborate caligraphy that was Fr. Rolfe's pride and hobby. Rolfe is, of course, identifiable with his own hero Nicholas Crabbe, and the method of the book is to submit Crabbe to the adventures and misfortunes of his creator (to the point of including actual and paraphrased correspondence) while superimposing these extracts from reality upon a charming imaginary love-affair with a hero-heroine of anomalous sex. Such a method, though it shows the completeness of Rolfe's self-dramatization, could hardly be expected to produce a perfect work of art; and it has not. *The Desire and Pursuit* is an incongruous compound of an exquisite, romantic dream-tale with undramatic and sordid details from Rolfe's life. And it is these actual details from life that seem improbable and out of place in the book. Rolfe's artistry conveys conviction when he narrates the adventures of Crabbe in his boat during the earthquake, and the discovery of Zildo, which are pure inventions; but the letters exchanged between the youthful Lieutenant of the Order of Sanctissima Sophia and the angry Nicholas, which are true, seem flimsy and exaggerated travesties. Nevertheless, when all that can be urged against *The Desire and Pursuit* has been weighed, it remains an admirable and astonishing book, a characteristic product of its author's genius, full of his unflagging zest for life and phrases, with hundreds of memorable and beautiful passages and sentences—as in the sage remark that 'Only beggars can be choosers,' or the Rochefoucauld-like severity of 'his closest friend or enemy—they are much the same in the long run,' or such descriptions as 'the rain streamed down in frigid lances.' There are not many writers who can say better things. Those who think otherwise are advised to try.

And Rolfe's punctuation is beautiful throughout. It was characteristic that he should take pains with his commas and semi-colons, as he did with the shape of his letters when he wrote. In many ways, indeed, the essential Rolfe reveals himself in the pages following; in his observations on enemies (p. 236, 'It never occurs to most people that a quarrel makes the other party much more interesting'); in his attitude to the boyish beauty of his heroine; in the cruel strain shown in his final treatment of the sot Butler; in his cold curiosity concerning the earthquake-horrors; in the attempt, so fitting in a man of the 'Nineties, to find an exact equivalent in words for Zildo's complexion; in his description of his attitude to women (p. 13); in the esteem that he sets on good looks; in his constant feeling for the changing Venice. And these instances could easily be multiplied. Most characteristic of all is his unquestioning assumption that his estate *must* yield a revenue which will easily produce 'a couple of hundreds sterling' (p. 172). If it won't produce 'so paltry a sum,' why then it must be mismanaged—'put it in the hands of someone else.'

Rolfe wrote this *Romance of Modern Venice* mainly in 1909, during the time that he was living as the guest of the late Dr van Someren at the Palazzo Mocenigo. For a time he was careful not to permit his hosts to see the work on which he was engaged, but in an unlucky moment for himself in the end he was moved by natural author's vanity to satisfy Mrs van Someren's equally natural curiosity. As the astonished lady turned the pages she recognized friend after friend—for even the minor characters, or most of them, are drawn from life. Naturally it was impossible for the intimate of Lady Layard, Horatio Brown, and the rest of the English colony to encourage this lampooning of most of her acquaintances. 'Fr. Rolfe' was given the alternatives of discontinuing his book, or leaving the house. Without an hour's hesitation he chose the latter course, and walked out into the streets. It was early March and bitterly cold. A month later he collapsed, and was taken to that Infirmary he had so bitterly attacked. He was given the Last Sacraments, but recovered—and finished *The Desire and Pursuit of the Whole.*

The Desire and Pursuit of the Whole, like all Rolfe's books, was written by a man who was nearly starving. That in itself is not a recommendation ; starving men may write good books or bad ones. But at least there is likely to be fire and feeling in what they write, and this book is no exception. It shows the intense passion of Rolfe's defeated but indomitable soul, his zest for life, his love of words and learning, his paranoia, and the twists and crannies of his strange mind, with the reflected exactness of a spiritual mirror.

Rolfe can have had little hope that his book would be published during his lifetime; it would have given ground for too many suits for libel: even in the present version drastic changes have been necessary in the presentment of one character. After Rolfe's death it was read by Horatio Brown on behalf of an unpaid creditor, and pronounced unpublishable; as, at that time, it undoubtedly was. The manuscripts were sent to England, to the Anglican clergyman who had befriended the Catholic outcast during the last years of his life, and locked away in a loft until, twelve years later, my own interest in Frederick William Rolfe set me rummaging for his remains. I hope that others may be found who will share my enthusiasm for this treasure trove.

THE DESIRE AND PURSUIT
OF THE WHOLE

In the *Symposion* of Plato, 193, you will find these words :—

'*Tou holou oun tei epithumiai kai dioxei eros onoma* ' :

THE DESIRE AND PURSUIT OF THE WHOLE IS CALLED LOVE.

The text chosen, o most affable reader, on which to hang these ana of Nicholas and Gilda for your admiration, will require such a lot of expounding that we must get at the heart of explanations (as to how it all happened) without undue delay. It is not my fault, I assure you, that things occurred in the order in which they did occur. I am not the regulator of this universe. If a conclusive series of events and energies is designed, whereby a man and a maid are brought together, demurrers against the said design need not be addressed to me: I am merely the recorder. I personally am not so very sure that there was a definite design for bringing this particular maid to this singular man. A certain deftness, which I notice about things in general, causes me shrewdly to imagine that this business might have been done without devastating a pair of provinces and massacring a couple of hundred thousand Christians. So, I do not propose to inquire into reasons, which neither I nor anyone else can possibly understand. I shall not attempt to account for coincidences, or to say why these things happened as they did happen. My job is simply to write down the bare facts concerning my friends Nicholas and Gilda as they were told by them to me. If the result seems to be unusually categorical, that (of course) is my fault as a bad story-teller; and I don't refuse to bear the blame of it. All I have to say is this, o most affable reader. These amazing events came about as I shew. As for me, I find them amusing, terrific, but witty. You may be blessed with a taste like to mine: or you mayn't.

Nicholas Crabbe, being bored (to the extent of a desire to do something violent) by the alternate screams and snarls of a Professor of Greek (with the voice of a half-strangled Punch) who had let him down, departed from Venice at the end of November. He went alone in his topo of six tons burden; and sailed southward along the Italian coast, with no idea in his head excepting that of thoroughly enjoying his own society and avoiding every kind of conversation with other human beings. He detested the whole lot of them, just then.

A topo is a bark belonging to one of the many kinds of clumsy-looking highly capable craft builded by the squeraiuoli of Ciozza or Castello for use on the lagoon and the vicinal Adriatic. It is a sturdy deep-bosomed flat-bottomed blunt-nosed thing, fitted with a great rudder curiously curved under the stern, which (in the hands of an adept) answers the purpose of keel combined with steering-gear, when one desires to speed the sail rather than to row standing in the mode Venetian. Nicholas Crabbe's (needless to say) had been made specially for him. He never did have the same sort of things as other people, but invariably individualistically revised versions. The outside of his bark was heavily pitched, like that of all topi: but the inside was neatly finished by a cabinet-maker after the squeraiuol had done his part; and the plain massive well-chiselled oak looked (and was) perennially sweet and clean beneath half a dozen glittering coats of good copal varnish. She carried a single sail aft, rather smaller than ordinary; and an original arrangement of cords and winches and pulleys enabled Nicholas to set or to put it without leaving the rudder. He called her *Selene,* the moon being his ruling planet. The ordinary topo is a vessel of carriage, decked only fore and aft: but, in Crabbe's, a low oblong cabin, wind-and-water-tight, had been constructed amidships. It contained a most comfortable couch formed of four kapok mattresses, and a small stove whose iron chimney projected through the roof in a knot which prevented the return of smoke or gases. There was a shelf full of books along the roof, and a chest of clothes and a chest of other things balancing the bed. There was also a roomy store-cupboard under the fore-deck for food and a cask each of fresh water and good old chianti. The space between it and the cabin was packed (under tarpaulin) with a stack of sweet wood for the stove. A second similar cupboard aft contained a tank of oil for the lanthorns, and a collection of miscellaneous necessaries.

It was rather a mad trick, to set out on a voyage like this, alone, so near the end of autumn, without any very particular sailor-man's knowledge—mad, that is to say, from the common point of view, the point of view of the profane vulgar who want hot water before breakfast, and tea-and-crumpet precisely three hours before dinner, and brown boots properly ronuked, and linen stiffly starched, and sock-suspenders meticulously aired. Crabbe's crabbed desires were otherwise. He was for fresh air, and open skies, and lovely loneliness. He wished (and intended himself) to breathe cleanly and freely, to hear no bestially blatant voices, to sleep, to think, all in the absolute liberty of wide horizons. And, notwithstanding the bitter biting blasts of autumn and winter on an inhospitable sea, he had his wish. A well-cut easy suit of blanket-overalls, worn under good English oilskins, kept him warm. Duplicates insured dryness. Half a dozen full-sized English blankets, sewn longways up the plain edges, provided a snug nest on the kapok mattresses down below; and, being open at both ends only, they neither stifled nor conduced to untucked misery. Water, coffee, and wine he boiled on the stove when he needed them: but chiefly he generated natural heat in his own rich blood by labouring at the long poop-oar, with every clever muscle working fully and joyously while his springing feet held and guided the rudder. Thus he passed the days. Generally, toward afternoon, he stayed at some small port. Never at any time more than a couple of miles from land, he contrived to go ashore as seldom as possible, and only to replenish his stores of water, wine, matches, tobacco, oil, meal for polenta, bread, eggs, Maggi soups, cheese, olives, beans, peas, raisins, nuts, oranges, fennel, dandelion, coffee, and salads. The whole coast-line of Italy (excepting, of course, the unexplored virgin beech-forests of Monte Gargano on the Adriatic) is girdled by the railway: which means that one is never out of touch with civilization, if one wishes (or is obliged) to touch the thing. Nicholas stopped only when he wished to stop, at such out-of-the-way places as Cervia and Giulianova and Vieste and Bisceglie and Gallipoli and Cariati and Gerace and Melito, catching a tame fisherboy at each place to be bribed to do his errands for him; and setting sail again, or rowing onward, to some lonely anchorage where he could spend moonless or inclement nights securely in solitude. He sat quite tight in harbours or roadsteads during tempests; not that he was very much afraid of them, or of anything, but simply because he was rather fed up with fighting and only sought to solace himself with a portion of peace. He had warred so long, and so bitterly.

Toward the end of December he rounded the Promontorio Erculeo, keeping his Christmas in the waste of waters—Christmas meant much to him, of the simplicity and the friendship and the love which the whole world totally denied to him, so he said, and not entirely without reason.

The weather was horrible: a gusty south wind blew, laden with the tepid stench of African enormities: rain poured incessantly. Nicholas had covered the whole topo with tarpaulin well laced down, making all snug below, a cosy nest for periods of anchorage. But he sat out, in his oilskins, at the rudder, with the sheet in his hand, letting the rain beat his face and wash all bitter ugly visions from his eyes.

On the evening of the twenty-seventh of December he sighted ancient Rhegium, Reggio di Calabria. His custom was to avoid large cities and their festering congeries of human beings, all with loves of their own, all with hates of their own, all with unintellectual indifference to and ignorance of him, his absence of love, his ravening appetite for it, his constant presence of odium. About eleven chilo-metres away, on the left and in front of him, was another large city, ancient Messana, Messina di Sicilia. He shunned both—shunned them as priests shun pestilence and the poor. With daylight, he would spread his sail and ply his heavy poop-oar, and get through the narrow channel as quickly as possible, emerging again into the open waters beyond Skylla and the Pharos. But, meanwhile, in the steady pouring rain and the warm gusts from southward, he anchored at a fair distance from the shore. It was not an ideally safe anchorage. Nineteen several lines of Italian steamships use that strait, to say nothing of the ships of other nations. But the season was winter, the weather was simply abominable, the current ran strongly from north to south, the wind came puffing from south to north; and Nicholas was bored and wet, and longèd for a spell below. He lighted hurricane-lanthorns at mast-head and prow and poop, after he had let down an anchor and had seen that the topo rode bravely on the swell. And then he blew up his fire; and stripped and dried himself; and refreshed his strength with food and wine and cigarettes and a decorated ode of Pindar about the Runner of Thessaly, before he nestled at length in his blankets ready for sleep. Sleep came with no wooing that night; and, on the soft warm breast of the dusky god, he attained thrice-blessed oblivion.

Like all great and singular men, Nicholas Crabbe maintained a familiar spirit. He called it his angel-guardian. [Please do not be a fool.] This being—(I intend to take for granted that Nicholas Crabbe knew as much, and very much more, about himself and his belongings as anyone else in this world; and he certainly never hesitated about connecting certain episodes of his career with this his angel-guardian)—this being, then, I say, habitually gave him warnings, so that crises never came upon him unawares, and not even his closest friend or enemy—(they are much the same in the long run)—ever was able to boast of having caught him napping.

He slept, rocked by the strongly-swelling sea, sanely and soundly till a little after half-past four in the morning. Then, suddenly, he became wide-awake and expectant, but of what he knew not precisely. He rolled and lighted another day's first cigarette; and peeped from the cabin-door.

The wind had dropped. The night was utterly dark and still. The rain streamed down in frigid lances. He stepped out, stark as he was; and climbed to trim the lanthorns, while the raging tears of pitiless heaven lashed his flesh, perhaps for two couples of minutes. Then he dived again into the cabin, and dried himself, and got into his blanket overalls and oilskins. He lighted the fire, and began to prepar his coffee,e intending to weigh anchor at dawn. And, yet once more, he peered, from the cabin-door, into the black, black profundity of night.

Suddenly, without further warning, four catastrophic phenomena of incredibly frightful violence tore his life in two.

The distant lights of Messina and of Reggio were blazing, through the rain-veil, on his left and on his right. Hundreds of thousands of shrieks of mortal agony pierced the black night like the yell of a Titan, and bored through his brain. His little clock struck five. He sprang out of the cabin, slamming its door behind him.

All the shore-lights in sight went out, as though blown by a gust. Silence heavily fell. He stood, alone, in impenetrable obscurity, waiting. The rain stopped, as though turned off at a tap. He counted his heart-beats.

Some enormous mouth beneath the whole world seemed to suck at him. He actually felt the being steadily sucked, with awful swiftness, down, down, down, down, all standing. In an instant he let go the anchor, and crouched, seizing the tiller, to keep her head to the current. He thought that his descent was never going to end. Ideas about Kharybdis flashed out of his memory. But, no: Kharybdis was at least ten chilometres in front of him. A blind man might have seen as much as he could see in the unpierceable darkness. Would he never reach the bottom of this green, dark, wall-less well in the world of ocean? No: never.

As awfully as he was sucked down, so, now, he began awfully to soar, spewed up (as it seemed) on the plane of a monstrous level billow. And a monstrous crashing of incalculably monstrous wreckage assailed his ears from all the distant shores which he knew to be on both sides of him.

Still, still, he ascended, evenly, with incredible celerity. All his nerves intensified as he clung to the rebellious rudder. Whatever was to happen, he prepared himself to meet it mindfully. The beating rain dashed down again in an icy sheet.

He was not only soaring. He knew that his prow pointed northward: but a breeze, from behind him, told him that a fearful current was sweeping him southward. Instantly, he reversed the rudder, to run back to where at least was the open sea which he knew.

Like unto oil, was the sea—the high sea, lifted high from its deepness. Never, no never before, had he sailed on a sea lifted so haughtily high as this sea, whose unfaltering billows rolled with velocity by, like high gods in pursuit.

II

WHEN white dawn crept up on his left, and he could trace the faint grey battlements of the Calabrian coast, he steered towards it: for he had a strange yearning to be near land. He set his sail, to catch such wind as there was in aid of the current. His brain hummed with the mysteries of the night; and every muscle and sinew ached with the force which he had spent on the tugging rudder. He had no curiosity to know details of what had happened. He says that his mind was informed that the nearest shores had been devastated, and that to him had been granted the privilege of witnessing some effects of seaquake and earthquake from a point just sufficiently secure—more than which he did not want to know. His plan, now, was to seek some lonely haven, and just to think things over, perhaps for hours, perhaps for weeks, perhaps for life. 'Do nothing,' he told himself, 'till you know precisely what and where and when and how you must do.'

Dawn greyed: the finger-like ranges of mountains, on the coast which he was nearing, displayed themselves in dull brown, greedily pointing at him through the driving rain. He looked for little white villages, which he had passed on the previous day: but none were visible. He steered nearer to the shore; and glided along at a good stone's throw from what in the dim light he took to be the observatory of Melito di Porto Salvo.

A few chilometres further on, his weariness became almost over-powering. He found a tiny cove, with a broken grove of olives lounging down a rocky ravine to the sea-shore; and, across the distorted railway-line, he thought that he could see the white gleam of a farm-house among the trees. Everything was as still as death, excepting the fierce patter of the rain. He got out his spare anchor; and moored in the middle of the cove, setting a barbed wire all round his gunwale for the discomfiture of chance intruders on his privacy.

After he had eaten, and smoked, and slept, it was after noon; and he was ready to move again—but not northward up the strait. No. That path would be crowded, not to say messy. Oh no. He would return to Venice now, quite slowly, with his mind easily digesting a hugely emotional experience; and then, some time in

February, he would read up all the facts in the files of the newspapers, and supplement knowledge thus gained with the pickings
of the brains of sailors to be met in the harbour of Marittima.

He had neither seen nor heard a single movement on the shore
since he came into the cove. It occurred to him that he might as
well take the opportunity of replenishing his water-cask, if he could
find a decent spring; and, no doubt, the people at the farm would
let him have some fresh eggs. He rowed inshore; and moored the
bark to her own oar stuck in the mud, as one does on the Venetian
lagoon.

The upward path through the wood (such as it was) was grossly
untidy. Trees and broken branches and split boulders littered it.
Gaunt black trunks, lamentably black-gleaming in the rain, were
torn and shivered: many were hideously uprooted. And, what he
had taken for the white walls of a house were the white walls of a
house thrown down and smashed to pieces. Horrible! He walked
up to the ruin. Had the place been inhabited? Where were the
inhabitants? There, was one.

A middle-aged man lay just round the first corner, with one end
of a slanting beam embedded in his hairy chest and the other leaning
on a tottering remnant of wall. Another beam lay sideways where
his neck should be, having switched off his head from his body.
The head reposed, at about a metre's distance, at beautiful white
peace in a puddle of rain and blood, with some pious oleographs.
Nicholas retched: but became violently interested. A great jagged
mound of broken bricks and stucco and splinters, variegated by
torn shawls and picture-frames and half a cheese, had human limbs
sticking out of its base. He inspected two right hands of babies,
four right legs of women splashed with polenta, and the upper half
of a thin boy with the eyelids closed as though by sleep, the left
arm and shoulder and breast torn sheer off, the extremities peeping
from a riot of pork-chop-bones and wood-ashes and tattered rags.
All the flesh was shredded in gobbets, as though it had been bitten
by beasts. Round another corner was an irregular stack of beams
and broken planks, piled up higgledy-piggledy amid heaps of dust
and the handles of saucepans. Emerging from an interstice of this
lumber was the whole length of a girl, excepting the head in a bundle
of shreds (once a chemise) which remained in the shadow of a gable
of beams. Nicholas took her by the feet, and dragged her gently
out, uncovering her head.

She was a strangely formed, very-well-grown child of about
sixteen years, straight-limbed, and strong, almost as sexless as a boy,

white as milk and honey with thick short light-brown hair flattened by rain. All her body was plastered with dust, which the pouring rain turned into mud and washed away. Her face was most strange, sexless, expressionless, unimpassioned, singularly ignorant and innocent, but fascinating—as fascinating as the slim magnificent body and limbs, with their splendidly muscular contours and pure but opulent colour. He appraised her inch by inch, the lithe sun-tanned feet and legs, the fine rich shoulder with a big blue bruise on it, the perfect flat cushion of the undeveloped white breast. Surely Nature had been interrupted when She made this creature, a grand broad-chested thin-flanked waistless boy by intention but a girl by defect. But—was she dead, like the others? A bruised shoulder does not slay. And she shewed no other wound. Nicholas laid his wet palm on her wet heart.

A moment later, his arms were round her knees, her head and arms were hanging over his shoulder, and he was stumbling downward through the wood to his topo. The floods of rain washed her, on the way, as clean as new ivory. The fragrance of her firm shining flesh was like that of early morning in a garden of wall-flowers and jasmine.

After another twenty minutes, wine and the warmth of the cabin revived her. Her eyes opened deliberately—large long eyes, childishly sweet yet wonderfully strong and wistful in expression, the irides greenish-blue with amber sparks in them, like the eyes of kittens or the waters of the Venetian lagoon, and seemingly set in the purest mother-o'-pearl. She looked up and round the cabin, lazily, seeing nothing, and, nestling again in the blankets, turned to sleep.

Nicholas watched and studied the strong resplendent pallor of her most intently. Now that her hair was dry, there was more gleam of yellow about it, but not a trace of shining gold or the warmth of copper. It was fine pale light hair, which grew thickly all over the nobly rounded skull, or cropped close at the back and top and sides like a boy's, with a waving ciuffo or tuft five or six inches long like a plume in front springing from and falling over the wide-arched white forehead down to the straightly planted serious long eyebrows. Nobly-chiselled also was the high-bridged ruthless delicate nose, with its dainty tip and close-winged sensitive nostrils curving artlessly to the short upper lip whose firm bow controlled the fulness of the lower. The bright coral mouth was a little open, the upper lip lifted and straight, the lower just drooping in the sweetest young dawn of a smile, giving glimpses of glittering magnificent teeth. Like all other features, her mouth was strong and long, but of splendid delicacy—capable of every passion, but unsullied, so innocent, so ignorant. Indeed, the whole face, grand in its perfect egg-like oval, down to the fine firm cheeks and jaw and chin, was ripe for devouring kisses: but never a kiss had brushed that flower-like bloom—never had those maidenly lips been offered, pressed, to another's. Of that he was certain. She lay at her length, straight, with her ankles lightly crossed, her body turned a little so that the cheek and the unbruised shoulder were hidden in the pillow. Her other arm was outside the blanket, displaying its bruise and part of her neck and breast. To just above the elbow this arm was sun-tanned to the glowing brown of honey. The palm of the hand turned upward: it was hardened like a Venetian's: it had the immensely-spaced thumb with the unmistakeable corn on its joint. But, above the tan, was the stainless softness of youth, the powerful shoulder, the muscular boyish breast, the supple moulded column of the throat. Her breath came deeply and easily.

Who was she? What was she? And what in the world was to be done with her? A sharp pang of annoyance stabbed Nicholas, as his own stupid situation flared before him.

He sat on the clothes-chest opposite, staring at the girl in his bed, and thinking forcibly. Anon, without noise, he rummaged under the lid of his seat, and produced a bath-gown, some black woollen socks, a new pair of brown leather slippers, a large black silk neck-square, and a couple of towels and pocket-handkerchiefs. He put every other loose thing in the cabin into the chests and locked them, leaving the garments lying invitingly on the lid. Then he quietly went out, closing the door behind him, and sat down upon the poop in the rain to smoke and continue his thinking.

He convicted himself of error in one particular, at least: He had been guilty of platitudinarianism in his mental description of his guest, comparing her with ivory and honey and milk and coral, pretty enough things in their place, but inanimate, and (therefore) unjustified here. To spatter with unjust epithets was, for a writer of his exacting taste, the sin unpardonable: for it signified that the user had let himself become too indolent for precise thinking. To what, then, should he liken her? Ivory, honey, milk, coral, forsooth! Where should he find a simile for the generous spread of her candour and softness and clarity and firmness and long strong vigorous pallor, for her naïve freshness and innocent unusedness, for her unstained stainableness? A simile must be found combining the tint with the texture of her, tint without texture or texture without tint being inconceivable.

She was like a flower. She was like a flower fragrant in vigorous serenity. She was like those marvellous Ghent-azaleas on the pleasaunce of Uskvale. In early summer, they offered huge tables of blossom quite comparable with her flesh, firm blossoming tables blooming with soft petals which could go black with decay on being touched or taken, soft pure petals flushing in the sun like the rich, sweet, wholesome flesh of a maid. And, there, having completed and closed a circle of thought, he stopped, satisfied. His simile approved itself just. He had started to find to what he might compare the tint and the texture of this maid. Memory brought him a flower, the flower of Ghent-azaleas. The perfect circle made him purr. And her form? The form of a noble boy, in all but sex. And her mind?

Who was she? What was she? Neither mattered an atom. What in the world was he to do with her? That mattered enormously.

Nicholas Crabbe, being Nicholas Crabbe, was as hard as adamant —outside. He tolerated the most fearful revilings, humiliations, losses, without turning a hair. He had none. Even his enemies (which means all the men and women with whom he ever had been intimate) freely admit (in their less excited moments) that nothing, at any time, ruffled his cruel and pitiless and altogether abominably self-possessed serenity of gait and carriage; and they account it to him for natural naughtiness. Of course they are imbecile idiots. What is to be expected of a man cased, cap-à-pie, like a crustacean, in hard armour of proof? Such a one has no means of exhibiting his feelings, excepting with his crookedly-curving, ferociously-snapping claws and (perhaps) with his bleak, rigid, glaring eyes. Crabbe was detested by people who habitually shewed their feelings. He couldn't shew his. He never shewed his real ones for that very reason. But boobies thought that he did—thought that his breakable but unbendable shell was his expression, a horrible expression because it gave no information whatever; and then, when (quite unexpectedly) the hitherto stilly-folded claws snatched and pinched and tore and tossed presumption, with a violence sudden and frightful which manifested some appalling sensibility hidden unsuspected within, the said boobies were gravely shocked or displeased and (when clerical) much pained or even deeply grieved. Pained, indeed! And what about the torments of Crabbe, which no one ever considered because no one ever saw them?

Have you, o most affable reader, ever dissected a crab? If not, pray do so at once, if possible, plunging him first into boiling water

to boil for five whole minutes and evitate unnecessary barbarity.
Lift the lid of his shell, and look inside. You will find it filled with
a substance like new cheese; and a magnifying-glass will shew you
that this is held together by a network ramification infinitely closer
and finer than spiders' webs. Under his shell, in fact, your crab is
as soft as butter, and just one labyrinthine mass of the most sensitive
of nerves. From which pleasing experiment you should learn to be
as merciful as God to all poor sinners born between the twenty-first
of June and the twenty-fourth of July: for they are born under
the constellation Cancer; and their nature is the nature of a crab.
They are the cleverest, tenderest, unhappiest, most dreadful of
all men.

Clever men and dreadful men and clever dreadful men are not
invariably unhappy: but crab-men are all three—excepting on a
sole condition. That condition is their union with a Saturnian, born
between the twentieth of December and the twenty-first of January,
who is their diametrical opposite and complement, soft outside,
hard within. Thus are things blended and balanced—at least, as far
as we know. For we know very little; and most of us are too
proud, and all of us are too hysterical, to sit down and work out a
really satisfying method of fitting together the parts of the puzzle
of life. People did make a beginning, once upon a time. Plato—
[I implore you, o most affable reader, not to be a fool]—Plato did
it. His ingenious theory was that, in the first beginning of all things,
the Father and King of gods and men created Man whole, 'totus
teres atque rotundus,' a whole smooth round man, complete in
himself and absolutely apt all ways, with two faces which looked
before and behind, and four arms which fought behind and before,
and four legs which went backward and forward, all at the bidding
of the one will: which whole round man, becoming very much
bucked by his own infinite potentiality, was misguided enough to
give himself airs and to get up and cough at the immortal gods,
making himself a most accented nuisance to those divine ones who
inhabit Olympian mansions: wherefore High Zeus, in ire, cut his
creature in half, leaving the trimming of the moieties to the tasty
fingers of Phoibos Apollon; and the healed halves he cast down, at
random, into the world, from the height of lofty Olympos, there
to wander to and fro while life should last, performing the punishment fitted to the crime of presumption. For, each half, being ware
of and ashamed of and ultimately discontented with its condition
of bisection, yearns most voraciously, and goes about most phrenetic-
ally, to seek and to be joined and knit to and intimately united to

and dissolved in its other half. Hence, says Plato, summing up his theory:

"The Desire and Pursuit of the Whole is called Love."

And, as far as I know (admitting freely, of course, that I don't know much), I really do think that Plato has touched the spot.

Nicholas Crabbe had forgotten as much Greek as any man of culture need know. He had read his Plato with the rest of us, and (like the rest of us) as an intellectual gymnastic, without receiving particular influence from Plato's now-obsolete notions. He certainly had no ideas about love, as that game is practised in decent society. The human female was to him a mysterious individual very much unlike himself. At the back of his mind, even when he bought her interest (and he never never had met one who had not her fixed price), he knew that she was something rather weak, rather tender, something to which it is a duty to be kind and helpful and attentive. On the whole, then, he treated the human female (meritorious or meretricious) on those lines. When, however, she laughed and talked and acted with him as an equal, he was by no means slow to caper along with her. And his frankness and simplicity and careless-ness and unsuspicious personality used to get him into the most awful trouble. That is the worst of the human female. She comes brazenly out; and jests and jousts with the male. He lets himself forget how strong he is. Suddenly, unknowingly, unintentionally, he hurts her. She runs back into her stronghold of feminality, and fills the circumambient air with howls. She is a martyr. He knows himself to be a foolish, much-wronged beast.

Such, in the main, had been Crabbe's relations with women. His natural bent was for treating them as goddesses in niches, with stately chivalry, and on his knees. He didn't in the least admire their physical beauty, as a rule. He looked upon them as he looked upon those very venerable black Madonnas who invariably work miracles. The form and ornament of them made him simply sick, ' usque ad nauseam,' by reason of its vapid bunchiness and vacuous inconsequent patchworkiness. You should have heard him on the pathetically anakolythose bonnets of spinsters and fashionable horse-faced dowagers. You should have observed his furious forbearance with the scraggy ladies of rectors, or with the tailor-made females who still hoped to allure a man with their motley mangy boas and hybrid hand-bags and clinking beads and heterogeneous high heels and foolish fat stockings and hard waists (o Aphrodite Anadyomene) and tabby hats like crumpled wrecks of flea-bitten birds' nests of felt plastered with the scratchings of rag-bags and gigantic withered old cauliflowers. But sometimes he did admire a young girl, at a distance, and only for her fresh wholesome youth, her lithe strength, her dainty adroitness. And, then, an appalling prevision of what she would have to hide, of what she was likely to become, made him wipe her from the mirror of his mind. He never had wanted one of these creatures for his very own. He never had tried to conceive himself irretrievably committed to the company of any one of them. Yet he knew that he was very far from being perfect in his loneliness. He used to gaze at other men, courting, marrying, living in apparent happiness; and he would wonder whether that was the right way. Anon he would distinguish a great gulf fixed between him and other men: they were content with so little, with what came to hand, with what they could get: he was not content with anything at all, the object of his desire and pursuit being simply the Unique and the signory of it.

He had tried friendship, with adolescents, with juniors, with seniors. Youths adored him for his strength, his wit, his extraordinary expertness, and left him for their own mates. Men of his own age, being human and entirely overwhelmed with the fulness and weight of the illimitable confidence which he generously lavished upon them, invariably took the most dastardly advantage of him, robbed him, wounded him, and departed, leaving him half-dead. Old men patronized him, or inspired him with pity and terror. Friendship was a failure, as it had been given him to try. People said that he asked too much of it. Certainly he did ask a lot. He asked for loyalty—the loyalty which demands and concedes no limit of self-sacrifice for the satisfaction of one's friend. He asked for honour—the honour which can quarrel freely for the sake of avoiding stagnation and as freely make peace for the sake of pleasurable repose: but never on any account will even listen to a single syllable from outsiders in one's friend's despite. And he asked for eternal, unflinching fidelity.

You see now, perhaps, what he was after? He was after his other (not his better) half. You behold him, a passionate pilgrim desiring and pursuing the whole. Pursuing? Yes—hastening slowly. Open wide was his heart, and extended his arms, and his breast bared, yearning with every fibre of body and soul, burning with eager desire to pursue, to attain, to unite with, melt, and dissolve in, the mate who should make, with him, One.

III

HE settled with himself that this unhandled slip of mulierity was not his, and that he had been rather silly in taking her. No one could have refused to give her such assistance as she needed: but, all the same, it would be right to get rid of her as soon as possible. The cure which he had proposed to himself for his soul's acidity had been three or four months' abstention from human society in favour of Mother Nature's. A companion of any other kind would interrupt this cure. And, a girl—o Lord! It was not a moral sense which caused him to refrain himself. He knew quite precisely how strong he was: he knew that he could live with his guest for as long as she pleased—that she could leave him at any moment, as she came to him. Why, he was even capable of living with her without so much as speaking a single word to her—he had done it frequently, for months together, with all sorts and conditions of persons, who (consequently) ascribed to him a genius for sulks. Also, he was absolutely careless as to what the world might say. People always did say the most awful things about him. He thoroughly enjoyed the very worst of reputations. Altogether abominable interpretations invariably were appended to his most innocent deeds; and, of course, sins and crimes, the very idea of committing which had never been submitted by his mind to his will, were habitually fathered upon him. His utter fearlessness, his utterly straightforward simplicity, his utterly boundless and blundering (but irresistible) audacity, never were understanded of his inferior fellow-creatures, who (in defect of intelligence) exercised their very nastiest imaginations and powers of invention.

The girl did not displease him. He did not covet her. Nor was he in the least uneasy about himself, or her, or anybody. But, nevertheless, he would send her away, because she was an interruption. And he would do it decently and kindly. Remark his selfishness (to say nothing of the other important factor in the problem which he totally omitted to consider), o most affable reader.

He climbed round the cabin, by the gunwale, over the wood-stack, to his store-cupboard at the peak; and got a litre of chianti, a few slabs of yesterday's polenta, and a large wedge of cheese, with some almonds and raisins. Returning to the poop, he made a gabled awning by drawing a flap of tarpaulin over the yard; and sat down under it to stay his appetite.

There was a little noise of movement in the cabin. After a while, the door opened; and the girl stood, looking gently straight into his eyes. She had put on the white bath-gown, tying the tasselled cords at throat and waist. On her head, she had twisted the black silk necksquare, knotting it on her nape as do the barcaiuoli of the lagoon. She had rejected the socks: but the brown slippers fitted her tanned feet. He noted how splendidly vivid her sweet flesh was in its white and black setting, how serene and slim and simple and brave was her poise, how utterly straight and artless her expression.

'Are you hungry?' he gravely asked.

'Sissior,' she answered, just as a Venetian would answer. Her voice had all the characteristics of her appearance, freshness, force, suppleness, with a most exquisitely full quiet vibrance. What (in the Name of Goodness) was she? He divided his food with her.

'Sior, prego,' she said, taking it into the cabin, where she sat on a chest by the open door in his view. She ate cleanly and heartily, not looking at him, as though unexercised by his proximity. When she had finished, she came to throw the crumbs from her lap carefully overboard; and leaned down to dip her fingers in the sea. Nicholas passed her the flask.

'Sior, prego,' she said again, taking it, and giving it a deft whisk with her wrist which sent the first few drops flying out of the ship. Then she stiffened, opening her pretty mouth and throat, holding the flask at a bent arm's length so that her lips did not touch it, and directing the stream of wine to wash her gullet. Nicholas watched the rhythmic swallowing in the throat as the liquid coursed down. She drank about a quarter of a litre. 'Grazie,' she simply said, returning the flask; and went back docilely to wait at the cabin-door.

'What do you call yourself?' Nicholas demanded.

'Falier Ermenegilda fu Bastian di Marin di Bastian di Marin.'

'Why are you here?'

'Mi no so miga.'

'Do you not know what terrible thing has occurred?'

'Mi no so gnente de gnente.' I don't know nothing about nothing (she was actually speaking the Venetian dialect) is a fairly exhaustive admission of ignorance.

'Tell me the last thing which you remember.'

She thought for a minute. 'I took a bad dream in the night, that the oar battered me and made me cascade out of the bark. When did I dream that?' She looked out on the wintry twilight. 'My shoulder is sore even now,' she added.

'You dreamed that in the past night.'

'But it is nearly night now. Where am I? What have I done this day?' she asked, quite calmly and without hesitation. Then she looked toward the shore. 'Why am I in a forestier's topo? They will be missing me at La Tasca, there, where I live. I do not know why I am here, or why I am vested like this. But I saw no clothes of my own.'

'With whom did you live at La Tasca?'

'With my uncle and my aunts and my cousins.'

She said 'barba' and 'amia' for 'zio' and 'zia,' which is most certainly Venetian.

'My dear,' said Nicholas, 'La Tasca is ruined by an awful earthquake, and no one is alive but you.'

'Poor little things! May they rest in peace. O Lord, grant them unending rest, and let everlasting light enlighten them,' she responded with astounding serenity and the Sign of the Cross.

As Nicholas watched her, a change came over her face. It was like nothing but a passing wave which seemed to leave her even newer than before. She stood, wistful, and waiting. He did not understand.

'I am going away now,' he said: 'but first I will make you a present and put you ashore; and you must go and find some of your neighbours.'

He went into the cabin, and put four fifty-lire notes and a handful of nickel twopences into a purse, which he gave to her, with an old frieze boat-cloak for protection against the cold of evening. 'I think,' he said, 'that you had better not return to La Tasca. It is not diverting there. But run as fast as you can to Melito; and try to find someone who will take care of you.'

'I take care of myself. Sior, I do not wish to go to Melito,' she said.

'It is my will,' he answered; and led the way.

The girl eyed him; and then followed without another word, flitting lightly along the gunwale to the prow, and leaping down (kitten-like) to the sandy beach.

'Addio! Keep along the railway,' he said, as he returned to the topo.

He pulled up the oar, and shoved well out into the middle of the little haven, about a hundred metres from the shore, where he anchored, intending to watch the girl's going out of sight, and then to take a good night's rest before resuming his journey to Venice.

He saw Ermenegilda climbing the beach till she came to the broken railway. There she sat awhile in the dusk; and, anon, he thought she rose and went skipping westward over the displaced sleepers.

He went into the cabin. The flower-like aroma of her seemed to haunt it. He left the door open while he arranged the bed, turning the blanket-bags inside out to air. Then he lighted a fire in the stove: got a stock of wood and provisions: changed into a dry suit of overalls, and shut himself up to enjoy a night of peace.

He was not particularly elated over what he had done: though, for the life of him, he did not know what better course he might have taken. It would have been possible to have sailed with the girl eastward along the coast, till he found someone willing to take care of her. But the coast eastward is very lonely, without a village before Brancaleone a good twenty-five chilometres away. He tried to persuade himself that he really had no business to interfere with other people's affairs, beyond giving such help as he could in their distress. That, however, he had done. He had the will, but not the power, to relieve the whole countryside from the results of the disaster. And he intuitively perceived that the lot of the first uninjured helper on that scene would be very far from enviable, and indeed absolutely impossible. He had done what he could. He loathed the gods who rendered him incapable of doing more. Had those divine ones had the wisdom to make him a supreme autocrat like the Pope of Rome and to dower him with the unexhausted riches of a Rockefeller, he was just the man to shew the world how to deal with disasters. But, impotent, he desired to get away from the scene without delay. Was it not, though, a slightly brutal thing to send a tender girl-child wandering about a devastated province at nightfall? Nonsense: she was a peasant, stalwart, heady, capable, perfectly self-possessed: she had enough money about her to keep her handsomely for a couple of months if necessary; and she had not opposed any very pointed resistance against his decision.

With these reflections he examined and soothed his conscience, while he made and ate a dream of an omelet flavoured with olives and cheese; and, at the time when he sipped his coffee and rolled a cigarette, he felt that he could read himself to sleep with Jean Lombard's *Byzance* very comfortably. It would then be about 20 o'clock.

But, just when he had pushed away his tray, and was preparing to strip for the night, he heard his late guest's voice crying faintly, quite close to him, 'Sior, Sior, for love of God do not send me away!'

He dashed out of the cabin.

There she was in the dark sea, clinging to a loose end of the tarpaulin which dangled over the ship's side. He hauled, till he could seize her hands; and hoisted her, dripping, on to the poop.

'You naughty girl,' he angrily began; 'how did you come there?'

'Sior, I swam, having seen your lanthorns: because I am afraid of staying on the land which shakes and smashes everything.' She fumbled for the soaked pocket of the cloak. 'Nor do I want this money,' she added, giving him back the purse.

What a piteous figure she was! The clinging wet gown marked every immature line of her. The slippers were tied to the cord of her waist. The frieze cloak was rolled and twisted round her neck. Rivers ran from her; and all of her quaked in the cold night air. She squeezed the plume on her brow flat with the palm of her hand; and threw it back while she looked ingenuously at Nicholas, and oh so humbly.

'Va ben. You may stay here tonight, and eat, and be dried and warmed: but tomorrow I must find some other place for you.'

'Sior, I will be your most leal servant. I pray you not to send me away.'

'But I don't want a servant. And it is impossible for you to stay here. That would be mortal sin. Come, now: slip off those wet clothes, and let me throw this blanket over you. And then you shall come inside and take some nutriment.'

He spread his arms wide, and held a dry blanket-bag high over his head, concealing himself and ready to envelop her when she should step back to it. He heard the sodden garments drop from her, and a slight sob which might have been only a quick indraught of breath caused by the impingement of chill night-air on wet flesh. But there was a momentary hesitation about her coming into the folds of the blanket.

'Sior, I have been to La Tasca. I have seen. You are my saviour. Pray do not send me away.'

'Get into the blanket,' he snapped.

'Sior, do not make me leave you.'

'Get into the blanket.'

'Sior, with permission, I will never leave you.'

'Get into the blanket. And I must give you much good advice.'

'Nòssiornò. All your things are here. I take nothing but leave to drown myself now.' And she slipped straight overboard as smoothly as a well-licked torpedo, before he could drop the blanket and look at her.

Of course he flashed after her.

The night was dark, but he saw the rippling rings of her disappearance, and dived right into them, and her. Her hands were
held lightly round her throat. He clutched one; and kicked out,
rising with her to the surface not far from the anchor-rope, butting
his head into her back so that he drove her against it.

'Catch hold,' he commanded. She instantly obeyed, shivering
dreadfully.

'Climb into the bark by my shoulders,' he growled fiercely.

She took both hands to the rope, and got on his shoulders: threw
up one long leg, and hooked it over the rope—then the other;
and went up, hand over hand, like a boy. The distance was not
more than a couple of metres: but in the dark it seemed a mile.
When she touched the poop, she turned, stretching herself, and drew
herself inboard the rocking ship.

'Take these things which I am going to throw to you,' Nicholas
shouted. He divested himself of his overalls, as he hung in the
cold sea by one arm hooked round the anchor-rope, treading water
violently to keep his blood from freezing. They were frightfully
heavy with wet. He rolled them into a bundle, which he squeezed
between his head and his free arm to lighten it as much as possible;
and, with a mighty heave which sent him under, he boosted it up
to the girl.

'Take the dry blanket, and cover yourself from head to foot,' he
roared at her, when he came (sputtering) up again.

A minute later, he swarmed up the rope, and dashed past her into
the cabin.

Nicholas no more knew false shame than did any of the Dia-
dymenoi. He gloried in his wholesome perfection, unconscious
of what the imperfect and diseased call indecency. But he was in
a blasting rage. His hand had been forced; and he instinctively
concealed himself from this victor, who was creeping far too near
him and must be taught the existence of sacrosanct arcana. He
jumped into a dry suit, tore three blanket-bags from the couch and
flung them on the chests, and came out to the girl.

'Uncover your eyes, and go inside, and get into bed,' he said,
moving aft, to see that the anchor still held. Then he also went in,
and shut the door.

She lay, covered to the throat, gazing at him with gentle wistful
eyes, her teeth chattering with cold. He made a blazing fire, and
gave her generous helpings of bread soaked in hot wine. The big
bruise on her white shoulder seemed bluer than ever. While she
was feeding, he went outside again, and wrang the water from her

discarded bath-gown and towel and neckerchief and slippers and cloak, bringing them into the warm cabin, and hanging them from the book-shelf opposite the bed to dry. Her eyes followed his every movement. She looked like incarnate docility.

He pulled two of the kapok mattresses from under her, and carried them round to the wood-stack between the cabin and the prow. Here he raised the tarpaulin, propping it with faggots, so as to cover a sort of shallow tomb in the stack, wherein he spread the mattresses for his own bed. Returning to the cabin, he trimmed the lanthorn to burn through the night, lighted another for himself, and took it with the three spare blanket-bags in his hand.

'Here is the key. Lock the door behind me. And sleep well,' he said to the girl, a little more humanely.

He went to his sheltered nook on the wood-stack, put two blanket-bags inside the third, stripped, and slid in, and stretched himself to sleep. 'Sin be damned,' he muttered; 'of course you can't commit sin unless you want to and deliberately mean to.'

His sleep was a lovely torpor.

Broad daylight woke him. A feeble well-meaning sun was struggling to peep over the shoulders of thin clouds which had fainted on the horizon, exhausted by long passionate weeping. There was a salt-smelling breeze from the sea. He got into his overalls, and came from under the tarpaulin to sniff the air and look round.

On the poop was Ermenegilda in the dry bath-gown, with the black silk necksquare tied under the back of the white hood and hanging triangularly on her breast like the kerchief of a gondoliere. Her head was bare, magnificently haughty and round, with its wonderfully vigorous pallor of skin over which the panache of lightening hair waved boyishly in the breeze. Her fingers were binding the end of a frayed rope very cleverly with string. As Nicholas came round the cabin, he noted that every cord was neatly coiled and stowed, not always in its proper place, though that had obviously been attempted. There was unusual order and symmetry everywhere. The loose water had been sponged out: the oar was laid conveniently.

Ermenegilda looked for a word.

Nicholas made up his mind, seeing everything visible and invisible; and passed her, without looking or speaking, just as though she had not been there. In the cabin he spotted more of her beguiling handiwork. She must have been up and about for hours, and it was only 9 o'clock now. The place was ridiculously tidy—the bed straightened and the blanket-bags separately folded on it—cups and plates and bowls and pan cleaned and arranged on the chests—the ashes gone from the stove and a new fire most artfully laid, the sticks standing wide apart at the base and leaning together at the top with a neat heap of loose dry chips in their midst—and not a speck of dust on any of the precious polished surfaces. He took the coffee-pan with a couple of handfuls of coffee from the small cupboard opposite the door.

A persuasive voice behind him said, 'Sior, with permission, that is my job.'

He gave her the coffee-pan, and shewed her where fresh water was. When she got to work at the stove, he locked her in the cabin, slipped out of his clothes and overboard and in again to freshen and sting and cool his wits. Oh, very well: if she wished to serve, serve she should, and nothing else—as long as she did it decently. But, ware of female wiles, if you please. No making herself indispensable. No translation of Cinderella from kitchen to library. 'Terrible is the Female,' as Canon Liddon always averred after he had made experience of Queen Victoria cross. Oh dolt: was that creature in the cabin a female? She was. And she wasn't. Mah! Treat her as one would treat a quiet strong nimble-fingered lad. And she would be one. She was young, malleable, plastic. One might mould her, if one could not get rid of her. Ah well, before making another mess of getting rid of her, it would be as well to find out a lot more about her.

He unlocked the cabin-door and entered. The coffee was delicious. He sipped two cupfuls of it—half the contents of the pan.

'Yours,' he said, pointing to the remainder, as he went out to sit on the poop and roll a cigarette.

When the girl had finished her job—she washed cup and pan over the side, and waved them for sun and air to dry them, before stowing them in the cupboard—she came and waited on the cabin threshold as though expecting orders. He only looked at her bare feet, fine supple straight-toed feet, with the second toe projecting further than the great toe and well parted from it, swift arching feet like the capable feet of the Hermes of Herculaneum. As he gave her no word, she went along the gunwale to the forepart, and began to wrestle with the tarpaulin, unlacing and rolling (not folding) it and stowing it on the cabin roof. She shook and aired the mattresses and blanket-bags, and restored them to their place indoors. Lastly, she busied herself with a rearrangement of the wood-stack. Every movement of hers was perfectly native and unerring, perfectly agile and puissant. She kilted the skirt of her gown to free her legs and feet. He got up to watch her, and he could not help admiring her ingenuity in building the faggots against the ship's sides, leaving an oblong space of about two metres by one by one, which (roofed with the laced tarpaulin and floored with the kapok mattresses) would form quite a snug little resting-place for the night.

Being up, and distinctly averse from attracting aboriginal attention (though no life had manifested itself on shore so far), he set sail and weighed anchor. The girl made no attempt to help him there. That was his job: not hers. Evidently, also, it was a job which she had not mastered: for she peered from her station on the wood-stack, eagerly noting his every action and effects of the causes which he put in motion. There was quite a pleasant little breeze freshening. Nicholas steered out of the cove, eastward, hugging the coast, in the direction of Cape Spartivento.

The girl put up her hands to her neck; and then went quietly hunting all over the ship.

'What have you lost?' Nicholas asked, at length.

'Sior, I had a cross and a coral on a string round my neck before I came here.'

'The earthquake must have torn it off with your clothes, when La Tasca fell in ruins.'

She flamed in scarlet; and returned to her vivid pallor.

'Sissior.'

'I will give you another cross and coral on a chain, when we come to the city where I am going to find a home for you.'

'Sior, with permission, I will never leave you.'

Who was she? What was she? What in the world was he to do with her?

'Feel if that boat-cloak is dry. If it is, wrap it close round your shoulders. Now come and sit down here, on the poop, near to me.'

Quickly she came at his word.

'Tell me now, who you are, please: tell me the whole of your story,' he tried to persuade.

IV

'MARIN FALIER' happens to have been the name of that Venetian Doge, who (despite his Serene Principate) was beheaded as a traitor to the Republic in the year of the Admirable Parturition of Madonna Saint Mary the Virgin 1354.

Before precipitately plunging into the bog of superior (but fatuous) sneers concerning the progeny of traitors, visiting (like Yahveh) the sins of the fathers upon the children, it may be wise, o most affable reader, to remember that your successful traitor is a laurelled patriot, and his treachery the purest Amor Patriae. As a matter of fact there was nothing particularly disgraceful about the treachery for which Duke Marin Falier paid the price with his hot head. He was 'disgraziato' only in the Italian (and first) intention of the term, in that he was so far 'out of the favour' of the irresponsible gods as to be what we call 'un-fortunate' in his undertaking. His enemies stole a march on him: his attempt, a simple and bloody one certainly, to purify corruption was foiled, equally bloodily, by people who preferred corruption. And he lives on history's roll of infamy because he was a clumsy victim, just as King Edward the Excellent of England lives on history's roll of fame because He is a most adroit master of His every situation.

Ermenegilda, daughter of Bastian son of Marin son of Bastian son of Marin, called herself Falier by cognomen no doubt for the best of all reasons. A person who (in these days) actually knows the name of father and grandfather and great-grandfather and great-great-grandfather, all in the male line—names which ascend alternately in the sane (but ancient) fashion of the steps of a ladder—may safely be suspected of possessing a notable ancestry. The Borgia (for example)—the original Borgia stem, which still flourishes in the descendants of that Pietrogorio Borgia of Velletri whose fortunes were made in gratitude by Duke Cesare, reputed son (and undoubted right-hand) of the invincible Pope Alexander the Sixth—still call themselves alternately 'Cesare Borgia' and 'Francesco Borgia.' Those are the two most illustrious names which their family has: Cesare was their benefactor: Francesco is their canonized saint.

It was borne in upon Nicholas Crabbe that he had scratched out of a rubbish heap nothing less than the daughter of a Doge—of three Doges, to be quite exact, namely, Vital Falier and Ordelaf Falier and Marin Falier of the eleventh, twelfth, and fourteenth centuries respectively. The dignity of serene principate was signed in the magnificent muscular curve of the neck and shoulder, as in every other physical contour, of Ermenegilda Falier. Most Venetian girls (certainly all those of pure undegenerate Venetian stock) have the gait of goddesses, the radiant splendour, and the sweet dainty opulent tranquillity of the sun and sea of their lagoon. But evidently Mother Nature had 'tried back' in the moulding of Ermenegilda, giving her also the superb saturnian form, the clear-souled gaze, the unwrung pluck and poise of those earlier ages when the world— the dust out of which sweet flesh is made—was half-a-thousand years younger and fresher and less trodden-to-exhaustion than it is now.

She told him her story—this daughter, through many generations, of the Doge of Venice and Dalmatia and Croatia, Hypatos and Protopedro and Protosebaste of Byzantion, Despot and Lord Of A Quarter And Half Of A Quarter Of All The Roman Empire, who had a right to wear vermilion buskins.

She was an orphan, seventeen years old in three days' time, the first of the coming January. Her father had been a gondoliere and gastaldo of the Traghetto of the Trinity in Venice, as also his parents had been before him. She had not seen her mother. But, when her father Bastian was massacred (about twopence) by the razor of a bancalo of the same ferry (who instantly scampered away to Argentina) in the year before the year before that in which the Patriarch Bepi went to be Pope in Rome, then, the brother of her mother, being her sole remaining parent, took her to his farm of La Tasca in Calabria which he inherited from the father of the wife to whom he had espoused himself in that province.

Nicholas was slightly puzzled about this strange 'Traghetto della Trinità.' He had thought that he knew all the Venetian ferries. And it was not till after his return to Venice that he discovered it to be the antique name (only used now by gondolieri) of the well-known Traghetto della Salute. How antique? Well, as antique as this. In 1256, the Serene Republic gave the then antique church and monastery of The Trinity to the Order of Teutonic Knights in payment for their services against Genova. After three hundred and thirty-six years, Pope Clement the Eighth suppressed that Trinity Priory of Teutonic Knights in 1592, and moved to it the patriarchal Seminary from San Cipriano di Murano. And, thirty-nine years later, the patriarchal seminary was shunted a little farther up the island to its present site, so that the Serene Republic might erect the great church of Santa Maria della Salute on the old Trinity Priory in thanksgiving for deliverance from the plague of 1631. Naturally a name, which has been embedded in human memory more than three hundred and seventy-five years, still persists after the lapse of a mere two hundred and sixty.

Ermenegilda continued, describing her first nine years of this life in the parish of Sanstefano, alone, with Bastian her father in his little house of four rooms (full of nut-wood bedsteads and antique pictures as large as walls) in the tiny court called Malatin which lies just under the distorted bell-tower of Sanstefano. Outside that parish, all the rest of the terra firma of Venice, excepting the Square of Saint Mark and his basilica and the markets of Rialto, seemed quite unknown by her: but her acquaintance with the city's labyrinth of waterways was of the most intimate nature.

The first thing which she had in memory occurred on a certain Lord's Day when she was about three years old. She and Bastian her father were eating cherries on the doorstep; and he picked her up, laughing, and jetted her into the canal, saying, like this, that he would give her a coral for her neck if she swam the length of the gondola which by chance was moored thereby. At which she took fear: but she contrived to swim the course; and she won the coral— the same coral which this cruel earthquake ravished from her. And she flushed, flashing a quick glance at Nicholas.

There was nothing much more to tell. No: she never played with other children. Bastian forbade it, saying, like this, that no one was fit to speak to his Zildo. He always called her 'Zildo' or 'fio mio': because he preferred making her a son rather than a daughter. That was why she never wore any but boys' clothes during her father's life-time; and, in Venice, she always passed for a boy. It annoyed her when her aunt in Calabria kept her in a petticoat, which hindered her and was incessantly tearing itself. Bastian, she must say, was a very sage, very brave man, adorned with nineteen bannerols and seventeen medals gained in regattas beside the municipal prize for his gondola. All forestieri, especially English, esteemed him. He taught her to read in the prayer-book, and to write her name, and to cook and sew like a gondoliere. Naturally the polishing of the gondola became her job, as soon as she could row. When? She could not clearly remember: but it must have been soon after the time when she found that she was able to swim.

She had nothing more to say: excepting (perhaps) this, which was a jocose story. At a proper time she took revenge of Bastian for jetting her into the rio. In this way. She being small, he cut down an antique oar and scraped it very slim with a slice of broken glass, because the heavy oar of the poppe was too heavy for her at that time. And he insigned her with the mystery of a gondoliere, at 4 o'clock on summer mornings, kneeling on the seat in front of her rowing, and cursing her when she let her oar slip from the forcola. So, one day, they were going like this down Canalazzo, when (suddenly) she took a temptation. Bastian by chance was standing on the seat for freedom in language, and a bark of sweet wood was coming out of Rio del Fornace; and she twitched the poppe aside so suddenly (to avoid it) that her father lost his equilibrium, made a grand capitombolo, and cascaded into Canalazzo. O Mariavergine, but he was comic! He banged her so uglily when he had retrieved himself that she flung away her oar and butted herself also into Canalazzo and swam back to the Traghetto, shouting (as she went) like this, that she would no longer row so ugly-humoured a person. But, when she saw him retrieving her rejected little oar, and coming back looking very unhappy lest any of the other gondolieri should criticize his humidity—he being their gastaldo —then she coursed to the house, and made him a risotto for his collation of every type of nutriment which she could find in the house. Now that she was grown up, she knew that that one must have been a risotto to poison a parish: for she mixed the rice with paste and raisins and oil and garlic and liver and cloves and pepper and red wine and salt and almonds and cheese and mustard and orange and vinegar and cuttle-fish and sugar and tomato and melon and fennel and all sorts of nutriments. But he ate it all, when she brought it very humbly to his station; and he called her a brave and a son again, being the best of all good fathers.

And the only other thing which she could remember was this. When she was a small creature, Bastian used to make her sit under the poop of his gondola while he rowed the forestiers, keeping as quiet as the good dead, and polishing antique coins and medals to be nailed to the portelle of the poppe for its embellishment. And, when (by chance) the forestiers noted her, in the inquisitive manner of the English, Bastian used to tell them, like this, that his little son was dumb and not to be spoken to, so that they would sniff and leave her alone. For he had a very proud heart, often telling her (like this) that, though the Falieri were low and much wronged, no one in all the Veneto had more honourable blood: for one of the family discovered the holy body of Saint Mark hidden in a column, and was himself interred in the porch of the basilica; and another of the family put up the Pala d'Oro in Saint Mark's, and builded the Arsenal, and made great wars in Dalmatia whence comes the firewood. Naturally one would be proud of parents of such a type. And, when she became larger and more expert, of course she always rowed the poop-oar while Bastian rowed at the prow, when rich forestiers wished to have two oars to take them to the glass-makers of Murano or the lace-makers of Burano, or Torxelo, or Saint Francis-in-the-Wilds, or Saint George-in-the-Seaweed, or Saint Angel-in-Dust, or the Lido, or other islets. In this way they earned many deniers, never less than three franchi a day and some-times as many as thirty when they put the gilded apparatus into the poppe for some rich lordo who desiderated a gondola of luxury. But, when Bastian was massacred dead, and sepultured, only ninety-one franchi of his were found in the bank: because they always had had the best of everything and as much as they wanted. Her uncle, calling himself Sior Polo Anapesto, chanced to be on a visit to salute her father at that very moment; and there was much to be told about him.

He was a very rich benign man, that poor uncle, with twenty-four cows and an olive-grove and nineteen hectares of a farm and innumerable congregations of turkeys, and his wife with her three old sisters in the house, and he was a treasure to everybody. Let him rest in peace. Why, when he had buried Bastian with a pomp costing two hundred franchi (which he paid from his own burse), imagine what beneficences he did for her now speaking. He sold the gondola for a thousand five hundred and fourteen franchi. An English, living on Zattere, bought the ferro of it alone for five hundred franchi, it being very antique and flexible as gum-elastic. And the coins adorning the portelle also had much value. Sior Polo also sold the pictures and bedsteads and other household stuff for a thousand four hundred and thirty-three franchi, which (with the ninety-one franchi in the bank) made a total of three thousand and thirty-eight franchi. Which immense riches he changed, at the Banca Commerciale, for gold sterlings each worth twenty-five franchi, one-hundred-and-twenty-two gold sterlings there were, most beautiful to see, beside a touch of thirteen loose franchi left over, which she asked him to accept as a handsel for his trouble.

'But he said to me, like this, "Sacramented Jesus! And am I the robber of an orphan!" And he took over twelve franchi out of his own burse; and added them to the thirteen; and made the gentleman of the bank give another gold sterling for them, making a hundred and twenty-three gold sterlings in all. These he caused to be put in a new leathern burse as large as a new-born creature's head; and it was sealed with the leaden sigils of the bank, four sigils there were, so that no one would dare to open it. And, when we two were alone in the waggon of the railway which transported us to Calabria, my uncle Sior Polo said to me, like this, "Zildo, this burse of gold sterlings is yours: but no one must know of it, save we two only; and, because you are young, I shall keep it: but, when you are fifteen years old, I shall give it to you, so that you may (if you wish) espouse yourself to a wife, and buy an oil-grove of your own in my vicinity, and get for yourself a bundle of sons before you go for a soldier, for your sons will take care of you in your old age." For Sior Polo thought that I was a boy, as indeed did all the living. So I told him how the thing stood. He laughed, saying like this, "Oysters!" first, and then, like this, "Ah Bastian!" Afterward, he said to me, like this, "A husband, then." I said, like this, that I desiderated nothing of that kind. And then he said, like this, "As you will, regarding that matter: but I believe that your aunt Alcmena will make you a proper girl; and it will be wise for you to shew yourself to her in a petticoat in the first beginning." So, when the train stopped at a city called Bari, my uncle bought certain feminile garments there; and I put them on me, over my habit of a gondoliere, rolling up my trousers to my knees, in the waggon wherein we were journeying. And, when the wife of my uncle, my aunt Alcmena, had seen me and had heard all, she said to me, like this, "Are you, Zilda, any things better than Maria Vergine whom Domeniddio chose to make a girl?" So Zildo of Venice became Zilda in Calabria, and good enough girl but for her awkwardness in the habit feminile.

'How did I occupy myself at La Tasca? Sior, like this. In the first beginning, I boxed the farm-boy—ping-pong-pang-pang-pang —because he dared to speak to me. In consequence, none of the vicinal peasants would send their sons to my uncle's service, for fear of (what they called) the savage girl who was of his family. "All the better," said I, like this, to Sior Polo; "and now I myself will be your farm-boy, being very strong, though feminile. And, when I am expert in the art and mystery of a farmer, I shall teach Archimede, my cousin." Sior, that one was the junior of me by two years; and now he lies torn in half longways at La Tasca. Brave, he was: but not half as strong as I am. Ah, the poor little one!

'I said also to my uncle, like this, "For the love of God, buy a bark; and I and Archimede will carry the milk in it, every morning to the Bars of Melito, and every evening to Bova Marina and the Tower of Saint John of Avolo, saving the expense of the railway." Thus we did. I also worked in the olive-grove: for Sior Polo said, like this, that my condition ameliorated that of the olives, which bore the best fruit in that vicinity when I took them in hand: for no one touched the trees but me, not even with a finger-tip, not even my cousin Archimede.

'What more? I helped my aunt, the Siora Alcmena, to do well by her babies, and to wait on her very old sister who was bedridden, through a bull which broke her back when she was young and prevented her from espousing herself to a husband. She was very holy, that old one; and she insigned me with the whole Christian Doctrine. Am I christian? Mah! What else, Sior, since Papa Bepi Himself chrisomed me in the basilica of Sammarco when he was our patriarch and before He went to Rome. And her other two sisters of my aunt Alcmena (also old, but not as old as the oldest, who was incredibly old), they taught me other cleanly and useful and virtuose mysteries, as Your Siora shall see. I say nothing more but that. I continue the history.

'Two years ago, on the first of January, being the day of my natalizio as well as a double festival of the first class with an octave, Sior Polo my uncle said to me, like this, "Zilda, this day you are grown up, having completed your fifteenth year; and here I consign to you your burse, containing one hundred and twenty-three gold sterlings, sealed with the four leaden sigils of the Commercial Bank." What a faithful brave man was that one! Me, I was rather frightened about those vast riches, having forgotten them. So I said to him, like this, "With permission, I wish to speak first with my aunt Eufemia on this matter," she being the holy oldest. And she said to me, like this, "Zilda, don't you know, the burse of gold sterling is your portion; and you must take it: but you may do a meritorious act if you take it from Santermenegildo your name-saint, and on his festival, the thirteenth of April next; and so you will have three months in which to pray to him to get you good advice as to what you ought to do with this your portion." Thus, then, I did: but Santermenegildo never deigned me a single instruction, though no doubt he would have told me something if I had been Ermenegildo instead of Ermenegilda. And, on the said thirteenth of April, which was the day of my onomastico, my uncle gave me the burse of one hundred and twenty-three gold sterlings; and I hid it in a hole in an olive in the middle of the grove, where it was most secure, because the very touching of the trees was prohibited to everyone but me. And that has been the bane of my life, that burse. I have no need of a mound of gold sterlings, being able to work: nor had my uncle: nor had his family of my uncle. We all worked: we were quite content: my uncle and my aunts and my cousins each had good portions of their own secured to them: I had my wages of all those years secured to me——'

She broke off suddenly with a gesture; and stared straight before her.

'Where is the burse now?' Nicholas quickly demanded.

'Sior, where should it be but in that hollow olive? It was there yesterday—no, I wish to say the day before yesterday; for I put in my hand to feel it; and the leather was so sodden-soft that I could plainly feel the gold sterlings through it. But now Santermenegildo has it; and (thanks to God) I am freed from it, though it seems that I have lost everything else.'

They had rounded Cape Spartivento; and were sailing north-eastward past the semaphore-station. Nicholas sternly moved the rudder, taking a tack to return by the way in which they had come.

'Sior, and where?' asked the girl, with apprehension.

'Back to La Tasca, for your portion,' he curtly said.

Instantly she sprang up. All her softness, all her sweetness, all her exquisite persuasive gentleness of exterior, became completely invisible; and her immutable mind shewed through a body as tense as an outraged cat's.

'Sior, for a favour, look away while I relinquish these your things: for I will not go back to La Tasca in this bark.' She tore off her neckerchief.

'How then will you go?'

'Sior, I will never go back to La Tasca alive.' She threw down the cloak.

'But your portion——'

'It is not mine. I said that I would take it from my saint: but he did not deign it to me. Let him keep it.' She untied the cord of the bath-gown at her pulsing throat. Bare-breasted, she bounded to the side to leap on the gunwale, slipping out a scarlet stalwart shoulder and arm—the other——

'Stand firm! Guard your head! Go and shut yourself in the cabin and weep for your sins, you mad thing!' cried Nicholas, as the yard swang over and he steered north-eastward again.

'Sior, prego,' whimpered Ermenegilda, purple, scrabbling at her coverings, and creeping away, meek as an inheritor of the earth all of a sudden.

His is an aspect cased cap-à-pie in mail adamantine. Tender and pliant she seems, as a lily in bloom. But, supple the sheath, it inshrouds an inflexible weapon. Soft is the sensitive soul which his armour conceals.

V

Nicholas Crabbe's position ought to be taken into account here. It must be understood that he already had been chased from two careers, and was fairly well settled in a third. Of course a man with his face and manner and taste and talent and Call ought to have been a priest. Elsewhere it is written why he was not. The fault was hardly his. When he was studying for the priesthood in the Scots College of Rome, he chanced to be of signal service to Mario Attendoli-Cesari, whose princely family shewed due appreciation. The Attendoli-Cesari were of royalist politics, lords-in-waiting and ladies-in-waiting at the Quirinale; and the Black Clericals (following their usual custom of pin-pricking White Monarchist patricians) quickly discovered that the friend of the Attendoli-Cesari had no vocation to the priesthood, and expelled him from college. Not to have a vocation is a misfortune: it cannot be called a crime: it is not even exasperating to anyone but the wretch who doesn't possess it. And one would have thought that a consolingly-worded invitation to take his name off the books would have suited the situation. But that is not the gentle clerical way. Crabbe was expelled with every sudden circumstance of rough abuse and indignity: he was flung out, at night, to penury and starvation, as the English consul of the 'nineties has testified. To furnish some small proof of his vocation, he vowed twenty years' celibacy; and, for twenty years, he proclaimed the barbaric absurdity of which he was the victim. Then, a very curious thing happened. The Spalding Club of Aberdeen, an amateur literary society, published a reprint of the Registers of the Scots Colleges on the Continent, including that of the Scots College of Rome. And Crabbe found therein only two records of expulsions since the reformation of the college some fifty years ago: in each case the cause of expulsion was stated, indolence in one, disobedience to rule in the other: but neither case was his. What did this portent signify? It would hardly do for ecclesiastical dignitaries to record that they had crucified a victim of their dirty venal spite toward secure impregnable princes who fought for the White Cross of Sabaudia against the Temporal Power of the Roman Pontiff. No. And so Nicholas Crabbe's record in the college

33

register simply consists of his name, date, diocese, and parentage, inaccurately stated (as one might expect, seeing that the new rector of the college himself supplied the copy from which the Spalding Club printed)—and then follow three plain dots such as are ordinarily used to signify incompletion. It is charitably supposed that the notorious details of the case being too shameful for publication while the rector who expelled Crabbe still infested this world, the record (as prepared for publication) was intended as a weak hint that his career had been merely°interrupted, and that he would be welcomed if he cared to resume it. He always was most anxious to resume it. He always was quite ready to bury the hatchet. He had no notion of defiling himself with ungenerosity—he was far too selfish for that. But, being a burnt child, he dreaded the fire: and insisted on an honourable and above-board understanding. He asked the present rector, he asked his own archbishop, he asked the cardinal-protector of the college, he even asked the English-aping cardinal-secretary-of-state who used to play cricket with him, to tell him definitely what he was to understand. They simply bit their tongues. So he wagged his.

Chased from priesthood, he painted arras. He painted for two years for a Jesuit, who obtained his services on false pretences, sold his work at the rate of fifteen hundred sterling, and offered him fifty. Crabbe took the fifty: flung it back: and began (from the gutter) to earn a living in literature. The histories of his two careers (the ecclesiastical and the artistic) are already written: so also is the history of his first literary period; and the curious may read who have the wit to find. It is his second literary period which concerns us here.

He published four books; and just half-lived on what he made by them, soured at heart, somewhat exhausted in body. To him entered (by means of an advertisement) an obese magenta colonel of militia with a black stub moustache and a Welsh tongue, an expert adviser of the Rhodon Trust and Constitutional Company of British South Libya, bearing a proposition. This Welshman wanted a literary man to edit his pamphlet. He had fought ninety engagements in the Boer War, with his thirteen-year-old son as his bugler; and K. of K. (hearing that he was owner or breeder of the Heaviest Ox) intrusted to him the establishment of all remount-farms in South Libya. Incidentally, and at a cost to himself of four thousand sterling, he had collected a mass of evidence concerning agricultural and pastoral prospects in that country; and he was employed to write a report thereon, for the Rhodon Trust's and Constitutional Company's private eye, and for subsequent bowdlerized publication.

But, simpered the agricultural or pastoral colonel, though he had facts in his mind and note-books, he couldn't write them readably; and the fee at stake was seven thousand sterling, with a footing in the Constitutional Company and in something called 'The Know,' in addition to lucrative amicity with the Rhodon Trust—of which lucre and advantages he offered Crabbe a half in return for literary services. 'You shall trust to the honour of a Welshman, whatever. I myself have to trust to the honour of the Duke of Cornaper and Earl Ashy and the Earl of Hippis; and so you shall trust me,' puffed the short-legged but military agriculturist. So it seemed necessary. Poor men take what they can get. Crabbe was obliged to trust to the honour of this Taffy, though he knew what Taffy used to be and what Mr Justice Grantham officially declares all Taffies to be now. He therefore digested the colonel's notes; and wrote the report, for eight months, in the form of a big bound book. But, when he was about half-way through it, the pastoral militiaman said something funny. He was expecting samples of Rhodonian corn and wool from Rhodonia, for an exhibition of Rhodonian produce which he was organizing for the advertisement of the company's shares in town. 'If they don't come by the beginning of next week, I shall just have to go and buy others in Mark Lane and Coleman Street, whatever,' said the scrupulously honest expert advisory colonel. Crabbe found this casual remark so illuminating that he dashed home and set down his conception of the terms of his own job in a letter, which he sent to his employer with a request for confirmation. The colonel briefly and mysteriously but undeniably confirmed it by return of post; and the book was finished, and immediately published by Warden at the instance of the Rhodon Trust's secretary. Taffy called on Crabbe, awkwardly offering a cheque for twelve sterling in discharge of all claims. And Crabbe rushed out of doors in search of a lawyer.

Messieurs Morlaix & Sartor of Lincoln's Inn Fields examined his case, and declared it to be one. They wanted security—a lien on his four published books and a great *Sforza Genealogy,* and on all other works which he should produce before the conclusion of his action against the Welshman. In return for such an assignation, they engaged to manage his literary property more profitably than he could, to give him (that thing desired of writers) a sufficient and regular allowance with freedom to do his job in peace and comfort, and also to pay costs of lawsuit. Which terms Crabbe accepted with joy and dances; and went to Oxford to write like blazes, and do the don's work of a blind friend. His lawsuit came on; and of course he lost it, owing to his solicitors' portentous imbecility in representing him as a mere hack whose brains anyone can plunder with impunity, and in omitting to call for production in court of the documents reciting and confirming terms of contract. However, grace to his case-hardened carapax, he gave no external sign of being much upset. The suit had dragged so long that it bored him —he had lost interest in it. His work had gone on, in a fashion, fairly uninterruptedly. His agents had kept to their agreement more or less punctiliously, enabling him to publish two new books, *Peter of England* and *Don Superbo*, to get two more accepted for publication, *Sieur Rènè* and *Songs of Gadara*, and to produce yet five others. So that they actually held a lien on, and for five years had complete management of, six published and eight unpublished books. Mark that point, if you please, o most affable reader. But you are not to think that Messieurs Morlaix & Sartor were the only persons with whom he had dealings. Beside his glaucomatic don at Oxford, he had two friends—O God of Love, o Saint Amys and Saint Amyl, o David and Jonathan, o Harmodios and Aristogeiton, forgive the abuse of the term! [1]

The Reverend Bobugo Bonsen was a stuttering little Chrysostom of a priest, with the Cambridge manners of a Vaughan's Dove, the face of the Mad Hatter out of *Alice in Wonderland*, and the figure of an Etonian who insanely neglects to take any pains at all with his temple of the Holy Ghost, but wears paper collars and a black straw alpine hat. As for his mind, it was vastly occupied with efforts to evade what theologians call ' admiratio.' By sensational novel-writing (his formula was to begin so that you must go on till there is nothing left for you to do but to end with a Bang [for choice of the slammed door of a Carthusian convent] behind the hero) and by perfervid preaching, he made enough money to buy a country-place, where he had the ambition to found a private establishment (not a religious order) for the smashing of individualities, the pieces of which he intended to put together again as per his own pattern. He did not exactly aspire to actual creation, but he certainly nourished the notion that several serious mistakes had resulted from his absence during the events described in the first chapter of Genesis. I do not pretend to be dogmatic on this point; and I merely offer the hypo-

---

[1] Readers of *The Quest for Corvo* will need no telling that Rolfe is following the lines of his own life very closely in the description he gives of Nicholas Crabbe's career. *Peter of England* is *Hadrian the Seventh*, *Don Superbo* is *Don Tarquinio*, *Sieur Rènè* is *Don Renato*, and *Songs of Gadara* represents *Songs of Meleager*.

thetical judgment that Bobugo's view was that the error in the
Creation of Man consisted in endowing him with Sense. The
kataleptic phantasm, opinion formed on evidence provided by your
senses, was (in his idea) abhorrently and repugnantly heretical, and
to be treated with far more subtile and poignant austerities than those
practised by experts of the Holy Office. The truth (according to
Bonsen) was that, God in His Infinite Wisdom having endowed
you with five admirable senses, your business was to neglect to use
the same till they atrophied or ossified or dropped off you (so to
speak), while you permitted yourself to see and hear and feel and
taste and smell nothing at all but the psychotherapeutic whimseys
of the Reverend Bobugo Bonsen. In short, he set up to be—unlike
T. Petronius Arbiter and the Jesuits, no one elected him—in sheer
fantastic arrogance he assumed the rank of Arbiter of Spiritual as
wellas Temporal Elegancies. Nay, more. If you hesitated for a
moment in performing acceptable kow-tows—if, gasping at his
audacity, you shewed the slightest unwillingness to shame and insult
and reneye your real Creator, this priest started in to coerce you
with a savage cruelty only conceivable by atheistic romances of the
Father Chiniquy and Alexandre Dumas and ultra-anti-Roman order.
'Feed My sheep—feed My lambs' was not good enough for him.
He followed Cardinal Baronius, 'Duplex est ministerium Petri, pascere
et occidere—The ministry of Peter is twofold, to feed and to kill';
and he put on the blouse of the butcher. Definitely, if you used your
senses, the Reverend Bobugo Bonsen recommended that you should
be so abominably insulted in mind and so barbarously man-handled
in body that, in despair, you would hang yourself, for him (hiding
behind the door) to cut down (just in time to evitate an inquest)
broken-in for ever to his appetite for tyranny. If, o most affable
reader, you doubt this mild presentment of his view-point, kindly
run away and study his novel called *The Sensiblist*, and form an
opinion of your own—if you dare.[1]

This priest very much admired Crabbe's books; sought him out;
and said so loudly. His engaging manners, and concealment of his
sadimaniac proclivities, induced my poor dear patron to give him
his very fullest confidence, in confession and out. It was so rare for
Crabbe to find a priest anxious as well as willing to stick up for him.
And Bonsen said, 'Never under any circumstances shall you ever

[1] Here again Rolfe is, of course, drawing from life. "Bonsen" is the late
Mgr. R. H. Benson; and *The Sensiblist* is *The Sentimentalist*, a novel
which aroused much discussion when it was first published. The central
character, Chris Dell, was in some part drawn from Rolfe.

have to go into the gutter any more,' and 'As soon as I am a bishop I'll instantly ordain you.' Moreover, he protested that he knew quite well how to quarrel fiercely and how to make it up again: which is, perhaps, the surest token of real earthly friendship. And, above all, he preliminarily assured Crabbe that he was incapable of the vice of complacency.

When they thought that they knew one another well, Bobugo voluntarily and spontaneously exploded with a proposition of his own. 'Your literary reputation,' he stuttered to Crabbe, 'is among the exquisite elect: mine is among the profane vulgar. I know. I make pots of money with my froth: you don't make anything like the value of your delicately carven crystals. I know. What I mean to say is that your books don't have half the circulation they deserve to have, and that mine have less than a quarter of what they would have if I could only write my stories with your pen of a clean keen angel. I know. Do let's collaborate. Let's collaborate a really start-ling novel about—oh—about Saint Thomas of Canterbury. You can't invent'—(the hybrist stupidity of that didn't pierce Crabbe's shell at the time)—so I will provide and write the story. I know. But you can tell a story more fascinatingly than any man alive: so your part shall be to give my story historic verisimilitude and literary form. I know. And we'll go halves in the profits.' Crabbe's answer was characteristic. 'I should love it,' he said; 'and I'm infinitely obliged to you, for I could do a thing or two with a pot of money: but, as I'm only to do a third of the work, I'll only take a third of the profit.' 'I know,' unctuously agreed Bobugo.

Only Domeniddio knows why so many proposers of propositions floated along by Crabbe his crevice. My own idea is that they couldn't help themselves. He was the most frantically interesting man alive.

C. H. Clontin Peary-Buthlaw was a large rude Scot, graduate of Christchurch, Lieutenant of the Grandmagistracy and Knight-Founder and Knight-Magnate and Prior of Saint George and Lord High Mostotherthings of the Splendid Order of Sanctissima Sophia, and Goodnessknowswhatbeside. This blood, in his turn, vastly admired Crabbe's books; and tremendously sought him out one midnight at Oxford to roar so, gigantically attired in coat-dress with high (but huge) vermilion heels. His gesture was as amplitudinous as his drawl and deep guffaw: but his wardrobe was brobdignagian, ranging from the street-garb of an English cardinal, through the corno of a Venetian Doge and the uniform of a Royal Archer of the Bodyguard, to the aprons and trinkets of the Eighteenth Degree of Freemasonry and the skimpy habit of a modern Knight Templar. In private life, he affected flappy scarlet waistcoats and very blood evening dress of white bound with violet moire, or rowing shorts only, during warm weather: but of his stars, garters, jewelled decorations, and unmarried frock-coated pyjamas, there was no end. Insignia of sovereign orders being not in his way, he designed his own; and had them made at the expense of an opulent maiden aunt. In fact, you may take it that his life was mainly occupied in conferring on himself the right to wear strange clothes and making opportunities to wear other people's. Crabbe was much touched by the homage of so stupendous a personage. But, when it largely invited him home, he hesitated. Everything did seem to be so roaringly gargantuan; and your crab prefers (as you know) tranquillity in a crevice. 'Thank you very much: but I must tell you frankly that I don't move in your world, and can't afford to go your pace: so please run away, and get someone else to play with,' he calmly replied. The Peary-Buthlaw vastly wouldn't. They really were only quiet country people, he averred, living the Simple Life sans motor-cars and men-servants; and he produced a moving invitation from his mother.

Crabbe went, and spent a summer month at Uskvale; and soon found out why he was wanted. The Peary-Buthlaws were the highest of high Anglicans. And Harricus was their only child, who never had anything but his own way, for whom alone his parents lived and moved and schemed (and pinched after a fashion) to consolidate a position in the country. He was not a bad sort of coxcomb: but he was a most colossal fool. And his father and mother and opulent aunt encouraged, and were responsible for, his colossal foolery. They knew it: and deplored it to themselves. For some years they had run about this world mending their child's broken toys and sweeping his messes out of sight. And, seeing the staid stable attractive personality which Crabbe's shell enclosed, they warmly welcomed him, and separately invited him to walks wherein their big son's adventures and misadventures were described and Crabbe's good influence most earnestly invoked. As for Harricus, his wants were of a more concrete order. He wanted a mediæval Rule for his order of Sanctissima Sophia, with designs for sigils, blazons, banners, and very blood dresses.

The month was blazing hot. The two lay naked on the shady banks of Usk when they were not actually bathing in that river; and Crabbe dictated a Rule, and allowed himself to join the five who constituted the Order on certain gladly conceded conditions. But, in justice to the father and mother, who detested (and encouraged) the Order, he also had a shot at trying to make their enormity of a son do something really worth while. It appeared that Harricus had written an immensely unsuccessful Mornington Prize Essay on the life and times of Pope Hadrian the Fourth. 'Of course it was unsuccessful,' said Crabbe, after perusal of it: 'no Oxford examiner would give more than a Gamma minus to gratuitously fantastic flummery of this species. But there's a certain quantity of new material in it; and, with some sobriety and rearrangement and a lot of extra stuff, we might very well make a nice little history-book of it.' 'As how?' asked Harricus. 'As thus,' said Crabbe; and he dictated his idea of a first chapter. The father and mother were delighted. Would not Mr Crabbe stay? Uskvale was pleasant. He stayed till the end of the long, revising and recasting and adding to the rejected essay, elongating it into quite a respectable book, and even designing its cover. And Messieurs Shortman Verde published it without ado. 'For the future, my child, I shall call you "Caliban",' Crabbe said to Harricus. 'And why?' ' "I pitied thee, Took pains to make thee speak, taught thee each hour One thing or other: when thou didst not (savage) know thine own meaning, but wouldst gabble like a thing most brutish, I endowed thy purposes With words":—ahem—Shakespeare, my sweet Caliban,' chanted the horrible Crabbe.

When Crabbe lost his lawsuit, his blind don's work at Oxford was interrupting his own work dreadfully. It appeared that he would have to give it up, and devote himself to earning the costs which fell upon him. 'Why in the world not become one of the Uskvale family and collaborate books with Caliban. It won't cost you more to live here than in that garret in town which you rave of.' Thus argued the father and the son. 'You must never live anywhere but at Uskvale, except for your betterment,' Lady Peary-Buthlaw passionately reiterated.

Crabbe consulted Bobugo, having got into the habit of trusting that priest to the full. His only difficulty about sharing Uskvale was a religious one. He had no ties elsewhere: he could work as well there as anywhere. But the place was seven miles from a catholic chapel. 'I know,' said Bobugo. Was a man justified in fixing his abode so far from means of grace? 'Undoubtedly,' purred Bobugo. Crabbe was fool enough to obey, though he felt that the priest was a compromiser. A marked deterioration of his character dates from this incident, a certain weakening of his serenity. He had let the wily

Bonsen get inside his shell and do all sorts of tricks with the softness therein.

So an arrangement was concluded, and Crabbe took up his abode at Uskvale. He and Caliban discussed subjects for books, historical novels written in a new manner, that is to say, History As It Ought To Have Been And Very Well Might Have Been, But Wasn't. It was frantically interesting and frightfully funny. They soon got to work on a couple of books. Caliban wrote one-tenth of each, to console his parents; and, during the rest of the time, he was either sprawling in the yellow drawing-room having his bare feet tickled by his "pater," or gadding about England peacocking in costume at pageants. And Crabbe sat night and day in the tapestry-room, writing the other nine-tenths, and thoroughly enjoying himself.

Summer came; and he felt that he wanted change of scene and society.

Crabbe gave his manuscript of one of the two collaborated books —*The Weird* was its name—to Caliban to be typed, saying that both manuscript and typescript were to be sent on a round among the publishers. His manuscript of the other, called *De Burgh's Delusion*, he took with him for leisurely revision and fair copying; and he set forth to spend six weeks in Venice with the professor of Greek, whom I mentioned at the beginning of these ana. He very much wished to pick his companion's brains, concerning the Hadrianic theatre at the Spartan temple of Artemis Orthia, with a view to a romance (a better one than Dr. Ebers's) about Antinoys—that most lovely and pathetic negroid, whom no one (though the Christian Fathers violently assailed his memory for it) ever yet thought of venerating as the founder of a religion of pure self-sacrifice untainted by promises of premiums eternal. Crabbe got what he wanted—yea, and more also. The professor (who had just inherited eighty thousand sterling and a house which he sold at once for fifteen thousand) displayed a niggardliness inconceivable on any hypothesis but mania. His screams, his stampings, his tripudiations, on the public Piazzetta when he found that he had tipped the hooker of the gondola a halfpenny ('xinque xentesimi') instead of two-fifths of a halfpenny ('do schei' in Venetian) made Crabbe sick to vomiting so often that he broke into rebellion. And, because the creature treated so many amiable gondolieri as though they were the basest slaves, half-starving and quarter-paying them, leaving vile impressions as well as debts of honour behind him, Crabbe felt bound in honour to extend his holiday, and pay, and otherwise do what he could to remove the abominable stigma from his race. It was quixotic, of course. But

Nicholas Crabbe was of that complexion. He could not sit meekly while foreigners, specially such childish ones as Venetians, nourished evil notions of the English nation. Venice is infested by Germans. That would be bad enough, if they were not detested. And Crabbe determined that the difference between English and Germans should be emphasized, as far as he could emphasize it. So he bought a pupparin and a barcheta-a-vele while his topo was being built at Castello, employed half a dozen gondolieri, fraternized with them, fed them and paid them munificently, and explored the whole lagoon. And then, in late autumn, he left the pupparin at a squero to be repainted and stored, sold the barcheta, and fled away in his new topo to cultivate the garden of his soul in the loneliness of sea and sky, amid the sweet salt air, where the winds were as a quire of singers.

Ermenegilda Falier you have seen, o most affable reader. See, now, and make up your mind about Nicholas Crabbe.

VI

THE breeze blew more freshly from the south-west, sending the topo scudding along with astonishing speed and easiness of motion for so ponderous and clumsy-looking a vessel. But the shipbuilders of Ciozza and Pelestrina and Castello have been building for more than a thousand years; and their burly blunt-nosed flat-bottomed barges, with the great curving timone which is centre-board as well as rudder, simply waltz upon the waves as lightly as a landlady of bucksome embonpoint. Crabbe ran a parallel course about a chilo-metre from the coast, passing Bianco and the ports of inland-lying Bovalino and Ardore, and nearing the classic region of Epizephyrian Lokre.

After one silent hour, he called to the girl in the cabin to prepare a midday-meal of polenta and cheese, and to bring his portion to him. He was frightfully angry with her for defying him. 'Stay within,' he snarled, when she would have come also to eat outside and admire the view. Opposition of any kind invariably hardened his hard exterior, and (within) set him frantically arguing every possible pro and many impossible cons with himself. For, while he was the most ruthless and ferocious of men, he was simultaneously the most fear-full and the most scrupulous—not scrupulous in the theological sense of the term (which is 'unscrupulous') but really and indeed inspired and refined and gubernated entirely by the delicate fastidious punctilio which is so soul-worrying a mark of true chivalrous probity. At the very moment when he was so furious that he could not speak civilly to her, he was wrapt in whole-hearted admiration of her scandalous indifference and concurrence on the money question. To chuck away a hundred and twenty-three sterlings because one doesn't quite know what to do with them, or because one has no imperative need of them, or because a spiritual disdain or a temporal point of honour repels one from incurring the taint of the touch of them, was a deed done so altogether in his own ideally unworldly manner, that it recommended her to him with amazing pressure. But, neverthe-less, the fact had to be faced—and all the afternoon and evening he sat at the rudder and faced it—that his life had been split in twain by an earthquake and seaquake, and that he was just at the beginning of the second half saddled with an unploughed field of female, seventeen years old, shaped like a boy and having a boy's abilities.

He bade her to keep the fire alight in the little stove, partly for the pleasure of seeing her poise as she went balancing round the cabin along the bounding gunwale to and from the wood-stack at the force. And every now and then he shouted a sharp command for coffee: which she promptly brewed and brought to him on the poop. Night came on. The breeze blew strongly. The topo skimmed from billow to billow. When the lanthorns were lighted, he called the girl out to him; and gave her the rudder and the sheet, shewing her how to govern them and the shore-lights by which he was steering. She gripped her gown between her legs, and sat down, with her smooth chin up and the wind blowing the pale plume back from her brow. He stood near the mast at the cabin-door, watching her for a few moments to observe her ability; and, being satisfied, he went within to make a pot full of soup of Maggi, a soup of double strength with a litre of chianti and half a dozen eggs in it, to be eaten with white polenta. When he had satiated his hunger, he relieved the girl. 'Go and eat,' he said, unconcernedly. And, from time to time, 'Coffee,' he cried: till he felt as though he never could sleep any more. About midnight, 'Go to bed,' said he. He desired, and would have, the dead of the night and the silence of dawn all to himself, for thinking.

What should he do with her? What, in the Name of Heaven, was he to do with her?

In describing the weird gymnastics in which his mind engaged during these wave-running fateful hours of darkness, he always laid singular and particular stress upon the influence of her phenomenally perfect boyishness—not her sexlessness, nor her masculinity, but her boyishness, he said with emphasis. She looked like a boy: she could do, and did do, boy's work, and did it well: she had been used to pass as a boy, and to act as a boy; and she preferred it: that way lay her taste and inclination: she was competent in that capacity. There was nothing in her to inspire passion, sexual or otherwise: no one could help noticing and admiring her qualities of spring-likeness, of frankness, of symmetry, of cogency: but, in other respects, she was negligible as a boy. A youth knows and asserts his uneasy virility: a girl assiduously insinuates her feminility. Ermenegilda Falier came into neither category. She was simply a splendid strapping boy—excepting for the single fact that she was not a boy, but a girl.

Crabbe pondered the problem of her future, absolutely without reference to codes, morals, or conventions. How could he dispose of her as a boy? Never having encountered such a case in life, he searched his memory for records of such in history and fiction. He remembered the sapient adage of Dr Samuel Clemens, 'Truth is stranger than Fiction: because Fiction is obliged to stick to possibilities, whereas Truth isn't.' He considered the Lord Baron Northcliffe's Amelia Vella, who called herself David James Lincoln Garfield McKinley, and served as an ordinary seaman for some months without disclosing her sex. And he soon cleared away newspaper instances: they were essentially unhygienic: they generally had to do with vulgar sordid intrigue, or with some undeniable lump of a female who went for a soldier or a sailor. There was an element of the animal, of coarseness, of sex, in all of them; and there was no element of that kind in Ermenegilda.

Shakespeare disguised a lot of his girls as boys: but that was merely his artful Jacobean stage-craft. The boy-actresses of his epoch were naturally more fitted to play the part of a boy than of a girl. The master made the best of his material, gave his boys their chance —sent them on, as Rosalind or Viola or Imogen, at the beginning of the play, in girl's attire, just to sign themselves and set the scene; and then let them do their real work in their own natural habiliments throughout the rest of the drama. The apparent deception was a frankly open one, which every guffin, mug, and noodle in the audience could understand. It was of no use here.

The girl in boy's guise is also a favourite literary eccentricity of the curious Mr Maurice Hewlett. Crabbe carefully reviewed evidence drawn from that writer's delicious stories. Firstly, Isoult, in *The Forest Lovers*. Slim and meagre as she was, who could have mistaken her girl's legs for a boy's legs in the long hosen of a page— consider the difference of shape and action of the knees? Dirty and disgraced as she was, what charcoal-burner could have handled her limp resistless body, or missed her girl's breast in her torn boy's vest and the shower of girl's knee-long hair hidden in her boy's cap —how hidden, unless the cap was a bag? And Ippolita of Padova in *Little Novels*. Did Padovan goatherds never touch, retire from, jostle, wrestle or engage in horse-play with one another? Yet What'shername successfully passed as a boy with her companion goatherds, actually was embraced till the moment when she herself (from sheer naïve desire) gave herself to the not even suspecting Whatdoyoucallhim. And Isolta of Mantua, who actually courted and married an amorous widow, and made a night-long journey from Venice to Mantua with his (her) bride, cuddling in one cloak, head on shoulder, without even suspicion. Crabbe pronounced these instances amusing, but quite unhelpful.

Shape and hair, he decided, were the chief reefs on which a girl disguised as a boy was bound to wreck her ship. Voice and manner and power of a boy conceivably might be counterfeited. Mice and nuts need not necessarily intervene. But hair and breast, and waist, and hip would give your ordinary girl away during four minutes' masquerade in boyish garb.

Ermenegilda Falier, however, was not an ordinary girl. She was a 'sport,' a freak of Nature who had made a very fine and noble sketch of a boy and failed to finish it. Her hair was cropped, always had been cropped. She was seventeen years old: but her pectoral muscles were as richly flat and vigorous as those of the Eros of Praxiteles on the newly-found 'Fanciulla di Arzio' which everyone makes such a fuss about. She had no more waist than a boy who has rowed all his life standing, and stretching to thrust, in the mode Venetian, filling and clothing his reins with that rippling belt of lovely muscle which Michelangelo admired (and is said to have invented)—that girdle which no 'strong man' has ever yet achieved with idiotic spring-dumb-bells or gum-elastic-exercisers. And hip, the horrible meaningless crupper, adored by kallipygs shaped like a little egg slipping off a big egg slipping off an inverted bluebell, accentuating hypertrophy caused and cultivated by straight-fronted corsets—she was close-packed, neat, rounded, and supple as the Narcissus of Pompeii. And her hard-palmed agile hands with the corn on the thumb-joint—and her long, large, sensitive, shapely springing feet. She should be a boy. She should be a servant. She should serve, serve only—oh yes, but she should surely serve. As she wished.

The wind dropped dead after daybreak, leaving a group of rain-clouds anxious to discharge floods on a sea which rolled like a drenched drunkard home; and Crabbe came to the close of his lucubrations.

'Coffee, Zildo!' he shouted, as he lowered the sail and let go the anchor by the green shore beyond the railway-station of the city of Gerace.

A clean fair face popped out of the cabin. 'His Sioria has called Zildo?' inquired the girl.

'Coffee, Zildo,' Nicholas unemotionally repeated.

'Ready immediately,' intoned Zilda, serenely returning to the stove, with lightened eyes.

Nicholas made the bark secure, drank his coffee, lighted a pipe upside-down because of the rain; and went and bribed a guard-of-the-finance to come and sit outside the locked door of the cabin in which he inclosed the girl, while he went on shore to do business.

From the barber, who shaved a week's beard from him, he learned that half Calabria and all Sicily and most of the rest of the world had been eaten by earthquake and seaquake; and that bread and sulphur were dear. He found a ship-chandler whom he bribed to get him a couple of fishermen to sail his topo to Venice. At a maritime sort of slop-shop he bought a pair of woollen socks and dago-drawers, and a vest, a black cotton guernsey, a suit of thick blue serge clothes, a black felt hat, a couple of metres of vermilion sateen for a waistband, a long furry-looking overcoat with cape and hood warranted waterproof, and a pair of stout alpine boots. At the station he bought two second-class tickets for Venice, and inquired about the next train.

He returned to his ship, dismissed the guard with a flask of chianti and a couple of lire, and entered the cabin. The girl had tidied it, and was sitting on the clothes-chest doing nothing at all, not even thinking. When Nicholas came in with his bundles, she stood: her firm, lightful, innocent eyes began wonderfully to lengthen, and her white teeth gave just a hint of the dawn of a sweet persuasive smile.

'Ciò, Biondo,' said Nicholas, 'I go this day to Venice; and I want a servant to serve me, and to row my pupparin, and to save me from trouble.' He used the masculine word for servant, not the feminine. The girl eyed him, wistfully and intensely.

'Mark well what I say,' he continued: 'my servant's special duty will be to save me from trouble. I have very much to occupy me. I am not rich—though you Venetians think that every English is rich——'

'It is so,' the girl interpolated.

'It is not so,' Crabbe asserted, rearing: 'and I will never have a servant who contradicts me.'

'It is my mistake. Every English is not rich,' she admitted.

'Very well. Understand, I pray, that I want more deniers than I have. To gain more deniers, I must work at my mystery of writing books. To write books, I must think many thoughts. To think thoughts, I must be quite quiet and undisturbed. Have you understood well? Good. Therefore, my servant must honestly and faithfully and always stand between me and any sort of interruption or annoyance. Also, he must always know what I want without words, and must have it ready at the moment when I call. Don't you know?'

'It goes well,' said the girl, comfortingly.

'My servant,' Nicholas continued, 'will be solely responsible for all my belongings: he will pay, from his wages, for everything lost or broken or stolen.'

'Naturally,' said the girl.

'I shall pay him five franchi a week, with a present of about twenty more if he deserves it: and also I shall give him lodging, nutriment, and habits.'

'It goes very well,' the girl commented.

'Do you well understand everything.'

'Most well, Sior.'

'Do you wish to enter to my service?'

'Sìssior.'

'And do you wish to stand between me and the rest of this wicked world?'

'Sior, I wish so to stand.'

'And do you wish to save me from trouble?'

'Sior, no trouble shall pass through me to you.'

'And do you wish to obey my will in all things without question?'

'Paron, with permission, I will never leave you, and I will never return to La Tasca: but, otherwise, I will obey you as though you were the Most Serene Prince the Doge, now dead.'

'Vest yourself, Zildo, my servant, in these vestments; and then clear everything eatable and drinkable out of this cabin, so that I may lock it up.'

He went out, to choke certain gulps. Ermenegilda shut the door. Nicholas sat under the tarpaulin by the poop and went on smoking. Ten minutes later, Ermenegildo emerged; and began bringing out odds and ends of nutriment.

Such an ordinary-looking working-boy, but so stalwart, Nicholas says Zildo was, with his vivid pallor clean above the collar of his black guernsey, and the blue serge jacket buttoned across his broad muscular chest, and his long legs lithe and twinkling in the blue serge trousers. He had given the regular gondoliere's twist to his black felt hat, the brim turned up behind and down before, airing his close-cropped nape and shading his ingenuous lagoon-coloured eyes—such an innocent, expert, well-knit, frank boy.

Nicholas changed his oilskins and overalls for the blue serge and peaked cap and grey burberry which was his shore-wear, and filled a bag with certain books and papers, his constant companions. He left his stores open, and made the two mariners (who came aboard an hour later) free of them, when they had signed the inventory of gear and furniture. But he sealed the locked cabin-door with lead in an impressively official manner before he gave his final orders. These were simple. The topo was to be sailed with all expedition to Venice, and there to be handed over to young John Spagnuol, the yacht-agent of the Wide Alley of Saint Mark, who would pay off the crew with a handsel according to merit.

And, by the afternoon train, he and Zildo went northward together; master and man, but truly two halves of one whole.

VII

THE Albergo Bellavista in Venice is so called because (from the front windows) you do get a most beautiful view of the Square of Saint Mark to your right, and the façade of Saint Mark's to your left, and (in front of you) the Campanile and the Piazzetta with its Columns and the Basin of Saint Mark with the distant islands of Sanzorzi and Spinalonga. Crabbe came there with the unnatural professor of Greek, who had so tormented his tympanum and temper in the previous summer; and he left his baggage there, when he set out to soothe his soul with maritime adventures. The first thing which flapped his return in his face was the hellish access of temperature. Modern comfort (as advertised) means (to Venetian Boniface) arid stifling heat of 80° Fahr. from hot-water pipes and windows hermetically sealed. The hotel was all but empty. But he could not have his old rooms, as that floor was occupied by a gentleman who was well known in Venice, his lady, her baby, its *bonne*. People were always upsetting Crabbe somehow. The rooms which he wanted were at the top, one on each side of a corridor-end; and there were two windows in each, which gave on a terrace commanding the eponymous fine view. He was annoyed, because these seemed to be the only rooms where he could regulate his own temperature by the windows, without being walked-on by Germans. It oozed out, though, that there was another room on the same level, with nearly the same outlook: but, disgraceful to say, it was in an unheated part of the house unused during winter. 'For the Love of God transport me thither instantly,' gasped Crabbe, sweating, headaching, and the odour of hot-iron pipes scratching his nostrils. It was a smaller room, No. 26, on the top floor approached by a side-stair, having two big windows, and a terrace adjoining his former one. Two tiny bedrooms were on the same landing, one of which would suit his servant; and he made a bargain for L. 16 a day all complete. This for the present. After a week, he would reconsider his plans. The plump little proprietor feared that he would be cold. 'Nonsense,' Crabbe snapped, 'we shall be out all day, and only use the rooms for sleeping; and we shall sleep with wide windows: so just give us four blankets apiece, and a couple of hot-water bottles in each bed every evening at 20 o'clock punctually; and I don't want to hear any more about pulmonitis,' he concluded.

There were a few changes downstairs. There was no secretary: the small dining-room was in use instead of the long one; and the talkative pigeon-chested waiter had gone to Florence to do his soldiering, so major-domo Elia snorted. But eager little Piero from Pordenone, with his athletic figure and sparkling brown eyes of a squirrel, was still second-waiter.

Crabbe remembered that he had left his servant upstairs, and uninstructed. He ran up. The boy was poised by the landing-window, observing a pair of facchini who made the two rooms ready for habitation. No words had been exchanged: Zildo's air sternly prohibited even the passing of the time of day, and the facchini laboured in full consciousness of being but worms of dust. Crabbe told the boy to unpack his luggage when the rooms were ready, and then to come to him in the hall.

The new waiter waited below for orders. He was very fair indeed, with blue eyes and an unusually white clean aspect, sturdily built, and quick and skilful in movement. Crabbe always admired dexterity in any kind of job. [Once (with a mouthful of blood) he spat compliments at a dentist who had nipped out a back tooth with one snatch and unexpectedly.] 'Do you speak English?' he inquired.

'O yes, sir.'

'Are you German?'

'O no, sir: Venetian, but my name is like German. I am Arturo Adolfo Einstein, to serve you.'

' "Einstein" is certainly German.'

'O yes, sir: but my father and my grandfather were natives of Venice.'

'Then you are Venetian, though your antecessors must have been German. And what am I to call you?'

'As you please, sir. I am Adolfo here.'

'I shall call you Arthur. You speak English beautifully.'

'O I hope so, sir. I was at the Holborn Restaurant in London for one year.'

'Very good. Now will you and little Piero look after me and my servant. That one is an orphan without a parent in the world: they have been swept away by the earthquake; and he is so shocked that he must not be spoken to by anyone but me. So, please get me a table by the window, and let him eat with me.'

'Yes, sir: I shall make it my business.'

'And how many people are in the hotel?'

'Only yourself, sir, and an English Protestant gentleman named Warden and his lady. There is only an English priest beside, a real priest, sir, who came today from Rome; and then yourself—thank you very much indeed, sir; and all shall be as you wish.'

Zildo came down; and Nicholas rushed him through Merceria to Barbaro's by Rialto for an outfit, a bag of his own, a couple of blue serge reefer jackets and trousers of a better cut and quality than those scratched up at Gerace, half a dozen white woollen high-collared guernseys, and a sufficiency of underclothes, handkerchiefs and boots with a plain toilet box. To these he added a couple of shiny-peaked caps from Semini's; and made the boy look (as he himself did) like an unpretending junior officer of the mercantile marine in mufti.

They had the dining-room to themselves for luncheon, excepting that the proprietor with his wife and children and nurse and cousin were gay at the other end. Plump little Evaristo would have renewed apologies for not letting Crabbe have his old rooms—'but not knowing when you would return, thinking also that you might drown yourself, and the Protestant gentleman being as good a bargain as I could get in this accursed winter season——' Crabbe put in that nothing mattered. He had not been intimate with his landlord. He didn't like the voice, twangy at high pressure, with a vibrant insistency which was maddening at the office-telephone close to the hall where he sat much in the evenings. But Parrucchiero always had been civil and obliging in return for the handsome sums paid, and was a good creature; and certainly maintained a coloured statuette of Saint Joseph in his office.

Directly after luncheon, the two went to the squero of Grassi by Sanzanipolo to get the pupparin. A pupparin is a smaller bark than a gondola, six to eight metres long against the other's eleven and without the twisted-up steel-armed fore and aft. It is flat-bottomed, like a gondola; and has the same curious but calculated curve in length, the same excess on the right which balances the weight of the gondoliere poised high on the left. Its prow is sharply beaked: its poop (from which it takes its name) is pertly spread and tilted like the tail of a merle at moments. Crabbe's pupparin was very long and slim: it would carry one passenger in ease with three oarsmen at pleasure. He always took three oars and three forcole: for (as he said) you never know what may happen—and squalls had been known to tear his craft from moorings to an oar stuck in the mud; and, but for the extra ones, he might have drifted idiotically.

He was pleased with the look of this slim ship. It was black and

smart and polished, and promised speed. Grassi had pitched and
tallowed it without, and painted it within; and had fitted it with
new gleaming-white floor-boards, and new oars and forcole nicely
oiled and brown. It had none of the rumpled carpets or greasy
brass-work or dusty cushions or funeral palls beloved of Venetians,
but just a very low cane arm-chair which could be thrown about and
used or not used. High on the prow rose a thin bright brazen rod,
surmounted by a hollow orb, and bearing a miniature vexilla of the
Royal Bucintoro Rowing Club in red silk and gold. Otherwise
the bark was bare, built for use and stripped for speed. Zildo surveyed it, as the squeraiuoli launched it on rollers into the stinking
canal: the Rio dei Mendicanti, where the Ospedal Xivile is, has
quite the most fancy stench in Venice at all seasons of the year and
at all stages of the tide. Zildo eyed the pupparin as one who knows
what should be, and is satisfied. The winter afternoon was bright
and sunny as most Venetian winter afternoons are.

'Row at the poop; and let us go on the lagoon beyond Sanzorzi,'
said Nicholas, as he took the prow-oar.

It was not far, after exciting twists through small canals into Rio
della Canonica, under the Bridge of Sighs, and out to the Basin of
Saint Mark. No collisions actually occurred. At the angle, where
the angel closes the hole in the wall by which the ape-devil bolted,
there was a narrow squeak of one: but Nicholas remembered that
seven years had lapsed since Zildo wriggled a bark through the city's
intricacies, and felt that the present test was severe. That, though,
was my dear patron's method. Tell him that you could do a thing,
and he implicitly believed you and trusted you, and set you to do
it without warning and never in the most favourable circumstances;
and (when you missed perfection) praised you, making the most
generous allowances for you.

'Sior,' said Zildo, 'it is very different rowing in these narrow
crowded ditches after the open sea of Calabria: but I shall do better
tomorrow, and still better next week.'

'It goes very well,' answered Nicholas: 'and now, uoa! uoa! regata!'

Both bounded at the oars; and the pupparin hissed like a javelin
across the broad basin, where steam-ferries pass from Canalazzo to
the Lido, and Austrian excursion boats anchor in seven or eight
metres of water. Between the islands of Sanzorzi and Spinalonga,
Nicholas knew that he rowed before the forcefullest and featliest
gondoliere who ever had rowed behind him.

As they went up the canal in the lagoon leading to the consumption-hospital of the province on the islet of La Grazia, a small sandolo came from the cross-canal on the south of Spinalonga. A monkeyish demon of distorted boy rowed antically on the poop. A litter of invalid men lounged wrapped on the cushions. A nurse rowed at the prow in the cardboard-model fashion permitted by starchy cuffs and aprons and streaming headgear. Nicholas sniffed some fun; and slowed to let the pageant pass. As they turned the palo at the corner and went up the canal of La Grazia, the nurse spotted the red and gold banner. She said something over her shoulder to her monkey, of course addressing him as 'Angelo.' 'Siora,' screamed that demon, 'it's a mad English trying to look like a Venetian.'

Nicholas stopped at the quintuple stakes marking the cross-canal and tied up there, turning the chair round to face the poop where Zildo was about to sit. 'Who are those lost souls?' he asked.

'Mi no so miga,' Zildo noncurantly responded.

'Did you hear what the demon said?'

'Siorsi' (with a slightly snarling twitch of nostril).

'And?'

'Gnente.'

Both were a little breathed, after the racing spurt which they had put on. Zildo's vivid pallor took the lovely rose of mother-o'-pearl, and his long green-blue eyes were bright. They sat still, looking over the glittering sunlit expanse of lagoon round them. Nicholas remembered that there was a private infirmary somewhere in Spinalonga, and when the sandola returned he stood up and called to the nurse as she passed.

'Pardon me: but, are you English?'

'O yes, do come and see us,' she bibbled, still rowing.

'I was about to propose it: because, you see, here is a pupparin and two stout gondolieri who will be pleased to row your convalescents these sunny afternoons, and save you trouble.'

'O thank you so much ; how frightfully good of you. Do come back with us now and have some tea.'

'Does English tea please you?' demanded Nicholas in a mischievous undertone of Zildo, as they cast off and followed the infirmary sandolo.

'Nòssiornò,' the boy responded with decision.

The British Infirmary, as Venice officially calls it—the Universal Infirmary as it dubs itself, in order to advertise its eagerness to take in lascars, Germans, and other dagos not afflicted with what its donnish old treasurer calls "sailors' disease"—is situate in Rio della Croxe on the island of Spinalonga, opposite to the Royal House of

Reclusion (or prison) which used to be the Benedictine monastery ruled by Saint Eufemia Giustiniani as abbess, the water of whose well proved miraculous against the pest of 1576. It is an historic house, formerly a summer palace of the Cornaro, but commonly known as 'Casa del Papa,' because no less supreme a personage than our Most Holy Lord Pope Pius the Seventh stayed there after His election by the conclave of 1800 on the neighbouring islet of Sanzorzi —that wonderful conclave of cardinals escaped helter-skelter from Napoleon's invasion of Rome—that specially wonderful conclave which (first and last in history so far) opened its walled-up door to admit an Englishman, Mr Robert Oakeley, emissary of Lord Minto the English Ambassador at Vienna, who bore (in noble answer to Cardinal Stefano Borgia's negotiations with Sir John Hippisley) an announcement that George the Third would make an annual allowance of four thousand sterlings to that pathetic figure 'Henry the Ninth of Great Britain, France, and Ireland, King, Defender of the Faith, by the Grace of God but Not by the Will of the People' —the Cardinal-Vicechancellor, the Cardinal Duke of York, Henry Benedict grandson of King James the Second, the last of the Stewarts, robbed of all in extreme old age by the brutal barbarity of Buonaparte. The Visit of Pope Pius the Seventh, exiled from His sovereign city, is commemorated on the antique stair of the Universal Infirmary by a marble tablet lettered in red gold with the following inscription, which (as far as I know) is singular in its ascription of the secular style 'Majesty' to God's Vicegerent here on earth.

NOMINI   MAJESTATIQ.
PII. SEPTIMI. PONT. MAX.
DICATUM
AD. MEMORIAM. GRATE. RECOLENDAM
ADVENTUS. REDITUSQ. EIUS
IN. HASCE. AEDES
X. KAL. MAIAS. AN. cIɔIɔccc. POMERIDIEM
QUUM. CATHARINUS. CORNELIUS. CUM. OMNI. FAMILIA
PRINCIPEM. INDULGENTISSIMUM
DEQUE. CORNELIORUM. GENTE. BENEMERENTISSIMUM
L.L. PRO. SUO. PUBLICOQ. TEMPORE
AD. SE. VISENDI. GRATIA
ACCEDENTEM. ACCEPIT
ITERUMQ. NONIS. JUN. MANE
AD. DOMESTICAM. ARAM. OPERATURUM
RECEPIT

In those days, a hundred and eleven years ago, the house must have been a charming little country villa on the verdant-gardened island of Spinalonga, not a quarter of an hour by water from the Square of Saint Mark. Even now it is possible to recover an impression of the quaint old low-pitched spacious rooms with their reticent stucco decorations at present cut up, or blurred by the dead white lead-pigment of people who do not want to know that whiteness is not necessary cleanliness, and that dark brown highly varnished is infinitely nicer to live and die with, reflects enough light, and instantly shews each speck of dust on its gleaming surface. But the infirmary is a private hobby; and (I presume) pleases its rider. It was originally founded by a committee of aliens resident in Venice; from one of whom I derive my information; and later, was captured entirely by a certain Lady Pash, who (being willing to pay for her pastimes) contrived to silence the committee and to oust British medical skill by making the directress acknowledge her sole sway. Mild old darlings, anxious to be charitable at the expense of a reputation for veridiction, used to say that as Lady Pash paid the piper she had a right to call the tune; and grumblers, who suggested that maintainers of infirmaries from motives of charity ought not to accept power as the price of their charity, were snubbed, and insulted, and (when possible) ruined. For Lady Pash was powerful, and Venice was her wash-pot, while (over Spinalonga) she certainly cast her shoe. She added a couple of wards to Palazzetto Cornaro, blotting out the splendid panorama of the Queen of the Adriatic which had met the Pope's apostolic eyes as He stood at the altar of the preserved chapel, gazing through the little windows flanking the triptych. No doubt she acted according to her lights. The pity is that they were farthing dips.

Zildo remained in the pupparin, while Nicholas followed the Directress to her private office under the roof. She had ribands of medals pinned on her bib; and was loquacious, garrulous, dicaculous, gushing incoherently and with such velocity that her words fell out of her, one over the other, with the distracting clack of the matrices of a linotype machine. By the bye, she meant well. Crabbe forced an opportunity, and said his little piece. He was English, living in Venice, liked to be useful, didn't like seeing women at rough work, would row convalescents on sunny afternoons, run errands, and do anything which a brain and two strong arms and oars and the fastest bark in Venice could do.

'How perfectly sweet of you!' the Directress gabbled. 'We shall be charmed. No one ever helps us. We shall be so charmed.

A man you can count on does help one so, you know. O, we shall be quite so charmed, you know. And now you positively must come and talk to the patients. And if you would only get up some entertainments for us. Conjuring tricks you know, or charades, or sing-songs, or a tombola, yes, a tombola—do write your name in the visitors' book, please; I don't know that name; what county are you? Kent? I'm a Somerset woman meself. Thank you so much—we should be quite so too much charmed.'

A grim calm hardened Crabbe's carapax as he was hustled through the wards. He began to wonder what in the world his impulse had let him in for. The patients turned out to be a chief engineer with a quarter of a kidney, a white-haired stoker with the sweet eyes and voice of a boy, with valvular disease of the heart, at whom the Directress yelled as "Daddy," and a little blackavized brigand from Bari minus a right leg. Crabbe reared reticently at a pattered description of himself as 'the kind gentleman who kindly offers to take you all out in his nice boat whenever it's fine—now let's all give him three cheers—hip, hip, hip, hooraaay'; and he got clear as soon as he could, saying, as the archgusher gushingly gushed at him from the door, 'Now look here, my dear good lady, please don't let me hear any more talk of that kind. Thanks are unnecessary and undesired. In fact I won't come near the place again unless you solemnly promise me never to acknowledge my services. Never mind why. Take it that it's my humour. So just agree to my conditions at once and be done with it. That's all right. Very well, then, there's the bark and the two barcaiuoli—damn the boy, of course he's handsome, they all are—listen—we shall row that bark every day, and we may just as well row it full as empty and usefully as uselessly. So please give orders. You can get at me on the telephone. Numero Due Quaranta. And try to get it into your head that I'm merely the handyman—nothing else, mind you. And I'll begin to work some day next week, as soon as I'm settled,' he shouted, lashing his oar at its forcola and sweeping away.

'Sior, did the lady insult you?' inquired Zildo as they popped under the bridge.

'Insult me? No. Why?'

'Sior excuses. I believed that you were scolding her.'

Nicholas laughed. 'I was teaching her Christian Doctrine,' he said.

It was getting dusky, and they hastened home—hastened, because the pupparin had no lanthorn, and Nicholas didn't want to be put in contravention of the law about lighting up. They dashed across the wide canal of Zuecca, and Canalazzo; turned out a trespassing gondola in Rio del Palazzo Reale; and moored at the pali of the Rowing Club which stands on the sea-front in the garden of the Royal Palace. The chain was secured by a Yale lock. Nicholas gave one of its keys to the boy, retaining the other himself, and took him into the club-house with him, so that the club-servants should know him; and shewed him where to store the oars and furniture of the pupparin when he had stripped it for the night. The servants were a dark diligent little marangon who was incessantly making or mending oars, and a foolish foul old idler who pottered pretending to clean when not begging of the only effective English member, or cutting his corns and patching his pantaloons in the billiard-room, or quarrelling with out-of-works infesting the Giardinetto Reale outside. They had seen so many of Crabbe's barcaiuoli about the place that this new one excited no special attention.

'Are you tired?' asked Nicholas, as Zildo's teeth dawned in a yawn.

'Never,' the boy promptly asseverated.

'You are licensed till dinner at 9 o'clock. If you have friends whom you wish to salute——'

'There is only one friend for me in all the world; and he is here——'

'Hummh!' said Nicholas, bleakly. 'Here are five lire of your wages for the pocket. Go and divert yourself at the kinematograph.'

There was an annoying accumulation of letters at the hotel, which made Crabbe sit thinking for an hour and examine his bank-book. Figures horribly bored him: his sums always came out wrong and in his own disfavour. Certain things would have to be pondered, and treated perhaps austerely: he put them away in mental pigeon-holes where consciousness might subconsciously nibble and chew them.

Zildo came in at $18\frac{1}{2}$ o'clock just as Nicholas was locking pigskin portfolios before changing for dinner.

'Sior,' he said, 'I have seen a kinematograph of the earthquake, pictures of pieces of naked women; and I have vomited; and I pray that I may go to bed, feeling a little evil.'

Nicholas regarded him with sudden anxiety. What a beastly coincidence. But the boy was as hard as nails; his indisposition was only superficial. Of course, tired with travelling and novel sights, it was enough to make him sick, to have the horror which slew his relations resurrected by the kinematograph's banal twitter.

'You must take nutriment.'

'Sior, with permission, I cannot eat now.'

'Go to your room, but do not despoil yourself till I come.'

Zildo obeyed. Nicholas summoned the squirrel-eyed little Piero and commanded a tray of soup, a roll, and red wine. 'Upstairs,' he said.

He and the tray found Zildo in the dark, not knowing how to switch the electric light at the door. Nicholas explained, as the food was placed on the dressing-table. 'Eat and drink, when you are hungry,' he said. 'And sleep and forget. Good-night.'

'Sior, you regale me with this? A thousand thanks. And good-night, Sior.'

Said Crabbe to little Piero, shutting the door, 'That boy feels ill, because he has seen scraps of naked women in a kinematograph of the earthquake which killed his parents.'

'O Caspita, and no wonder,' replied the athletic waiter; 'I myself saw them yesterday at the Cinematografo Sammarco, and they are shameful. Ladies ululated at the view; and I hear that the Municipality is involved to suppress.'

'I must go immediately after dinner,' said Crabbe. But he never did.

He took a book, as he was to dine alone; and read as he munched at his table by the window. Only one other guest was in the room, at the door end. Nicholas collected an impression in a corner of his eye as he passed—a priest (evidently), plain, polished, rather handsome, undeniably scholarly, and with the large manner—and then buried himself in his book while burying his dinner. You understand that he was not on speaking terms with any Roman Catholic clergyman, excepting the Reverend Bobugo. He avoided them, because of the dedecorous way in which some of them had treated him; and because (excepting the aforesaid B.B.) as far as he knew, he had never encountered an honest faithful one. He was frightened of them; for he knew quite well that there must be some decent priests somewhere; and it hurt him dreadfully to have illusions dispelled by never meeting any but indecent ones—using the word 'indecent' solely in its first intention. Beside, he had published a book of personal experiments with priests, *Peter of England,* an awful audacious book which flayed whom it did not scald; and his mood was not to compete for reprisals. 'It is not I who have lost the Athenians; it is the Athenians who have lost me,' he superbly said. So, when priests slank up to him, he civilly warned them off: if they merited kindness and persisted, he gave them double: but, never any more would he admit them beyond the barbican of his lifted draw-bridge, never any more would he go beyond parleys from the height of his impregnable battlements—unless they should come, at high noon, with a flag of truce and suitable gages—never any more would he on any account seek them, but to serve him as ministers of means of grace. He dallied with his tasty dinner, and his book—that really huge romance *Antichrist the Humanitarian* which his friend Bobugo wrote with such reprehensible slapdashery—noting plagiarisms of manner and of phrase from his own books, regretting the adoption of the literary trick (of interweaving the events of the last chapter with a sacramental hymn) played with perfect success by the obsessed author of *The Gadfly*.

When he left the table, the priest had vanished. He went to take coffee in the hall, where cane arm-chairs suited him. His Paternity was there. As Crabbe lighted up, the inquiry came, 'Have you been here long, sir?'

'I beg your pardon: I am rather deaf; and I was musing about my book.'

'I thought you were deaf,' said the priest, 'for I asked you the same question in the dining-room. I said, Have you been here long?'

'Frightfully sorry,' answered Crabbe. 'Indeed I did not hear you, or I should have replied that I have been here six months.'

Conversation welled from this boring, and began to flow over cigarettes and coffee. The priest named himself—Father Hugh Pontifex of the English Preachers, returning from preliminary examination for the Roman doctorate: he wanted to know how much, which really was worth while, could be seen of Venice in two days. His admirable manner, so Englishly Ecclesiastical (the finest manner in the world apart from that of sailors and stockbrokers of naval proclivities) made Crabbe happy enough to say formally, 'I shall be pleased to be useful. But, first, I ought to tell you my name, and that I wrote *Peter of England;* for I understand that I am eschewed as *persona ingratissima* by gentlemen of your Paternity's profession.'

'My dear man!' cried the other. 'What a meeting! What modesty! And, what a mistake! Why, lots of us think your book splendid; and would ask you to go into retreat for Holy Orders tomorrow, if we were bishops. And so I can return to England and say that I have met the Great Crabbe!'

Naturally, conversation flowed faster. The Dominican had seen Saint Mark's and the Doge's Palace. Crabbe named Sanzanipolo of the Dominicans, the Frari, Saint Mary of Miracles, Saint George of the Slovenes, Saint George the Great, and the Grand Canal. Those, for one day. And on no account could one go away without collecting impressions of the blue blue blue lagoon and the two byzantine basilicas on deserted Torxelo the grandmother of Venice.

While he was speaking, the Erastian Mr Warden and his lady passed, on the way to tardy dinner. The lady was a sour withered meagre lath of smirking female with the thinnest of pinched lips and nose-nippers, exquisitely dressed autumnally, clanking with narrow chains, famishing and parching for worshipful attention. The ghostly gentleman was meagre also, and knock-kneed: his face and head (by aid of goggles, nostrils at 45°, a flat, long upper-lip, and a thin, wide, rather abject grin), were the face and head of a skull, abnormally philoprogenitive. His gait was harassed, but obsequious. He cast a timid glance at the two English-speaking men as he went by; and would have moved, if he could have caught an eye. None was tossed his way.

'And now,' Crabbe continued, 'I will make a suggestion. I have a desire to be an object lesson; and this seems to be a chance of shewing that I'm not really the priest-eater which I'm said to be. I have nothing particular to do these next two days. So, will you let me run you round in my bark, and shew you what I call characteristic tid-bits? I promise you that you shall have the rarest time.'

'It's very good——'

Little Piero ran out of the dining-room bringing printed cards announcing service-hours at a dissenting temple in the city; and laid them with a roguish smile on the coffee-table of the two.

'This,' laughed Crabbe, on savouring them, 'is a juicy lark. This Mr Warden, who is, I understand, something of a light in the Erastian chapel here, is making a desperate bid for a nod, on the mistaken notion that your Paternity is a brother pastor who might, perhaps, preach in his conventicle on Sunday.'

'Not the first time that mistake has been made. But, do I look so patently Protestant?'

'O no, indeed: excepting perhaps that you are clean, and neatly shaven, and don't slink, and are neither puffed-up nor cringing, and don't wear those satin or velvet stocks with pearl buttons with which some priests are so violently enamoured.'

'I don't mind speaking to this thiasarkh, this Warden,' the Dominican continued: 'I've known many people of his persuasion who were quite passable.'

'So have I,' cried Crabbe. 'Some of the best men I ever knew. "Thiasarkh," though, is delicious—"President of a religious community" I take it—so vague, so defining, so sneering, so inoffensive.

He is not the actual President, the residing minister, but his name of Warden is enough to warrant the title. I shall call him the Thiasarkh if I have a chance. But I am not making any new acquaintances.'

'You kindly made no bones about making mine.'

'Touché! I'll owe your Paternity one. But, you know, you spoke first; and you have said nice things to me. All the same, I'm going to hold aloof here; specially from these dissenters. I've been here six months: I'm not unknown: but no one has thought it worth while to call. Even if they had—well, you know what British metoikoi in continental cities generally are—absent from the motherland by advice of the police, invalids, cranks, or resident aliens from purely selfish motives. People of that type make me rear; and I'll keep them at arm's length. And I've another reason. I've a game of my own to play, not an easy one by any means; and I shall play it properly only if my hands are not tied up in social obligations.'

They went on to talk of books. Friar Pontifex described questionable customs of British Roman Catholic publishers, instancing his own treatment at the hands of Messrs Paternoster. Crabbe told the inner history of the writing of *His Eminency's Vinaigrette*, and of the 'Deo Gratias' ring of its author, scribe of a single theme, four times repeated in *Towers near Hispana, His Eminency's Vinaigrette, The Dame Dominant,* and *My Friend Fortunato*. Conversation eddied over the defunct *Blue Volume*.[1]

'By the by, talking of the *Blue Volume*, I wonder whether you ever met a most admirable book of folklore called *Tales of my Toso* ' said the friar.

'O my Goodness Gracious, I wrote it,' Crabbe roared, with an upheaving gesture.

Cheers and loud laughter. The *Tales* [2] had appeared pseudonymously; and this mention of them was spontaneous enough to be gratifying. The Thiasarkh and his lady passed, anxiously cock-a-whoop to be funny with anyone. They were not invited to caper.

'Tomorrow then,' Crabbe concluded, 'you say mass at Saint Mark's; and the next day, at Sanzanipolo. So, tomorrow, I'll shew you Venice; and, the day after, I'll pack luncheon for three in my

---

[1] The *Blue Volume* is easily translated as the famous *Yellow Book*; and the works of which Crabbe relates the " inner history " are those of Henry Harland, i.e., *The Cardinal's Snuff-box, The Lady Paramount,* and *My Friend Prospero*.

[2] i.e., *Stories Toto told Me*, Fr. Rolfe's first book, published as by " Frederick Baron Corvo."

pupparin, and take you to Sanzanipolo for your mass at 7 on the way to Torxelo: which will give us a good ten hours on the lagoon. And now I'm off to bed.'

When he reached his top-landing, Zildo's door opened; and the boy came out, barefooted, in blue trousers and white guernsey. 'Sior, I pray one word,' he said.

'Còssa?' Crabbe shortly inquired.

'Sior, for gentility tell me who saw me when you found me swooned in the massacre of La Tasca?'

'I only.'

'Sior, with permission, was there no one who made kinematographs of me?'

'I did not. Nor was there a live Christian save I and you.'

'Sior excuses—did I resemble the pieces of woman shewn in the kinematograph?'

'I have not seen the kinematograph. Therefore I do not know. But all I remember of your appearance is a bruise on your left shoulder. Does it give you pain, Zildo?'

The boy ripped open the buttoned neck and shoulders of his guernsey, and twisted out his grand arm. The bruise had yellowed, and was fading fast.

'It goes well. It does nothing. So many thanks, Sior, and good night.'

'Good night.'

He who desires must pursue his desire though the whole world obstructs him. He who pursues has his path with obstructions bestrewed.

VIII

CRABBE sat in the sun, in his pupparin moored to a palo of the canal of La Grazia where the Three Wistful Eyes of the quire of Sanzorzi continually regarded him. He was to ponder matters contained in his pigskin portfolios, which had points of interest about them.

"I find," wrote the Reverend Bobugo, "that the purchase of my new house and estate has cost me more money than I anticipated. And what I am going to do for a regular income I really do not know. As for my people, they think me criminally rash to spend my capital as I have done, and I may not expect any help from them. The archbishop (very wise and holy) allows me to do as I am doing so long as I promise to preach and give missions during four months of each year. As I'm already famous enough to be refusing nine out of every ten invitations to preach that I get—Fact! Comments, please?—I think I can make almost enough at a tenner and expenses per sermon in those four months to live on during the other eight, but nothing like enough to carry out all the divinely-inspired plans with which my brain positively seethes. For example—I must have a minstrel's gallery in my hall communicating with another gallery in my chapel, which I certainly must build at once in the late Tudor manner, where my quire of boys (which I must establish) will discourse madrigals and antiphons (respectively) to the musick of archlutes and virginals. (Send me instantly the address of the man who said that the South Kensington archlutes were faked of bits of fiddles glued together—Dol. something was his name.) And I want to put up an altar made of a single block of slate at a cross-path in my pine-wood, where I can say my mass on fine summer mornings like the priest in *Forest Lovers*. And lastly (for the present) I must have my tomb made without delay—just a plain marble altar, with me in marble in Tudor vestments lying longways under an ogee canopy on a shelf at the back. Here is a sketch of what I mean. Admire it at once. Well: so you see my need of money is serious; and I can't make anything like the sum I want by books, or ghost-stories for the Yankees, or reviewing for the *Dublin*. Which brings me round quite naturally to the question of St. Thomas of Canterbury.

Now I have been talking to my publishers about our collaboration; and they say that, if my name appears with anybody else's, I shall only make about half what I should make otherwise. I didn't know this when I asked you to collaborate with me; and of course you can't hold me to an agreement, which you haven't. And I'm also sorry to say that I have so many things in hand now, as you see, that I shan't be able to give as much time to writing the Thos. book as I intended. This you won't fail to understand. So what you have to do is this—you must sign me a bond consenting to the suppression of your name altogether and to my name appearing as sole author of the book; and you must be prompt about it, and word it cheerfully as though the suggestion came from you and not from me, for I'm not going to give anyone a chance of saying that I take unfair advantage of you. That's one thing. This is another—I haven't, as I've told you, time to write the story as I proposed: but here is the Synopsis, which of course you'll agree to; and I'll engage to do this much—I will write chap. I: you must write chaps. II, III: I will write chap. IIII: you must write chaps. V, VI, and so on: but you will have to write all the most important chapters, St. Thomas's consecration as primate, and his martyrdom, for example. And of course you must revise and shape and give the real Plantagenet flavour to the whole; no one but you could in fact do that. Of course I shall want a second signed bond from you engaging to do all this. Now you clearly understand that it is simply a question of money. And, if you fall in with what I say without giving me any bother, I'll promise to pay you on day of publication One Hundred Pounds on account of your third of the profits—the third which you yourself stipulated for. I suppose you can see that, if you hesitate at all, you'll place me in a rather difficult position. I must be plain with you. I mean you would set me wondering whether I have been mistaken about your Vocation or not, and whether I should ever be able to collaborate with you again. I do not say that I will collaborate with you in other books if you do what I wish in this case. I don't bind myself or make any promises. I simply state my requirements and leave it for you to decide on which side your bread is buttered. ☞ Take care that the bonds are witnessed. It is not necessary or desirable that your witness should know their contents. All he has to do is to see you write your name and then append his own with the word 'Witness'."

That was the first of the three sweet screeds which Crabbe considered.

Harricus Peary-Buthlaw wrote, "I'm afraid I haven't done any-thing with the two-typed copies of *The Weird* nor yet with your manuscript of it. I've been too busy. As soon as you send me your manuscript of *De Burgh's Delusion* Mother shall type it and I'll try and see Shortmans. Up to now I've really had no time. I send you your vermilion habit as Provost of the Order. Be sure and get as many members as you can, and then I'll create a Grand Priory of Saint Mark with you as its prior. I've had four most haughty new sigils made. Please draw up a Latin office for the coronation of a Grandmaster. We must have a coronation next June positively. It's impossible for the Order to flourish while it has only a Lieutenant of the Grandmagistracy. The sovereigns of other orders are liable to cough at us. I'm sure the Patriarch of Hierusalem would have conferred the Order of the Holy Sepulchre on me last spring if I had gone to him as Grandmaster of our Order instead of merely as Lieutenant—he was so affable and frightfully bucked about our honorary cross of Lesser Wisdom which I conferred upon him. And when I sent father to Buda-Pesth as Chancellor of the Order to carry the same decoration to the Grandmaster of Malta, that prince as good as said that he would return the compliment to a brother-grandmaster. I suppose I shall be elected to the Grand-magistracy next June. There doesn't seem to be anyone else likely. So don't yon see why I want to have a function imposing enough to make Freemasons and Knights Templars perfectly goitrous with envy. I'm having my crown made, silver set with violet cairngorms and an ermine cap; and my nun-aunt is making my mantle of silver llama-lined ermine. My sceptre is going to be ivory, a narwhal-horn I think, and long—a staff not a mere stick, embellished with silver and violet cairngorms! I shall also have that big egg-shaped crystal in the drawing-room banded with the same metal and gems and a very long high silver flame and cross rising out of it for my orb. We shall call it the Egg of Wisdom. Now do draw me a design for the Great Seal of the Order under my Grandmagistracy—Obverse, me enthroned and wearing all my regalia—Reverse, me on horse-back ditto. And for my sake hurry and finish up and send me *De Burgh's Delusion.* We must have some money, and we can only get it by going to Shortmans with the two books which I've made them promise to take on sight. And, by the by, you being absent from England can't vote at curial meetings, so send me your proxy so that I can do the trick. Illuminet te Sanctissima Sapientia. P.S. You'll be interested to know that I'm engaged to marry Betty Bombazine this time next year."

That was the second of three sweet screeds which Crabbe considered.

Messieurs Morlaix and Sartor wrote, "We have to inform you that we do not feel justified in continuing your allowance on the present security."

That was the third of three sweet screeds which Crabbe considered. And his bank-book shewed that he had paid about a hundred and fifty sterling to the landlord of Albergo Bellavista, owed about twenty to him, and had about eleven left to his credit in the bank with possibility of an overdraft for about twenty-five.

As he sat in the sun of the lagoon, he wrote to Messieurs Morlaix and Sartor:

"Absence from Venice has delayed me in replying to your letter of December. I do not understand why the security of my six published books and of my eight unpublished books (of which you had sole and absolute management for five years) has suddenly lost its value. Please explain. Meanwhile, you have my life-insurance policy worth four hundred and fifty sterling: please increase the amount of it so that you can borrow ready money for my present need. I have here all the corrected proofs of my seventh book *Sieur Réné*: in the circumstances I think it safer not to send them to England for publication, but to retain them."

He wrote to Harricus in a form beloved of that sovereign: "Nicholas, by Divine Lenience knight-founder and knight-magnate and provost of the Order of Sanctissima Sophia, to Harricus, by Divine Tolerance lieutenant of the grandmagistracy, etc., of the same Order, greeting, kissing the splendid sceptre. Absence from Venice has delayed me in replying to Your December letter. Whereas Morlaix and Sartor have stopped my allowance without explanation: And, whereas Bobugo dictatorially commands me cheerfully to give him signed and witnessed bonds, first, that I will write two-thirds of that book about Saint Thomas of Canterbury on the same terms which were to have been mine for writing a third of it; second, that I will joyfully consent to his name appearing as sole author instead of both our names so appearing as he spontaneously projected in the beginning: And, whereas I am stony-broke, chiefly through paying Macpawkins's debts, and with no certainty of money coming in: I demand that Your Splendour instantly shall come to my aid, taking order that none shall do me wrong. And I blame Your Splendour for neglecting to dispose of *The Weird* which You have had in trust these six months past: and I pray you no longer to sin against diligence. And I at once will finish *De Burgh's Delusion,* which You shall receive early in February. And as for the Egg of Wisdom, I pray you to suck it assiduously. Illuminet te Sanctissima Sapientia. Given in my bark by the Islet of Saint George the Great at Venice in the Octave of The Lord's Nativity, mcnıviiii."

He wrote to Bobugo as gently as he could, putting his feelings in the form of hypotheses so as not to offend: "Absence from Venice has delayed me in replying to your December letter. Why all this bellowing about bonds for me and none for you? What's the meaning of this new fashion of letter? I've never heard such stuff in my life. If you're going to start in as a tyrant with your menacing roars, let me tell you that I defy and detest them and you. If you really mean to ask me to do what you ask me to do, I denounce you as an invader of voluntarily-proposed obligations, a breaker of spontaneous promises, and an attempter (somewhat sneakish in type) of the trick of paying for your ill-omened place and unchristian phantasies, and of otherwise aggrandizing yourself at my expense. I'm willing to believe that your head has been swelled by the adulation which (you say) your preachments procure for you. You must know that you are not the first young priest who has whispered to me (smacking his chops) of royal princesses rushing after him to sit veiled under his pulpit, and of Spanish bishops pursuing him to take his mind as to accepting a mitre and a pontifical breve of appointment as keeper of the conscience of Queen Victoria of Spain. So I am willing also to wait till the wet-cupping of this admonition has reduced your swelling and cooled you down to think over what you asked me to do, when, I am sure, you will realize that nothing of the sort ought to have been suggested. And, by the by, please note that you have not sent me your usual New Year Benediction."

That seemed all, for the moment, in those directions. Crabbe, feeling slightly touchy, preached to himself the duty of a strong rein on imagination, for avoidance of suspicion. As for means to go on with—as for the future of Zildo—his pockets were not quite empty, he had excellent credit, his assets were as valuable as ever though there seemed to be some hitch in their management, and the topo was coming from Calabria which had cost him 10,000 lire all told and could and should be sold for half that sum at least. As for other matters —"Never try to cross a bridge till you come to it," he warned himself.

When they reached the hotel for luncheon, the Thiasarkh was screaming through the office telephone, 'Per piacere, per piacere.'

He pleasingly varied his pronunciation from 'Pap pitch hairy' to 'Pippy cheery.' On seeing Crabbe, he beckoned him to the instrument with a goggling grin. 'Dear man,' he said, 'I do so think that the Directress of our infirmary is anxious to speak to you.'

She wanted him to row her and a nurse to all the English vessels lying in the canal of Zuecca and the harbour of Marittima directly after luncheon. He said that he would be with her before 14 o'clock; and turned to go into the dining-room.

Mr Warden waylaid him with, 'Dear person, I do so hope you have forgiven me for taking your rooms': and, in certain circumstances, a pat on the shoulder might have been perpetrated.

'Oh yes,' said Crabbe, stung by an instinct of dyspathy and not concealing it, 'I have forgiven: but it is too early for me to tell you that I have forgotten.'

'Thank you so much,' murmured the other, with a newer and sicklier and a more earnestly slap-requiring grin.

Winter suddenly vindicated itself after luncheon. A smart breeze sprang up with flesh-nipping gusts; and the sea rolled, tossing up actual waves, when the pupparin shot from the Bucintoro Club across the wide canal of Zuecca to the infirmary. The long light bark leaped saucily, but not agreeably, after the first hour of it. Nicholas and Zildo fitted her with carpet and cushions and took the two women aboard with an awful and apparently very bacterial white poodle, darling of the Directress.

'How truly sweet of you to come!' she bibbled; and explained that she wanted personally to invite all officers of the English Mercantile Marine then in Venice to the usual New Year's sing-song at the infirmary. Crabbe wondered why such functions did not take place at the Sailors' Institute. She had a lapful of invitations; and was fixed up in the frowsy moth-alluring furs and crumpled putrefaction-coloured flannelly garb affected by virtuous females. Crabbe found the voyage diverting. The fight with choppy rollers, adverse currents, gusty wind, filled his muscles with joy. The mousey little nurse was distinctly frightened: but she sat quietly, with none of the writhing and wriggling and spasmodic jerking offered by the Directress in token of active sociability. The latter, indeed, was so intempestively lively in bounding to ascend rope-ladders up grimy-sided coal-tramps that Crabbe presently inquired about swimming. 'I haven't the slightest objection,' he said, 'to your hurling yourself overboard, and I'll guarantee to get you out within half an hour.'

'Half an hour!' she screamed. 'Why, I should be drowned!'

'No,' he pointed out. 'You see, we couldn't heave you into the boat with all your fur and flannel water-weighted: so I should swim you to the quay-steps. But don't be disturbed. I'm quite able.'

She opined that she and hers would land near the oil-tanks on the quay of Marittima, and board the various vessels from terra firma. Crabbe accompanied them; and Zildo followed in the pupparin as they made the whole passage of the great oblong harbour. Captains and mates (whom they visited) were flabbergasted, but civil: though Crabbe knew that they suspected him of philanthropy, a pocketful of tracts, and a liability to burst out unprovokedly into a flat hymn. But they were not half so demonstrative as the Directress. She was accentedly hearty, bright also even to the smacking of a thigh for jocular emphasis. They took to the bark again at the quay-end under Sylos, and Zildo ferried them across the canal of Scomenzera. The visitation terminated at a particularly coaly tramp lying off the coal-heaps at the mouth of Rio di Sanbaxegio. The only officer here visible was the steward, who said that the ship would sail on the following morning, but (with a squint at the now grey poodle) he'd gladly see that the old man had the lady's letter.

Sixteen o'clock sounded from the bell-towers of Sambastian and Santareanzoloraffael as the party climbed down to make their way to the steps by the bridge where Zildo held the pupparin.

'O thank you so much,' the Directress bibbled, with a grimace and a fawn-gloved hand protruded. Crabbe looked surprisedly.

'No, we won't trouble you to take us back: we're going to tea with dear Lady Pash at Ca' Pachello; and we'll cross to Spinalonga by ferry after, you know. I've such a budget of news for dear Lady Pash. And of course you'll come and help us with the sailors tomorrow night now, won't you? I'm sure you know all kinds of funny tricks. So dear, so good, so trotty of you!' she finished.

Zildo's fresh face looked utterly serene, innocently ignorant, as he put away a rolled-up cleaning-rag which he was hugging, and stood up to arm his master into the bark.

'Ten centesimi for your thoughts about that lady,' Nicholas offered.

'Sior, I have many thoughts,' said the calm boy, skipping back to his perch on the poop.

'Tell one,' insisted Nicholas, frowningly annoyed by delayed obedience.

'Sior, Mariavergine would like to see her directing a small house of her own containing one bed and one cot.'

'Noa! Noa!' cried Nicholas, thrusting at his oar poised on the forcola, mightily beginning to row. Zildo was not to know that he had perpetrated a blazing epigram—that he had power to reckon up a superior (God help her) in one windy afternoon. Certainly Zildo would have to be considered seriously.

Crabbe considered him all the way back to the club. The atrium there, where racks of skiffs and pairs and fours and eights are stored with slim shallow valesane of Venetian origin and sheaves of oars like an army of lances stand and are made or mended, was unusually crowded in the vicinity of the notice-boards. Crabbe saluted his acquaintances, sumptuous lieutenants from the Arsenal, and insinuated himself into the focus of interest. The earthquake, of course. The Bucintoro as usual was to lead young Venice to victories—this time, of beneficence. On three appointed days, athletes were to meet at dawn in squadrons in the Royal Little Garden by the club. Each squadron would have a band and a fleet of barks to accompany house-to-house visitation of assigned districts. The whole city was to be ransacked for contributions of money, clothes, nutriments, building-wood for the starving, naked, homeless of Calabria and Sicily. Crabbe saw strenuous joys before him, involving the pupparin as a vessel of carriage; and away went all the worry of his difficulties.

The Thiasarkh (who had dined at the ordinary and alone) took a chair and a cigarette near him in the hall that night. Crabs are not bears. There were words about the voyage round Marittima, and the coming Beneficenza of the Bucintoro.

'Lady Pash, who perhaps you know is the chief member of our congregation, such a mother in Israel, is working very hard for these earthquake sufferers,' said the gentleman with the mildest tentativity.

'I ought to tell you that I'm a Roman Catholic——' Crabbe began. The Thiasarkh supplied arched eyebrows and a grin which said 'I flatly feel so unshocked.' Crabbe's instinctive aversion of dyspathy surged up: he sensed the toady odour of tuft-hunting; perhaps it would be as well to test the buttery-sugary swallow of this example. 'And I don't know any members of your congregation,' he continued; 'but I heard this Lady Pash mentioned in connection with beneficence at the rowing-club today; and I noticed that, when the name was uttered, every head instantly became bare.'

'Myiphmh! How truly touching! Dear person, do excuse me a moment. I've just remembered that I must telephone to my wife about the gondola. She is working at Lady Pash's.' He turned gleaming to the telephone, and began to ring and scream 'Pap pitch hairy, pippy cheery, noomerowd yea chick wattaw ditchy. Signorina,

per piacere, numero dieci quattordici. Prontaw. Prontawk heap
ah lah? Pronto, chi parla? Who is speaking. Ah, is that you,
dearest—yes, I was just going to ask you—he shall start directly.
Yes. And are you very tired? That's so brave of you. Three hot-
water bottles? Yes. And how is dear Lady Pash bearing up? That's
right. Give her my respectful love. Yes. Wait a minute. I haven't
finished——' He peered out to Crabbe. 'You don't mind if I tell
my wife what you just told me?'

'Not if you leave me out.'

'Thank you so much, she would so like to hear it. Dearest!
Dearest! Are you still there? So brave of you. I want to tell you
something so sweet. I've just heard such an interesting tribute to our
sweet friend. I'm sure you'll be glad to hear it too. Are you there?
Well, it seems that dear Lady Pash's name was mentioned this afternoon at the Bucintoro—Bucintoro—Boo-chin-taw-raw—the rowing-
club, you know, in the Royal Little Garden—her dear name was
mentioned—at a meeting, I think—in reference to the Beneficenza—
her name—you needn't repeat it unless you think it wise. Oh
Seen your eener, Signorina, pray go, prego io non ho finito, pippy
cheery, prontaw—ah, there you are, dearest—the silly girl cut me
off—I was saying her name—you know whom I mean—Lady Pash's
name came up in connection with Benny Fechenza, and instantly
all the young men raised their caps—yes—such a noble act of homage,
wasn't it? I thought you might tell—I thought our friends and our
sweet friend· might like to hear—yes, yes, of course—I'm sending
Vincenzo at once—ah river derchy!'

Crabbe hardened in his cane arm-chair, afflicted by verification of
his instinct. There came a mouth-taste of sour milk mixed with
very bad egg and rancid oil in a rusty old meat-tin; and a warm
ache gasped inside of him. It was, of course, indigestion, caused by
angry contempt temporarily paralyzing intestinal muscular action—
peristalsis, in short. He commanded boiling water, and moodily
sipped the potion. His obsequious neighbour gave orders to a
gondoliere in waiting, and resumed his place and conversation.
Crabbe incubated a fierce (but purely academic) interest in the
cringing little creature, and dabbed him (so to speak) for good
between a couple of glasses of deliberately microscopic observation.

I have already tried to hint how my patron was in regard to priests
and all others connected or interested in church matters. 'Bōzu ga
nikukereba, kesa made nikui,' says the Japanese proverb, 'Hate the
priest, and you will hate his very hood.' Always, everywhere, and

by all, it must be remembered that he himself, by choice, by call, by formal rite of tonsure, belonged to the estate ecclesiastical. He himself refused (for twenty years) the freedom of returning to the secular state by the footworn way of matrimony. Churchman and clerk he was: clerk and churchman he made himself remain while he patiently waited for the word to come up higher. Do just think, o most affable reader, what wild tenacity, what perdurable determination, what blind mad unreasoning fortitude, kept him clinging to that lowest rung of the ecclesiastical ladder for twenty years, with the hoofs of the hierarchy and the pads of the priesthood above him capering on his knuckles and stamping on his face, while the world with its devils and its flesh snatched at his heels, all to drag him down. Was (o most affable reader) that fortitude and determination and tenacity merely human? Or was it superhuman? I'm asking you. . . . In his soul's solitude, sheared from the laity, rejected by the clergy, he found for himself an ideal. I believe that he could have and would have lived very nearly up to that. I will go further. In my (merely my) opinion, had the blind guides had the gumption to legitimate (by ordination) the public practice of Crabbe's ideal, somewhere in this world (in as obscure a corner as possible) there would have been a fairly vivid and serene portent of virtue ecclesiastical, sowing immortal seeds in pastures cleared of tares, letting a light shine before men instead of advertising comparatively paltry experiments in illumination. But, these things being as they were, clerk Crabbe's front towards other clergymen was painted with unmitigated detestation, generally envious, often aggressive, always impatient and indignant. He knew so well how to walk in the world without in the least being of the world; and his pity for those who couldn't, or didn't, was more offensive than scorn. He had 'arete,' the poise necessary for tripping easily, airily, like a winged one, along the swaying slack-wire stretched across the seething gulf of sins. People—such a lot of respectable priests and people held their breath at his antics, away, up there, hoping to see him take some appalling toss. Such a satisfaction it would be to see pride taken down a peg or two. But he went unwaveringly on, sometimes reeling, but never other than superbly erect; and no one ever took him down anywhere —no, not even when they gagged and fettered him. Yet, while he thus detested clergymen and their kind collectively (Nonconformists for their meek hats and priest-ridden consciences and biblical criticism, Erastians for accepting catholic endowments in return for performance of catholic functions, and Catholics for their fussy, tawdry, sordid, worldly anxiety for acatholic testimonials and recognition), all the time he was scanning their ranks on every opportunity for the apparition of a specimen conformant with his romantic and simply scriptural ideal. That the good priest—the honest, honourable, fearless priest, the priest unspotted from the world, the priest unselfish who hoped and believed all things, whose charity never failed—the faithful servant, solely, and in simplicity—existed—Crabbe never for one instant doubted. He was not a narrow vulgar fool. But he never had met that priest: he had nothing but his ideal. For the strengthening of his astounding faith (the substance of things hoped for, the evidence of things not seen), Domeniddio seemed to be offering him the cautionary collection of clergymen and their church supporters with whom his life was infested, by whom it was (humanly speaking) spoiled, whose cantrips and squirmings and squealings defile these (and many other) pages. I trust that I have now explained, or (at least) described, an attitude which I should not dream of pretending to justify.

Warden talked of the earthquake: no one in Italy talked of anything but the earthquake, excepting of course, 'L'amore' and 'pajanche' and 'pojenta,' during that month of January. Crabbe tidily disposed his claws, shot out stark imperscrutable eyes to see, and set his feelers quivering to collect impressions. All crabs are deaf, you know: they have no ears and not even a rudimentary aural apparatus. That is why mere words sung by a Chrysostom, bawled by a bully, whispered by a Judas, never have the smallest effect on a crab. Your crab has no use for words: he must have deeds. Crabbe carefully concealed from this man his own recent experiments in Calabria, treating them as though they had not been.

Crabbe soon had enough of Warden's talk, and interpolated a lingering yawn.

'I wonder,' said his neighbour, a little awkwardly, 'if you could be so good as to advise me. There was a collection in our church on New Year's Day for Calabria and Sicily; and I'm so pleased to say that it amounted to more than that of any other church in Venice save Saint Mark's. How do you think I ought to dispose of it?'

'Why ask a Catholic? I'll answer you. I won't resist the temptation to answer you. All religious offerings ought to be placed in the hands of the local religious chief. Write a nice little note to the Cardinal-Patriarch: tell him that you want to pay him money: and don't omit to remain " Kissing the Sacred Purple".'

'Alas, dear person. I did something very much like that.'

'No!' Crabbe enthusiastically exclaimed. 'My compliments for behaving like an unembarrassed Christian. And?'

'The Patriarch received me so kindly. He thanked me quite too effusively: but he said it would be as much as his place was worth to take a public offering from schismatics.'

Crabbe smashed the glass which had held the boiling water, and commanded another. 'Silly idiotic old sheep, masquerading as pastor!' he ejaculated. 'Why didn't you give your money to him privately?'

'Oh, I don't think that would do. You see our congregation expects public acknowledgment.'

Crabbe sniffed. 'Of course, if you yearn to dish the Cardinal-Patriarch, if you still burn to place your contribution in catholic hands——'

'I won't send it to the National Fund, because of the shocking way the last National Earthquake Fund was maladministered; and of course I agree that the church of the country has the best right to administer to the christians of the country. Yes, if there is any public way——'

'Catholic journalism has a fund which it will lay at the feet of our Most Holy Father and Lord Pope Pius the Tenth. Send your money to the Venetian catholic journal *La Dipesa* "from the British Erastians in Venice," and you'll get your advertisement gratis.'

'Thank you so much. I will.'

Crabbe had a bourgeoning of urbanity. 'It's very sporting and christian of you,' he said. 'But I confess that I'm intrigued about you. May I ask what—thinking as correctly as you do about the rights of the church of the country—what your church and what your minister are doing here? What is your own justification of their official position here?'

'I fancy,' mildly murmured the other, 'they are here not, I do so hope, to intrude, but merely to administer British Erastian rites to British Erastians.'

'M-yes,' Crabbe concluded. The illumination afforded by a Roman candle surpasses that of a night-light. He provisionally pigeon-holed this zealous churchman as a consistent walker in the rays of his vouchsafed night-light. It did just keep him on the path, though it did not take him far. But, better a night-light than no light. The Wardeness swirled into the hall, a lady of impeccable principle with shallow peepers and miauly mouth in a brown stamped-velvet tea-gown and a fur cape. Seeing her property talking to Crabbe she came toward them, her tight exiguous smile of a public performer shewing tiny gold-speckled teeth in a line round the front of her visage. She swept a bow to Crabbe and sat by him. No presentation was attempted. The Thiasarkh's toad-like mouth opened and shut with delight.

'Dearest,' he mooed, 'Mr Crabbe has been so kind about our little earthquake collection; he has given me such a good idea!'

'Oh Exeter, do run out and get some cigarettes—the long ones with gilt cardboard tips,' she interrupted him, 'and Mr Crabbe shall flirt with me. We're going on to Fenice presently where our kind friend has lent us a box, to hear the last act of *Aida*,' she added.

Patently tactful and diplomatic, she proceeded to put Crabbe to the usual inquisition as to who and what he was, and where he had been, and whom he knew: from the answers to which, catechizers of her type are wont to extract their own image of what the catechumen pecuniarily is worth. For that is what they want to know— whether there is enough gilt on the calf to justify obeisances.

Crabbe instantly made a clean breast, so as to strip her stark of all hallucinations at the very beginning. He was a nobody, son of four generations of poor respectable tradesmen, privately schooled till fourteen, and thereafter quite on his own, no university, no even desirable connections, wrote (for a living) history when he got the chance, perverse historical novels when he didn't—he had particular friends, knew nobody worth knowing, and was not worth anybody's while. In fact, he tried to choke her off—or, perhaps this will be nearer truth, he let her know that he was neither jam nor treacle nor yet sweet flesh, so that she might go and hum in someone else's ear if she so chose.

Her man came back, and the three smoked. Dearest was to be told of an incident which had occurred about tea-time. 'A young gentleman,' Warden began, 'called to appeal for my help. He said he was in such a ridiculous plight. He left his fur-coat at Bologna, and didn't want to buy one here, because he had telegraphed for his own. Would I lend him something, anything, to keep him warm for a day or two. He's staying at the Britannica. Oh yes, he gave me his card.'

The lady tightened her nippers to look at it. 'D'you think he's alright?' she snapped. 'Rather a funny card, isn't it? What do you think, Mr Crabbe?' She shewed it over. He read *The Honourable V. Fitzgerald-Vepner.*

'I've never seen an honourable's card: but I've heard that such bloods always call themselves, not "Hon." and not "Honourable" but "Honble", and never on their cards. It's quite out of my line, though,' said Crabbe.

'Now I do hope, Exeter, that you've not let yourself be taken in again,' the Wardeness querulously ejaculated.

Another awful wave of dyspathy swept across Crabbe's mind, obliterating the sand-castle of the other man's christianity. This meagre female was prompt to think evil. Ghastly creature! Then what in the world was her tuft-hunting game with him? He hastily glimpsed his old grey velvet dinner-jacket for tufts which might have attracted so shameless a fly. No. He was a model of quiet shabbiness. Then, why had this pair barged into him? He hardened his shell, and felt for impressions more alertly than ever.

'Oh, I think he's all right, dearest,' Warden apologized; 'he was so well dressed, and his manners were quite nice, and he was so frank, too, about himself. It seems that his father was the eighth son of the tenth Duke of Drogheda——'

'They're Fitzgeralds. But what about "Vepner"? That's not even Irish,' slurred the lady.

'But he's the adopted heir of a Swedish general who has made him take his name.'

'Myiphmh!' she suspired. 'I'd better look at Debrett. And what did you do about the coat?' she added.

'I lent him,' her husband put it, 'that old pelerine with the hood. It only cost fifteen lire new, but I assure you it looked worth double when he put it on. Oh yes, I feel so sure that he's all right. If he isn't he's missed such a fine chance of robbing me. I took him to the Sailors' Institute after tea, as I had business there. I thought we could have our talk on the way, quite forgetting that I was to bring back last quarter's subscriptions to bank tomorrow. They were rather better than usual—L. 1,300 odd in fact, and he saw Royce count them over for me. Now, you know, he could easily have robbed me of all that current coin in any of those dark little alleys between the institute and Rialto. Couldn't he? So I'm sure he's all right, dearest. In fact, I've asked him to run round about 22 o'clock to go to the opera with us.'

The two, wreathed with simpers, went upstairs to satisfy wants and titivate. It was nearly 22 o'clock. Crabbe sat meditatively smoking. He was very far from keen on these Erastians. His instinct warned him against them. His aversion, from their blatant manner of thrusting themselves into his life, was poignant. What in the world did they see in him? What in the world did they want of him? Anyhow, they wouldn't get anything. It might, of course, be the case that they were merely dull, that they only meant to be decent, that they only pined for novelty in the way of cultured conversation. It was annoying, tedious beyond words, but human. And he would have to live in the same hotel with them, to be continually tumbling over them. If he wished to sit in that hall—and he intended not only to sit there, but to do quite a lot of literary work in the comfortable cane arm-chairs there—it would be impossible to avoid these bores, unless he could bribe some undertaker to bury them. Perhaps, then, a modicum of the 'hither shalt thou come but no further' type of civility, the passing of information about the weather, the submission of a literary point (she had written a book about sausage-fed females or something of that sort), or a discreetly witty story over a cigarette, now and then, might be not inconveniently conceded. But no more—oh dear no, with his hands as full as they were of involved affairs, and the yet to be finished *De Burgh's Delusion*, and the delicate delightful dangerous problem of Zildo.

To him there entered the most elegant young stranger, say of twenty, faultlessly dressed, exquisitely noncurant in carriage, not handsome, not fetching in any way, a perfect specimen of the undergraduate species, clean, cool, immaculately turned-out, draped in the most unpretendingly picturesque pelerine. This pattern had a little difficulty in making Bruno, the hall-boy, understand his Italian.

'I believe, sir,' Crabbe called to him, 'that Mr Exeter Warden is expecting you. He will be down in a minute.'

With modest acknowledgment, the youth sat to wait. Crabbe took him in hand, for the purpose of gaining a personal impression. Did he know Venice? Was he staying long? About a week would see him through. It was his first visit. He produced his pastime, a tiny cigarette-case, quite simple, quite golden. Never was dinner-suit more loosely and beautifully cut and worn. Never were seen such lovely plain linen, such masterful carelessness in the tying of a black silk bow. And the voice and the manner were so fine. For the lark of the thing, he should have a fair and independent show.

'I wonder,' said Crabbe, 'whether you'd care to come in my bark tomorrow? My rowing-club, The Royal Bucintoro, collects relief for Calabria and Sicily from every house in the city, and I am going to be a carrier.'

'I couldn't undertake to row a Venetian boat, you know, but I should be delighted to come and carry.'

'I do the rowing—I and my servant. And, if it amuses you to sit in the bark, and to take on board what the collectors bring us, you would help us hugely, and you certainly would see a lot of the city!'

'It's simply rippin of you to propose it——'

'Then, do me the pleasure of lunching here at noon.   And, afterward, we can go to the club for instructions.'

The skull of Mr Warden appeared: he said that his lady felt tired
and would remain at home.   Might he present the Honourable
Fitzgerald-Vepner.   He might.   And he and the youth, with nods,
set forth to the opera—Crabbe to his bed, where (for an hour) he
pondered the problem of Zildo—pondered it, pondered it, till, with
a sigh, he wooed Sleep.

IX

A LARGE card, proclaiming Lady Pash At Home on Twelfth Night, was what the morning mail spat at him. This was the limit. He had been a fool for having proffered aid to the infirmary. None of these people had the slightest notion of doing their own altruistic jobs for the sole sake of doing t.o.a.j. It's always the amateur and the egoist who does the real artistic thing for the sole sake of the art of it, and the real beneficent thing for the sole joy of doing it, without thought or care for (and with every high disdain and angry avoidance of) the social advantages which repay the professional. Oh, what a fool he (desirous of secrecy and solitude) had been, in letting these people even begin to discuss the Desirability of admitting him to their professionally altruistic economy! Was he going to submit to be sampled by these panting resident aliens of Venice? No, but no. His mind's ear instinctively heard the gossip which procured this invitation, and it made him wince and shudder. Acceptance would be a formal act of placing himself under somewhat exacting sway: it would be a voluntary numbering of himself among the appanage of yearning females (with little private axes to grind) and dull petits maitres (unable to give light and glad to glimmer in a reflected one) who throng such salons at command, grateful even for intolerable tedium. Oh, what a fool he had been! He wrote a frigid refusal, on the cool ground that (as a transient) he had brought no evening dress with him.

When he went to drop his letter in the hall-box, the Warden was pottering near. Crabbe firmly nodded: 'I'm just declining Lady Pash's invitation, which (I suppose) I owe in great part to you,' he said.

'Oh, I am so sorry——'

'I haven't the proper clothes with me, and I've frankly said so, so that your friend can't take offence. But I may as well make it quite plain to you at once that I don't want to know anybody here.'

The Thiasarkh oozed, 'I had so hoped——'

'How did you get on with your honourable?' Crabbe switched to inquire.

The change of subject was seized with alacrity. 'Capitally, quite capitally. I don't think we need have any apprehension. You know there was absolutely nothing to prevent him from absquatulating with that institute money.'

'Did you find him in Debrett?'

'No, but then ours is a very old copy. Mrs Warden is going to try to look at someone's Burke today. But I'm sure it'll be all right. In fact I've just telephoned to ask the lad to come with us to Lady Pash's weekly reception. I only wish that I could persuade—— Oh! Must you go? Good-bye!'

Zildo put away a very clean-looking roll of cleaning rag when Nicholas appeared, and they rushed across the Zuecca Canal to take infirmary orders for performance that morning, leaving the afternoon free for the Beneficenza. The pupparin looked brilliantly polished: the boy was evidently an expert who took his duty seriously.

By the steps in the niffy silted-up little Rio della Croxe the Directress was bouncing on the quayside, excitedly demanding her ever-bacterical poodle.

'I haven't got your poodle. You took him with you from the last coal-tramp, when you went to tea at La Pachello.'

'No, no, he didn't follow us, and we naturally thought you were sweet enough to take him home in your bark!'

'Thought that I was going to cross that tempestuous canal just for the sake of a dog? Well, I am—— He's evidently lost us both, and now I'd better go and trace him. Noa, noa, Zildo!'

He pushed off, leaving an agitated female flapping aprons and veil, incoherently jibbering on the quay. Up the long Zuecca Canal and across to the Zattere they swept, to the coal-tramp by Ponte Sanbaxegio, site of the beast's evanishment, Crabbe's intention being to work backward from that. There was confusion, on decks dirtier (but a little tidier) than on the previous evening. 'Have you come for your dog, sir,' the steward roared, as Crabbe climbed the grimy rope-ladder: 'we sail in ten minutes, and I've just put him ashore down there, by the coal-heaps.'

A coal-black poodle ecstatically demonstrated relief of mind, leaping at the ladder-foot. Crabbe incontinently dejected him into the pupparin. Barking which became strident at the Ponte della Croxe brought the Directress to kiss her truant's ebony nose and suffer the smirking of starchy caparisons. 'O, Mr Crabbe, how good of you, how sweet of you, how dear of you, how too truly trotty of you,' she began to hiccough.

'Good-bye for three days,' he cried, shoving off; 'I'm working for the Beneficenza.'

'Eat at a trattoria today,' he said, giving a lira to Zildo at the club, 'and have the bark polished of the poodle and ready here at the stroke of one.'

While he sat in the hall of the Bellavista, waiting for his guest, a little before noon, the Warden entered from the street, a gloomy pained skull. 'I'm so sorry, but that young man is a wrong 'un,' he twittered.

'Lord!' Crabbe cheerfully aspired. 'What a silly wrong 'un not to have hocussed you last night! And to think that I've asked him to luncheon! Do tell me what you've discovered, so that I may know what I should like to do.'

'I think it might be as well not to put him off,' mused the other; 'that might make him suspicious, and it would be so unpleasant to have a scene here which might be avoided. I fancy he'll get his deserts, without us, elsewhere; and one need not mix oneself up unnecessarily with undesirables, need one?'

'What have you actually found out about him?' Crabbe inquired.

'Well, we went, as I say, to our dear Lady Pash's to look at her Burke, and it didn't tally at all with his tale. And our sweet friend then made us tell her what she could see was perturbing us. And it appeared that she, last week, at the very time when the young man admits he was at Bologna, received from Bologna a telegram, as from an intimate, signed Captain Alured Baldcock, of whom she's never even heard, asking for fifty sterlings by wire, he being in difficulties at an hotel there. But, by the Mercy of God (Whom we both commonly adore) our dear sweet friend was sharp enough to wire, not to the sender but to the proprietor of the hotel, saying that she didn't know this Captain Baldcock. Whereupon that gentleman vanished from Bologna, leaving his luggage at the hotel; and we sadly fear that he is identical with your friend.'

Crabbe, for his own purposes, shelved that neat 'your friend' for the moment. 'Where is the connection?' he merely inquired.

'Ah!' sighed the Warden, 'that's what pains me so. Of course I instantly called upon Gaultier at the Britannica, who tells me that the feller did go to Bologna, and came back without his fur-coat and a hand-bag.'

'But that's exactly what he himself told you. Hardly the act of a leg, is it? Hardly more the act of a leg than the letting you get your fifty-two sterling home safely last night, now is it?'

'B-but he was at Bologna at the very time when this Captain Baldock was wiring from Bologna.'

'Isn't there a remote possibility—is it utterly inconceivable that there also may have been just one other person knowing enough English for telegraphic purposes there too? I frankly should not conclude a syllogism on your present premises, unless you particularly want to. For conviction, you must get the Bologna hotel-porter to identify his Captain Baldcock with your honourable.'

The Thiasarkh produced a martyr's obstinate grin. 'Gaultier,' he began, 'is afraid——'

'Naturally,' supplied Crabbe, 'hotel-keepers always are, when the best intentions go nosing their guests.'

The Warden still patiently edged in his word: 'But, you see, the feller hasn't got any money. In fact he borrowed fifty lire of Gaultier.'

'Unfortunate young owl! Still, that's not evidence of crime. Heaps of nice, honest people find themselves in pickles. I'm in one myself. But—well, now I'll tell you what I'm liable to do. Your honourable friend' (he prinked his man full, this time) 'will be here to lunch in a minute, and will spend the afternoon with me. I've a fairly cultivated intelligence and carefully sharpened sensibility, and I've made experiments in reckoning-up several scores of undergraduates (though I'm not a university-man) and I've heard several hundreds reckoned up by proctors and examiners. I believe that I can form a provisional judgment of this youth by about 19 o'clock. But I warn you that I start with a prejudice in his favour, chiefly because I perceive that he's going to be another example of the One and the Many, and secondly because I really do not credit him with the astuteness necessary for the bold buccaneer and gentleman-adventurer which you've got on the brain. He may be in difficulties, but he's far too young and simple to be your accomplished and fearsome rogue. Anyhow, I've never to my knowledge entertained a blackmailer; and perhaps this is my opportunity—ἔυφημαι, hush!' he concluded, in Ciceronian Greek, as the gun of Sanzorzi and all the bells in the city announced noon; and the Honourable strolled through the hall toward him.

That enigma was as well done as ever, in a reserved grey morning-garb—quietly and nonchalantly and perfectly put on, neat to flower-likeness and not new. He looked like nothing else than what he made himself out to be, a slightly elegant and not a bit precious lounger, as he shook hands with Crabbe.

'Luncheon is ready,' said Crabbe.

'I'm to come to you after dinner tonight?' his guest passed to the Warden.

'Myiphmh,' softly sighed that touched one, 'Myiphmh, no; I'm so sorry to say that Lady Pash isn't receiving as usual this week, so it were useless to trouble you.'

'My misfortune!' came the assent, with a step Crabbe-ward.

'Myiphmh,' sighed the Warden again, 'do excuse me—I was trying to recall what you told me yesterday. Your father, you said, was——'

The youth conceived the germ of faint interest in his inquisitor. Looking him straight in the eyes, he filled in, 'Eighth son of the tenth Duke of Drogheda.'

'Thank you so much. I suppose it would be in Debrett or Burke?'

'I suppose so.'

'Yes. Myiphmh. Well then, good morning.'

As they entered the dining-room Crabbe remarked, 'Resident aliens are always frightfully inquisitive about new-comers.'

'I generally get on pretty well with 'em, and with most people,' the other informed him, glancing at the menu.

It was an ordinary hotel-luncheon, gnocchi, a cutlet, salad, cheese, and fruit, and half a litre of white Corvo.[1] The two told each other about each other, and exchanged cards. The Honourable was roaming for a year, before settling with the Swedish general who had adopted him. It was all very likely. He couldn't talk Crabbe's subject: the only books which he seemed to know were the novels of Dorothea Gerard. After coffee, they meandered down the Piazzetta to the bark lying off the Bucintoro. The suspect shewed not the slightest concern at the really gorgeous display of prizes, monstrous silver krateras from the Athenian Olympic Games, the golden Bucintoro and targes and statues; and Crabbe felt that he had nothing heavier than a comparatively innocent and subvacuous undergraduate in charge.

His orders were to go to the desecrate church in Campo Santamargarita, which was used as a receiving house, and to carry thence as many bark-loads of goods as possible to the barracks of Sanzaccaria. He and Zildo drove the long, light pupparin, all that sunny afternoon, up Canalazzo to Santamargarita, and back across the Basin of Saint Mark to the water-gate of the barracks in Rio dei Grexi. During the passages empty, the Honourable lounged amidships, smoking or chatting. When loads were taken in at Santamargarita—amazingly heterogeneous loads, clothes old and new, mattresses, bales of cloth

[1] The wine of Corvo is made on the estate of the Duke of Salaparuta, and has no connection with Rolfe's earlier assumption of Corvo as his own baronial title. But this reference to Corvo wine shows that he was acquainted with the fact that the word has a territorial reference.

and linen and flannel, boots and hats and bathing-dresses—the suspected character worked with the concentrated fury and simplicity of a football quarter-back of Trojan extraction, catching miscellaneous masses indiscriminately hurled from the quay, stowing them in the frail bark scitulously and securely, leaving space for the two oarsmen and no more. On the return voyages to Sanzaccaria, he airily perched on mounds of millinery and tottering towers of trousers, covered with dusty fluff and justly jocund as a slender sand-boy. Arriving, after swiftly cautelous passage with gunwale not more than clear of the canal, he joined at the great barracks (with gusto) in the game of unloading and tossing the freight to the arms of Italy's splendid soldiers, for classification in that vast magazine, whence Italy's even more splendid sailors were to load Venetia's offering on the marine bastiments anchored in the Basin, for quick conveyance to Calabria and Sicily.

About 18½ o'clock, all very wearied in the dusk, with the last load (half a bark-ful) from Santamargarita, Crabbe said, as they approached the Albergo Britannica, 'Shall I drop you here, or would you care to finish the journey?'

'Just as you like,' the Honourable answered.

Nicholas called back to Zildo to steer inshore. 'I'm frightfully obliged for your help; we've done about double the work of any other pupparin,' he said to his guest.

'We've had a rippin time,' rejoiced the other one; 'do come in and have a cup of tea with me.'

Crabbe declined, for he wanted to finish, and was really tired, and felt that he must have time and solitude for pondering the items and producing the sum of his experiment. After delivering his burthen at Sanzaccaria, he had a mental impulse to collect Zildo's impressions for his assistance. But he refrained himself sharply. The awful promptitude with which his servant had furnished a summary just judgment of the infirmary-gusher darted from memory to will as a bolt to bar a door. He bade himself to do his own thinking, and not to be so confoundedly lazy as to count on the opinions of others. And he took himself severely to task about his propensity to be familiar with Zildo. It would not do. It ought to be checked. This was a new half of his life, and everything in it was different from the things of the first half.

He called for tea when he got home. Elia, the major-domo, provided it. He spoke a weird type of English, this one, and would ask whether Crabbe knew the young gentleman who had lunched with him.

'Only that he was introduced to me by Mr Warden,' Nicholas answered, with gleeful malignance and a feeling that there were fourteen possibilities in the air. 'And he has been working with me for the Beneficenza this afternoon. But why do you ask?' he added.

'Well, sir, you see, sir, he was followed here by a detective who waited outside, sir, you see, sir, while he lunched, you see, sir, and followed you both after, you see, sir, when you went across the Piazzetta, sir, you see, sir.'

Crabbe said that it was comical, and he buried himself in the perusal of the *Gazzettino*, that charming little journal of Venice which gives, not only a decent summary of the world's and the country and the city's news, but a really liberal education in Venetian manners, customs, and delicious dialect, all for the sum of three schei, less than three-fifths of a halfpenny. Through and after dinner he mentally reviewed the afternoon's tests. Taken in sum, they amounted to confirmation of his instinctive first opinion—that the Honourable hadn't it in him to be an undesirable of that particular type which vulgar, sordid imaginations could no doubt make of him. He neither bragged nor lamented, neither asked nor hinted: his carriage and conversation had been confined (quite without effort) to the plane of the ordinary, though undeniably embellished by the natural elegance of his personality. And—let this be vociferously intoned to the clamour of clarions and the bray of bassoons, he was young enough, and unembarrassed enough, to have thrown himself whole-heartedly, for four good hours on end, into the somewhat sweaty game of bodily poise while catching-in and storing-in and tossing from a dancing pupparin ponderous amorphous baggage collected for the Beneficenza. Crabbe compared the specimen with several historical land-sharks, bandits, piqueerers, rapscallions, rapparees, riggers, rooks, Greeks, sharpers, light-fingered gentry, and other varieties of legs. All these, as he remembered, possessed one common salient feature at least, the eye of the public performer—the same eye which the popular clergy and their ladies share with conjurers, welchers, singers, actors, politicians, tradesmen, and all kind of mummers—the nervous inquiring eye with a 'what price this?' expression—the anxious eye which watches, with would-be good-humoured equanimity, the effect of offered goods, and is eagerly ready to substitute fresh samples at any sign of disinterest or disapproval. The Honourable had not that kind of eye; he hadn't shewn any concern about other people's opinions. If he was bad, he was bad with the cleverness of a very master of badness and not at all prone to take a toss over a paltry fifty sterling. And Crabbe conceived it probable, being himself a mysterious unit (because simple in a complex society) that this other unit might be suffering involution in webs of mystery because he was (as he seemed) simply simple. He was just thinking of taking this judgment to bed when the Wardens came from dining out, with discreet and chastened sumptuosity.

'Oh!' the Thiasarkh gleamed, 'have you, oh have you, heard of the Honourable?'

Crabbe shifted his great ferocious pincers into position, shooting out his rigid eyes to glare at a silk-faced, frogged and braided dress-coat clothing an aspect of lamblike gaiety which indicated capacity for being really sprightly on a well-waxed floor at festive seasons. 'I've had him with me all the afternoon,' he answered, and quietly collected his forces to resist impact of something intended to stun.

Mistress Thin-lips looked on, with a slit smirk of smile. She was festooned with very narrow chains on black lace over blue, and her dove-coloured coat foamed with feathers.

The Thiasarkh made the Venetian gesture which signifies in-carceration, crossing his wrists. 'Tonight, he sleeps (if he can) at Sansevero,' he toadily mouthed.

'Lord!' Crabbe threw at the pair.

'Gaultier did it,' the man newsfully burbled; 'he, you know, has sons himself, and he tells me that he took a fatherly interest in the young man. So, when he had thought over the Bologna affair, and saw our friend going about quite calmly, he had him watched all day——'

'That explains what Elia said about a detective who was following us about.'

'I do hope you were not annoyed,' the lady aspired.

'Not a bit. I wasn't conscious,' Crabbe guffawed; 'if your Gaultier's detective ran about on our heels all the afternoon he'll have earned a handsome tip as well as his wages.' He sketched speed and action. 'And what next?' he inquired.

'Well, then, when Gaultier found that nothing suspicious could be learned this way, he asked him tonight to pay his week's bill and the fifty lire which he borrowed, and, when he couldn't, Gaultier says that he felt it his duty (as a father) to prevent the youth from running into debt. So he sent for the vigili and had him arrested.'

'I always knew,' Crabbe commented to the round world, 'that Germans were quaint in their ideas: but your Gaultier's conception of the duty of a German father strikes me as purely weird. Do German fathers always strike their sons impotent with public disgrace

to prevent public disgrace from rendering their sons impotent?
And, what are you going to do about it?' he further inquired.

'Give me a cigarette, Exeter,' said the lady, taking a chair near
Crabbe who turned to illuminate her. She sucked. 'I don't see that
my husband'——she began, turning up her cigarette (as false-pre-
tentious women always do) to assure their sight (of what their taste
and smell and touch perceive not) that kindling successfully has
been accomplished.

'What,' the Thiasarkh cut in, 'do you think I ought to do?'

'What indeed?' Crabbe quietly murmured, producing the most
recondite and exacerbating sword of smile in his whole armoury.
For he nourished predilection for the trained intelligent expert,
who knows his proper job, and intelligently and methodically does
it; and he impatiently scorned your mere modern mechanisms,
which are always slipping for want of winding, and every now and
then break down till some chance passer-by jogs or jolts or jerks them
into feverish but only intermittent activity.

'It's such a difficult question,' the Warden opined, when that
immutable reckoning smile began to have the effect on him of the
smile of a headless Irish nightmare.

'Is it?'

'Oh, isn't it?'

'No. It's as easy as eating. It's merely functional. Your friend,
who (you've freely admitted) safely might have robbed you of
fifty-two sterlings, and didn't—your friend is a member of your
Church, one of those very errant Erastians to whom the Church you
and others have established in Venice is bound to administer Erastian
rites. See?'

'But what would you do?'

'If I were a priest, I should have been at the prison within five
minutes after news of the arrest was sprung upon me. I'm presuming,
for your sake, that it was sprung upon you. I should have
demanded my right as an Englishman and a Church official. If
they made difficulties, I would have had in our capable consul.
But they wouldn't. The Italians always behave magnificently to
the English. I should have said to the prisoner that I had come
as a friend: he might confess, if he felt moved to confess, or
he might call upon me to perform friendly offices. I certainly
should have tried to persuade him to confess. No one is
ever the worse for having his soul cleaned. But, apart from
confession, if he liked to tell me about money difficulties, I
would have scratched up (out of the congregation) enough filthy

lucre—what's money? what's (say) a hundred or two sterling in comparison with the branding and wrecking of a young male life?— to set him free, for the sake of the reputation of England in Italy.' Crabbe blazed with fervent emphasis. 'But,' he added, 'I ought not to preach what I'm not prepared to practise. This is another of the occasions (about the nine hundred and sixty-ninth) when I curse the infernally vacuous miscreants who prevent me from priesthood. But, even as I am, I'm gravely thinking that your friend has a call on me. He hasn't had me alone in a maze of dark alleys where he quite comfortably could have taken L. 1,300 from me, it's true: but I'm gravely thinking that the slight relations of this afternoon oblige me to visit him at Sansevero, saying just this—that I come as a friend if he wishes to use me, telling him all which is being said or suspected, inviting his confidence, and offering to advise or to help in any way. Yes, I'm gravely thinking that I'm bound to do as much as that.'

'Oh, pray don't!'

'Someone once said, "I was in prison and ye visited Me not".'

The debatable Warden writhed, agonizingly gurgling. His arrant lady skimmed round the edge of a sneer at unheard of shop. 'But, don't you see,' he squeezed out of his silken all-round waistcoat, 'I've been so mixed up with the young man——'

'Yes. He protected you when your pockets bulged with convertible coin, instead of bashing your face in with the usual chloroformed handkerchief and scooting with your spoils.'

'Oh, well, but, you know, it's extremely likely that the Questore may call me as a witness. And you, too, for that matter——'

Crabbe broke in. 'And then? And then? You can't say anything against him, excepting that he's such a besotted idiot that he didn't rob you when he might. And your being called as a civil witness doesn't absolve you from performing a Christian duty. As for me, I know nothing certain about the boy, excepting what is highly in his favour; and I'm prepared to proclaim it, if I'm given an opportunity, and to take or make an opportunity if I'm not offered one.'

'Lady Pash, Exeter, ought to be asked——' the Wardeness began.

Crabbe felt his mind becoming unhinged. 'I'm not arguing with you, I'm just telling you,' he announced with perfectly horrible austerity. 'And I've tired myself slightly today: so I'll say good night, if you'll permit me,' he serenely added. Why should he wabble with windbags like these, who so fawningly flattered fortune, and snatched from misfortune the hem of their skirts?

X

He rose at 6 o'clock, after a frightfully restless night, and hurried with Zildo into Sammarco to find a mass. One thing which had been worrying him was the health of the boy's immortal soul. His private habit of sneaking a quiet mass in a dark corner every morning, absorbing a little vigour to nerve him for the day, was his own affair; and he preferred to keep his privacy. But he did intend to see that his servant heard mass, at least on holidays, like a decent Christian. They slipped into the cavernous brown-gold shade of the basilica, already twinkling with the primrose stars of lofty tapers, whispering with the sound of entering feet. Outside they left the wonderful deep cold blue which heralds dawn. A mass of Epiphany was beginning at the little octagonal shrine of The Cross. They stood, with their backs to the opposite column, slim, strong forms, one half a head shorter than the other, in indigo opened on the white triangle of guernseys. Nicholas noticed that Zildo was perfectly motionless, not signing triply at the Gospel, standing entranced, with childlike gaze fixed on the heart of the mystery. Nor did the bell awaken him. The approaching Elevation was proclaimed. Nicholas gave a flat bang on the back, whispering, 'Here is God: kneel, if you are a Christian'; and master and servant kneeled side by side. After the Last Gospel, Nicholas went to make his special compliments to Madonna of Nikopoieia. Mass was being said at her altar; and the Host was present. He made his reverence on both knees: Zildo, accompanying him, crooked one. "Down!" said Nicholas sharply; and saw it done. When they moved away, he insisted on the proper genuflection. As they emerged into the atrium, he issued commandments: 'In a church you will imitate me—both knees on the floor to the Lord God exposed—one knee on the floor to salute Him in His tabernacle when passing—and fortify your soul with the Sign, my boy.'

'Sìssior. Very religious are the English.'

'They are not ashamed of anything, or afraid of anybody, as are some Italians.'

'Nòssior. Nor am I.'

Have you ever considered, o most affable reader, Nature's slow, slow, sure process of making a flower, her long preparation of the ground, fallowing, manuring, digging, harrowing, irrigating it, setting it and its circumstances in order, before the sown seed will peep out, and shoot to growth and leaf and bloom and flower? I ask, in case your perspicacity has not perceived that I follow Nature's method here. I am writing this book, preparing my ground, sowing my seed. Give me time, then, and you shall see a flower, that transcendent flower called Amaranth—Christ's Scourge, or Love-Lies-Bleeding.

After coffee, Zildo was sent scudding to the club to polish the pupparin. Nicholas rolled a cigarette.

There was no news from England. It was too soon for letters. Why didn't people wire. If they were going to be wretches in England!

The great claws clashed. Moreover, this inglorious crew, among whom he was mixing himself in Venice, were going to annoy him still further. What, in the Name of Heaven (he had beaten into his brain in the wakeful watches of night), was the duty or the use or the good of having any truck at all with these new people, when interesting affairs needed every ounce of resources and energy. But, if friends in England, Bobugo and the Peary-Buthlaws, by chance should choose to be blackguards, would it not be well to make new friends? How can one in trouble make friends? What sort of comment attends action of that species? Consider people like the Wardens, chorus-masters of resident aliens in Venice—benign gods had shewn him their notion of treatment due to disaster. They arrogated inquisitorial powers, judging, and condemning unheard, a fellow-mortal. They behaved like bullocks who stamp on the fallen. And was he benighted enough to supply them with chance, or material, for weaving for him such another damning web of gossipy suspicion as that with which they were enmeshing the (perhaps naughty, but certainly) unfortunate Fitzgerald-Vepner. O Lord, forbid! What then? Take no thought. And, for today, there was the Beneficenza.

He was still dawdling with the *Gazettino* in the hall, so that Zildo might have his time to do the job, when, all of a sudden, the infirmary directress bounded in and swooped at him. 'Maaah! You dear thing,' she mouthed; 'how could you have the heart to refuse our sweet Lady Pash?'

Crabbe froze stiff. 'This is most irregular. Lady Pash—God knows why—asked me to her party. I said I couldn't come because I hadn't the proper clothes. And there's an end of it. So run away like a good girl.'

'Not at all; think how disappointed we shall be.'

Crabbe sincerely hoped they would—'we, indeed'—and he would do his very best to disappoint them as deckle-edgedly as possible. He didn't say so, but just affronted the bibbler with his senseless carapax.

'Oh, but surely, surely you could get some clothes?'

'In Venice? To fit? By tonight? Not if I tried. But I'm not trying.'

'Oh, you must. You can't think how hurt dear Lady Pash is.'

'Sorry.'

'She does so want to know you, to thank you for your sweetness to her infirmary.'

'Quite unnecessary.'

'She says she's never been refused by anyone before.'

'For my part, I simply wallow in strange experiments.'

'But you will reconsider? I must run off and do some shopping in Merceria. You will now; won't you?'

'Impossible.'

'She says she was never so snubbed in her life.'

'Nonsense. Ambassadorial ladies can't be snubbed by anyone below the rank of a sovereign regnant.'

'Well, I'm to tell you that she won't take your No for an answer.'

'Won't she really? Well, thank you very much for coming. Ring me up on the telephone, next time. I'm just off to the Beneficenza. You shall tell me all about the party the day after tomorrow.'

No sooner had he got rid of the woman than the Wardens came downstairs, holding opened letters.

'Ah, there you are. Good morning,' baaed the Thiasarkh. 'May I—I wanted to say that we do so hope you've altered your mind——'

'If it's about Lady Pash's party, I haven't.'

'Oh, I am so grieved. Can't we persuade you? The fact is I've got a note——'

'Thank you very much. I know all about it already and I've said No loud. I really can't wait now,' Crabbe added, rushing upstairs.

He was bleak with rage. Confronted by interference, threats, force, or any kind of opposition, he was terrific, a monster absolutely ununderstanded of the profane vulgar. Most men give in under the third degree of importunity, after a show of resistance, or at some stage. Crabbe never gave in, any more than he ever let go. He was very very long-suffering, he hesitated hideously: but, when once he went forth to war, he persisted. Right, wrong, success, failure, expediency, inexpediency, had no significance to him then. He just tenaciously and idiorrhythmically persisted. When you smashed his shell, and broke his ferocious pincers, and tore off his feelers and claws, in handfuls or one by one, with deliberately Christian cruelty or charity (the terms are synonymous, the method and effect of both are identical) he lay quite still—if he could, he limped, or dragged his mutilated remains, into some crevice—and grew new armour wherewith relentlessly to continue the affray.

The uproarious indecorum of this importunate widow's messages finally crystallized his determination. He didn't know Lady Pash, excepting by sight as one of those gaunt but flocculent females with a horse's long face, which she (of course) prolonged by a tall, thin bonnet perched aloft and set with rigid vertical bows resembling the ears of an obstinate mare—the kind of female liable to wear Mary Stuart caps by night and to fly in the face of Saint Paul's explicit command concerning feminine head-gear (as recorded in canonical scripture) by sporting the price of a life in the shape of a pear-shaped pearl-drop on her parting. How much of her real self was pictured in the fulsome fuss of the infirmary directress and the fawning of the sycophantic Wardens he neither knew nor cared to inquire. At any rate, a woman (allowing her full discount) content not to take a besom to the puffers and earwigs and clawbacks and parasites surrounding her, and willing to snatch and scuffle for yet another one, was far too odious for the taste of Nicholas Crabbe. That he would make plain. At the same time, he might as well make an end of the Wardens and their honourable friend. The infirmary directress should be taught her place, and kept there; and he need not break his promise to visit and help the charity. But, beyond that, and the Beneficenza, everyone else in Venice should be wiped clean off the slate which he wanted for the inscription of his sole affairs. He wrote to Lady Pash, regretting that the conventional half-truth with which he had veiled the cause of his refusal of her invitation had not been accepted, and offering the naked and unpleasing fact which (he felt sure) would be efficacious in protecting him against further persecution. He had been living beyond his means: something seemed to have gone wrong with his affairs in England: he fancied that he was about to be ruined: anyhow, he was extremely likely to be without an income during the current year at least. These disabilities (he judged) sufficed to disqualify him for association with persons more securely situated. 'I beg Your Ladyship to confine Her attentions to those, and be pleased to leave me alone,' he ruthlessly concluded with flaming sincerity. He was rather pleased with the manner in which he had piled up the agony and pitched it strong. 'That ought to keep her out of harm's way,' he said to himself, as he took a second sheet of paper and wrote, 'Dear Sir, I do not pretend to inquire why you and your lady have been so obliging as to notice me: but I think it well to warn you that you would be better advised to let our intimacy grow no closer. I really wish not to make new acquaintances at present, my affairs appearing to be in serious disorder, and there being a likelihood of my having no income at all at least for this year. It would pain me to involve you in a replica of the Fitzgerald-Vepner imbroglio; and I sincerely advise you (for your own convenience) to sever our connection here and now, without fear of offence, Faithfully yours, Nicholas Crabbe.' And, rejoicing as a bird who escapes from the snare of a fowler, he put Lady Pash's letter in the letter-box and the Warden's on the numbered key-frame in the hall of the hotel, and sidled hilariously toward the Bucintoro.

The terrace of the Royal Little Garden was all alive and thronged with athletes, forming in squadrons. Young Venice has as superb a physique as can be found anywhere. In a city where everyone swims from his cradle and almost everyone above five years old has rowed (poised and pushing more than pulling) for twenty or thirty generations—a movement which includes balance with force thrust forward and incessant adaptation to fluent circumstances—you may see (without search) the keen, prompt, level eyes, the noble firm necks, the opulent shoulders, the stalwart arms, the utterly magnificent breasts, the lithely muscular bodies inserted in (and springing from) the well-compacted hips, the long, slim, sinewy-rounded legs, the large, agile, sensible feet of that immortal youth to which Hellas once gave diadems. Painters like Tuke, and sculptors like Wheatley, neglect their privileges. The negligent ignorance of the common (or squat) professional 'strong man' (who never even heard of the *Agias* of Delphi, the canon of form of Lysippos) is a matter of course. But the indifference of trainers of champion oarsmen is purely inexplicable. For, in each of the six sexters of Venice, at least three young barcaiuoli could be found who (liberally trained and taught) could clear the world of its chief rowing trophies within three years.

Every kind of athletic association was represented in the Giardinetto Reale: the glorious Bucintoro in black and white, the valorous Querini (who scoop all prizes) in white and blue, rowing clubs, football clubs, bicycle clubs, walking clubs, fencing clubs, gymnastic clubs, companies from schools and palestre, a battalion from the Technical Institute in quaint green, red-slashed mediæval berettas copied from the university of Padova. White armlets with the legend 'Pro Calabria e Sicilia' were being served out to all. Bands were proving brazen. Money-collectors clanked tins or rattled wooden boxes. Shoals of barks, topi, valesane, pupparini, barchette, cavalline, floated by the terrace steps. And, every now and then, a squadron got its route, and marched away in the sharp sunlight, with music to move and enliven the merciful.

Venetian courtesy avoided offering burthens to an Englishman, and Crabbe had to insist on his right to work. 'If His Sioria would repeat his labour of yesterday——' was insinuated. He looked round for a third oarsman, with a view of accelerating speed. A tiny coxswain of the Bucintoro volunteered, Hebrew, shrill-voiced as a jay, active as an ape, with a lovely thirteenth-century Hebrew name, William Grace-of-God, Memi Graziadei. Crabbe looked him over, vivacious gait and expression, haughty little nose, devilish little eyes, already-darkened little upper lip, and nodded assent.

'Cio, Biondo! Hi, Fair Male!' the imp cried to Zildo, 'this English takes me to row poop-oar!'

Zildo went to row at prow, where the red and gold vexillo of the club waved its six streamers in the morning sun. Nicholas took a third oar amidships, and the long, light bark slid off on pious errands. All two- (or more) oared barks in Venice need force forward. A pair of lusty rowers, like Nicholas and Zildo, can be steered by an expert infant. The speed with three oars was swifter than ever. The miniature Jew steered as adroitly as a devil, chattering amazing Venetian to all, in all barks, on all quays and bridges, encountered in passage. Thus were made the journeys to Santa-margarita. In returning, loaded, to Sanzaccaria, little Graziadei amused himself with cigarettes, perched along on the cargo, while Nicholas and Zildo rowed at prow and poop. At noon, all tired and smutty, Crabbe proposed luncheon for three at a trattoria and instant resumption of labour. But either the Hebrew funked the the latter, or (perhaps) he feared to eat unholy ham with Christians, though Nicholas had in his mind the delicious kosher place of Fano Lazzaro, in the Alley of the Waters. Anyhow, Memi excused himself on the plea that he wished to bathe his hands and change his shirtlet. He fled: the others snatched nutriments, and returned to seek a new third at the club.

A tall, grave boy came from the crowds reassembling on the terrace. He looked nice and straight and capable, and was put to row at prow. He called himself Beltramio Hernando Giuseppe Maria. Nicholas pronounced that too long and dubbed him 'Ghezzo' from his small blue-black, green-hatted head and large blue-black eyes of a Moor. In Venice, personal appearance is noticed and named. Ghezzo rowed like an Englishman, with placid forceful self-possessed concentration. He always turned an eye, however, on passing girls. 'Why do you ogle those shes like this?' asked Nicholas, supplying a grotesque imitation. 'I wish to observe them, Signore.' Nicholas laughed aloud. 'And why?' inquired Ghezzo. 'In English, the word observe signifies careful inspection as through a microscope.' Ghezzo chuckled: 'Thus I observe them,' he cockily said. Nicholas was inclined to approve of this youth: he contrasted well with ordinary Venetians, who do much, but chatter more than much, and always keep a vain, anxious outlook for spectators of their prowess.

The afternoon journeys were diversified by miscellaneous collecting. Nicholas and Ghezzo left Zildo in the pupparin, while they pervaded narrow alleys to scratch up what they could. Venetian private charity is astounding. It is very like the real thing in its lavishness and its frantic efforts for secrecy. The mere apparition of Nicholas and Ghezzo in slums, with their white armlets and the boy's strong grave maiden-like resonant cry 'For Calabria and Sicily,' set the most amazing springs of piety in flow. A little haberdasher sneaked out and burthened them with a bale of twenty brand-new blankets. 'Tue nuoe—tutte nuove,' commented Zildo with Venetian amazement as he stowed them in the bark. A dreadfully scanty old seamstress mysteriously beckoned and brought them by innumerable stairs to an indescribable attic; and offered two good thick shawls, imploring that the neighbours might not see. Anywhere else, of course, such a gift would have been stolen goods. 'How to hide them?' Nicholas asked. His arms happened to be empty. 'Hi, old She!' cried the ready Ghezzo, 'I'll give you a lira for your counterpane.' A Venetian will always sell anything. Nicholas laughed. 'No,' he said, 'the price is five.' He laid down a note to a din of benedictions; and the shawls went veiled to the pupparin. As the bark came rocketing and ramping along the narrow Rio Sanluca about tea-time, a very painted lady screamed from a passing gondola petitions that they would go for a gift to the house with a grated door by the Bridge of the Cloaks. There was no mistaking the nature of the place: but ten notes worth five franchi each were taken there and handed to a passing money-collector—Nicholas avoided money-grabbing—not very precious ointment, not even an alabaster box, but only another humble offering from the Sisters of Saint Mary of Magdala to the poor of her Lord. Oh, why not, most affable reader?

Ghezzo had a roguish young eye in moving away, and a certain pause.

'And now?' Nicholas inquired, unsuspicious, impatient.

'Here one takes diversions,' the youngster smilingly asserted, merely as a small contribution to the sum of human knowledge.

Instantly Crabbe became very sick in his mind: not because of offended morals (he had none), but because precocity offended his clean instinct. He gripped Ghezzo's slender wiry biceps and bunted him up the Calle delle Veste to the pastry-cooks in Twenty-second of March Street.

'Take an English tea? The tea at this place is excellent. No? Then take a coffee.' He commanded a tea and a coffee, with ham sandwiches and a dozen gorgeous sorts of tartlets better than Quadri's or Florian's. 'Now,' he continued, when Ghezzo's white teeth were well-set in the pastry, 'how dare you speak of that bordel?'

'It is the best in Venice, Signore.'

'How do you know?'

The other smiled with perfect knowledge.

'How often have you committed this mortal sin?'

It was quite a joke. 'About twice in a month.'

'Since when?'

'About a year.'

'What do you pay?'

'The price is five franchi: but we students pay three.'

'Where do you get the money?'

'I have three franchi a week for the pocket: and I save half of it.'

'How old are you?'

'Fifteen years and two months.'

'How long have you been breeched?'

'About half a year.'

'So you began to commit mortal sin when you were a little chap in socks with bare legs! And who first took you there?'

'No one, Signore: I went by myself.'

'Now why?'

'I had a wish. And one of my friends went when he was thirteen.'

'Little pieces of great pigs, both of you!' Nicholas rolled a cigarette, and began to smoke it displeasedly. Ghezzo wilted a little. Had he deserved that this English should cease from esteeming him? He was worried.

'Tell me about your family,' Nicholas suddenly continued. 'What's your father? Where do you live? How many brothers and sisters have you? And what do they do?'

'Signore, my father is a captain-engineer in the Royal Marine at Livorno. And I live with my uncle and aunt by the Arsenal. And I have two brothers and two sisters, all at school.'

'And your mother?'

'Signore, she lives in the city' (said with hesitation).

'Go on.'

'There is a divorce, Signore.'

'Why?'

'My father and my mother cannot agree in their temperaments. But no one is to blame.'

'Is it a judicial divorce?'

'Nòssignore: they agree to live apart.'

'And you go to school?'

'Sìssignore: to the New Commercial School. Signore, I pray you not to speak of my mother as divorced.'

'I know nothing about it.'

Ghezzo's smile came back, a naïve roguish smile which lighted the grave young face. 'Signore, I demand excuse for disturbing you in the Alley of the Cloaks.'

'You didn't disturb me: you disgusted me.'

The boy blankly stared. 'It is most strange,' he said.

Nicholas stared now: but grimly. 'Tell me who first taught you these tricks.'

'No one, Signore. I found them out, I think. Everyone at school talks of them. It is a custom.'

'Thanks be to God, it isn't an English custom,' he ejaculated. 'Do you know that an English boy, who spoke as you did to a casual acquaintance, would get such a thrashing that he couldn't sit comfortably for a fortnight.' The large blue-black eyes opened more widely.

Nicholas, in high disdain and indignation, went on. 'Precocious little touches of pig that you all are! English boys of your age play football and cricket and baseball and fives and tennis, or they run and swim and row and jump and hunt. They don't go snouting in mud-puddles like swine. Most of them don't even know the sin of which you speak so gaily till they're twenty years old. And the result is health and strength.'

'My father says that English and American sailors are the strongest in the world——'

'Of course. And you Italians with your wholesome food and excellent wine might be the next strongest, if they didn't play the fool with horrible incurable disease when they are little boys like you—much stronger, and much more enduring than those filthily low-necked German sailors whom you see lingering about the city every now and then.'

'Is it true?'

'It is true. Now, get a dozen of these tartlets in a bag for my servant; and let us finish our work,' Nicholas said as he went to pay the bill.

Twilight was deepening, when they rejoined the pupparin. The bark lay low in the narrow dark canal. There had been an addition to the cargo; and Zildo paid no attention to the tartlets in his anxiety to supervise embarkation.

'Siori, with permission, tread with eyes in your toes, I pray, for the love of God: for there are treasures of flasks in every hole and corner.'

'Flasks? What flasks?'

'Twenty of Marsala, Sior, and twenty of pure oil of olive most fine. For, while Their Siori were absent, came a certain one demanding, like this, whether this was the bark of the English brave of the Bucintoro. To whom I responded Yes. And he said, like this, The respectable firm Sozogno and Salvini, out of friendship for the English, have made this offering of their merchandise for the beneficenza of Calabria and Sicily. To whom I responded, like this, The master thanks the said firm. Sior, with permission.'

It was quite the most periculous journey of the pupparin. Zildo had packed the flasks very cleverly, wedging them between folds of stuffs: but forty quart flasks and a mountain of textiles, in a very light bark built to hold five persons with perhaps the slight baggage of two—and, in the dark, through that dreadful little ditch of a canal by Sammoise which is lined on both sides with the gondole of the most disagreeable extortionate nasty-tempered gondolieri in Venice—and then the sudden bulge-out into Canalazzo by the steam-boat pontoon of Calle Vallaresco, and the hard push against wind and tide across the Basin of Sammarco to Sanzaccaria—well, as Nicholas cheerfully said, all three could swim; and the cargo was not his.

'Pray, Signore, may I come tomorrow?' Ghezzo inquired, when Zildo chained and locked the bark to the pali of the club for the night.

'If you are clean, and will work as well as you have worked today,' Nicholas coldly assented.

He took Zildo to dine at the Bonvecchiati. It occurred to him to keep clear of the Wardens for the present, certainly till after Lady Pash's party where (of course) his two deliberately rebuffing notes would be compared and judgement concerted regarding them.

Nicholas chose chicken and an insalad of mixed vegetables; and passed the list for Zildo to choose his own repast. The arrangement of eating together did not work quite easily. Not that the boy's manners mattered. They were exquisite, unnotable—he had a healthy appetite, ate his portions with gusto and finished movement— but he was not happy. Nicholas wondered why; and gave him this chance of selecting his own food. The waiter went for a litre of old Valpolicella. Zildo looked up from the list; and began to speak suddenly and quickly.

'Sior, pray hear. When I eat one thousand nine hundred and thirty-seven different plates for my lunch and for my dinner like a Sior, turkey, upon capons, upon fry, with mustard-tart, and zabajon to follow, then I always vomit at two o'clock in the morning from the window of my bedroom into the alley below. So, Sior, with permission, for gentility's sake let me eat like a gondoliere as I am accustomed, o blessed he of God!'

'How does a gondoliere eat?'

'Sior, one massed plate, with a mound of bread or polenta, and a little beaker of wine with water at pleasure; and after, nothing.'

'Do as you please.'

Zildo beamed thanks; and turned back to the list. Presently he cried, 'Hi! Black male!'

A rather perturbed cameriere hurried: but the pair were decently dressed, and had an air, and the wine-order had been a decent one. Zildo issued commands: 'One portion of sepia, and a double of maize-porridge; and bid the cook to be free with the fish's juice.'

Nicholas eyed this mess when it came, brown and yellow. It looked beastly: but its odour was that of sanctity, unctuous. He had a natural dyspathy against fish; and had never tasted it even. But 'seppe con pojenta' seemed unfishy: the brown lumps might have been rich truffles. Zildo enjoyed it immensely.

After coffee and the bill of L. 3·45, Nicholas proposed a gentle hour on the water. It was a dark-blue night with a waning moon. He wrapped himself in a thick blue boat-cloak; and sat in his cane arm-chair in the prow of the pupparin, as he did not wish to row.

He had a mania for cane arm-chairs, and called them sane—which they are, and far more comfortable than any other arm-chairs.

'Sior, indove?' Zildo inquired, when he had lighted the fanale and was poised at the lofty poop.

Toward La Grazia, very smoothly, for I wish to use my thoughts.'

'Sissior.'

No words can be combined to produce an exact impression of the nights in Venice, though they assuredly can do it better than paint. This was only one of the myriad different kinds of night in Venice— a wonderful blue blue night of velvety calm and fresh odour and magnificent width and breadth, splashed with bluer bluer masses of basilica and palace and bell-tower, sprinkled and flecked with dots and lines of lemon light from the squares and quays, flared with torches and starred with lanthorns gliding back on black-blue water. Read that, and look on Venetian night—only one type of Venetian night, remember—and then cut off to Palazzo Pesaro, and see what the Gallery of modern Art can do with night in Venice. It can do everything but the blue and the undulous starry light, and the breadth and tranquillity and smell, and the velvety brilliant profundity. I except Miti-Zanetti: he can present on canvas the verisimilitude of several sorts of night in Venice—but he doesn't exhibit at Palazzo Pesaro, and his pictures (though coloured) are not worked in oil or water or pastel. They are unique.

The quiet transcendent beauty of the scene was soothing. The bark swam easily and gently. Zildo's slender richness, finely poised aloft against the limitless sky, swayed and retired, dark-blue on blue. The glitter of his eyes in the moonlight, the gleam of his teeth, the white triangle of his guernsey, came clean from shade. Nicholas made no task of thinking: he was content to let thoughts come and go. Beyond Sanzorzi, the boy made fast to the usual palo. Behind, was the starred blaze of the lace-like Piazzetta streaked by the Columns of Mark and Theodore, reflected in the silent sea. Before, was the white wide silvery sheen of the south lagoon, buttoned with black islets, La Grazia, Sanctemente, Saccasessoja, Santospirito, Poveglia, Santangelo in Polvere, Sanzorzi in Alga, and the various pirogues of the finance. Zildo got a cloth from the cupboard under the poop; and began to dry up the night-dews which moistened the gunwale. All things of this species he did functionally: every spare moment he instantly and automatically devoted to polishing. Nicholas watched him minutely always, desiring to envisage and know him, his calm meaningless face, his infallible carriage and gait, his bearing to the strange boys brought to row, his faultless performance of his

part, his conception of his place and beauty, his comprehension of
and unquestioning submission to his master's mind. What a marvellous creature he was! That grave persuasive face seemed to
mask no mind at all; and yet it wasn't inane, it wasn't null—it was
full and alive with itself. It had the perfection and splendour and
purity and serenity of a precious gem: it had the added quality of
the tremendous dormant potency of a soul unawakened. There was
not another face in the world so utterly satisfying—no, not one,
among the lovely clever good ugly silly wicked faces of this world,
all anxious, all selfish, all mean, all unsatisfied and unsatisfying.
The wistful flower-like face of Zildo took no thought, it knew no
want—yes, that was the huge and pregnant note of it, it knew no
want, no want—it was confident in itself. Was it by any chance
(Nicholas wondered) confident also in him? Mah——. And the
quiet alertness, the vivid prompt vigour, never (so far) caught
napping, set in silent motion by a glance—a word rarely was needed
by that ready intuition. After the amusing but tiresome servants
who had agitated Nicholas in the past—strong buxom mindless
venal creatures, who had to be prodded continually, who gaily
cried 'Pronto!' when they were only just thinking about beginning
to prepare, who argued, who discussed orders, who invariably lied
blatantly and stupidly in self-excuse—it was queer, and disconcerting,
but most comforting, to let responsibility slide. How did this boy
know (not his job—of course he couldn't help knowing that—but),
how did he precisely know what his master would want, before his
master himself solidly knew that? If things should go on like this,
many bars would be removed for the prisoned mind's activity.
And yet, Zildo shewed no extraordinary concern about anything,
asked few questions, never quivered all agog with the doggy fidelity
of the good slave. He was as far above all servants whom Nicholas
ever had seen, as he was far above all other human creatures—those
lads of the Beneficenza, for example. How deftly he had dealt with
them—that charming but chattering jay of a Graziadei, who could
not think without gabbling, to whom Zildo imperturbably and
instantly paid just the attention due to a jay. The tiny Jew's preliminary shriek, 'Ciò, Biondo! This English takes me to row poop-
oar!'—how adscititious it was! Naturally the smallest oarsman in
the bark would row the poop-oar. And Zildo answered him
nothing, having left the poop-oar on seeing the screeching shrimp
engaged; and was lightly dancing along the rocking gunwale to
the prow, before instructions were even formulated. And, while
once they waited for cargo at Santamargarita, when Memi would

have chitchatted with him about his English master—how rich that
one was, how much he paid, why he diverted himself always in a
bark—what a fine lazy smile Zildo spread, furnishing the deliciously-
apt and indescribably-squashing gesture (the quick gesture of chin-
brushing with a hand-back) which signifies, 'O you chatterbox,
jabberer, prattler, cackler, twaddler, poll-parrot, and bibble-babbler,'
and strikes dumb. How amusing it was. Venetians, certainly all
members of the Bucintoro, laboured under the fixed idea that
Nicholas could not understand their tongue—I know not why:
unless, perhaps, it was because he always made them speak his own,
when possible; and took an impish pleasure in giving them in return
a very archaic Italian ungrammatically constructed and atrociously
pronounced. But, on suitable occasions, he showed a disconcertingly
accurate comprehension of what was said in his presence; and he
was used to pour forth volumes of purely Venetian abuse of stupid
persons in pungent idiomatic Venetian dialect. Nevertheless it was
the custom to agonize to make him understand, by nasal roaring
in his face, and to discuss him and his doings in the free delusion that
he could not follow. He heard all Graziadei's impertinences:
approved the rebuff wherewith Zildo flattened him and disqualified
him for further intimacy. Beltramio the Ghezzo, on the other hand,
had had the sense of decency to say little or nothing to Zildo. His
business was with the patron, not with the barcaiuolo. The Jew
would have fraternized with the servant: the Christian assumed that
he was the guest of the master. That was as it should be. But there
was a quality common to both Zildo and Ghezzo—the fresh serious-
ness of their youth. But Ghezzo was extremely male: while
Zildo——. What about pairing them presently, dark and light,
sinew and muscle, knowledge and innocence—great heavens, no—
keep them universes apart. No—no: do nothing. Why worry?
Leave it to Zildo (with his beloved clean rolls of cleaning-rag stowed
so neatly under the poop). Zildo would do what was to be done.
Actually, Nicholas felt quite secure in leaving things to Zildo—that
one was perfectly to be trusted in any circumstances, in any developments. He did indeed stand admirably, within the scope afforded
so far, between his patron and the rest of this wicked world. Who
else, in the whole world, mattered an atom? Morlaix and Sartor,
Caliban, Bobugo, supposing that that little lot were going to start
in as traitors? What did they signify? With Zildo, he knew himself
to be a match for any combination of annoyers. M-yes. But
(mark, o most affable reader, how the essential interior softness of
the crab came into play)—he must keep well in mind this one con-

sideration, that his affairs were his and Zildo's were Zildo's; and, in honour, he might not let the unpleasantness of his affairs (if they should become efficaciously unpleasant) affect that ignorant innocent who so meekly and so incorrigibly had confided in him. That confidence must be deserved. True, Zildo had wished to serve— to serve, how far? Nicholas knew that he had not the shadow of a right to count on the service of a—friend : but only on the service of a servant. He could not count on more than that, without infringing Zildo's rights. For as much as that, he would be thankful, and pay, and ask no more. For Zildo had rights which, in childlike simplicity, he might not guard, or use, or know. Certainly he must have the protection which he claimed. His honour and his life must be secured to him. He insisted on serving; and he should serve. Would he wish more than that? It was not permitted to contemplate even the possibility. His life had been saved: he was in possession of food and clothes and lodging and good pay and a favourite occupation; and, in return, he served; and served well. Gratitude? There is no such thing. Be content with willing and perfect service, Nicholas exhorted himself.

'Con permesso,' murmured Zildo. His cleansing operations brought him near his master's chair. He crept balancing along the gunwale with his cloth, to polish the prow. As he came crawling back, a little shy breath of night sighingly lifted and spread the splendour of the fair plume waving in noble ripples on his brow. Nicholas had a sudden impulse to blow it, just for the sensuous pleasure of seeing its beauty in movement again—it was within a hand's length of his lips.

'To land,' he instantly commanded, checking himself with a shock, sternly governing mind with will. For what species of snub had he been on the very verge of competing?—a snub from his servant. But, perhaps Zildo would not have snubbed him? 'So much the worse, o fool! Hast thou time or occasion for dalliance?' Thus, he reined up his soul, prone to sink, prompt to soar.

XI

AND the third day of the Beneficenza was like to those which had
gone before. Beltramio the Ghezzo worked admirably. When all
was over, Crabbe (not certain whether a boy of his rank would be
insulted by a tip) put on his finger a little ring set with an intagliate
honey-sard. 'We are friends,' he said. 'Per sempre' came quick
reply in the fine firm voice which Crabbe immensely admired.
They saluted; and parted: Crabbe never expected to see him again.

As he was likely to fall over the Wardens at the hotel, he gave
Zildo a lira for dinner elsewhere, with license till 9 o'clock on the
morrow, when the bark was to be ready at the club. He himself,
cleansed and changed and cheerfully armed for affrays, went to the
ordinary dinner; and read the winter-part of the *Pastoral* of Longus,
all alone, excepting for the landlord and his family at the door-end
of the room. The Wardens came in much earlier than usual,
while he still sipped soup. He kept his gaze stolidly on the page
before him.

'Good evening,' the lady called, grinning and bonily bridling from
her table.

He hoisted up his regard; and bowed, not coldly, but with what
is called Common Politeness. The gentleman, about to subside into
a seat, oozed, 'I do so hope you had a good day with the Beneficenza.'

'Thank you, yes—a little tiring.'

'Oh!' the Thiasarkh sympathized, squirming round to his dinner.

Crabbe relapsed into his duodecimo. A situation was about to
call for treatment. Usual pace would place him in the hall, to
drink coffee and to smoke, just in time for these people to catch
him apparently waylaying them. That would not do. It was
annoying of them to net him like this. Perhaps, though, they were
not personally on his track, but were dining earlier than usual merely
to suit some evening engagement. They were always gadding about
somewhere.

So, he made much of walnuts. But the Wardens did not hurry.
It was plain that they were pacing him. Nothing was left but to
sprint. That failed. As he rose, they (evangelically) left all and
rose too. But their table was nearer the door; and he was forced,
not only to let them precede him but, to follow close on their heels.

It was awkward, and totally damnable. But, passing the landlord's table, he snatched an opportunity of taking a decent pause.

'And what have you done for the Beneficenza?' he inquired of Parrucchiero, noting (with the tail of a happy eye) the outgoing of his hunters.

'Gnente. E lei?' puffed the merry little man.

'I've been gadding about in my pupparin, as usual.'

'But Signore, why do you, an English, thus excite yourself about an Italian matter?'

Crabbe was disgusted. 'I think,' he said, 'that the relief of suffering is neither English nor Italian, but human. Beside, I must have physical exercise.'

'Most strange are the ratiocinations of the English,' the well-fed landlord commented.

What could be said to such an one? The coast, however, should be clear, now. Crabbe went out; and found Mistress Thin-lips seated in the hall, and the Thiasarkh attending with a packet of her favourite cigarettes. 'Here is your chair, and we want you to have coffee with us,' she cried, as soon as Crabbe appeared.

'Do try one of these cigarettes: you'll find them so nice,' the Warden bleated.

'Very happy: but I always make my own, of Maryland, thank you,' Crabbe murmured. There was nothing to be done but to make the best of his usual chair, now effusively butted at him. The Thiasarkh commanded three coffees.

'I want to know,' said the lady, making play with the rings on the bones which she used for a hand, 'why you sent that shocking note to my husband.'

'Matter of duty.'

'I don't think so. Anyhow, please understand that we're not going to take any notice of it. Are we, Exeter?'

'No, indeed no.'

'Most unwise and most annoying of you,' Crabbe chucked out. 'I really mean it. I'm in a pickle. And you don't know me. And I utterly refuse to be classed with Fitzgerald-Vepner, should things turn out as I'm prepared for them to turn out. So I insist upon trumpeting beforehand to warn you of the danger of having anything to do with me.'

'Thank you very much. You've done your part. And you'll have the goodness to let us do ours. You don't know us yet, either. And we intend you to. And now, please, we want to be friends with you.'

She took his note from her bead-bag: tore it into bits: beckoned squirrel-eyed little Piero to furnish a wastepaper-basket: and disposed the fragments there with emphatic finality.

This seemed all right. The speech was quite charming. They had ugly aspects—this pair. They had unpleasing features. But apart from their push, their fawning, what fault could be found with their conduct to him? Oh, were they, were they by any chance sent? (Crabbe was always fatalistically on the look-out for sendings). He didn't know. He was not a little morsel attracted to them—very much the reverse. And, why should Erastians be sent to a Papist? He saw no points but of difference, excepting this clean-cut refusal to let him go. But he didn't want them a bit. All he did want was that ideal of his, that Other Half of him which he knew he lacked. He did not know whether that Other Half was a person or a position. He always thought it was priesthood, though he was not unprepared to find that it was a friend; and, failure after failure (to find a friend with the faintest trace of faithfulness) had made him more and more convinced that priesthood was the one thing lacking to his happy completion. And now here was another parcel asking for his friendship. Well: he was certain that his much desired Other Half didn't consist of officious Erastians already paired.

He kept himself inside his shell, all but his stark eyes and undulating feelers: neatly folded his fierce talons; and sat still to collect impressions which might light and guide him. Truth emerges from Error sooner than from Confusion. He might have made a mistake. So he talked, and listened, and waited for Truth to emerge.

It seemed that all three were writers. The Wardens had read *Peter of England*. More curious still, they also had read its author's earlier books, which had been published under a pseudonym. Ha-ha! So, then, they had taken the trouble to root about rather extensively to inform themselves in his regard. And still they thought him worth knowing. Oh, very well, then.

Not a word was said of La Pash. Crabbe never knew more than here is written of her rejected party. It looked as though she (wounded in the vitals) kept her sore concealed, and as though the Wardens were acting in this instance entirely on their own. It did not occur to his blunt simplicity that he could have taken no more certain means, for exciting feverish interest, than his cold, rude, ruthless rejection of advances. He had not the most rudimentary suspicion that people of the Warden's calibre are, in solemn fact, incapable, incapable of believing such news as he had given of himself. Their habit (in circumstances similar to this) is to whine while laying traps for pity, mustard, relief, and beef. And, when a man roughly roars, 'Shoo! For I wish to be ruined all by myself!' they look on such horrid words as a merely individualistic fashion-of-speech barbed-wiring desirable possessions—into which (by persistence) they may obtain admission and of which a share. Crabbe knew nothing of this. The only impression which his feelers gathered was that (for some reason, apparently a correct and sublaudable one) these two Erastians were determined to come barging into his life. Remained, then, for him to determine dimensions. And he decided that such intimacy as life in the same house ordained would be about the thing. He was not minded to open more widely than that.

John Spagnuol Junior announced the arrival of the topo *Selene* from Gerace. He had had her tied up to the pali next to Francis Leland's yacht by the custom-house. Crabbe accompanied him on board to pay off the crew, and to do other business.

'She's for sale,' he said to the yacht agent.

'Have you got a customer, sir?'

'No: you must find one.'

'It may be a little difficult, sir. You see, sir, she isn't a yacht and she isn't a cargo boat.'

'But she's a jolly good sailer, and a jolly comfortable ship for an artist to live and paint on.'

'How much did you want for her, sir?'

'As much as I can get. She cost me L. 10,000.'

'I'm afraid I couldn't get that for you, sir.'

'How much could you get?'

'Perhaps half what you gave, sir.'

'L. 5,000? Look here: if you can get me more than L. 6,000 within a week, I'll pay you 10 per cent commission.'

'I'll give you L. 6,000 myself, sir; and risk finding a purchaser.'

Crabbe realized that the usual Venetian game of combination was to be played and didn't refuse to join in. 'No,' he said, 'I said more than L. 6,000, if I have to pay commission. Offer me L. 7,000 and I'll give you back L. 600.'

'Would you take L. 6,000 net, without commission, sir?'

'Yes: if you come ashore and give me a cheque now.'

'Are you Castellano or Nicolotto?' he demanded of Zildo, who was handling a rag while waiting in the pupparin off the Piazzetta.

'O Dio, but Castellano, Sior.'

'Let us go through all the small canals of the Castellani.'

'Va benissimo.'

The tone-horror of Zildo's asseveration may be explained by the custom of the Castellani of alluding to the other party, in songs and sayings, as 'swine of low-born Nicolotti.' A short elucidation is in order here. It should be understood that the Venetians divide themselves into two factions—have divided themselves thus for a thousand years or so. The Castellani colour is red; and the Castellani faction occupies half the city east of an imaginary line drawn from Sanzanipolo to Rialto, and thence down the middle of the Grand Canal Rio Santrovaso to the canal Zuecca, as well as all islets. The Nicolotti colour is black; and the Nicolotti faction occupies the remaining half of the city as well as the island of Spinalonga. Foreigners are Castellani, or Nicolotti, according to the district where they first come to land. Nicholas was Castellano by interrament: Zildo by birth.

They swept eastward along the Molo; and through a network of small canals, beginning with Rio del Canonica—Santamaria, Formosa, Sanzanlateran, Sansevero, Sanlorenzo, Santazustina, Fontego, Greci, Sanfrancesco, Sammartin, Gorne, Sanzanbragora, Arsenale, Tana, Sandaniel, Santanna, Vergini, Sampiero. Passing along the Fondamente Nuove north of the city, they entered the canal of the Mendicants, and (thence) proceeded to Canalazzo by Barcariol and Sammoise, when they turned westward and worked up as far as Rio dei Todeschi beyond Rialto. All the way, Nicholas looked for windows bearing a blank sheet of note-paper pasted on them. He saw perhaps half a dozen: twice he stopped, and went ashore, apparently to no purpose.

After luncheon, he rowed over to the infirmary for a convalescent passenger. The directress gave him the quarter-kidneyed engineer, at whom she splutted the nickname of 'Chief.' He was a red-nosed wan wreck, with a drooping moustache, pretensions to being a blood, and no particular chin or character. He kindly offered Crabbe a Macedonian cigarette.

'I can't tell you how trotty we think it of you! Do keep in the shade and bring him back in an hour or so, you darlings!' bibbled the woman from the quay.

They crossed the wide canal into the web of little waterways, Salute, Fornaxe, Toresela, Sanvio, Santrovaso, which pierce the city between Canal Grande and the quays of the Zattere. Nicholas continued to inspect the window-shutters. In Rio di Santrovaso, he went ashore for about a quarter of an hour. On his return, the Chief was weary. Crabbe made an effort to amuse the poor thing, who gave watery unintelligent acknowledgment. Nothing but kidneys and similar clockwork really interested him. They rowed him home. As they got him on to the infirmary doorstep, a gondola with two royal-blue sashed gondolieri came up the Rio della Croxe behind. Crabbe spotted the long-eared bonnet and the horse-face of Lady Pash in it. 'Uoa! Uoa! Zildo! Forward, on to the lagoon; and return by Ponte Lungo to Santrovaso,' he cried, in a hurry to evitate encounter with that dame.

He landed at Santrovaso; and once more entered a house whose top window-shutters were embellished with blank paper. A written or printed 'To Let' must be stamped in Italy; and no one dreams of paying stamp-taxes when blank paper conveys a meaning. Here he settled on a lodging for Zildo; and got the keys of it—a private door and stair with magazine on the ground-floor, a fourth story of two rooms and a closet on a landing, and a cockloft above all. The rent was L. 30 a month: he took a receipt for twelve months in advance. He went upstairs and looked about him. The front room was of comfortable size; it had a stone-hooded fireplace between two west windows, which gave a view of the rio in front flanked by the lovely old squero with the trees and green and church, and the Rio di Ognisanti with the Long Bridge and the Zuecca canal, to right, and left, respectively. All the sun of the day from noon to sunset would pour in these windows. The next room, across the landing, had one window eastward. There was a tap with adequate water and a sink on the landing. The cockloft was spacious, fit even for habitation, with good windows north and south. The whole apartment, avoiding palaces but perched aloft above the neighbouring dwellings, simply swam in air and light and was not overlooked. No one could wish for a more convenient abode. Zildo being what he was, should live here, alone, with perfect privacy and a fixed income. He should come to the hotel daily for orders, as was proper; and the bark could be kept at the club, where it was always accessible. This arrangement would enable Nicholas to get *De Burgh's Delusion* off his chest, while trying to reduce his affairs to some sort of order. Instinct was impressing upon him that he really must prepare himself to find Morlaix and Sartor, and his two friends, behaving queerly. He intended to make quite certain; and then—well, he felt that he was just the man to provide any number of beautiful and sacred subjects for morning meditation.

In the morning he hired a cavallina and a couple of porters, and set them under Zildo's supervision to remove from the *Selene* all books, clothes, furniture, and loose stores, to the apartment of Santrovaso. He himself did some business at the Savings Bank. After luncheon, he took the boy there with him. They were received in a parlour, by an official who took cognizance of Zildo, and made him write 'Falier Ermenegildo' four times on the front page of a blank account book. This done, Nicholas said, 'Listen, Zildo, to my commandments, which you will obey.'

'Sior, naturally.'

'You will come here every Monday at 8 o'clock, and inquire for this signore, Signor Caloprin. You are prohibited from dealing with any other person here. Signor Caloprin will give you thirty-five franchi, and you will write your name like this in this book every Monday at 8 o'clock. Every fourth Monday, Signor Caloprin will give you a hundred franchi as well as the usual five and thirty. Today is Friday, and you will begin on Monday following. Do you understand?'

'Nòssior.'

'What?'

'I do not understand why this eximious Signor Caloprin will pay me thirty-five franchi every Monday at 8 o'clock, and also a hundred more at 8 of every fourth Monday, just for writing my name.'

'You need not understand. But you will obey?'

The long greenish-blue eyes fixed their regard, like a cat's, upon the man, for an instant. 'Sior, I will obey.'

Nicholas (satisfied) nodded to the high-shouldered official, who wore the big red beard of Nazarite; and rushed his servant over the Academy Bridge to the apartment in Santrovaso. The goods from the topo were heaped neatly on the floors of the large room and landing. 'Now,' he said, 'I shall give you some explanations, and some more commandments.'

'Sior, please,' said the boy, standing very straight and attentive, with his wonderful innocent eyes set singly toward his master.

Nicholas rolled a cigarette; and began, 'First, my books and clothes must come to the hotel. I want to use them there. You will pack them in these leathern bags, and bring them, one at a time.'

'Va bene.'

'Second: this apartment is yours, and yours only. Here are the three keys of it, the key of the door in the street below, the key of the magazine under the stair, and the key of the door at the top of the stair. Do not lose them, for there are no others. And you will live here, by yourself: while I shall live at the hotel.'

A vivid rosy tide began to flow and deepen under the pure smooth skin. The clean eyes glittered in flooding vermilion. 'Sior, I understand; and I will obey, with so many thanks,' Zildo said as he took the keys; and the flush slowly faded.

'You are a brave boy; and you understand that you save me from trouble by your obedience,' added Nicholas, kindly: but he was holding himself very rigidly.

'Sior, be assured of my obedience.'

'Third,' Nicholas continued, 'you will use the money which you gain from Signor Caloprin of the Cassa de Risparmio in this manner. The five and thirty franchi which you will take every Monday, are for eating and drinking and wood and candles. The hundred, which you will take every fourth Monday, are for clothes and for the pocket. You have nothing else to pay. The rent is paid for a year. Signor Caloprin pays rates and water. You have only to take care of yourself. If anyone demands money of you, send him to Signor Caloprin. Pay nothing but for nutriment and fire and light and clothes and pleasure. And if anyone annoys you, instantly inform Signor Caloprin.'

'It is too much, Sior.'

'It is my commandment.'

'Li xe paron—you are the master.'

'Benissimo.' Nicholas looked at and rummaged among the heaped goods on the floor; and went on speaking: 'You have here mattresses, blankets, plenty of towels, lots of aluminium pots and pans and plates and mugs, and so on. Let us now go and buy what else is needed.'

'Sior, nothing else is needed, in fact.'

Nicholas looked. The calm eyes were crystally bright, and the rose-leaf lips had a little quiver. 'You need a chain for your keys,' he said, as they came downstairs together.

The beauty of the Venetian fireplace (I am not speaking of the block-like closed stoves) is that you can make a cheerful fire of logs upon it, to warm your hands and gladden your heart, in those bitter wintry days, when they sweep the snow off the Piazza into cocks of a man's height, and the horrible wind called Bora rages across the Adriatic from Trieste. And, at all times, in a corner of it, you can stand a dear little terra-cotta stove (or two, or three, according to the number of your pans) burning charcoal whereon to cook your nutriments. And the quaint stone chimney-hood wafts away smoke or noxious gases. Nicholas bought a terra-cotta stove, and a bundle of palm-leaf fans for keeping it in blast. He made no resistance to a bargain which shot up at him—on an occasion of this kind he always acted as a led blind man—a bargain of a bed, a chest of drawers, a wardrobe, and a mirror, all of fine massive uncarved old nutwood (such as gondolieri love and have used for centuries) which cost L. 380, better than new because matured, and fit to last out several lifetimes. In Sanlio, he got a rug and a couple of cane tables and a cane arm-chair, naturally. And, at the ironmonger's in Merceria he bought a lanthorn and a pair of copper-shaded candlesticks, and a swivel-chain for the house-keys. In all, he spent (that day) about L. 5000 of the L. 6000 which Spagnuol had paid him; and he felt entirely satisfied. He had the overwhelming joy of him who gives overwhelmingly, of him who has the enormous luck to find a taker who can take as generously as the giver can give. No penny-farthing inquisitorial charity-monger shedding his drop-pings on the deserving ever touches the supreme bliss of him who casts bread on the waters, giving away, with lavish abandonment, his all. It is more blessed to give than to receive. Who believes that? Who knows that? Well, it's true.

Zildo was safe for a year. Nicholas was quite cock-a-hoop with the knowledge that he had done his part to deserve the confidence forced upon him, and with the success of his experiment proving that Zildo was no meanly-modest hanging-back protesting annoying uncorresponding fool. In the course of a year, developments would take place: by the end of it, no doubt, Nicholas would have torn and slashed and bitten a way through his private difficulties; and then fresh plans could be formulated. Anyhow, his hands were quite free, now. Free? He had provided himself with a devoted squire who would cost nothing, to arm him for coming affrays. Was not that enough? No, not quite.

The boy had gone to Santrovaso with the purchases. Nicholas changed the balance of the topo's price into ten-lire notes. It would be as well to provide against one other contingency. So he mouched about the city till tea-time, mischievously slipping the notes into the boxes for Saint Anthony's Bread in all the churches which he found open. He finished at the church of Santi Gervasio e Protasio on the boundary. There were two doors to this church, one on the south for the Nicolotti, the other on the east for the Castellani.

As he came forth to the east, there shot long yellow beams, from behind him, out of the setting sun, and across the canal: bright-haired Zildo stood there, in the light, ready, waiting—straight as a taper, and tall with a flame for its crown.

XII

Between 2 and 3 o'clock in the morning, Nicholas was jerked awake by what he vainly imagined to be a dog-fight under his bed. There generally was a couple of hounds or so sleeping there when he had a home in England. 'Down, dog, down!' he shouted, automatically.

A second shock made bed and house and city reel.

'Thank you very much,' he serenely said: 'that will do quite nicely,' and skipped out of bed, into bath-gown and slippers, and on to his balcony.

As he came, the Warden (in pyjamas and astrakan coat, with spiky hair) bounded on his, the next one. 'Myiphmh-myiphmh-myiphmh,' he babbled: 'do you know, dear man, I fancy I felt such an earthquake!'

As he spoke, his lady shot out in a magenta-quilted dressing-gown, rat-tailed hair to wind, pressing her hands on her wizened chest. 'Exeter,' she squawked, 'I've got all the money. Do go and get the baby!'

As far as Crabbe was concerned, that settled it. When you wish to classify people according to their characters, o most affable reader, you must see them naked and God gripping them by the short hair and giving them a sudden and nasty shaking. Their comportment and their clutchings in those circumstances will tell you what you want to know. 'It is finished,' he smilingly asserted. The Erastians were going to be instructive as well as diverting.

'I presume it was an earthquake?'

'Oh, without doubt—Venice sobbing with a ripple of a hiccough for Calabria.'

'What ye think we'd better do?'

'What can you do? Look!'

They were high on fifth-floor balconies, above the Square of Saint Mark, which was vastly dark, and vastly empty. As Nicholas pointed, lights flashed in every window; and, up the Piazzetta, and out of all the arches round the Piazza, the whole population of Venice (dressed at a snatch) swarmed, pouring, prancing, capering, roaring, 'O Dio! O Domeniddio! O Mariavergine!' Nothing could have been more comical on touching a button.

'Bubbubbubbubbubib . . . !' sputtered the lady.

'Don't you think we'd better get downstairs?' cackled the Warden.

'On the whole, no,' Crabbe decided.

'But suppose there should be another shock which made the house fall down, dear man?'

Crabbe deliberately struck a match and lighted up, before he otiosely drawled, 'How do houses fall in Venice? How did the Campanile fall? They collapse. They subside upon themselves. They don't topple over. They just sit quietly and dustily down on their proper seats. And, if a shock comes to wreck this house, where would you rather be? Squashed under it? Squelched in that seething mob down there? Or comfortably enthroned on the height of its ruins? For my part, I'm inclined to bring out my bed, and watch the ballet from this comfortable balcony. Just look at that girl's leg. May I offer you a cigarette?'

After that, the three stood where they were, and smoked a little. The Erastians swallowed copiously, and became less jerky. The crowd below was comical to a degree. With Calabria and Sicily fresh in mind, Venice went stark staring raving mad that night. Fat fathers of families careered in fichus and hip-boots: but bed-gowns and felt-hats and carpets were the ordinary wear. You couldn't have slid a lottery-ticket into the monstrous mass of very leggy citizens which writhed and wrestled in the middle of the square. It had no interstices at all. No football scrimmage could have been more closely packed than this congeries of terrified semi-nudity. Crabbe fetched himself a cloak: for his own drapery was sensibly ventilated. After a little, the lady remembered her baby and retired. The Warden lingered longer looking down, murmuring 'Myiphmh' from time to time.

'Well, that's all,' Crabbe cheerfully announced after half an hour; 'and perhaps we might as well go back to bed.'

'Dear person, don't you care at all?'

'Care? Lord, yes: I care desperately about what I do myself. But I don't do earthquakes. Why should I care about them?'

'Myiphmh: good night,' purred the Warden.

Crabbe went back to bed. And immediately vaulted out again, and into clothes and slippers. Zildo! Zildo in a second earthquake! Host! What was that poor child suffering!

He grabbed tobacco and matches, and fled the hotel; and hustled and butted his way through the fringe of the crowd, across the front of the basilica and down the Piazzetta, to the Bucintoro. The club was closed, but its terrified nightwarden stood on the terrace.

'Oar and fork and footbridge, instantly!' Nicholas shouted as he clinched the rails on the sea-wall and went to unlock his pupparin. And he furiously swept up the Grand Canal to Santrovaso. People were rushing along the side-quays there, to the wider spaces of the Zattere. It was 3½ o'clock.

What had he done so impetuously? What should he do next? Of course he never was going to enter Zildo's door. Suppose the boy had slept through it all. Gondolieri always sleep like logs. Why worry him with the clangour of his bell? Had he missed Zildo on the way? Had the boy started to come on foot to him?

He chained the bark to the quay-steps below the house, thinking. He rolled a cigarette, and began to smoke it; and sat down on the poop, surmising. Why did not his angel-guardian say something? A numbness came upon him. He rolled another cigarette and smoked it, waiting for a word. And another, waiting—And another, waiting, numb. . . .

'Sior, buon zorno!' said the clear calm voice of Zildo in an opalescent dawn, from just above him.

He looked up as the boy lightly vaulted over the low quay-parapet and dropped a leather bag of books into the bark.

'Sior, you commanded the pupparin for 9 o'clock; and 7 is sounding but now.' He spoke with an air of concern and reproach.

'Where were you going at this hour?'

'Sior, I was going to the club to do my duty. Very dirty is the pupparin.'

'Have you slept well?'

'Sior, very well.'

Nicholas looked him over, in his neat blue clothes and white guernsey, from his serene attentive gaze to his shoes with their smart ties. He was quite undisturbed, quite ignorant. Better to give him the news than to let him have the shock of hearing it.

'Let us go by the canal of Zuecca.'

Zildo rowed under the Long Bridge and out to the wide expanse of flowing tide. They were all to themselves, there, when they had passed the ferry-pontoons: for there was an unusual absence of ordinary water traffic that day. All the quays, however, were black with human beings. The pupparin was bare of furniture, and Nicholas perched on the seat which struts the poop-end in front of the oarsman.

'It might be said to be a festival today, yet I cannot remember the Saint,' Zildo commented, noticing the crowds which they had cleared.

'Have you really slept well?' Nicholas repeated.

'Sissior.'

'And nothing disturbed you?'

'Nòssior. What should disturb me?'

'There has been an earthquake here, this night.'

'Mariavergine! At what hour?'

'Half-past two.'

'To me it has done nothing.'

Suddenly the boy stepped down from the poop, trailing his oar to rest, and came close to Nicholas. His face had whitened and his great eyes strained open wide. 'Sior, with permission, has the earthquake done ill to you? Don't you know? Has it broken your hotel? Like La Tasca? O, Sior, are you wounded? Why, my master, are you here, like this, at this hour? Sa?'

'No one is wounded; and nothing is broken. But foolish people are mad with fear. Therefore, I came that you might take the news from me. You must not be frightened, Zildo.'

'Sior, I have no fear.'

'Bravo! Then give me the oar and let me row, for I am cold.'

Zildo changed places in silence; and Nicholas mounted and rowed viciously toward the club. He wanted coffee and a razor.

As they slipped by the Istrian firewood boats moored off the Dagonale, the boy softly said: 'Sior, I understand that you have waited, during several hours, in the cold, at Santrovaso, so that I might not be frightened.'

'It is nothing,' Nicholas repeated, rowing on.

They both became mute and rigid as they crossed the Grand Canal: for the most usual unusual thing had happened. They have told me of it separately and together: so I know. I will try to explain. So far, Nicholas had known himself for Nicholas. He was himself; and his body was his own habitation—his own. Other people's were theirs. One could deal with other people's, take them, use them, given or by force: but they remained other people's: they never became one's own. They never could become one's own. One was not the person who owned them, any more than one was the person who inhabited them. Just that. Zildo, on his part, had never examined the problem: never had been conscious of it, so far. He says that he made a certain discovery, on the topo, at the moment when Nicholas told him that he was absolutely alone in the world. For the rest, he was called Zildo; and that was all about it. And then, all of a sudden, on this iridescent morning of opals in January, when the lips of Zildo touched the hand of Nicholas, owner of lips and owner of hand experienced a single definite shock: an electric shiver tingled through their veins: hot blood went surging and romping through their hearts: a blast, as of rams' horns, sang in their ears and rang in their beings, and down went all sorts of separations. They were bewitched. They were startled beyond measure. Of course we others are well aware that this was merely the commonplace casting of the commonplace spell by their millions of dead ancestors recognizing (in these two) the possessors by inheritance of the multitudinous charm of all other own dead loves—that it was nothing more than the quickening in these separated entities of the dormant prenatal knowledge of homogeneity. At the moment of recognition, Zildo says that he felt only satisfaction. He had faith from that moment the day after La Tasca: now he had the evidence which he had hoped for. Then, he attained knowledge of something unseen: now, he gained the substance of it. For him, fact had replaced theory. But Nicholas only knew that something had happened to him, something liable to appal him unless he was careful, something absolutely antecedent to any previous experiment of his. It was far more awful than an earthquake. It was the dragging of all anchors. It was the breaching of innermost bulwarks. He had nothing to hold on by. He was naked and unarmed to all the world. His citadel was open. Crab-like, he instantly shut himself up in his shell, throwing up ramparts and earthworks to conceal and protect his individuality. So, while Nicholas landed at the club, wearing an aspect rather more stark (not to say forbidding) than usual, Zildo (simple also, but firmer and not in the very least dependent on external fortifications) was sensible of no fear, of no abashment, of no revolt; and sedately performed his duties with the bark, fetching up the leathern bag of books, and following his master to the hotel as docilely as ever. For Nicholas, the experience was a revelation. For Zildo, it had been a confirmation. That was all the difference.

'You are licensed till the stroke. Walk about the city and hear what people say, so that you may divert me with their cackle. And at 13 o'clock, be ready at the Bucintoro.'

Crabbe wanted some hours to himself. There was not going to be any nonsense. He would not even permit himself to think of (much less to analyse) this latest phenomenon. It stood this way. Its very rarity worried this lover of the concrete. It impeded him.

And NENE ME INPEDIAS NENE LONGIUS PERSEQUARIS was the ruthless motto with which George Meredith (that accurate reckoner of men) once had fitted him. He thrust the whole affair out of his mind. Zildo was worthy of all praise—as a servant. And — custodia òculorum—it might be as well not to look at Zildo quite so much.

Work was his panacea. He got out the huge pigskin portfolio of rough drafts and notes of his unfinished book, and the tall slim white buckram-bound volume of blank bank-paper already half-filled with fair copy. He read over what he had already done. It seemed to be almost as far above the ordinary as he wished it to be —history as it wasn't but as it very well might have been. For example, there is no direct evidence of the mysterious murder of Arthur fitz-Geoffrey, Duke of Armorica, by or at the instance of his wicked uncle John. Young Arthur was rightful King of England, not only by primogeniture but also by will of King Richard Lion-heart. Consequently, it was very necessary to John Softsword (who usurped his crown) that he should disappear. And he did disappear at Rouen. And John is credited with his murder. But— suppose that he did not really disappear, that he was not murdered, that he actually escaped from his wicked uncle, the history of England (as we have it from the monkish chroniclers) might be quite another story. This was Crabbe's idea. Young Arthur was not murdered at all. By help of Hubert de Burgh, he escaped the tormentors sent to put out his eye-lights, he escaped from John when that assassin tried to drown him in the Seine, he escaped (half-crucified), from the Giwen of Bristol to whom John-Judas had sold him for thirty thousand marks of silver. Innocent the Third, that astute steel pontiff with the eye of a squinting lambkin, though frightfully excited about the boy, didn't see his pontifical way at the moment to depose the rich oldster John (who was in possession of the crown of the English) in favour of the poor youngster Arthur (who so far hadn't a doughty deed to his name). Arthur, accordingly, in an access of Angevin anger, went and did deeds in the Holy Land, as the shortest cut into Innocent's valuable affections, returning (as King-Consort of Hierusalem) just in time to find the Pope bored to death with John's abominations, and only too happy (now) to do the straight thing. Armed with bulls and what not, and supported by Earl Hubert de Burgh, admiral and warden and regent of England, Arthur conquered England, drove John into life-sanctuary at his Cistercian Abbey of Beaulieu, fought young Henry Lackland (commonly called Henry the Third) for the crown in ordeal of

battle at Oxford, and reigned with enormous glory till the year of
our Lord 1255. And the history of it all was written, on King
Arthur's death, by old Hubert de Burgh, Constable of the Tower,
who had been and done everything in England for a matter of
sixty years or so, and (in extreme old age) fancied that he naturally
knew more about facts than a certain little monk, Mr Matthew
(formerly of Paris), who only listened to gossip and spied through
the keyhole of his monastery, and wrote the stuff thus gleaned
as what he had the insolence to call *The Chronicle of England*. This,
Hubert de Burgh's astoundingly circumstantial Delusion, bristling
with personal knowledge of men famous and infamous, with statesmanlike policy, heraldry, archæology, love, wit, sorrow, humour,
courage, suffering, every high and noble human interest and activity,
all illumined by the insight and pathos and power of his own personality, was embodied in a manuscript written in a very individual
sort of Latin, which Nicholas Crabbe pretended to have discovered
in the Tower of London and to be translating in collaboration with
his friend Harricus Peary-Buthlaw. I say 'pretended,' because he
himself firmly averred it so. But (with reverence may the words
be spoken) I never for a single instant believed him. I have written
a book or two myself. I have translated several. And I happen to
be fairly cognisant of Thirteenth Century History and of English
Thirteenth Century Manuscript. Also, I have seen a lot of the Peary-
Buthlaw's work—it reads like the slap-dash translation of a showy
presumptuous Harrow cub—and I have seen all of Nicholas Crabbe's.
And I am of opinion—that my head spins round and round. But—
if the book called *De Burgh's Delusion* was not actually written in an
old knight's limping but vivid Latin, was not actually the source of
lots of Shakespeare's Arthurian verses and lots of Tennyson's verses
about the other Arthur, and so on, and so on—I simply say Who,
Who wrote the Latin from which my patron pretends to have
translated? For there it is; and there's no getting away from it.
Perhaps when the book is published—it is not published yet,[1] for
reasons about to be elucidated—some kind critic may give us
his views, unless in the meantime Nicholas, that monument of
mysterious simplicity, has seen his way to make the matter clear.

That was the task to which Crabbe sat down. He flung his
concentrated forces on the job.

Every morning, after mass and coffee, he sloomed down to the

---

[1] Though lost to sight for many years, the manuscript of this remarkable
work has been discovered, and, it is hoped, may follow the present volume
into publication.

club. If the day was fair, Zildo rowed him on the quiet Lagoon, where, sitting in the cane arm-chair of the pupparin, with a writing-board across his knees, he pondered and judged every word of his rough drafts, and transcribed the result in the fair copy. If the day was foul he worked in the club, where solitude reigned in the mornings. The fine saloon, with its balcony on the mouth of the Grand Canal, made a decent workshop. Zildo would light the fire, and arrange with the servants that his master should be undisturbed, and then come and sit by his side, to rub into lissomness the hand which was not wielding the enormous Waterman fountain-pen. For Crabbe's hands had been damaged for fine writing by use of the twenty-two-foot oar of the topo during that voyage down the Adriatic. It was not a mere case of blisters and callosities. Long gripping of the oar had hardened the palm-muscles, stiffening fingers and thumbs from knuckle to tip, so that each hand was cramped in a certain large definite curve of the circumference of an oar-handle, seriously interfering with the light quick effortless finger-bending necessary for its job. He could write equally well, however, with both hands, that extraordinary plain implacable kheirography which he invented (from Cesare Borgia's and Pope Clement the Seventh's) for the benefit of printers tired of smudgy misspelt illiterate illegible typescript. And so, while he wrote in his book with one hand, the other hung down at his side, to be warmed and pressed and twisted and pinched and moulded into flexibility by the gentle force of Zildo. He deliberately submitted himself to this test, danced along this slack-wire, taking horrible, useless risks, as usual. Defiant of weakness, daring danger, he hardened himself by means of these very thrills of contact, making his citadel anew impregnable. If he thought of the effect on Zildo, he only thought of him as undergoing discipline together with his master. As a matter of fact, it was discipline for Zildo—very salutary discipline, discipline of the species which inspires kissing of the rod. Zildo quietly enjoyed his proper emotions. Nicholas permitted himself to have none.

Every afternoon, fair or foul, he and his servant rowed to the infirmary for orders. On fine days he carried patients desirous of air—the nephritic 'Chief' who seemed to have made up his mind to live and die on La Pash, the little brigand from Bari who offered his hand to the nurse-assistant at the amputation of his leg, the hoary pneumoniac donkey-man who used Mrs S. A. Allen's Hair Restorer, the Greek artist who wouldn't be parted from the needle in his sole, and innumerable phthisical or carbuncular or impos-

thumish sailors and footmen of La Pash. He acted, at all times, as
ferryman to the nurses or the female guests of the bibbling directress.
On wet days he did the infirmary's shopping in the city, importing
panettone for its tea-fights, or bargained for firewood among the
Istrian trabaccoli and counting the logs when brought to the infirmary
door, or bought its coals, seeing them duly weighed on delivery.
Perceiving how barefacedly and successfully the infirmary was
cheated by its purveyors—its own cook, as a matter of course,
accepted eighty quintals for a hundred—Crabbe often used to wonder
where the committee, or the management, so ingeniously concealed
itself, and, also, whether females really are quite as almightily competent and adequate as they advertise themselves to be. When he
had once discovered that the establishment wasn't an official or
professional institution, it became easy to understand why it was
so absurdly undermanned and overwomanned. It was La Pash's
private preserve. The house-surgeon was Italian and non-resident,
with a penchant for powders. The operating-surgeon was the
chief in the city, and strong enough to bargain for sole use of the
theatre. Other doctors shied at the place, because they never knew
that their directions would be obeyed by the nurses. In the absence
of such guarantees, two German doctors refused to send patients
there. They had good reason. One of the two English medical
men in the city, an original member of the once-a-year-meeting
committee, had been hunted out by La Pash's interference with his
professional practice. She (at the instance of the fussy directress,
her nominee) forced a consultation where neither doctor nor patient's
relations deemed a second opinion either necessary or desirable.
Naturally he sent in his resignation, though his treatment was
approved. And the other English doctor, a recent arrival, supported
his colleague by declining connection with La Pash's infirmary.
Had the place posed modestly as a private clinic, public criticism
would have of course been muzzled. But, on the contrary, notwithstanding the fact that the four most eminent physicians in
Venice had shunned it, while most of the others hardly noticed it
at all, La Pash's infirmary advertised and exploited itself with every
circumstance of publicity. A notice-board flared at the ferry-pontoon,
directing the way to it. English and German ships, entering the
port, were attracted to it. Its garden and blue-room and directress's
office were made a rendezvous place for residents and transients.
Its afternoon teas were erected into social functions. Its collecting-
boxes on staircase and in hall appealed to every visitor. And the
pachydermatous figurante, who directed it as an evening rival to

the Sailor's Institute, frantically demanded a public lottery, pesca, tombola, or beneficenza on behalf of its funds, when she saw what Venetian charity had done for Calabria and Sicily. This sort of thing was irregular. A private clinic or a private nursing-home or even a private hobby mustn't scramble for and take public subscriptions. If it does it mustn't pose as a private charity managed and maintained by an irresponsible old lady masked by a committee of doddering nonentities. But the Universal Infirmary actually was that—a private hobby of La Pash's, an admirable one (no doubt) in intention, administered on lines which were purely amateur. An example will serve to point. The second engineer of an English coal-tramp was brought in on a wet Sunday afternoon, his third day of double-pneumonia. The directress was capering in England, leaving two young but very capable nurses in her room. Rain poured in torrents. The patient was put to bed in the outer ward and duly compressed; and the Italian house-surgeon was summoned by telephone from his residence at the far end of the canal. Crabbe arrived just as the house-boy (the jibbering ape Angelo) was being hurried to the farmaxia (a quarter-mile off) with the doctor's prescription. Crabbe wondered why ordinary drugs were not kept on the premises: but he waited in the hall, ready to serve in any way. The nurses seemed dreadfully worried, and the case was said to be a grave one. After three-quarters of an hour Angelo had not returned, and Zildo was sent flying to the pharmacy to make inquiries. Most gondolieri are awkward with their beautiful legs on terra firma, though there's no poise too delicate and no pose too elaborate for them on a bark on the water. But Zildo could stretch himself out and run like Pheidippides shot with the sandals of wing-footed Hermes. He was back in ten minutes. The ape had not been, and was not to be seen. Confusion: the patient in collapse: the Italian doctor calmly absent on his private rounds and inaccessible even by telephone: no prescription excepting the unread one in the hands of Angelo. Crabbe himself rushed out, through the deluge, to seek the little devil. There's only one street on the island of Spinalonga, a quay half a mile long which runs from end to end with blind alleys running out of it like the teeth of a comb. In a filthy court, half-way down, he unearthed Angelo's father and raged: 'Where's your son? A life depends on him!' 'Ma-ah! What do I know? No doubt he plays with his companions in some alley, today being Sunday and a festival.' 'If death occurs, he will be an assassin!' 'Me don't know nothing about nothing!' the oaf concluded, returning to his vomit. Thence Crabbe fled onward to the farmaxia. The pharmacist knew the toso of the infirmary well: yes: he hadn't been there that day. At which, Angelo casually strolled in with the prescription. It was made up in an instant, being only camomile; and the little beast was booted, howling, at full pelt back to the infirmary, where the patient had that moment died, surprisingly like a victim of well-meaning but amateur inadequacy. This incident gave Crabbe such a sickener that he passionately asked himself what the devil he was doing in that galley. Yet, the place was supposed to be English; and for that reason alone, though he denounced its absurdities, he continued to serve it. He would give it his very best: its shortcomings were not his affair.

He returned to the hotel about tea-time, dismissing his servant for the day; and wrote letters or read the papers in his room till dinner at 19 o'clock. At $19\frac{3}{4}$ o'clock he brought his work and coffee into the hall, and wrote there steadily till 1 o'clock in the morning when the house was closed.

As a rule he made more progress by night than by day. He used to feel as though his tide had risen and was in full flood during those five last hours. Whereas in the morning he was listless and dry and had to force his power; at night, he was clear-headed, quick to create and to judge and to select, and his hands flew with unnoticeable facility. The hall was nearly always empty, after he had dismissed the gossipy Wardens, till the midnight train from Milano sometimes disgorged a belated visitor. The plump little landlord used to go and play a billiard with spillikins at his father-in-law's Albergo Diana, variegated with rounds among the kinematographs. Crabbe then had the place to himself, excepting for the waiters who watched alternately. On the nights when old Elia and Little Piero were on duty, he hardly had an interruption. The maestro-di-casa sneaked out of doors on private errands round the corner perhaps half a dozen times in the course of the evening, and returned ten minutes later to snooze festively behind the *Corriere della Sera*. During his absence Crabbe used to pass a kind word with Little Piero, a nimble willing wonderfully-deft good-hearted youthlet of eighteen, who toiled nineteen hours out of every twenty-four to support a widowed mother and half a dozen brothers and sisters with his scanty earnings. On other nights, when Arthur had his turn alone, Crabbe often talked for half an hour at a time. This waiter was really anxious to improve. He was astonishingly intelligent and even well read, with quite a fair knowledge of the literature of the four modern languages which he knew. Once, Nicholas happened to say something about long words. Instantly, 'One of our popular axioms, "Chi troppo in alto sal' cade sovente, precipitevolissimevolmente" is not as long by one letter as "honori- ficabilitudinitatibus" in your Shakespeare's *Love's Labour's Lost*,' came from the waiter. Nicholas gasped; and became keener than ever on picking Arthur's brains. The mental method and manner of life of pleasant-looking people always was his constant study, partly because of his acquisitive temperament which snatched at everything likely to serve his trade of a writer, partly because of his rejective habit which prompted him to give away. As he once said, he liked to get people to tell him about themselves, as it gave him an opportunity of shewing off. Never before had he known anything about waiters, excepting as useful automata. From this one he learned how much a good waiter must actually have at the tip of his fingers and tongue, the day's dishes and their composition, innumerable details of the place and sights and the times and ways to things, with a nice appreciation of and ability to satiate the mis- cellaneous tempers and heterogeneous idiosyncracies of multi- tudinous travellers all to be anticipated and ready at the moment of expression. This, for eighteen hours at least on each of the seven days of the week, and in return for what? Perhaps fifty franchi a month for wages, and another fifty in hardly-earned tips, with poor exiguous nutriment snatched anyhow and anywhere, and a dirty densely populated dog-kennel of a garret (boiling in summer, freezing in winter, with a thin thigh's girth of space between the almost wicked beds) to herd in at night. Such is the lot of waiters at the chief hotels of Venice; and naturally they jump at a chance of a place in less pretentious alberghi where they are treated as human beings. There's a law in Italy ordaining that all the employed (excepting domestic servants) must have a Riposo Festivo of twenty- four consecutive hours in each week at least. Most have it on Sunday. All barbers have it on Monday. And so on, by arrange- ment. But pious persons (the Wardens, for instance) not only make their gondolieri work seven days a week on the plea that they are domestic servants, but they don't even give their maids a chance of going decently to Mass or Communion on Sundays. And the managers of company hotels which are run only to earn dividends for professional philanthropists (generally Jews or Free- masons) not only give their waiters no Festive Repose at all—for an occasional afternoon hour or so is not the consecutive period demanded by the law—but they force their slaves (on pain of instant dismissal) to state formally to the legal inquisitors that they in fact enjoy their legal privileges. It took a great deal of time and trouble to extract information from Arthur. He was one of those active, adept modest somewhat courageous creatures who have no notion of kicking against pricks. They do their job: never complain: generally better themselves: and are the phlegmatic salt of the earth. Nicholas had to win his confidence. He couldn't understand, at first, that an English collects knowledge for its own sake. He was far too respectably minded to mix himself with venal wretches who sow discontent among the working-classes; and all sorts of suspicion had to be cleared away before he could open his heart. But, when once he realized that Nicholas was not an Austrian spy (the Venetians, with good cause, are desperately on guard against Austria) or the salaried inquisitor of secret societies like the socialists and the charity-organizations, but a friend, a well-wisher, as well as a mine of desirable information, then he used to speak freely from his naïve and interesting and really very well-stored mind.

Nicholas Crabbe was incapable of refraining from the mixture of his life with other people's. We know why. His watery temperament craved earthy support. He was always seeking his Other Half. And his own hard Life, while sharpening his natural ferocity to an utterly inhuman point, had given him a superhuman faculty of pity. He fell into philanthropy as easily as a black-beetle falls into a basin—'tanquam blatta in pelvim.' His immense proclivity for redressing wrongs, for succouring the oppressed, for protecting the helpless, for cultivating the lovely and good, was detrimental (humanly speaking) to his own interests. But he simply could not be practically selfish. Hence all sorts of unpleasing predicaments. His was the knightly soul; and his deeds were the deeds of a champion fighting the battles of others, neglecting his own.

XIII

Parrucchiero requested a private interview. He had a number of bills to meet.

'Something seems to have gone awry with my affairs in England, and I haven't any money to spare at present; but, as soon as my book's done, there'll be plenty for both of us,' Crabbe serenely said.

He was annoyed, though. He had paid handsomely, had brought visitors there, had kept others there by shewing hospitality when they were good-looking and a whole army of brutally ugly Russians by the simple expedient of rejecting their advances. Of course he was a bit touchy: one always is when asked for money. The landlord's manner, however, left nothing to be desired. He merely mentioned his little bill.

Bobugo at length wrote, haughtily. His offer remained open: though he had grave doubts as to the corollaries of Crabbe's reception of it, and fervently hoped that he would not have to make them unpleasant ones. He purposely omitted, and continued omitting, his usual New Year's Benediction of his friend, not being at all sure that that friend was in a fit state to receive it. Meanwhile, he had been talking about Crabbe's exquisite writings to his particular friend Lord Arthur Baliol Kingsbury, the editor of *The Lykeion*, who begged the favour of some for his weekly.

Harricus at length wrote, as Lieutenant of the Order of Grand-magistracy of Sanctissima Sophia. He abolished vermilion as a curial colour; and knights of every grade were to wear violet and white henceforward. He enclosed a lot of new forms of inquisition, to be used for the yanking-in of as many Italian naval officers as possible. He had conferred honorary knighthood on several Free-masons and Knights-templars (list of names enclosed) in a church at Hampstead, lent by its Freemasonic vicar, who also had joined the Order, with awful and sinful pomp and dignity. Said church was suitable for ordinal functions, and would be willingly lent when wanted. Said functions must instantly be devised. Nicholas, being beyond the narrow seas, was temporarily suspended from provostry: the Lieutenant would assume the office of Provost for the time being.

And he howled for designs for great sigils, and the Latin office for his own coronation. As for Crabbe's present plight, perhaps Bobugo Bonsen had better be invited to Uskvale for conference. Nicholas was not to take umbrage where none was intended, but Harricus considered him rather a mucker of his own business affairs, and therefore implored him and commanded him to let his friends manage them for him. On no account was he to write letters about them meanwhile, especially to Bobugo or to his agents. The latter should be brought to their senses instanter. No one but a fool would pay another man's debts of honour, certainly not those of a gobbler like Macpawkins, of whom the Peary-Buthlaws never wished to hear again. Harricus was sorry that he had neglected *The Weird*. He would neglect it no longer. But let Crabbe just hurry up *De Burgh's Delusion*, as money in mounds would be forthcoming immediately on its receipt in England.

Morlaix and Sartor didn't write anything at all.

At the same time some bills came in: which Crabbe, rearing with fury, paid, to the exhaustion of his small stock of cash. No one but he would have paid them. They were some nasty little accounts which the professor of Greek (mentioned at the beginning of this history) had left behind him. Crabbe already had spent lavishly in making good the name which association with that carroty obscenity had gained for him in the previous autumn. He had been absurdly generous to a whole parcel of gondolieri, whom the skunk had enslaved, half-paid, and more than half-starved by sharing two lunches among five habitually. He had paid for broken and lost oars, and for damages to barks, solely because he had been seen in the professor's company and did not choose to be known as the equal of a screeching niggard. No doubt he disbursed very much more filthy lucre than was necessary: we know what Venetians always have been. But he paid for honour and reputation, to emphasize the severest severance of every sort of connection. And after this, for ready money, there was nothing to do but to overdraw his account. The bank knew him well; and, after all, tightness could only be temporary.

Sitting in his bark at the traghetto of Santasofia, he wrote to Bobugo. "I must say that I am amazed at your mention of me to such a person as your friend Lord Arthur Baliol Kingsbury. You know you are not giving me any particular cause for confidence just now, and I beg that you will take no more hare-brained steps on my behalf without my permission. However, not to make you look more like a fool in the present instance, I am sending half a dozen short things of about three thousand words each to your lord, stating my price is five guineas a thousand. About our collaboration and your astounding demands for bonds, I am waiting for your answer to my last. And permit me to remind you again that you are still withholding your New Year's Benediction."

Next, he wrote to Caliban. "I should only be too delighted if my friends would manage my affairs. I suppose you may be considered a friend of Bobugo, seeing that I had him with us at Uskvale last year; and I suppose you're free to invite him again, if you yearn to. You're fully aware of the questionable manner in which he's treating me, and I shall be curious to see what you will do. Of course you're your own master. If you ask for my wishes, I say No: specially as, you remember, he's a scorner of the Order. But do as you please. I know just what will happen. You'll have to settle whether you'll be my friend or his; and that's a tough task for any Christchurch man, even a Lieutenant of a Grandmagistracy. In obedience to your command, I cease from writing to Bobugo, and Morlaix and Sartor. If you suspend me from my provostship—oh, very well. The moment seems rather singularly chosen: that's all. Why abolish vermilion immediately after sending me my vermilion smock to wear here? For the present, I reserve remarks about the Freemasonic absorption of the Order, save only these: I object to it with every force at my command—and, use not that Lombard church till you have the written permission of Mr A. W. Ingram. You will get no designs for sigils or Latin offices till I have finished *De Burgh's Delusion*. I'm putting all my power on that, for things are becoming serious. The blind and naked fact is that I've paid another lot of Machawkin's beastly bills, and my landlord is beginning to cough; and I actually have but *diesi jenche* to go on with: which means that I shall have to overdraw at the bank. Morlaix and Sartor are lying low. So please be quick and see what devilry they're up to. I'm getting rather anxious; and of course I shall keep the proofs of *Sieur René* till some decent explanation is forthcoming. I'm not going to have that book mucked, if (as I suspect) they've been mucking its predecessors. Now mark—this is a case of knight of the Order invoking the Lieutenant to his aid. Haro! Haro! Mon Prince! Illuminet te Sanctissima Sapientia."

Afterward, he made a visit to the church across the Campo. It's a miserable old place, though well enough formed, squarish, capable of extremely pompous functions in its nave: but it's piteously neglected and tawdry; and, being in a populous slum and overshadowed by its neighbours Santapostol and Sanfelice, no one seems to care a pajanca about it. It pleased and suited Crabbe immensely, though. He was not a born creator, but he was a born constructor. All his life long, in every branch of activity provided for (or grabbed by) him, he proceeded on a single principle. He invariably began by stripping. He insisted on clearing off all accretions, good and bad, so that he might get down and see the thing as it is. Such was his curious cultivated capability in this direction that (as a rule) he actually saw people and things stark naked. He had a disconcerting knowledge of what mere passers-by looked like without their clothes; and very few minutes' casual inspection would tell him the proportions of the skeleton of the person to whom he happened to be speaking. By this faculty, he formed ideas as to the diet, diversion, and decoration, which would produce a pleasing peel or pod upon such frameworks; and, of course, with buildings (whose proportions satisfied him) he simply revelled in planning their adaptation to their proper purpose and their adornment in a manner suitable. In churches, where he went to pray—in open air, as he walked in the city or rowed across the blue lagoon—anywhere where silence was and solitude (for, as will have been perceived, he prayed without ceasing)—he proceeded on a method of his own. Long practice and unstifled genius makes as near perfection as imperfect man can attain. He was no novice, but an adept, now. He had been at the pains of inventing a formula of initiation. The vulgar wallowing stage of verbal prayer (extempore, whining, suggestive, didactic, dictatorial, generally impertinent and particularly bathotic), he had left far, far behind him. He had passed the stage of repetitions, liturgical or otherwise, commonly vain. He had gone beyond formal meditation, with its stumpy "firstly and secondly and thirdly let us consider" platitudinous obviousnesses which no decent Christian ever lost sight of for a single blink. Quite aware of his own unimportant high importance—perfectly conscious of being merely one of quintillions, one (though) for whom the Maker of the Stars had deigned to die the atrociously comic death reserved for criminal slaves—he simply hadn't the desire (much less the stupid cheek) to approach the Presence by any way but the road of wordless submission. With that means, only, could he preserve his individual dignity. He came with boldness, with childlike boldness: for he was no errant alien, keeping back more than he gave, preferring his own will, miring himself with the fond delusion that he (that he, untold), knew what he wanted. But he came as one to whom Mystery has a meaning and a method, as one of the intimate, and fortunate, as one who belonged, as a son to the Father. Liberated from the bondage and dubiety of human speech (that trap of the unwary, that stumbling-block to truth)—using words solely as an incantation, for casting himself off this earthly plane, stark, up to the Presence Divine, where all his praise, all his worship, love, hope, faith, fear, aspiration lay quite open, known clearly through and through without expression—thus then he was wont to pray. Kneeling in some desert fane like Santasofia, standing in the huge brown gold-gleaming gloom of thronged Sammarco, steering his speedy course through the human current swirling in the city's narrow alleys, rowing with regular rhythm on the sun-kissed lagoon—he would say his spell, Deus meus et Omnia, again and again and again and again, like another Blessed Brother Francis of Assisi. And, at first, his gaze would wander, appreciating his environment, analyzing, stripping, selecting Deus meus et Omnia. Next, his god-given faculty of imagination would come into play, reconstructing, regulating, ordering, adorning, Deus meus et Omnia. And, having thus used to the very uttermost his singular endowment and peculiar gift (which he knew to be given to be used), surrounding himself with an image of his ultimate ideal of earthly beauty, he made this—his very best—a spring-board; his eyes became fixed, his body rigid and insensible; and on the wings of the incessant spell Deus meus et Omnia, he shot with impetus onward, soaring away till, somewhere very high, beyond illimitable space, he floated, in face-to-face communion. Deus meus——. Then after eternities of endless ages, silent eternities, he would take leave, and come softly down, corrected, cleaned, his problems solved, his soul inspired with necessary news and necessary strength and necessary knowledge for guidance on the way, to complete his rune—et Omnia, in celestial serenity.

When he came from the church of Santasofia, with the delightful consciousness of knowing a thing or two, Zildo was engaged in a tafferuglio at the traghetto. Zildo in a rage, a white and vermilion fulguration, was a spectacle for gods and men.

On the wooden steps stood the old ganzero of the ferry, chattering at the top of his voice, like the ravidest orang-outang, 'È divieto! È proibito! È vietato!' punctuated by noises as of hyæna violently vomiting. Also he threw his wrists into the air, dancing stiff-leggedly.

Zildo sat on the edge of the poop, with a roll of rag across his knees; and he held one of the piles close at hand. He was intense and pallid as Death: his great long eyes blazed; and the set teeth glittered between his scarlet lips.

The hooker hiccoughed for breath, as Nicholas came down to them; and Zildo snatched the chance of slipping in a pointed word or two, cursing with low vibrance which scorched like vitriol by the suddenness of its suitability, fulminating an abusive torrent to which it was a joy to listen: 'Che macàco che ti xe! Marionetta! Goffo! Sciocco! Oca! Cretino! Imbecille! Pandolo! Bertoldin! Scimiotto! Sa! Oh what a fool thou art! Dancing Doll! Awkward! Insipid! Goose! Idiot! Imbecile! Stick! Stupid! Great ape! Don't you know! I have said that this is the bark of an English! Know it! Thou thyself hast seen him! Know it! O vile one! who wantest not to be regaled with a good handsel by an illustrious English——'

Nicholas cut in: 'And now?'

'Mariavergine!' ejaculated the hooker; and seizing his ganzo, he executed a change of front with ludicrous celerity. 'Hi! Fair Male!' he shrieked to Zildo: 'the bark for the most noble master immediately, o lazy idle inattentive potato!'

Zildo bunted him aside, and assisted Nicholas to step in, with a single dexterous movement. 'Sior,' he said, 'that touch of putridity blasphemed me for doing my duty. More, also, he spat on my shoe. And I call him una bestia de ome che noxe bon degnente.' The boy was very angry.

'Bad old male, ignorant of thine art, scratch up and wed a ghost of some good manners!' scolded Nicholas, pitching no more than the usual five schei, and taking up his oar.

Zildo had got another rag, and was cleansing his shoe. He flung the rag at the hooker. And 'In dove?' he asked, like a lamb.

'To the Bucintoro via Canalazzo.'

The swift bark swept by the Fish and Fruit Markets, through the always tossing currents, below Rialto. When they had passed the landing-stages, and were in a less crowded stretch of Canal Grande, Nicholas demanded explanations.

'Sior, the ganzero of that ferry is an ugly type, so evilly created as to wish to bully strange gondolieri, specially young ones such as I am, saying, like this, that none but ferrymen of that traghetto may moor at that traghetto for a moment. And I first gave him genteel words, saying that my patron was an Englishman who habitually bestowed pence instead of half-pence upon commodious hookers——'

'But, in fact, one really has no right——'

'In fact, nòssior. But, when there is a vacancy between the pali, one may moor there without detriment to the rights of the ferrymen; and none but an ill-created hooker would send a stranger's bark to toss outside the pali, among the vaporetti and lancecececette——'

Nicholas reared and roared. 'Launchchchchch' was a lovely new onomatopy for the motor-boats which make the Grand Canal a surging peril to Venetian barks.

'Còssa?' demanded Zildo in uncertainty.

'A beautiful new word—and many thanks for it.'

The boy was grave for a moment. Then, 'Thus they sound, and thus I call them: so also a dear little baby-angel, unable to speak, says "Mamma, Mamma," desiring to drink of his mother's breast. So, Sior, with permission, I did not loosen my hold from the palo, though that ugly individual arrabiated himself, foaming at the mouth like an epileptic, outraging my new shoe, for, though I am only una——!'

'No nò: Un——!'

'Sior, excuses. I forgot. Un toso—for, though I am a lad, I am the gondoliere of an English, with respects to his face; and I will not let my master be defrauded of his rights. Wherefore I, in my turn, offered certain descriptions to that hooker. But I see, Sior, that these have not disturbed you who have gained so blessed an aspect from Santasofia. And that pleases me, o blessed one of God!'

Nicholas held his peace. They were passing by Ca' Pachello where La Pash kept court. The abrupt revelation of Zildo's consciousness of sex, in that quite unintentional application of the feminine 'una' to himself, struck his master dumb. What sort of a game was this which was being played? Here was this girl acting the boy, and acting it perfectly successfully before a whole city. Crabbe saw that all was clear on that score. So far there had been no suspicion or cause for suspicion. Even Zildo's splendour and vigour went unnoticed in Venice, where forty out of fifty young people of both sexes would make the world turn to look at them in (say) Aberdeen. His stalwart boyish figure, in its revealing white guernsey and clinging dark-blue clothes, was by no means singular even among gondolieri. Many second gondoliere (who row the poop-oar) are from twelve to eighteen years old, as well-favoured as Zildo and much more screechingly attired in uniforms of fantastic cut and colour—the Wardens' (for example) in crimson and blue, and Lady Pash's in white and royal blue, and the priest's (who unpriested himself because he found priesthood a tie) in Rio Manir, and that dear little imp of Palazzo Sciebante (well-named Alessandro—helper of men) in two shades of white, who plunged headlong to save a spoiled baby off the quay of the Zattere. No. Of course Zildo was unique. But people seemed unaware of it—excepting—horror—perhaps the directress of the infirmary, who undoubtedly eyed him with alluring grimaces from the quay: but—Gracious Powers—would that hag look twice at a female inferior in position? Wasn't her ogling of Zildo plain proof that she took him for a male meet for palpation with patronizing paw? His carriage, his quiet impenetrable reserve, his serene inoffensive avoidance of unnecessary people, his strictly official communication with waiters at the hotel or the servants at the club—oh no: no one dreamed of suspecting his secret. For his own part, Nicholas was resolutely adhering to his determination to treat his servant as a boy. It had not cost him nothing. Gruffness was an effort. He loathed to expect of his servant rough dirty work and violent exertion. But Zildo had preferred it. No matter how much drawn in other ways his master might be fool enough to feel at times, honour could not yield one inch to chivalry in this case. Thus Nicholas frigidly admonished himself. There was always danger. There was an ever-present danger: for here upsprang the disconcerting (but most natural) news that Zildo never lost sight of his femininity. Host! If he ever unconsciously betrayed himself to another, as to Nicholas just now, how could that exquisite young life bear the unthinkable sequels?

'I wish to know something,' said Nicholas very grimly.

'Servo suo.'

'What friends have you?'

'Sior, ninsun.'

'To how many people do you speak?'

'Sior, I speak to my paron, to the servants of the Bucintoro, to the merchant from whom I buy nutriment, but no longer to little Piero or Arthur the Blonde of the hotel. Otherwise, I shout 'That' or 'Nigger' to barcajuoli who come in the road of the pupparin. And, upon occasions, I give of 'Imbecile' and similar outrages, to gents companions to that hooker there.'

'That is all?'

'Sìssior. But why? Have I done a fault?'

'No.' Nicholas shipped his oar. They were nearing the Abbey of Sannegrorio which is for sale for eight thousand sterling (and dirt cheap). He came and sat on the seat in face of the boy. 'Tell me, Zildo, how many people know what you are?'

The youngster looked down from the poop, his face aflare with a vermeil flush in which his eyes took the piercing radiance of blue stars: but he didn't shrink an atom. 'Sior, my master knows, and I know, and Domeniddio knows. No more: for we never linger at the traghetto of the Trinità, though I am grown beyond knowledge after so many years.'

'And the priest, to whom you confess yourself?'

'Sior, with permission, I should give to a priest not my secrets but

my sins. But I confessed myself with my relatives at Melito at
Nativity. Therefore they had a happy death; and I am here. And
I shall not confess myself here till Pasch—unless, Sior, I may confess
to my paron now?'

'What? Why?'

'Sior, I hanker after something. And my paron is secret, his face
is clean, his hair white, his mien grave, his wisdom vast, but he is not
old, nor severe, nor terrifying, nor——'

'Nonsense.' Not to be wheedled. 'No.'

'And why, Sior, do you ask me these questions? Has someone my
secret?' The tone was one of alarm.

'No one, as far as I know: excepting the three whom you named.
But, are you certain? Have you never, by carelessness, betrayed——'

The pretty teeth shewed in a smile. 'Now I understand well.
Nòssiornò—excepting to you just now, and of course always to the
Lord God when I pray 'Make me a good——'

'Yes, yes. And to Mariavergine? And to Santermenegildo?

'Mah! Scherza coi fanti Ma lasa star i santi. Play with the police,
but not with the saints. Those are quite trustworthy. And of course
Domeniddio told His Mother and my patron all about me when I was
baptized, so that they might eye me now and then. But I tell not
my secrets to the living; for a secret told to the living is trumpeted
from the little porphyry column called Il Bando to all in the Piazza
and in the Piazzetta. No xe ver, Sior?'

'It is true. And this is a commandment—your paron is one of the
living, to whom the secret may not be named. Understand?'

They had crossed Canalazzo; and the bark was being chained in
the little rio by the club. Nicholas had a hand on the iron rungs in
the sea-wall, and was about to climb up. He looked round. Zildo's
face was earnest, but his lips had a certain gently mischievous disposition to smile. His confession could not be very hair-raising. (It was,
though, that, precisely).

'Speak.'

Zildo bared his fair head. 'Sior, do a favour and view my hairs.
'I see them.'

'Sior, with permission, they grow, quickly-quickly. And for
discretion, I do not wish to be touched by a barber. Therefore, I
ask permission. For, at La Tasca, my aunt Elettra cut them every
fortnight with her scissors; and that is what I cannot do neatly by
myself. But, I have remembered a little machine, which my father
used for me and for himself, a very brave little machine to cut in
the dark, being a comb with tiny knives moved by two handles——'

'Good. I quite understand. Your discretion is admirable. You shall have such a little machine, and cut your hair yourself.'

'Sior, I pray. The cost I will reimburse from your money which I have gained from the Sior Caloprin.'

'No, I regale you with the little machine. But be discreet.'

'Sior, trust me; and so many thanks.'

Nicholas went to the barber's opposite to the hotel and bought a hair-clipper as he went home. The price was L. 15. 'I'll pay for it after lunch,' he said.

This meant beginning his overdraft. After luncheon he got his cheque-book and drew two pounds. Elia gave him L. 50 for the cheque and he sent Little Piero flying across the alley to pay for the hair-clipper. As he was replacing his cheque-book in the pigskin portfolio, the Thiasarkh crept up.

'Myiphmh!' he purred: 'money!—my compliments!'

Crabbe celebrated a sardonic snort. 'You may as well know,' he said, 'that I've just begun to overdraw at the bank: for I gave one of my last ten halfpennies to a hooker this very morning.'

The skull goggled commiseratingly. 'Do you think it quite safe?'

'I've no doubt they'll let me overdraw for—well—say a tenner. But look now—I'm open with you—you see how I am——'

'I couldn't help fancying that I saw that you had some letters this morning. Dear person, I do so hope they brought you some good news?'

'Neither good nor bad. Things seem to be hung up. And goodness only knows how they are to be got down, and what they'll look like when they are down. So I warn you again. Take a friendly tip and sheer off, and don't burn your fingers over me.'

'Oh, dear person, I couldn't really do it. Could I?'

'Quite comfortably, since it is I who warn you.'

'Myiphmh-myiphmh: no, dear person: you won't mind, will you? But you mustn't ask me.'

'All right. So much the better of you. And thank you very much,' said Nicholas, comfortable with the notion that others beside himself were capable of unselfish behaviour. This is the might of the Moon on the life of the native of Cancer, softening what should be hard, making weak what is strong.

XIV

WHAT grievously harrowed Crabbe's soul was the defect of Bobugo, specially in the matter of the benediction. It made him rear, clashing his awful claws. He had seen so many priests comporting themselves usuriously or venally that (although it excruciated his sense of decency) it only strengthened his faith: for he never permitted himself to forget that there was a Judas among the apostles; and so he was able to contemplate Bobugo's shameless proposal about the collaboration with comparative complacency. That priest would sin in a numerous company; and, no doubt, knew it. Crabbe's ridiculous habit of lenience in regard to men and priests whom he liked—which habit was also one of Michelangelo's—his absurd confidence in their honour, the exasperating injustice of his implicit belief in everything which they chose to tell him—his ever-readiness to slave for them, to lavish the charm of his individuality (with the stores of his experiments and his knowledge) upon them, to adorn their houses and churches, to edit their ideas, to write their books, to serve them as clerk-of-the-works, agent, steward, designer, gardener, poultry-farmer, secretary, coach, reader, eyes, hands, buffer, handyman, all without a thought of protecting his own interest by demanding preliminary agreements in writing—naturally could have only one result. People used him, his time, his means, his strength, his talents, freely—seeing how willingly he slaved, with what ingenious joy he flung himself into ingenious activity, they conceived the sacred and beautiful notion that they were his benefactors in bestowing upon him so much pleasure. And when, one day, his job done, himself and his resources exhausted by it, he naïvely looked for a due reward, his benefactors (deeply pained) would try to gag and paralyse him with alms. They meant it as a kindness: the man had no legal claim. (They took good care of that.) Well then— could anything be more infuriating than to have appeals made to one's honour, and one's charity hurled back with resounding smacks ? A man who could behave in that way was a nuisance. The man who habitually trusted in his friend's honour had his own opinion on this point: an opinion which, at length picturesquely enunciated, rustily rasped the self-respect and left it raw and envenomed. Crabbe in his path through life left festering carcases (of this kind) writhing on both sides of the way, hacked and torn and mangled with his ferocious pincers. Of late years he had become a little bored by the monotony of such exercitations. He did so earnestly desire reason for thinking well of some, at least, of his fellow-creatures. As for poor things who must needs have their honour corseted by law before they could hold a straight backbone—oh, well, they were not the kind of people which he cared to know. It was impossible for him to alter his own conduct; and, if it brought him suffering, he was content to deal with that—and competent. When Bobugo voluntarily proposed public collaboration, Crabbe never dreamed of serving himself by demanding legal agreements. And, when Bobugo (tempted by avarice and fortified by confidences, confessional or otherwise, as to the impunity with which his friend, and penitent, had been and might be safely wronged) thought fit to hector, demanding renunciation of his share of the credit of collaboration without equivalent—then Crabbe shot out stark eyes and twitched his terrible talons into working order. Bobugo, in the capacity of unscrupulous tyrant, was unfit for his society, and he steeled himself to lose another friend. Bobugo should have a chance of retraction, and traces of the slip (if slip it should be acknowledged to be) would be generously obliterated: but the iniquitous proposition was to be rejected, anyhow. Crabbe was rearing violently, as I have said. He was bored with the role of victim—ultimately bored. And, if Bobugo persisted in his dedecorous exactions and shewed metal too base to stand the acid test of Crabbe's criticisms, then (of course) he would prance off and number himself with all the other former friends of Crabbe whose examples he was but imitating. No doubt he would congratulate himself on being secure among a number. Most men prefer the Many to the One. Few men will second another in a duel; no seconds ever dream of engaging their principal's opponent's seconds just for friendship's sake and as a matter of course. And your common (or vain) man, facinorous cringer for nods and sanctions, having lapsed from the narrow ridge of righteousness, contentedly wallows where other lapsed crowd thickest, preferring (like bugs) quantity to quality. Crabbe anticipated that this would be Bobugo's procedure; and did not worry himself with fears of causing the priest unhappiness.

But he worried himself frightfully about the benediction. That yet another trusted priest should misuse ghostly power to gain profane advantage pierced his heart. That was what Bobugo seemed to be doing—his usual New Year's Benediction was the price of consent to write the greater part of the book (of which he was to pose as sole author) on the same terms as those proffered for equal collaboration and credit. It was an awfully keen weapon, coercive to some, intimidating to all. Bobugo was well aware that a Jesuit had once used it to Crabbe with appalling but unexpected effect. For, when a small thing like the Rite of benediction was refused, Crabbe publicly understood that the greater Sacraments also would be denied; and, for two whole years, went openly deprived of these means of grace—informally deprived, no species of excommunication being dared to be pronounced—until rigorous insistence on right forced his persecutors' bishop in person to bring him rites and sacraments both. Bobugo knew, in confession and out, the agonies which Crabbe manfully endured in these two years; and, speaking humanly —I believe, though, that le mot juste is 'diabolically'—it was an adroit stratagem to furbish up the same old thumbscrew of compulsion. That he should defend himself with the plea of Crabbe's unfitness for benediction only made matters more uproariously ludicrously worse. I am not discussing this question on the plane of Christianity (be it clearly understood), but only in its relation to ecclesiastical practice, which ordains that all things under the Curse are to be restored by Blessing. If, then, Crabbe, by refusing to be cheated by this priest, became accursed, so much the more reason was there why he should be precipitately blessed. Accursed, he was recalcitrant and incorrigible: blessed (logically) he would be at least disposed to submission. Would you not have thought so, o most affable reader? And, if (as was not unnatural) he should happen to be turning his own attention toward an exquisite and recherché and meticulous anathematization of this hairy priest who wouldn't bless him—well, at the risk of the howl 'Two-edged,' I will simply say, What about 'Bless them that curse you'? However, Bobugo (misguided and mad enough to blind himself to these considerations) might do his worst. He should be amply informed of the corollaries of his contemplated crime. And Crabbe would resist the devil till he fled.

An unsigned telegram interrupted these speculations, and flopped Crabbe flat in his cane arm-chair in the hall to perpend it. MIXI V LIBRXX XD CVLINX PXR VOX VXNI XD VXKVXLXM INXTXNTXR CONFIDXTX OMNIX IN MX.

Barbolan popped out his head from the office, hoping that it was not bad news. Crabbe distractedly waved the sheet with its two gummed strips of typescript at him.

'It's cipher,' discontentedly declared the landlord.

'But I don't know any ciphers,' Crabbe complained.

He sat, weakly wavering over the hideous thing, feeling that (very shortly) his mind would become unhinged. It was 18½ o'clock, and he was tired, after an afternoon's hard rowing of a loaded bark and a noisy tea-fight at the infirmary.

Elia brought a handsome flaxen young man across the hall, who addressed him in English by name. He had the sturdy air and the thighs and calves of a football player. Crabbe admitted his identity.

'I have to pay you L. 125.65 on behalf of Messrs Thomas Cook and Son,' said his visitor.

'Lord!' Crabbe murmured. 'But why? They don't owe me anything.'

'It's a remittance through our London house.'

'From whom?'

'I'm not at liberty to say.'

'Thank you very much. I decline to snatch mysterious remittances. Kindly retain it till I've made a few inquiries.'

The incident pondered, at length produced the needed clue. A hundred and twenty-five lire and sixty-five centesimi represented the equivalent of a fiver; and there was a V LBRXX in the unsigned telegram. Of course the thing was the majestuous (but cubbish) Latin of the Lieutenant of the Grandmagistracy of the Order of Sanctissima Sophia, transmogrified (by a Venetian telegraphic dattilographer) from switch-deserving prose to frantic nonsense by the substitution of X for S and E and A. It was thus construable: MISI I have sent V LIBRAS five pound-weights AD CULINAM to the kitchen (Cook?) PER VOS for you (Ouch!) VENITE come AD USKVALEM to Uskvale INSTANTER instantly CONFIDETE trust OMNIA all IN ME to me (Ouph!). Come instantly? Leave Zildo? Ha-ha! Not for ninety millions! He told himself not to be a fool, and planned a letter during dinner: afterward, he wrote and posted it, having kept Zildo entirely out of his considerations.

This is what went to Caliban. "This night I have received an illegible telegram; and have told Cook that I won't accept a remittance of five sterling from a mysterious stranger. I'm not coming back to England in any circumstances, at least till I've finished *De Burgh's Delusion*. Nothing shall stop me in that. I do confide in You, and already have entrusted my business to You. Do not neglect it, I implore You, as I have stopped action on my account in obedience to You. Make Morlaix and Sartor explain their silence and their failure to account for their management of my property. They promised (and have paid) me an allowance, so far. Make them continue it. And for Heaven's Sake dispose of *The Weird*. Now I will speak of ordinal matters. Your Splendour is a Freemason, and you have been conferring honorary knighthood on a parcel of Freemasons. This news, and that about Your Freemasonic parson, who lends his church to the Order, vastly have perturbed me. I am not provost any more: but, as an articulate knight, You will still hear me keeping keepership of Your Splendid conscience, admonishing, exhorting, and (in fact) keeping the article for all I'm worth, in accordance with Part I, Chap. iii, Clause 32, of the Rule of the Order. And I am moved to utter these four sayings following. (*a*) As long as I, a catholic, ruled religious exercises within the Order, I had no objection to the assistance of acatholics, freemasonic or otherwise. (*b*) But I, a catholic, will not assist at any but functions conducted by catholics. (*c*) And I view this incursion of Freemasons and other Loyal shepherds or Antient Buffalos with dismay mingled with distaste. (*d*) Lastly, I implore Your Splendour to go slow. Say 'No, thank you' to the Hampstead church definitely. Avoid public ceremonial and ostentation of any kind. The object of our Order is the pursuit of Wisdom. Let us pursue it singly, avidly, quite quietly, and very humbly. Not till we have justified our existence, by some notable contribution to human knowledge, dare we court attention. Even then, three-times and four-times blessed is he who can contrive to escape the attention of Lord Elmwood's young men. Conceive an idea of the appalling way in which the ha'penny papers would write up (or down, you pay your pajanca and you take your copy) an automatic autonomous sovereign order creeping with Freemasons, functionizing heraldically in that temple of the Church of England As By Law Established, about which You (as I dare to deem) ill-advisedly have been smacking Your Splendid Chops. I'm really concerned about this. And I pray you to ponder my opinion; and to stick strictly to business. I.T.SS. S."

Thus relieved, his mind felt easier. His poignant mode of expression by no means indicated cantankerous temper. As a matter of fact he was rather keen on the Order, and took it, and his connection with it, extremely seriously. Despite his peculiarities, there's no denying that Nicholas Crabbe was a man of insight and intelligence: though I admit that there is a great deal of difficulty in making this point clear, seeing that he entered into such very close relations with priests and Scotchmen. Caliban's passion for pageants and pompous paraphernalia was phenomenal in a young Oxford graduate, of county-family and no particular endowments beyond a gigantic form and fascinating manners, who had his way to make in the world. Still, though sovereign of the Order (more than less self-chosen) he was biddable, or had been biddable so far; and the Order itself was an admirable scheme for reviving the military-monastic life in connection with modern research. Far better and far more tasty, said Crabbe, to unite in study, under a military-monastic discipline, pooling discoveries and special knowledge, and producing worthy results in perdurable form for the race's benefit, than to dissipate time and energy and ability in compromising with socialistic free-thoughts or other crazes affected by the ordinary altruistic crank. And the scheme of the Order of Sanctissima Sophia was neither bad nor foolish—if worked by a wise autocrat, in the beginning. Caliban, by himself, was too fantastically-minded: but (weird to say) he was willing and thankful to be coached and crammed by Crabbe, who (conscious of his own power) had a preference for remaining in the background. 'Savoir' and 'Pouvoir' are very rarely found united. And 'To make us respectable, we want, among us, a J.P. or something equally vulgar and sober. Why not elect your father : knight him; and name him chancellor of the Order?' said the Power-Behind to the Throne. 'I should like it awfully: but I'm not sure whether he would,' responded the Lieutenant. 'Take my tip and try,' suggested the Keeper of the Splendid Conscience, who had machiavellianly made preliminary soundings. Hence, Edward Chancellor, with curial rank and a veto on foolery and foolish ex-penditure, to keep young blood flowing coolly in the channel of wisdom—as one would have thought. Crabbe was rather bucked at his adroitness in thus placing the father as a check upon the son; and of course he hadn't the faintest notion that the father was without exception the very tallest of all stupid dolts which God in His Infinite Wisdom gives us as awful examples. The religious question also had been difficult. Most of the knights were ritualistic Erastians, by no means inclined to cough at Rome. They had no objection to, and they rather enjoyed, the sane simple symbolic offices and observances which Provost Nicholas ordained: for, as he said, 'Though catholics may not pray with acatholics, it is possible and preferable for acatholics to pray with catholics catholically. And so he joined the Order, on condition that he, as hierarch, gave catholic character to ordinal functions. Bounders, of course, called it presumption that a mere tonsured clerk should insist on such predominance : but he was the only catholic member of the Order, and catholics of higher ecclesi-astical grade than his were ineligible for election. He, therefore, made the best of material and circumstances; and, as long as he was present, all went well. As for the work of the Order, it was carried on in this way. Members were only admitted on shewing tokens of pursuing some serious branch of knowledge. The earliest members had been after history and archæology: each had his special subject, excavation, or archivial research. The Lieutenant—it was preferred to have a Lieutenant of the Grandmagistracy until a Grandmaster could be duly elected—undoubtedly had a talent for adapting designs of habits, coats-of-arms, note-paper headings, vellum forms for patents with sigils appended in circular oaken saucers, collars, stars, ribands, badges, sashes, for himself and his knights to disport with; and on such gauds he meditated day and night. But, being so far on the road to wisdom as to be biddable, he clenched his teeth at Crabbe's jobations and consented to set an example. Crabbe bade him to qualify for the Oxford degree of B.Litt., by producing a thesis on Roman remains in N. Africa. He agreed: and carried his family and fancy-dresses as freemason, knight-templar, and sovereign of his own order (for the confounding of consuls, Druses, and œcumenical patriarchs), together with no knowledge of photography, on a Cook's tour of seven months through the regions designated. In time, he brought back masses of notes and measurements of the amazing masonry sprinkled over the East by the fourth crusade, and some hundreds of random negatives. Crabbe then gave a couple of months to the development and printing of these last; and left Caliban safe at work on the thesis, when he first came holiday-making to Venice. The literary work which they had done, and were doing, together has been described already; and, regarding the Order of Sanctissima Sophia, your mind should by now be informed, o most affable reader. Crabbe felt fairly comfortable. He regarded Caliban as fit to run alone; and, finding himself in a pickle, had no hesitation in trusting the Lieutenant to do the knightly thing. He had formally proclaimed his rigour on the religious question. He had set the Peary-Buthlaw in action against his faulty agents. And there really seemed to be no particular reason (apart from Bobugo) why all should not turn out to be all beer and skittles.

Crabbe went into Cook's and got his money. 'Here is Lire 100 on account; and I'll keep the odd L. 25.65 for my pocket,' he said to his obsequious landlord. Then he plunged back into his book. Not in absolute comfort, though, even now. The Wardens barged up against him more than ever, and were so gushing with geniality, that they made him take himself gravely to task as a suspicacious brute far too prompt to attribute ugly characters to ugly persons. And the infirmary tea-fights at which the directress required him to assist twice and thrice a week, when he brought back convalescents confided to his oar, irritated him almost to frenzy. The only joke obtainable on the Island of Spinalonga sprang from the excitement of dodging La Pash, sidling out of the side-door of the infirmary as she pranced in at the front. It was as good as a play; and Zildo was the most alert and intelligent of call-boys. He soon perceived what game was afoot; and, at the moment when the royal-blue liveries and long-eared bonnet hove in sight at the end of the rio, he (on watch in the pupparin at the infirmary steps) would look the other way and cry a low-resounding 'Ciò Paron!' which pierced his master's ears at the directress's tea-table, and brought him scudding by backstairs into the laundry. Meanwhile, Zildo moved higher up, to let the lady land from her gondola; and, as she passed through the doorway, a second softer 'Ciò' shot Nicholas from nook to bark and swept him out of the dyspathetic area. For the more he heard of the proprietor of the infirmary, her wit, her wisdom, her pathos, her pity, her charity, her umbrella, her manufacture of enamelled trinkets for the embellishment of her toad-eaters, her gargantuan appetite for incense and subservience and adulation, so much the more he prayed and schemed and intrigued that, by hook or by crook, he might be spared her. Her gracious thanks for his services— 'In generous sympathy and practical help you are a larger subscriber to the infirmary than anyone else has ever been'—frequently conveyed to him by the directress on cushions bibbling with bad taste, glanced off his mail of total disregard. Even 'Ask Mr Crabbe,' reported to him through the same channel as La Pash's invariable solution of every difficulty connected with the conduct of her hobby, failed to elicit from him any glow but of disgust and a request for silence. As for the difficulties, they were only the stupid irritating fatuities which inevitably itch in a hen-house; and he patiently (or ruthlessly) cracked or expunged them. It was his small service to England— only that.

Another communication from Caliban tore him up by the roots again. Was it absolutely impossible to leave him alone to finish his book? A short official letter of pompous form, a grandmagisterial breve engrossed and sigilled in vermilion, intoned in his face "Harricus, etc., to Nicholas, etc., greeting. We, in virtue of Our sovereignty, do hereby claim your obedience, requiring you to leave your wrongs in Our hands, and We promise and warrant, as a Christian and as a knight and as your Sovereign Liege, that no injury shall touch you in your honour or your person or your property. Illuminet te Sanctissima Sapientia."

At first, it made him rear. Things, whose inmost significance he could not perceive at a glance, always did set him up on end, clashing his portentous pincers. Of course he would give obedience. He had said so from the beginning. It was easy to obey commandments which one inspired. Caliban had been told to do some business in England; and was willing to do it. If the Lieutenant liked to be obeyed in that manner—why, both subject and sovereign were satisfactorily amused. But why try to howl down the thunderings of Sinai?

This was why. (And Crabbe turned round on himself, and punched his own head hard, on the score of his impulse to stupid suspicion.) He had been at his old game of taking a would-be friend for an ambushed enemy. Caliban, in fact, was behaving most entirely decently, within his limits. Lucidity was not to be looked for in an enthusiast inebriated with the exuberance of mediæval verbosity. Penitent for having neglected *The Weird* and anxious to make amend, he was exciting himself about the present problem like a champion. Guessing that Crabbe might be harassed by creditors and prevented from working on *De Burgh's Delusion*, he was sending very fine and large assurance of support for purposes of public exhibition. No doubt that was his simple meaning. Silly owl! Being fat-witted, and (at the same time) impulsive in action, he naturally was emitting such assurances in crescendo, as they occurred to him, from the pianissimo 'Don't cough: but you know you always do muck up your own affairs and therefore We implore and command you just to sit still and let your friends manage them for you,' to the mezzoforte 'Confide all to me,' to the present imposing breve in fortissimo, claiming obedience and solemnly promising a happy issue out of all afflictions. Yes. Crabbe gave himself a thorough shaking: wrote a renewal of his oath of allegiance; and made another resolution to refrain his nerves. And then, like a fool, he went into the office to shew the breve to his landlord.

'About my bill,' he said. 'I ought to let you know that my London agents seem to be behaving mischievously in regard to my property. And, as I happen to be a member of this Order, I have asked my superior to put the matter straight for me. This is his answer. I shew it to you, that you may see that something is likely to be done.'

Barbolan spelled it over, grinning obsequiously at the promise and the monstrous vermilion sigil; and expressed perfect satisfaction.

An incident of this kind, occurring at a day's beginning, completely stopped Crabbe's morning work. He took his materials out as usual, and strolled down the Piazzetta, trying to pull himself together. By the time he reached the club, he thought that he might perhaps look over a few pages and do a little retouching. There were no letters for him in the atrium; and he passed along the balcony, and climbed down the rungs in the sea-wall to his waiting pupparin. Zildo caught the pigskin portfolio; and stowed it under the seat. A brilliant sun made writing in the open possible, until the hands got chilly. Just as they were moving off, Nicholas remembered that he had left his enormous Waterman pen (without which he positively refused to make a single mark) on the cane-table in the hall. And, of course, he at once became seized with a most imperative desire to write; and sent his servant flying for the pen.

Meanwhile he took a turn of a rope round the nearest palo; and sat in the bark to wait. The mad gondoliere sneaked alongside, mooring a little further up; and flung himself prone on his poop, groaning, 'Ai-vant-manni, ai-vant-manni, I want money,' for the Englishman to hear him. Mendicancy is most severely suppressed in Venice: but it is surprising how many curved palms crop up in unexpected places. Nicholas, notwithstanding his faculty of un-reasoning and unreasonable pity, which tore great gashes in his heart and emptied his pockets on boys out of work and starving old women in winter, abhorred, and was rough with most of this class, from the nasty whining ragamuffin (with two fingers in a red void eye-socket) who chases you along the Riva dei Schiavoni, to the shawled beldam with the gold necklace and a mask of smut in the angle of the Ponte dei Baratteri. Presently, he could stand the moaning pest no longer. 'Go, fox, to thy proper ferry, and honestly ply there for hire: or the municipio shall snatch away thy license,' he flashed in Venetian to the intruder.

A pigeon perched on the Istrian marble balustrade just above the pupparin, expressed itself freely, and began to coo, 'Lookatthefool, lookatthefool lookatthefool lookatthefool! Yooou fooool! Yooou fooool! O lookatthefool!' Nicholas swore. He detested a spotty bark; and went to the cupboard under the poop, where Zildo kept brush and baler and sponge and rags for cleaning. He pulled open the panel—even there all was neat and orderly—and put in his hand. The most suitable thing for wiping up the mess would be that roll half-wrapped in blue linen. The wrapper was loose, and fell off, leaving a roll of old blanket. How nice and dry, and how extremely clean, it was. As he was about to dip it in the water, something in its appearance arrested him; and he examined it more closely. It was a close roll, about ten inches long and three in diameter, curiously tied with thread at three inches from the top and again in the middle. In the top part were stuck two little black tacks—resembling eyes. Why, it was not unlike a rag-doll. Host! And the dainty bit of blue linen which had enshrouded it? He quickly went back to the cupboard. The other roll, there, was the one used for the bark: it also was a roll of old blanket, but not tied—wrung out, and still damp. This one, the doll, had lain in a place by itself. He folded it in its shawl again; and put it reverently back, closing the panel. The defiled prow would have to go unpolished, as far as he was concerned. And he must not pry again under the poop of his own pupparin, where his servant kept private and sacred affairs. Zildo's baby was cradled there.

Man may not meddle with Nature's law; she laughs and defies him. Motherhood cannot be kept from the mind of a maid.

XV

The lieutenantial flux of Latin telegrams persisted with unabated amorphousness. Translated from Venetian telegraphese the next one ran thus: FECI CONIVRATIONEM CUM BOBVGONE MACPAWKINSQUE ET NOS TRES CONTRIBVEBIMVS NOSTRUM PARUVM OMNE PER UESTRVM AVXILIVM RECEPEBITIS NVLLAM REM PERSONALITER SED BONIFACIVS UESTRAE TABERNAE RECEPEBIT DVAS LIBRAS OMNEM HEBDOMADEM PER DVODECIM HEBDOMADES PER UESTROS EXPENSOS UIA MORLAIXENSE ET SARTORE ET UESTER PARS EST SIMPLICITER UIUERE IN ISTVM LIMITEM ET PROCEDERE CVM UESTRAM SCRIPTVRAM QUAM PROMPTAM POSSIBILEM ILLVMINET TE SANCTISSIMA SAPIENTIA. Fifty-nine words and four of an address, at threepence each, gave fifteen shillings and ninepence to as good as the gutter: though no doubt Caliban got his money's worth in importance at the Uskvale post-office. But the horrible portent, when meaning was picked out of the unspeakable Latin—that was what inflamed Crabbe—"I have made a conspiracy"—(conspiracy was excellent)—"with Bobugo"—(as might have been expected)—"and Macpawkins"—(damnable presumption)—"and we three will contribute our little all for your help"—(nothing of the kind)—"you will receive nothing personally but the landlord of your pub. will receive one pound (weight) every week for twelve weeks by way of Morlaix and Sartor"—(never!)—"and your part is simply to live within that limit and to go on with your writing as promptly as possible"—(snorts)—"may the Most Holy Wisdom illuminate you." Here, Crabbe went so blind, so speechless, so boiling in the brain, with fury and disgust and disappointment, that he tore madly out and across into Saint Mark's, lest he should make somebody untidy. Haha! He would satiate himself with the society and illumination of that same Most Holy Wisdom so besottedly and sacrilegiously insulted by inclusion in such a bestial telegram.

If you, o most affable reader, will walk from the narthex up the side of the basilica, entering the door in face of you, you will find yourself confronted by the altar of the Virgin-Mother of Nikopoieia. Approach, passing the great rood and the columns to right and left with their fonts of hallowed water for lustration; and note that the angle of the north transept (just by the chantry door) has a narrow marble seat in an obscure inconspicuous situation. Here, Crabbe sat down, panting, palpitating. Not that he was affrighted—o Lord, no! On the contrary, he felt poignantly because he was fearless. Want of courage indicates want of sense. But he was raging at himself for having counted on Caliban's sense of obligation and personal affection—for forgetting that sovereigns cannot be their subject's friends, that a Scotchman's faith is invariably Punic, that a beggar set on horse-back rides to the very devil.—Sedes Sapientiae, ora pro nobis, was his incantation now, as he himself formerly had made it the Order's. He raged at the Lieutenant's weakness in dancing (no doubt glittering with tinsel) straight into the clutch of Bobugo. The introduction of the unmentionable Macpawkins at first seemed inexplicable. Crabbe had loaded him with fetters of contempt: and Caliban himself had pitched him overboard in disgust. But the stench of the ecclesiastical paw was apparent from the outset.—Sedes Sapientiae, ora pro nobis.—Crabbe's gaze soared to the huge silver rose of the south transept, that delicious window in the mode Venetian, simply filled with hundreds of crystal bull's eyes leaded together, through which daylight streams with silvery radiance into golden gloom, cooling and purifying the sight of man's three eyes.—Sedes Sapientiae, ora pro nobis.—And he gazed into that argent candour, till (in it) all things became quite plain. Caliban was a mechanical dummy, unable to perform without direct compulsion. Hence, the summoning of Bobugo: that had not been specifically forbidden; and though aware of a priest's behaviour, an acatholic never permits himself to know the turpitude of which a priest is capable. The Lieutenant wanted an audience and an elbow-jogger. Bobugo was invoked, as a friend and collaborator of Crabbe. Summoned, then, to conclave, Bobugo (that diplomatic little fanatic) grabbed at so gorgeous a chance of serving God—it being understood that his particular divinity was of the Moloch-cum-Kali type. One must explain.

A certain sin of omission lies to the score of the Prince of the Apostles. Saint Peter, P.M., has failed to leave us either a syllabus of His infallible utterances or a compendium of His pontifical gests on the occasion when Saint Paul "withstood Him to the face." This information is wanting in canonical scripture; and that is a great pity. For, knowing (as we do) that Christians, smitten on one cheek, are bound to offer the other, regardless of the merit of the smiter, a record of the example of the first and chief of Christian clergymen would form a valuable standard for appreciating the action of the dedecorous Bobugo. Crabbe, rearing and lashing out in his customary manner, had sought to save that priest from a slip into shocking shame, by catching him a scornfully sounding slap on his proposition about the book which they were to write and sign together. Bobugo (having started in business as a section of the day of judgement) had that slap to avenge; and, knowing how terrifically up and down Crabbe's life was wont to be, he saw (here) a charming possibility of oiling a new descent for him, whereby he might be forced to glide into a hole which had no outlet save the hack-writing of that novel about Saint Thomas of Canterbury of which Bobugo wished to pose as sole author. That was the glimpse of Bobugo's mind which Crabbe had.

Next, the priest and the Freemason conspire—the word is Caliban's—and I agree that to go into Crabbe's grievance against Morlaix and Sartor would partake of the nature of a Task. (Who suggests, and who adopts suggestion, is obvious.) 'Do you want him home again at Uskvale?' 'Of course: but what I really want is the book we're doing together.' 'I know. Then let's help him to finish that; and then he can come home and punish his agents himself.' Those seemed the salient preliminaries. Their diabolically adroit intention cannot fail to be perceived. Now, to find a means of capturing De Burgh's Delusion and playing upon Crabbe's temperament so that he should rid himself of all resources. The priest is alert: the decorative dummy stertorously blows out that he is in a maze. ' 'I know. Let's do it like this. Crabbe lives a simple life, can't handle money, mustn't be worried. Let's allow him a pound or so a week so that he may write in peace—and through his agents so that he may have no trouble.' 'I'm rather short just now; and can only manage a tenner.' 'I know. And, being a poor priest, I can only manage a fiver. But what about the friend who went to Venice with him?' 'Macpawkins? Yes: he inherited our neighbour Boyle's place and a cool ninety-five thousand; and, from what I can make out, Crabbe's been paying his debts!' 'I know. D'ye think he'd bleed?' 'One might try.'

So the money was raised—twenty-five sterling from the three of the recreant Lieutenant's coniuratio—for paying Crabbe's landlord two sterling a week for twelve weeks (which Bobugo knew would be rejected) and for imbroiling him further with Morlaix and Sartor while putting a sterling in their pockets.

Why 'imbroiling him further'? Tell me this, o most affable reader. When defaulting agents find that the two best friends of their victim (one a popular preacher, the other a county gentleman) do not defend and support him, but pay to keep him low and away, are they or are they not formally encouraged in their questionable malfeasance?

It was Saturday. The little triptych on the altar lay open.— Sedes Sapientiae, ora pro nobis.—How altogether lovely these byzantine eikons are! That is because they have Christian tradition— they alone, in religious art. Undoubtedly that council of the Church was inspired divinely which uttered the canon prohibiting painters from producing any ideals save those ecclesiastically dictated. Who ever dreams of praying (with expectation of response) for the prayer of a Tintoretto or a Titian, or a Bellini, or a Botticelli? But who can refrain from crying 'O Mother!' to these unruffleable wan dolls in indigo on gold?—Sedes Sapientiae, ora pro nobis.—Crabbe gazed into the pure brown everlasting eyes of the tiny picture, where Mary Virgin ostends her Son and God, both so sweet and so sprightly and so changeless, laced with great pearl ropes over cope and cowl of blue, on gold embossed with big gems and sixteen times saintlily enamelled, all enclosed in its shrine of jewelled silver with bordures of massive gold.—Sedes Sapientiae, ora pro nobis. He, this so-called hater of women, this most loyal but unconscious lover, gazed, gazed—till wrath gave place to firm serenity, till he knew precisely what to say and do.

He wrote to Caliban. "I have your telegram. What you propose is out of the question. In no circumstances will I have anything to do with Macpawkins, or with Bobugo to whom you forbid me to write, excepting personally. Kindly get me (at once) Morlaix and Sartor's answers to these inquiries: Why they do not send my allowance: Why they do not send accounts due to me last June and last December: Why they do not attend to my instructions about increasing my insurance as security for a loan for my immediate needs: Why they do not write to me. All this ought to have been done long ago. Please do not delay it now. I continue to overdraw my account. . . . And now do you know that neither your mother nor Chancellor Edward your father wrote to me at the beginning of the year? Why? When I was leaving for Venice, your mother begged me not to be so fascinated as to stay—'You must never leave Uskvale except for betterment,' she repeatedly reiterated. And what have my relations with your father always been? Then, why, at such a time as this, these portentous silences? You are not to think that I hint suspicion. I don't. But I am in the dark; and I ask for light. Nor will I any longer disguise from you that these last weeks have hurt me, in more ways than one. I.T.SS.S."

His present information was that the Lieutenant of the Grandmagistracy of the Order of Sanctissima Sophia actually was a pretty puppet, no more and no less, to be coaxed amoenely and adroitly to do its antics, and not to be banged about on account of essential insanity. To treat Caliban as an intellectual equal, or as a trustworthy friend, was simply waste of time. Undoubtedly he had certain capabilities: but their scope depended on the will and skill of whoever pulled the strings. Crabbe (rather fed-up with the role of string-puller) had left the fantoccino alone, fondly crediting it with (at least) reflected intelligence; but now, conscious of his blunder, he made a quiet innocuous grab at the strings. How strong a hold on them that serpentine Bobugo had, he was without present means of ascertaining: but he thought that the answer to his letter would be instructive. He, however, permitted himself very little hope. He felt very much inclined to remind himself that he who makes a sovereign prince out of a child of man must not put confidence where there is no hope. The boisterous blatant inadequacy of the Peary-Buthlaw shot out rootlets to batten on the remnants of his trust. What can you expect from a pig but a grunt? The creature is incapable—yes, incapable—so far, incapable only.

Non possum togam praetextam sperare cum exordium pullum nideam.

The landlord invited him into the office to inspect a letter from Morlaix and Sartor. Acting on instructions from Mr Peary-Buthlaw, they inclosed cheque worth eight sterling in payment for Mr Crabbe's total expenses for four weeks in advance, and a similar cheque would be sent at beginning of two succeeding periods of four weeks each. Barbolan was astonished. 'Who are these who write?' he asked.

'Lawyers. My agents in London. I assigned to them the management of my property: and they agreed to make me a sufficient allowance. They have stopped it, giving no reason. So I placed the matter in the hands of the Lieutenant of my Order, Mr Peary-Buthlaw. You saw his answer.'

'Yes. But this——'

'He has made a mistake. I will not permit it. I have told him so, giving him definite instructions.'

'Will he follow them?'

'But certainly.'

'It may be difficult. Lawyers are thieves.'

'These are not. They are quite respectable.'

'Is this respectable behaviour?'

'It appears not. But there is some misunderstanding.'

'I feel that you are in the hands of thieves.'

'No. No.'

'But—I do not want this cheque in advance: I want my past bill. I trust you. I have confidence in you. I do not want your lawyers. They are thieves, furbi, Signore, furbi, furbi. I will not have them.'

'Very good. Send back this cheque, and tell them your reason.'

'The letter is already written. See it here!'

'Bravo! Stick to that. Support me. Refuse to deal with anyone but me. No one in the world shall act over my head like this. I have assets; and they shall be made to produce money, if not by Morlaix and Sartor, then by someone else. But I must know first what Morlaix and Sartor mean. And Mr Peary-Buthlaw shall tell me. Is that clear?'

'Perfectly. You are being robbed by brigands, and you call out the carabinieri. Never fear: you shall be saved, Signore.'

Each succeeding hour made Crabbe more apprehensive of impending peril. He invoked Saint Theodylos, the patron of all who suffer from cruel apprehension; and he wrote again and more insistently to the Wardens that his news from England was becoming worse and worse; and he repeated his request to be dropped. They scoffed at the bare notion, quite boldly this time; and apparently they chattered at the infirmary: for, at his next visit, the directress plumped upon him a coy and bibbling demand for his confidence, as between friends. 'You're getting pale and thin about something, you darling man! So trotty you used to look—too! And there's the line of worry on your brow. Do come here for a month and make a rest cure. We should so enjoy nursing you!'

'Nonsense. Whom shall I have in the pupparin today?'

'Would you mind a couple of Salvation Lasses with poisoned fingers? They're putting on their bonnets.'

'Not a bit. But—whisper—impress upon them that nothing can persuade me to smite their timbrels. In fact, you'd better say that I'm so saved that I'm dumb.'

The directress chortled: but began again. 'Do, though, tell your friends about your troubles. Let's bear one another's burthens you dear thing. It would be such a joy. Think of what we owe you. How could we let you have a pain without wanting half of it?'

'Oh, very well.' (Crabbe always made a point of bunging this spout with the very pattest of replies; and he thought that he could do so now by flapping the blind and naked truth over her mouth.) 'My agents seem to have made some sort of a mess with my property; and I shan't be at all surprised to find myself without an income, at least for this year.'

'But surely your friends——'

'I only know of two, and I fancy that one is a beast and the other a fool.'

'Oh, but we're always your friends anyhow——'

The Salvation Lasses crept out, one a Tuscan, tusky, spectacled, anæmic, and flat, the other quite beautiful. Crabbe shut his head, and wouldn't say another word.

Zildo had no easy time of it that while. His master worked him hard, and barely noticed him, giving (indeed) no attention to anyone or anything but the infirmary work and the finishing the last pages of *De Burgh's Delusion*. And, at length, the book stood, one night, in the hall, displayed to the admiring expectant eyes of Parrucchiero— two tall narrow-paged beautifully written volumes bound in white buckram, containing the knowledge and the experiments of several lifetimes, and representing Crabbe's only immediate hope of pecuniary solvency. He had Caliban's word for it: 'We must have some money; and we can only get it by going to Shortmans with the two books which I've made them promise to take on sight.'

'What's its worth?' asked Parrucchiero.

'I won't take less than a thousand sterling for my share of it,' said Crabbe, beginning to pack it in tissue and damp-proof, canvas-lined pitch-paper for transmission to England. The landlord was so vastly concerned that Crabbe consulted him as to methods; and the two ran all over Venice in the pupparin seeking an insurance company to police its safe transit. Such business was unusual: the Venetians are the slaves of custom; and the attempt failed. So Crabbe himself gave the parcel to Cook to send to Caliban 'carriage forward': which is a safer and cheaper method than official registra-tion, for no delivery means no pay. And a telegraph went to Uskvale, 'Cook delivering Delusion Monday.'

Deprived of the book, Crabbe experienced sensations very similar to those which follow parturition. He was relieved of a weight, which he missed so much that he felt light-headed and feeble and quite languid. A longish spell of cold weather ensued. Snow fell thickly, and was heaped into cocks in the Piazza of Saint Mark. Zildo flourished exceedingly: his young flesh took the roseate tints of mother-o'-pearl in the snowy sunlight. The pupparin being snow-logged and ice-bound, master and servant walked fast on the mushy football islet between Santelena and the Public Gardens, engaging with snowballs when alone. Zildo's joy was enthusiastic: the exquisite smile, which half closed his long bright eyes, heaping his rosy cheeks, widening his lovely lips, gleamed like great sunbursts on the snow. He hurled his missiles over-arm, just like a boy—only, unlike a boy, he knew exactly the moment before that when his master began to be bored; and, from larking long-leggedly with far-flung whirling hands all over the field, he subsided (at a look) into his usual alert sedateness, prompt to obey. Once, when they were both drenched to the skin, Nicholas would have sent him home to change: but he said that nothing did anything.

'Nonsense. I go to change my own clothes; and you will do the same. I have no use for a servant sniffling with a fever.'

'It is very meet, right, and their bounden duty, that the Siori should take fever from wet clothes: but we, never, o blessed of God.'

Nicholas took the rebuke with a meekness baldly grim. Nothing exasperated him more than a reflection on his physical fitness and hardness—excepting perhaps being mistaken for a "gentleman." He walked his boy, lengthily striding, through the Public Gardens and along the mile of Riva to the club, where he helped to rid the pupparin of snow and ice; and then he rowed at full speed round three sexters of Venice, Dorsoduro, Sampolo, and Santacruce, going by Canalazzo, through the Rio della Scomenzera, and returning by the Canal of Zuecca with not a damp thread on him. This ebullience strung him up again. He took interest in imagining what would happen next. Something to do seemed his need while waiting for a manifestation. His fat pen enticed him. And, after talking matters over with his angel-guardian, he began to write.

It was granted him to know four causes which pushed him—intolerable fidgets: a growing prevision of evil: a temperamental horror of appearing idle at a time when people were more or less gazing at him: and a desire of arranging perfectly secret caches upon which to fall back in case of necessity. So he went to work with wile, and wrote (of course he wrote) on the backs of the rough drafts of *De Burgh's Delusion*. The sanctimonious Warden, caterpillaring in the hall of the hotel, presumed that he was preparing additions for his expected proof-sheets. (There is a type of writer incapable of writing his own book till he has seen it in print.) Crabbe hastened to answer the fool according to his folly—which, permitted to flourish, served its sly purpose. Also, the new unsuspected book, which he began, was just the kind of book which no one would expect from him. I said, at the beginning, that the appalling shock of the Calabrian Earthquake tore his life in two. This was actually so. From that event he emerged (not a different man, but) a man who has entered on a second period. He was still Crabbe, and as crabby as ever: but he began to exercise his crabbiness in directions which he had never tried or cared to try. His books, for instance, dealt with history, with one dry shot at agricultural and pastoral Libya. Now he broke fresh ground, with a subject and an environment of which he was supposed to be totally and uninterestedly ignorant—a study of character, the Sagittarius character, the character of the brilliant long-enduring marksman who never sends his shaft till he can hit the bull; and he set it in commonwealthy surroundings. Sebastian Archer, a nice boy stupidly misused by ultra-religious relations, was scrapped (at eighteen) into the dust-bin of Australia. His aim had been the episcopalian ministry; and he never lost sight of it. He was a large healthy athletic intelligent witty fellow, clean to look at, and good enough for anyone's society. His job was to build a career out of nothing with his naked hands. Assistant-masterships in vulgar private schools of the commonwealth under sottish illiterate principals, variegated by bush-tutorships, kept him alive and led him nowhere. His English public school had placed him far above all his new neighbours. Squatter parents liked him: his pups adored him: his principals left all to him while they danced drunk in doubtful dwellings: the female sex unicorporally strewed itself before him. Being extremely young and sanguine, in mind as in body, rascals (and commonwealthy rascals) invaded him all along. Being also sound and sane, he rejected much—kind to all, he chose no one. A one-eyed episcopalian bishop ordained him deacon. His sermons (and personality) cut out those of his archidiaconal vicar. Naturally, success became a butt for the darts of scandal. The archdeacon's daughter played *Lady Potiphar*, Act III, Scene i; and was abruptly married to the right man. But, pierced by archidiaconal arrows, Sebastian found himself minus his curacy. A fresh shower of shafts hurtled at him naked. His bishop—(I mentioned that His Lordship was a one-eyed man)—refused to hear him, withdrew his licence, leaving him (as it were) bound to a tree and transfixed like a pincushion. The One She appeared, and loosed his bonds. Together they drew out the arrows. Twelve silent years, in the diocese next door, cicatrized his wounds and put a nimbus to his name. Then—wise general, reserving fire—Archer drew his bowstring to his ear—his bolts fell fast: one by one his would-be murderers bit the dust. And, on the day when Death shut the one-eyed bishop's other eye, his episcopal next-door neighbour wired to Sebastian Archer: 'I have admired you all along, although I can only say so now: come and take your licence and appointment as my examining chaplain.' It sounds washy in summary. Nice simple human stories always do. They need artistic telling; and Crabbe was a real artist with a style, poignant and nude and athletic, shrewdly humorous and trenchant. But his most artistic stroke on this canvas was secrecy. The tale once hewn out on scraps of old paper, he even went so far as to produce the fair copy in a form unrecognizable as his. No more long white volumes filled with his large straight-margined script: but a small fat quarto covered with tiny square fearfully-legible writing was the new disguise of him. He was inspired to feverish activity. Stuff poured from his monstrous pen. He wrote in his room, chiefly at night, never in public. By day, he seemed to lounge drowsily, deceiving many. How long his overdraft at the bank would last he did not know: it was essential to provide cash in hand, even while he toiled at forming his cache: so, at intervals, he stepped out into the gutter and wrote feuilletons for farthing rags and short stories for provincial syndicates—the type of trash which unearths little lumps of guineas at unexpected moments—the kind of rubbish which the monstrous married mob reads, believing it to be the work of a pair of themselves, and he signed these "Geltruda and Bevis Mauleverer."

His phenomenal mental activity made him impatient (even to rearing and roaring in private) with the inferiorly inspired—the Wardens, for example. Their feeble fecklessness drove him ramping with such fury that he couldn't refrain a shove to galvanize them into concentrated exertion. He let them say what they always were trying to say. She wondered so much whether she could write a tale—they were tired of Italy and wanted to go and live in England, whence they had hitherto been exiles on account of the cost of living. An opportunity had arisen in an infinitesimal village, no pub, no work, but good chance of writing, a nice house, resident agreeable noble squire, good society: but, being poor, they wanted money for moving—in fact, she had written a tale—tales. Could Mr Crabbe advise? He advised; and revised; and packed her off to *Chambers's Journal*. And the Warden—he stammered that he had purred a pious text-book on commission, about Society in Early Christian Days, and was being staggered by the proofs. So Crabbe savoured that; and, raging at seeing a fair field fouled, thrust himself in to edit, taking the work in hand for a couple of hours a day. Why, the Warden didn't even know that that dear delightful Domitian obliged his procurators to begin their official instructions, "Dominus et Deus noster Domitianus hoc fieri iubet," till Crabbe flourished Suetonius *Dom.* 13 in his toad-face! Truth is tarter than taradiddles; and nothing is tarter, terser, than truth on the track of tired trash in a trance.

XVI

THREE letters came in one envelope; and three answers went in another. The worst of a fountain-pen is that (if you drop it point-blank on the street) it becomes irremediably cross-nibbed, and spits.

These were the three letters :

" DEAR MR CRABBE, I am writing to wish you a happy new year. It grieves me to hear from my son that you are in trouble again. One knows so much and one can't help hearing more. It does seem such a strange thing that a man of your undoubted genius should be always quarrelling and getting into difficulties. A rolling stone gathers no moss, you know. Could you not manage somehow to keep out of debt? Why do you not try and get a situation at a photographer's, where your knowledge and experience should at least enable you to live. You must not mind beginning low, for I am sure your talent would soon make you rise. I throw out the suggestion for what it is worth, for I cannot bear to think of how it all will end. So with renewed good wishes,—Yours sincerely, ELIZA PEARY-BUTHLAW."

"DEAR KNIGHT NICHOLAS, Afraid I forgot to write you at com-mencement of year, being rather busy with building new wing. Kennels are something of a business too just now. We have had several good runs. On Wednesday got my feet wet. Did pretty well with turkeys at Christmas, but not as well as last year. Pilgrim says they missed you. He is getting rid of all old fowls but Buff Orping-tons and White Wyandottes. Poor old Dingo is dead. We shall never have another dog. The peacock was lost for two days last week. Harry has invented a new savoury, bacon and walnuts on disks of muffin. The Tretowers can't keep up the abbey now they're smashed. They have to leave it for a cottage, and one of the Jackson-Maitlands has taken it for the fishing. I think the J-M's will be pleasant neigh-bours. Bible-class has two new members from the mill. Well, here's end of paper. Compliments of the season.

Yrs. E. P.-B. CHANCELLOR."

"HARRICUS, etc., to NICHOLAS, etc.,—Greeting. Don't cough so bitterly at what we offered. We meant well. You are so suspicious. Anyone would think we were addicted to goitre. I have had to

PURSUIT OF THE WHOLE

return their money to Bobugo and Macpawkins, and they are mewing
horribly. It is such a pity of you to quarrel with everybody before
you have made your fortune. I told you that I was going to be married
and you haven't said a word. Why don't you marry some nice girl
with money, instead of sneezing at them all   Heaps would jump at
you if you'd condescend to ask them nicely, as you can, if you choose.
I don't know what to do with Morlaix and Sartor. I was very haughty
with them, so don't blame me, but I couldn't get much out of them.
They complain that you won't write to them, and say that they
intend to cut their losses on you. What has made them cough loudest
is your retention of the proofs of *Sieur René*. They say they would
continue your allowance if you give those up so that the book can
be published immediately. I fancy they think you want to defraud
them, and you know you have given them a lien on it. So I managed
to get this much from them as well. If you will send me the proofs
of *Sieur René* so that I can arrange to get the book out at once, they
will make no claim on the profits of it but leave them entirely to you.
It doesn't sound consistent and I haven't a notion what their game is,
but that's what they said, and We hereby command you in virtue of
your oath of obedience to Us to fall in with it. I don't see what else
you can do. Have you any idea? Oh, and they said that they had
delayed considering the question of increasing your insurance till it
was too late to do so without a fresh medical examination in England,
and your company won't take the reports of niggers, and I don't
suppose you've got an English doctor there. *De Burgh's Delusion*
came all safe. It looks as if you'd been at some pains over it. I'll see
what can be done with it as soon as I can. What follows now is
Ordinal. You are mistaken in being offended at your suspension
from provostship. If you deserved punishment We should have
deprived you, but suspension is really a mark of Our sovereign confidence in you and Our consideration for your present unfortunate
plight. Also, We have no desire to shove Catholicism out of the
Order as you seem to fear. So keep calm. Furthermore, We entertain no alarms about undesirable Press interference. For, be it known
that We intend to have a fair number of Freemasons in the Order, so
that when the Press pokes its snout in wanting to know, you know—
the said Press being, as you are aware, amenable to freemasonic compulsion—We shall instantly be able to muzzle it or any other Peeping
Tom with the statement that members of the Order (no need to state
numbers) are prominent Freemasons desirous of privacy. So you see
you have been snorting at what is really a measure of high and statesmanlike policy. Are you satisfied? I.T.SS.S."

These were the three answers :

"DEAR LADY PEARY-BUTHLAW,—Many thanks for your good wishes for the new year, which I hasten perhaps a little tardily to reciprocate. 'Better late than never,' you know. There is not much news here. 'Out of sight, out of mind,' you know. And, indeed, the only thing which I can tell you, or which I can trust myself to tell you civilly, in reply to the rest of your letter, is that if I had written it I should think it my duty to make it the subject of my next confession, and would drive into Abergavenny at once to get the guilt of mortal sins of Superbia and Avarizia and Invidia off my soul. The weather is fine but cold. So, with renewed good wishes, I remain yours sincerely, NICHOLAS CRABBE."

"DEAR CHANCELLOR EDWARD,—Glad of chance of answering your first letter of year as have nothing particular to do today. There's very good fishing (cuttle-fish) in Canal of Freganzorzi. It's rather a bore, though, taking off one's boots. Venetian turkeys are tiny. Give my love to Pilgrim and tell him I hope the poultry-farm will bear up. Poor old Dingo! But he's better off where he is than you could make him. Do try cats next. I should chain the peacock up, and give him sponge cake soaked in maraschino. Don't let Harry overdo himself. Bacon and walnut and muffin involve too much thought. There's a mustard and jam cake here, which is simpler, and quite as fat. I suppose you'll continue to know the Tretowers. An occasional nod might please them. They weren't a bad sort before their smash, and it wasn't their fault. Congratulations on increase in your Bible-class. Why, you must actually have three members by now. Well, do you know I simply haven't the energy to begin another page. I can't and won't be bored. Compts. of season returned with thanks. Yrs. N.C., KNIGHT."

"NICHOLAS, etc., to HARRICUS, etc.,—Greeting. Thanks for your parents' insults. Enclosed please find retorts according to samples as nearly as I can match them. Please do not offer me alms, or go schnorring on my account, ever again. You blunder horribly in having anything to do with Bobugo. How could you blunder so, being aware of his treatment of Your Splendour's Knight? And, how could you touch the Macpawkins after what you said of him? About Morlaix and Sartor, mark this well. I have done nothing offensive but to ask for my agreed portion of my own property. You yourself stopped me from writing to them; and you must not let them complain of my silence. The affair is in your hands. Your duty is to arrange it before you give it back to me. Yes it is. You assumed it. And you swore as a Christian and a knight and a sovereign that I should not suffer in my honour or my person or my property. Very well, then. Get a statement in writing from Morlaix and Sartor that they are going to chuck me and cut their losses (what losses?) and let us at once transfer my property to some more decent agents. But, of course, they're bluffing; and this looks shady. However, in faith of what you say, I send you the proofs of *Sieur René* by this post; and I expect you to make Morlaix and Sartor send a remittance by return. Oh yes, indeed you ought to champion your knight much more chivalrously against agents who neglect a client's instructions as those boobies have neglected mine about my insurance. Can't you see that you should make them understand that it is they who are arraigned—not me: that the tone which they are taking is most unbecoming in agents who refuse his accounts to their principal: that it will not do with me. And kindly hurry with *De Burgh's Delusion.* As for my having an idea of what I'm going to do, of course I haven't. That's your affair, now that you have claimed and received my obedience. I'm your knight. Ain't I? Meanwhile, I certainly shan't think of getting married till I'm free from this imbroglione—if then. The twenty celibate years, which I vowed to offer in proof of my Vocation, expire this year. After that, I deem myself free to look around me. But I'm not keen. Now for Ordinal matters. Very well: I must accept your Splendid explanation of my suspension from provostship: but I still think it a significant step to have taken at the moment of my pecuniary difficulties. Such as the mark of confidence is, I thank You for it. I am calmed by Your assurance about catholicism, being firmly determined never to incur any kind of acatholic taint by religious association where the catholic flavour is not predominant. But Your high and statesmanlike policy makes me smile. I never heard anything more fatuous. Either You are going to make the Order a private succursale of freemasonry, in which case You can (I suppose) muzzle the Press—or You are going to keep the Order unconnected with freemasonry and secret societies, as the Fundamental Constitutions (unalterable, excepting by unanimous consent of the whole Order) expressly declare, in which case You can't use freemasonry for muzzling the Press. No. Your scheme, Splendour, will not do. Even the Press is not quite unintelligent; and one believes Freemasonry to be ordinarily honest. And it will simply make You more of a mock than I do, if You even begin to dream about thinking of playing so idiotically double a game as that. Why not be a little less ingenious, and a little more modest and honest. Illuminet te Sanctissima Sapienta."

Zildo noticed that Nicholas was depressed by reading and writing these documents: he watched his master intently for some time, unostentatiously and spontaneously proffering welcome attentions. Presently he said, 'Sior, with permission, you are disturbed.'

'It is not your fault,' said Nicholas.

'Sior, for gentility's sake, tell me who disturbs you. Is it some swine of the ill-born Nicolotti?'

'No one whom you know.'

'If you would make me know, Sior, after ten minutes I would have eaten his heart and there would be no more disturbance.'

'Row! Row!'

'Sissior.'

Even the Wardens noticed his grimmer face and his balder manner: they put it down to the tremendous quantity of work which they had seen him do, and to the worry of his unsettled affairs. They laid themselves out to entertain him with ghoulish cheer. It wasn't wise to shut himself up as he did. Man was a gregarious animal, and needed the society of his kind sometimes. Besides, had not one some sort of a duty to one's fellows? And there were such a lot of quite nice people in Venice, who were just dying to know him.

'No doubt,' he snapped, 'but I don't see my way to make acquaintances. I should be certain to crash straight into Lady Pash; and, after what I said to her, I don't intend to compete for snubs——'

'Oh no! She wouldn't. She is so sweet. And she does so want——'

'Not on any account. I've quite finished with Lady Pash. And another consideration weighs with me, though it doesn't seem to have occurred to you—how can I possibly begin to mix with strange people while my affairs are in the mess in which they are? Suppose that I am ruined, as I really expect to be—what would people say if I'd just been thrusting myself among them?'

'No question of thrusting, dear person. You keep back far too much, if I may say so. And, may I—thank you so much—how will you find friends in need if you refuse to make friends now?'

Crabbe reared. 'That's precisely my point. I don't try to make friends now, just because I'm in violent danger of wanting friends soon. See? How could I look at my own face when I shave if I did such a thing as that?'

The Warden purred a bit. Then, 'I do so wish you'd let me

persuade you for once—no, please listen—let me take you to one
of Nelson Mactavish's Mondays—you know him by name—tonight, you know—a writer like yourself—knows your books, and
does so want to know you. He only receives men; and they are
so interesting, writers, artists, or quite the best people. I'm sure
you'd be amused. And, you know, he's on the infirmary committee.'

Crabbe gave way at that. Perhaps he might pinch the management of La Pash's hobby. He could go in his hardest shell, defiant
of penetration: he need not go twice—it might pass an hour—might
make him sleepy.

After dinner, he went on foot with Exeter Warden to the big
Palazzo dei Incurabili on the Zattere, where Nelson Mactavish
humped shoulders up to a bluish smack-of-cheek-red face, with
invisible (or wandering) eyes, a pursed mouth, a tight waistcoat
splayed over a pudding, and longish knock-kneed shanks. He was
very gracious, with hesitating utterance; and presented an assortment
of miscellanies—a long flaxen pair of scissors who handled little
books, a German prince with onyx studs who talked of little red
houses in excellent English, a white and scarlet rolling-footed
crumpled-skirted Academician, a shy reader of archives with a
cockney twang, a dyspathetic featureless old-youngster whom
Crabbe most felicitously snubbed by imperative instinct from the
very beginning, and the usual make-weight of nonentities. A side-
table afforded wines and whisky. Tobacco was generally used.
Conversation spluttered donnishly. There's no more putrid sight
in the world than a pack of adult males stalking round and shewing
off to each other. Crabbe sat well back on a couch for two, smoking
the disgracefully short pipe which he kept for the insulting of fools,
and attending only to people who came to sit beside him. The
Academician maundered meaningless memorials of models. Mactavish and the scissors and the prince talked lagoon-exploration, the
marvels of unknown marshy Commacchio and Pomposa. At the
piano mooned the Warden: asked to sing, he favoured the company
with Aida's *Lament*, at which Crabbe bucked up and thoroughly
enjoyed himself. His atrocious sense of the ridiculous set his very
marrow chuckling at the spectacle of the ghostly gentleman, gleaming, toad-mouthed, moaning pianissimo, 'My pew! My pe-ew!
My pe-e-ew!' 'Mai piu.'—Nevermore—nevermore (simply shaking)
would Crabbe refuse to let this pastor entertain him. Nevermore!
Someone told the tale of the artless illiterate Cambridge don who,
hearing his combination-room fellows discussing Keats, naïvely and
mildly inquired, 'What *are* Keats?' The poet's name made Crabbe

rear. Mactavish seemed to think it time to pay him a little attention, and came to sit beside him. Everyone banally beatified Keats. 'Much over-rated,' was Crabbe's picric acid opinion. The long saloon suddenly sat upon its hind legs and glared. Crabbe, in defence, spurted certain sloshy quotations, 'the fill and airy feel of a light mantle,' 'what is more soothing than the pretty hummer that stays one moment in an open flower,' and 'like a blank idiot' from the *Hymn to Apollo*, demanding whether such lazy lapses into bathos deserved the name of poetry. Doubting Scissors strode for another little volume; and, at sad altitudes, verified the quoted passages. Ravers of Keats rarely know all their Keats. Crabbe became eyed. Mactavish hoped to see him every Monday. The coy old gossip from Sambastian asked him in a high treble to tea. A rosy doctor, with a perpetual crumb on his chin and a smear of egg under his eye, named lunch. And the prince took him and the Warden home in his gondola.

'What do you do when you are not with me?' Nicholas inquired of Zildo.

'Sior, listen. I have polished my house and the things which are in it, till you might say, "All mirrors!" And now I do not know how I shall occupy myself when you do not want me. Sior, command me.'

The German Emperor was coming to Venice that day, incognito (of course)—which means that he was accepting what all men but Germans would call a semi-state reception. Every palace bannered itself: balconies on the Grand Canal dripped with arras and hearth-rugs. Nicholas had ordered his pupparin to fly the Red Cross of Saint George of England and the Union Jack, as ostentatiously as possible, for the teasing of tetchy Teutons. He dawdled on the terrace of the Bucintoro before embarking to see the pageant. There was plenty of time. The view of the great curved Basin of Saint Mark, streaked with the tracks of moving barks, was quite enchanting. The big white rather-clumsy imperial yacht *Hohenzollern*, pretentiously attended by its cruiser *Hamburgh* and a lean destroyer, had been anchored off the Molo some days waiting for the emperor's arrival at the railway station.

A launch, manned by awfully low-necked sailors, smokily puffed up Canalazzo to fetch His Majesty; and the gondole of sightseers began to range themselves in lines along the sparkling water. Nicholas thought that he might as well be taking up his own position. He was about to descend to his bark when he heard a most feminine voice quite near being extremely explanatory in very imperfect Italian. There were a lot of members of the club with him on the terrace; and they politely passed a lady in his direction, signing that he was the man to understand her.

The Royal Bucintoro Rowing Club is curiously situated. It cuts right across the end of the Royal Little Garden; and beyond it is the narrow canal of the Royal Palace. Fifty-four times a day, strangers (generally Germans) prance along the Giardinetto Reale, imagining that the club ambuscades a bridge (to be forced) across the small canal, by which they can emerge on the ferry-pontoon of Calle Vallaresco. These creatures have to be assured that the club is private and actually part of the King's palace, the canal bridgeless, and themselves nothing more nor less than gratuitously truculent trespassers; and they curse quite noisily at having to go all the way back and round by the Piazzetta and the Piazza and Ascension.

The lady was in this predicament: only—she happened to be amazingly pretty, of an utterly unheard-of chic, and obviously on the verge of dewy tears. Naturally, she encountered the floored hearts and hats of susceptible members of the club instead of the usual chucker-out. Nicholas lent her his gravest attention, while she explained (in the American tongue) that she wanted to reach her friends who were waiting around for her at the new Palazzo Massarol next to the abbey on the far side of Canal Grande.

'There's no road,' he said, 'in this direction, and no bridge till you come to the Academy; and I fear that you cannot even get a gondola now to ferry you over: but, if you will do me the honour, my pupparin——'

Her gratitude was emphatic, but sincere. The members of the club (cerise with envy) escorted her to the royal steps; and the short passage by Salute and Sannegrorio was made amid much talking. On the spot the lady fell in love with the light swift bark and the long lithe boy. She deemed them both verry verrry cute, asking nothing better than that heaven should vouchsafe her such a bark and such a boy for her painting.

Now Nicholas, in handing her in, had viewed (on the block which she was carrying) such an impression in aquarelle of the Istrian firewood barks off the Zattere shrouded and shrined in a sunset of flame, that he conceived a notable respect unto her. People who can see Venice are rare: those who can express Her with pigments may be counted on one hand.

'Sente, Zildo,' he shouted in Venetian over his shoulder: 'after we have annoyed that Tedesco Emperor, you will attend at this American young lady's palace and obey her commandments.' And then, in English, to his passenger, 'I have told the boy to come to your palace in an hour, for orders; and I pray you to use him, and the bark, mornings and evenings, at your pleasure.'

The sweet thing yelped with glee. But wouldn't he just step in right away and be presented to her friends? Thank her, no: he had a certain fish to fry. (And he wasn't going to make any more new acquaintances.)

During the next crowded hour he manœuvred his pupparin so that the banner of England blotted out (in the big photograph) no more than the figure of the German Emperor after His ascension of the brazen stair of the *Hohenzollern*. This being satisfactorily accomplished—not because he didn't admire the Kaiser (for he really admired him immensely), but just to console the Kaiser's nation (which he loathed)—he sent Zildo off; and complacently returned to incubate new and more horrible correspondence.

The following day he heard an opinion. 'That blessed of God my young-lady American,' said Zildo possessively, as they rowed to the infirmary in the afternoon, 'as well as being Christian and the most beautiful among the living, is (I wish to say) an angel, or would be if she were masculine. For, Sior, yesterday evening at 17 o'clock she commanded me to row her through little canals with a touch of sunset and antique palaces; and we went by Rio di Santamargarita and Rio Malcanton, where there are also gardens, cats, and kittens. And she wept with joy, on account of beauty, while she painted it, like this, with two hundred and ninety-four dabs in five minutes, not making one blunder. And, after, she wished to regale me with a billet of xinque franchi: but I said to her, like this, "Never, young-lady, with permission!" She then said to me, like this—but—it is nothing, Sior——'

'What did she say?' Nicholas suddenly looked behind him. The boy was one blaze of vermilion.

'Sior, she said, like this, "Then I will give you a kiss." '

Nicholas reared, and shrieked.

'Sior, indeed she said it.'

'And you?'

'And me, Sior, I said to her, like this, "So many thanks, young-lady: but my Paron would not permit it." '

'Why?'

Zildo hesitated; and then, 'Because I—because he——' And paled, trembling a little.

Nicholas imitated the woman of Samaria, and made haste to change the subject. 'And then?'

'Sior, she laughed; and I understood that she esteemed me. So I said to her, like this, "But, if you wish for pleasure to give me a certain thing, then I will take your collar."'

'O Dio!' gasped Nicholas, shipping his oar and sinking back on the seat. 'And then?'

'Sior, she gave it to me instantly.'

'Where is it? Why did you want it?'

'Sior, she also asked that. And I said to her, like this, that I wanted it because it was beautiful—but most beautiful—being made of little beads, silver and pearl, woven together on threads in a pattern of pomegranates; and I believed that (if I could have it in my hands for a night and a day) I could make its companion. Therefore I demanded and took it. And, at night, I informed myself of its confection. And, this morning, I rowed my young-lady American, from 8 o'clock to mid-day, on the lagoon by Sacca Sessola; and she painted the Island of Spinalonga, all like ivory, floating on its own image in a lavender haze of heat. She asked me, then, whether I had given her collar to my She-Benjamin. Me, I answered her, like this, that there was no such person; and also I said to her, like this, "Very genteel and most beautiful young-lady American, here is your collar: but, if you will confide it to me for one week only, I shall buy beads and certain things on the Bridge of Rialto, and make a companion for it." She said to me, like this, "Va ben: but you may buy the best beads at the shop of such a Berengo-Gardin in the Wide Alley of Saint Mark; and, if you make a companion, I will buy it of you for fourteen-fifty and as many more as you please at that price, even hundreds; and I shall rest at Albergo Danieli during fifteen days or more, but (after) I shall be in America at the address stamped on this card, where you shall send your collars: but now I desire to return to my hotel." So, Sior, I rowed like a regatta of champions to her hotel; and, at 17 o'clock, I am to row her to seek another sunset at the point of Rio di Santeufemia, which I have remembered for lonely beauty. And, while she paints, I shall observe the collar; and, tomorrow, I shall course to Calle Larga San Marco to buy mounds of beads, needles, thread, and things. Then I shall begin to weave collars, in every empty moment, at first resembling the collar dela mia zentijisima Siorina Americana, and (after) different in colour and in design, so that I may gain many deniers—even sacks full.'

Nicholas got up to row again, pondering these news. Oh, very

well, then—let it be so. The boy was going to preserve himself
from idleness. And knew quite well how to retain his secret and
his dignity. Ha-ha! And, if he could earn money through this
acute (but blind) though most benign American, and wanted to,
so much the better. If affairs went on as horribly as they were
going on, it would be a comfort to know that Zildo at least had a
lucrative and chosen occupation.

'Sior,' said a tiny bland honeyed voice from the poop behind him,
as they approached the Ponte della Croxe.

'Eco to paròn,' he replied, still rowing.

'Sior,' insinuated Zildo, stopping, and creeping down to speak
with dulcet persuasion, 'do me a favour, do me a pleasure. I pray.
The sheets of paper, Sior, on which you write are signed with
lines making squares like the squares which I must make with thread
weaving my beads into collars. And—Sior—if I had such a sheet
of paper—Sior—I could sign its squares with a new design, demon-
strating where I must put beads of one colour, and where of another.
For I believe and it seems to me that innumerable are the various
weavings of beads into collars.'

'It is true. And I will regale you with a whole packet of my
paper, as a handsel, if (now) you will row and give me a touch of
silence.'

'Sìssior. Servo suo.'

Light to the wretched is granted, and life to the bitter in spirit.
Thus said the patient Job. It was true. It's true now.

XVII

Caliban to Crabbe: "Oh why will you be so crabby? Don't you understand that mother and father only hadn't written because, knowing your troubles and being unable to help, they found it hard to find anything to say. But you took offence at their silence, and when they did their best to oblige you, you rear up and tear them into tatters with your awful talons and make them your bitter enemies. It's very hard on me. However, here's another proposition for you; and I do hope you'll be sensible enough to accept it. If you do, there'll be no difficulty about funds for your first-class journey with every comfort. I'm afraid you'll have to make a discreet departure and leave your things behind, but as you only took a few things when you left home which must be worn out by now, you won't mind losing them. Bobugo says come back and live with him and do that book about *Saint Thomas of Canterbury*. He will not insult you by offering to take you in out of charity, but says that he'll consider it an equivalent for board, lodging, and washing if you'll do such work about the house and poultry-yard and putting his gardens in order as he may require. He promises not to speak to you except on business, and the book can be done in your spare time. Now there you have an offer of exactly what you want, viz. an open-air life and a chance of writing in peace where your creditors can't get at you. So I send you the proverbial guinea, which I want you to use like this. Go and have a good dinner for a change, for I guess you're starving yourself as usual when things don't go quite as you like. After that, swear violently at and tip heavily a cheap gondoliere. And wire me your consent with the balance. I'll instantly instruct Cook to secretly give you the necessary tickets, etc. I.T.SS.S."

Crabbe to Caliban: "You do make me smile. Your parents wrote to me as to a merely casual acquaintance, and an undesirable one at that. It was stupefying: but, not being slow at taking hints, I sent them the kind of answers they seemed to want. And you say they're coughing horribly. Well, I say that they must be comical people: for it does strike me as extremely comical when people say that they don't know what to say to a most intimate friend in trouble, being unable to help him—and not being either asked or expected to help

him, mind you. (Damn you.) Of course, I, being peculiar (thank
Heaven and The Black Cat), think that the moment when a partner
and most intimate friend is in trouble is just the very moment of
all others when kind consoling encouraging words are far more
suitable than stony silence. But your people (who used to pretend
that they were mine too) 'found it hard to find anything to say.'
Quite so. Admirable. Delicious. That clears up mysteries. Do
you know why they f.i.h.t.f.a.t.s.? I'll tell you. They haven't got
it, my dear. That's all. And one knows precisely what sort of
people people are who f.i.h.t.f.a.t.s. to a friend in trouble. They
are people who have most magnificently mucked the most gorgeous
opportunity of their lives. No doubt they're biting with rage. But—
are they raging wholly at me? Archbishop Laud bless Your Splendour, no! Ha-ha! Ha-ha! And, no, thank you very much, I will
not run away from Venice, at your expense, and leave my debts
unpaid. And I will not on any account go and live with your
Bobugo. It's ridiculous (and perhaps sinful) to use a razor for
chopping stone: but I haven't the slightest objection to polishing
his boots and emptying his pails, and scrubbing his floors and creating
his capons, and trenching his celery and manuring his marrows, in
certain circumstances. And it's not that I altogether refuse to write
a book for him to sign. No. I won't go and live with him for
another reason. You just sit down while papa tickles your toes at
tea-time, and read Bobugo's book *The Sensiblist* over again. You'll
find my reason there (in the character of his 'Mr Rhodes') for refusing
the offer of which his sadimaniac effrontery makes your blank in-
eptitude the medium. That is a character which he invented—he
thinks it like God (Who said, 'Come unto Me, all ye that are weary
and heavy-laden, and I will refresh you') and got an archbishop's
widow to think so too—he also thinks it himself, and lives and
labours to make himself it. No, thank you: I will not incarcerate
myself in the lonely country-house dungeon of a despot, whose
fixed idea is to break in pieces men's minds and natures by physical
torment and mental torture, so that he may gum them together
again on a model of his own and exhibit them on crimson carpets
at garden-parties as perfect cures, all for his own greater glory. No,
thank you, and your Bobugo. This is Century XX; and this fly
will not walk into the parlour of that spider. Think of something
else. But, by the by, why not stick to the matter in hand? Why
not fulfil Your Splendid promise that You wouldn't let me suffer
in honour, person, or property? Why not reclaim Morlaix and
Sartor from their evil courses? Yes, why not? And, haven't you

received *Sieur René* yet? Then why haven't you sent (or seen sent) the remittance promised for it? Eh? By the by, here's your infernal guinea. I.T.SS.S."

The plump face of Parrucchiero became longer and longer. Crabbe, invited to conferences and aware that the envelopes of his correspondence were not unnaturally scrutinized before they reached him, had no news of pleasing nature to bestow. A sort of indignant serenity encased him: he was indignant that his torment should be prolonged by his own consideration for an imbecile: but he was serene, with the two types of serenity produced respectively from the conviction that one's facts are substantial, and from the consciousness of merit gained in the attempt to win a man from dishonour by confiding in his honour. But indignant serenity on the part of a debtor doesn't prevent his creditor from baying him; and Parrucchiero's became strained with the apparently insusceptible Crabbe.

Caliban wrote by return: "I wish I'd never heard of Bobugo. And I'm getting quite uneasy about you. For goodness' sake do something. You can't go on running up a bill at your hotel, you know. No one suggests that you should do anything dishonourable: but I do wish you'd run away—I suppose you move about Venice as you like and could slip off from the station without a row—and go somewhere into the mountains just across the frontier. There are heaps of villages in the Austrian Tyrol where you could live on nothing. And, once safe out of Italy, write and tell your landlord that you'll pay him when you can. There is nothing dishonourable in that. Pray do it. I have sent your manuscript of *De Burgh's Delusion* to friend Wallace for an opinion and revision, which he says he'll gladly give. When he has trimmed it, mother shall type it. You know it's ripping to get a man like Wallace to do this for us: his last book, which I suppose you haven't seen, *Annals of an Individual of Condition*, is selling like hot cakes, and that's just what we want ours to do. I say—please take my advice for once. I.T.SS.S."

Crabbe instantly replied: "Your jests (or gests) are becoming clumsier than ever, my Caliban. My purely personal opinion is that jesting hardly is opportune. As sovereign of the Order, You can claim my obedience to Your mandates—if You dare to issue mandates: but I utterly refuse even to ponder such requests and such advice as you lately have seen fit to spue upon me. I just toss them back at you. Once for all, be it known that I won't leave Venice till I've paid my debts—if then. They don't amount to a couple of hundred sterling; and it's inconceivable why such a fuss should

be made about so paltry a sum. Make those treacherous Judases
who keep my bag render the last two half-years' accounts; and let's
see how I stand. If they've been mismanaging, put my property
in the hands of someone who'll manage better. If You, my Sovereign
—one of 'em, anyhow—hadn't made me stop action on Your spontaneous promise that I shouldn't suffer, I could have got things straight
by myself weeks and weeks ago. As for sending my MS. of *De
Burgh's Delusion* to Wallace, I don't think I ever heard of anything
so truly and lusciously fat. Fancy letting a Quaker go rooting and
snouting in my lovely catholic garden! Man alive! Why, he'll
tusk up every single flower which I so artfully planted and brought
to bloom there! Ajuto! Take it away from him at once; and send
it, with *The Weird*, to Shortmans. You yourself said, in January,
that there was our only way of getting ready money; and here we
are at the end of March; and still you play the giddy—Lieutenant.
And, what about *Sieur René*? My dear, I'm becoming a bit tired.
I.T.SS.S."

You'll admit, o most affable reader, that Crabbe had sufficient
cause for boredom. His overdrafts, amounting to about twenty-five
sterling, went entirely in tobacco and postage of the shoals of night-
born manuscripts which he secretly was sowing in England. For
living expenses, he went in debt to his landlord; and denied himself
everything else. But nothing was coming in. He had no certain
knowledge of when anything was likely to come in. And he was
convinced that delay in bringing his agents to book confirmed
them in their position while it weakened his. But the experiment
was fascinating to his temperament; and he resolved to bear these
intolerable conditions till he had completed *Sebastian Archer*, but not
a moment longer. Once let that book be safely and secretly sent
direct to a decent publisher, and then he would discomfit several
and stop all hanky-panky. So he worked on, harder than ever.
Luckily his bedroom had electric light, and abnormal consumption
of it (not being separately registered) did not betray him. The
diminution of his meals (for which he actually had a conscientious
motive) excited remarks—he refused the various courses of the table
d'hôte, and ate one plate only at luncheon and dinner: but he
explained that the work which everyone saw him do (on the book
of Mr Exeter Warden) necessitated a brain unimpeded by the
functions of a delightfully-employed interior. Little Piero of the
squirrel eyes offered to steal walnuts for him, all the same; and
Arthur the Blond saw that he never lacked bread and butter. And,

of course, a certain wan anxiety in his gaze did not pass unnoticed: but it was generally known now, in the hotel, that something was wrong; and, on the whole, he was rather admired and pitied than suspected. The fierce and banausic Venetians have the most tender heart-commoving pity for misfortune, and are not a bit ashamed of shewing it. But gentle pity only excited Crabbe to fury. He went in most horrible and ghastly fear of suspicion. The bare idea of it goaded him into frenzied activity at night, when the rest of Venice slept; and the customary quaking of the mud, on which the miraculous city is poised—not a proper earthquake, but a gentle ripple as of a swayed jelly or (if one must be literary) the pleasured sighing of a maiden breast—gave him a most wonderful understanding of that ever-moving instability of human things, an infinitesimal morsel of which (now and again) some persistent genius contrives to consolidate and to crystallize for all time by the force of irreversibly resolute human will. But he need not have feared. He was not suspected then. Your regular swindler doesn't deny himself kinematographs and society. And Crabbe shewed a shell-like adamant to all diversions. He went for an hour sometimes to Mactavish's Mondays, sitting and smoking and listening, sometimes speaking with incisiveness, but making no friends, and acquiring the reputation of a swordstick. That was his sole dissipation. And then, one sunny spring day, La Pash pounced upon him.

He had been rowing infirmary people on the lagoon throughout the afternoon, and the nurses offered a quiet cup of tea when he returned. La Pash, they said, had been and was gone, taking the bibbling directress with her to do some shopping. The nurses' room was in the garden at the back of the hall: one door opened in the kitchen corridor, the other in the paved court at the beginning of the garden. And Crabbe, thinking the coast clear, was just drawing up his chair when Her Ladyship pranced in from the corridor, ostensibly to neigh farewell at the nurse who was pouring tea. The open garden door was but a step behind him: but escape in full face he could not. Incivility was not one of his habits. He merely reared while the nurse lisped a presentation. La Pash bridled: she was charmed, gracious, and suppliant. Her nephew, young Hoste, staying with her, was mad on learning to row in the mode Venetian. She had borrowed the sandolo of the infirmary for him; and (curvetting) could Mr Crabbe be so kind as to send a nice boy, expert with the oar, to act as his instructor. Crabbe didn't like the look of the white of her eye, and remained all shell, with enormous pincers tidily disposed but visible. He would try. What would she pay? Anything which he thought right: if he would send the boy to Ca' Pachello, with a card saying what, that would be enough and admirable. Crabbe said that a boy would appear on the following morning. And he whispered to himself that that boy would not be Zildo, no matter what La Pash's little game was. On the whole, he was rather pleased. He saw that she was vicious: he guessed that she hadn't forgotten his thwacking 'Please leave me alone': he fully intended to avoid her as carefully as ever; and the notion of bows (now obligatory) from a distance (minimum 15 metres) did not perturb him unduly. For he had scooped two points. He had gained a chance of making one of these aliens (who treated their gondolieri so meanly) pay handsomely by way of a change. And he had gained a chance of giving a job to one of a crowd of delightful, capable, but (perforce) idle youngsters, always hanging about the door of the club in the hope of being taken into the service of the English, whose former gondolieri were reported to have wallowed in illimitable luxury.

At 8 o'clock the next day, the only idler at the Bucintoro was a leggy lissome creature of fifteen, all pink and white with a round black poll and comic chinese eyes, who called himself Richard of the Knights.

'Ciò, toso,' cried Nicholas, 'would it please you to serve an English?'

'Sìssiorsì, but willingly.'

The job was explained to him; and he was armed with a card inscribed 'This is Riccardo Cavalieri. Engagement for one month at least. Payment L. 21 a week, with handsel (according to merit) up to L. 25.'

Zildo observed these proceedings with his usual gentle imperturbability. When the stranger had dashed eagerly off to Ca' Pachello, 'Sior,' he said, 'will it not please you to use the pupparin this morning: for my young-lady American voyaged to her place yesterday?'

Nicholas surveyed the tempting water. It was one of those shouting spring days which offer celestial bliss in the open sunlight. He was sick of indoor. Oh, to get out—to go far——

'Yes,' he said, 'let us go to Burano, where I had much pleasure last year.'

The two swirled through the city, entering by Rio della Canonica, rocking and ramping through little canals, with Zildo's clanging bell-like 'E-oe,' and 'Pre-i' or 'Sta-i' booming at the turnings; and emerged, by the Rio dei Mendicanti, on the northern lagoon. They swept at full speed along the cemetery-islands of Sammichele and Sancristoforo, and through the Canale Ordello by the glass-making island of Murano to the long stretch of the Canale di Giustizia beyond. At the islet of Saint James in the Marsh, where Madonna sits in her altar-shrine on the sea-wall, Nicholas called for a halt. The pace had been terrific: but his magnificent strength (sapped though it was by night-work and by the strain of making and wearing a daunt-less defiant front to the world), and perhaps also his unconquerable sense of superiority which answered to every call and kept him taut and erect, enabled him not to shew signs of distress before the boy. As for Zildo, flushed and beaming, his fair head bare and crowned with its waving plume, he exulted in using the force of his insuperable youth.

'Sior,' he said, roping to the stake by the shrine, 'many banners have been gained for courses of a quarter of our speed and a half of our length.'

'Do you desire to gain a banner?'

'Nòssior—not without His Sioria.'

'But I do not wish to gain banners from the Venetians.'

'Also me: the banner of the English contents me.'

Nicholas went to the prow, and twisted straight the little Red Ensign which a breeze was wrapping round the shining brazen flagstaff. He was flying England now, in place of the Bucintoro vexillo, because Venice simply creeps with Germans in late spring. Then he sank into the cane arm-chair amidships, and began to roll a cigarette.

A hand curved from the poop behind him, laying four notes of ten lire each with three silver lire and five pajanche in copper on his lap.

'Còssa xe?' he blankly demanded.

'Sior,' answered a voice of infinite young jubilation, 'that is the price of three collars of pomegranates, in silver beads on pearls, in pearl beads on silver, and in silver beads on gold, which I wove for my young-lady American. And here, also, is a design' (shewing a paper) 'for a new collar of tiny feathers of peacocks, which tomorrow I shall weave in gold beads with green and blue, for sending to America to the same.'

'Benissimo.' He folded the coins in the notes, and, turning round, placed them in the boy's hand.

'But—Sior——'

'Put your deniers in your pocket.'

'Nòssior.'

'I am not disputing. I am telling you.'

'Sior, listen' (gabbling hurriedly), 'I wove the collars with beads which I bought with your deniers which I took from Sior Caloprin of the Cassa di Risparmio——'

'Zildo, listen. There are no deniers of mine in the Cassa di Risparmio.—The deniers which you take from Sior Caloprin are your earned wages.—You have woven collars of beads bought with your own deniers, not with mine. Bravo, my Zildo. Do it again. I am very contented with you. Make some more, and yet some more. Fill your pockets with deniers while you can. Good auguries to you. That is all. Understand? Good. And, now, do me the pleasure of rowing me to Burano: for I wish to repose myself with my thoughts——'

Tears welled in unchecked flood from the boy's frank wistful innocent eyes. Nicholas felt like a perfect beast: but he set his teeth against any sort of putrid foolery. Better feel like one than be one; and he shuddered to think how near to the verge of an embrace his heart had so suddenly thrust him. He hardened, and struck a match for his cigarette.

Zildo blinked a bit, without wile, that he might see his way to cast off; and his ripe young lips closed courageously against so ruthlessly bitter and cruel a disappointment. But he obeyed his master implicitly, saying not another word. In half a minute the bark was flying on, driven by the long regular sweeps of his oar. He says that this was when he first knew that he must wait and wait.

Nicholas remained rigid, facing prow-ward, thankful that only his back was visible to his servant: for certain emotions were beginning to play a fierce game with him. The love and the lealty, the gentle delicate honour, the unswerving faith and trust, the grave deliberate singleness of purpose, of the exquisite soul which inhabited that splendidly young and vigorous and alluring form behind him, rang echoing through every secret cavern of his being. Zildo was minded to give. For his own part, he also yearned to give. But he yearned to take as well. And Zildo! Light of light! What would be the unravelling of this tangle, in which he had involved himself and Zildo? Why had Zildo so conclusively refused to leave him. Why had he, with such unusual weakness, acquiesced in that refusal? What portended this content with the position—this content —this—no, not content—this suppressed consuming longing to take and to give, to give and to take all, all, to mingle and dissolve in as one? What was this hunger, this thirst, this ravenous sense of desire for the $\chi\tau\eta\mu\alpha$ ες αει of that soul and body? It was not mere everyday lust: his admiration was as great for the naïve spring-like soul, for the mind as gently and firmly bright as a star, as for the long lithe limbs, the soft firm fragrant flesh, the noble features, the stalwart grace, the virginal freshness (all once seen, and never for a moment forgotten); and his admiration (for beauty pure and simple) was refrained by impregnable virtue proclaiming its object sacrosanct and inviolable. Nor was it mere vulgar recognition, in the humble manner of Christians (that latebrosa et lucifuga, natio, as Minucius Felix calls them) of any inferiority in his own soul or in his own body. He was ware of his own distinction and force and untainted excellence of form and feature, of his own inexhaustible youth and strength. He knew himself to be capable of thoughts and deeds as worthy as Zildo's, fine and rare and cardinal as those undoubtedly were. Was it, then, only the effect of the shock, the appulse, the thunderclap of joy, at the knowledge that he had (actually in his hand and devoted to him) one so completely sympathetic, so precisely resembling the majestic eternal primaveral ideal which he formed for his own attainment? His friends—never, in all his life, had he had such a friend—never had he even seen anyone capable of being such a friend as Zildo seemed to wish to be, and might be— one and all of them had taken the most hideous and egregious tosses at the very first approach to his ideal. Sympathy—oh yes, they said that they sympathized with him. They roared it. But they knew no Greek: they hadn't the faintest notion of what they were saying. Asked to define, they whimpered that they felt for him. Felt for him—yes, they felt feelings of their own; and expected him to feel them too. The idea of feeling his feelings never entered their fat heads. They felt for, not with, him; and, what they thought was sym-pathy, actually was dys-pathy. No one had ever felt with him. No one had ever been able to take his part. What heaps of miawling minnocks thought themselves so beastly virtuose for taking—and one admits that they took it with both hands—was, not his part but, that which they thought ought to be his part; and their precious taking of it was their gain and his loss. Bobugo, whom he had really wished to love—pheuph!—the stench of his shame!—Caliban, monstrous farcical buffoon, victim of inordinate vanity and the foot disease called Talipes Plantaris!—And now, here, was an ideal friend, whose form and thought and word and deed and very being were as his own: whom all laws, divine and human, forbade him to have for a friend. Human law held Zildo out of his reach. Nor did he really want Zildo for his friend. That slim strong brave-breasted athlete, aloft there in blue trousers and white guernsey, was his servant, inadmissible to friendship. Co-operation is a different relation from union. But, after all, Zildo was not Zildo—not-Zildo. And honour and reverence forbade him to begin to think of taking not-Zildo for his friend.—What had Caliban spluttered, 'marry some nice girl—instead of sneezing at them all—heaps would jump at you, if you would condescend to ask them nicely, as you can, if you choose.' Ouph! 'Marry some nice girl with money!'— some 'nice girl'—some 'fille repugnante, la femelle du male, un chose horrible, tout en tignasse, en pattes rougeaudes, yeux ravages, bouche défraichie, talons éculés—ci-devant provinciale, nippé comme une Hottentot—puis bonne a tout faire, feignante, voleuse, sale—brrr!'— Some coarse, raucous, short-legged hockey—or hunting—female hideous in hairy felt—some bulgy kallipyg with swung skirts and cardboard waist and glass-balled hat-pins and fat open-work stockings and isosceles shoes—something pink-nosed and round-eyed and frisky, as inane and selfish and snappy-mannered as a lap-dog—some leek-shaped latest thing, heaving herself up from long tight lambrequins to her own bursting bosom and bonneted with a hearse-plumed jungle-crowned bath—some pretentious pompadoured image trailing satin, moving (apparently leglessly) in society—all of the mental and physical consistency of parrots crossed with jelly-fish. O god of Love, never! Infinitely far better to marry not-Zildo— if not-Zildo would. But—would not-Zildo? Well, why not? 'He, who dispenses with woman, lives in sin,' said Maimonides.

He stood up; and turned round, as though to look back at Venice. Zildo, poised, swaying at the oar in the centre of vision, looked down, straight at him, as he turned, with the usual gentle persuasive welcoming smile. There must have been, in the aspect of Nicholas at that moment, something of the aspect of a conquistador sampling a spoil of damsels: for the boy flushed vividly, and returned his bright gaze to the dancing prow to keep it straight with infinitesimally-calculated wrist-turns, pushing or feathering the oar. Nicholas attentively observed him, from the proudly-floating panache of his hair like candle-flames, to the rosy tips of his arching honey-hued feet—the candid wistful visage, the long lovely form full of promise, full of joy, the slim magnificent membrature, all alive, all supple, all indefectible, all without trace of sex. Oh, to take!—Marry? Rather than anything else in this world. Oh, to take the offered bud, which taking would bring to bloom. Buds neglected wither. Was so halcyon a bud to be left—to wither?

Yes: he must leave it, to wither: because he might not take it. He might not take it against its will. And—sordid horror—he dared not to ask leave to take it: for he had no garden wherein to plant it. O fool, to dally thus!

He threw himself headlong down again to the world of things as they were—to the staggering priest scheming to batten on his brains—to the coxcomb, catarrhic with incompetence, who juggled with his trust—to the agents squalling stolidly on his means—to his creditors, his empty purse, his empty hungry heart, his empty lonely life. These, these, were what he had to face. He might not indulge in dreams.—His mind was still ecclesiastically tinged.—He was still very very young.

He picked up his oar; and began to row, as the pupparin approached the canal which enters the islet of Mazzorbo. 'Sta-i,' he commanded.

Zildo steered to the right, along the sea-wall painted with a lace-maker's advertisement; and would have turned sharply to the left, into the canal where a long wooden bridge connects Mazzorbo with Burano.

'No,' cried his master, 'keep straight on.'

'Sior, there is no canal across this lagoon; and we shall be stranded.' (Gondolieri are dreadfully nervous about leaving the staked water-ways for short cuts across tempting but unmarked expanses.)

'It is true that there is no canal: but I will not go in dry. Do me the pleasure of obeying me.'

'Sissior.'

They struck a more or less diagonal course toward their nearing goal. Nicholas kept vigilant watch on the shallows at the end of his own oar, and held the bark in depths just out of reach of them with shouts of ' Pre-i,' or 'Sta-i,' to the steersman; and, so, slightly zigzagging along the short-cut used by fishermen, they came to the south end of the canal which penetrates Burano. Zildo's panting anxiety, lest his Paron's prepotence should have run the bark aground, gave place to an admiring smile worth millions. Nicholas shipped his oar; and went to the prow to shove aside barks impeding the way, the canal being narrow and crowded.

As they went under the iron bridge, a sturdy islander (of the Re Galantuomo type) saluted from the quay. Nicholas recognized him as one who used to take a modest nightly potion at the inn where he had often stayed in the previous autumn. They glided on, turning the corner, and going under the second bridge, tying up the bark at the Albergo di Roma. Nicholas went in; and was welcomed by all, from the pursy paron to shock-headed Scimiotto the waiter: he ordered luncheon—something fortunately fried and a flask of white chianti.

Zildo remained at the door, shewing his teeth, keeping an eye like a knife on the pupparin. The quay swarmed with ragamuffins, cubs, cinderellas, and slubberdegullions, eager to snatch from the well-known English. 'All the Buranelli, who are not mendicants, are brigands,' said the boy, citing the aristocratic opinion of serene Venice, when his master came out to lounge beside him.

'And the Buranelle?'

'Mah! Like this like that, and all verminous (pidocchiose)': he said with disgusted indifference.

Now the girls of Burano really are wonderfully handsome. ('O che beo biondo!' screamed a jade in Zildo's ear. 'Go away, Blessed She,' growled that Beautiful Fair-He). Of course they're as bold as brass, as they spadge about the quays of their tiny island-city, arm in arm, with clattering of clogs; and their taste in dress is alarming and vulgar beyond words. But Nicholas had not investigated their personal cleanliness. Judging from the density of the population and the stench of their canals, possibly Zildo's sentence was just.

'See that fisher-boy with the black eyes, who walks on his hands for our diversion?' asked Nicholas abruptly.

'Sissior.'

'Go and say to him, like this, "Emilio, the paron wishes you to guard his bark." '

Zildo stepped across the quay; and delivered the message. Active-footed Emilio vaulted upright, brown-gleaming thighs bare, mud-green trunks, black shirt open, arms to shoulders and breast to waist bare and brown as a cigar, brown face, sparkling eyes, glittering teeth—a wicked merry mercurial muscular slip of tatterdemalion, clean because amphibious, prompt to do anything (blessed or damned) for tenpence, a born slave. His naked arms and legs whirled: there were shrieks, yells, thuds, a patter of feet, as he cleared away the rabble of riff-raff. Nicholas laughed: and chucked him a couple of cigarettes. He deftly caught and stuck them over his ears; and, bounding to a post-top, sat there to smoke on guard, legs open, one ankle laid on the other knee and one leg dangling down, in the exact pose of the fine bronze called *Intervallo* which a Venetian sculptor, Ugo Bottassi, once exhibited to unappreciative London. Nicholas wondered where that bronze was now.

While they ate their luncheon, the sturdy citizen (who saluted their arrival) passed through the inn to imbibe at the back. Catching a glance, he paused at their table: and presented a black-bordered visiting-card. 'With permission, Siore,' he said, 'seeing that gentility leads you to revisit this island, I affright myself to demand the honour of shewing you some pictures.'

'You will give me a pleasure,' Nicholas replied: 'but I ought to say that I am that strange thing called a poor English, who cannot afford to buy pictures.'

'That is of no import, Siore: I only wish to give you a pleasure.'

'And I accept it with many thanks.'

'Then, when you are ready, I will conduct you to my little house.'

'Permit me, meanwhile, to offer you calcosa a bere.'

'Grazienò, Siore,' with a noble retiring gesture worthy of a renunciating exarkh.

Nicholas read on the card 'Novello Ermenegildo,' as he paid his bill. 'Here is a namesake of yours, who is going to shew you some pictures,' he said to his servant.

'Sior, he is a brave, and very beneficent; and, as for me, I am appassionated for pictures.'

Nicholas sat up. 'What do you know about pictures?'

'Much, Sior: for, always when I spy a painter, I creep near to peep over his shoulder: but I forget all those pictures: though I never have forgotten certain pictures, which I used to see on festivals, while Bastian my father had life, before I went into Calabria.

'And those?'

The boy's big long blue eyes explored past memories. 'Sior, there was, in a corridor of the Accademia, a very celestial azure picture of an angel—o be-o!—And, in a hall—yes—a picture of ten thousand martyrs—o be-issimi!'—He became rapt in mental contemplation.

Nicholas knew the Ten Thousand Crucified Martyrs of Mount Ararat by Carpaccio, a myriad of the ordinary stalwart Venetian nudes who adorn all time, dilated in divers demeanours on the trees of wooded hills. 'Why did that picture please you?' he inquired.

'Because, Sior, the martyrs were so amiable; and I wished them alive to hug me, I being then an infant. And also, Sior, there was a picture with his patron of my father, Sambastian, very sane and vegete, very sedate and noble, with an arrow in his left belly and another in his left calf.' (This, no doubt, was the Giambellini.)— Then, Sior, there was a picture of Sancristoforo in the church of Sanzancristostom: but my father said he was a Buranello, being of that type, but beautiful—and, also, I remember a picture of a toso, amiable, amiable, amiable and brave like my Paron, at Santamaria Odorifera, on the wall by the altar of Sanlorenzo——'

Sior Novello reappeared, and led them along the quays to his house, Emilio following (at a beckon) with the bark.

It was a tiny three-floored cottage, one of a row, entered (from the quay) to a room which was parlour and cobbler's shop. On the right, were Sior Novello's bench and apron and tools of trade with a medley of finished and unfinished cobbling. Three walls were covered with religious or national chromos and family photographs. Furniture and ornament were of the most undistinguished taste imaginable. On the left wall was a very large oblong curtain. The cobbler drew it aside. He was as sober and as staid a respectability as one could find anywhere.

Nicholas gasped; and stared. He never praised anything without a but: but this was astounding. It was a finely framed picture of a perfectly feminine female nude asleep, simply and grandly depicted by a master. No accessories jumped or buzzed. Nothing disturbed your unique impression. You were struck (with one blow) unconscious of anything but her.

'Ma che!' Zildo ejaculated. He glared: went gradually hot and red; and, turning his back, picked up a waxed thread from the bench to twiddle.

'Who—who—is the painter?' Nicholas demanded.

'Siore, my dead brother, Luigi Novello, professor of the Roman Academy, to serve you,' superbly said the cobbler.

He led them over the three floors of his little house. Every foot of wall, of stair and landing and room was covered with pictures and studies—a Dead Christ watched by Modern Maries embellished the stair. Everywhere was exquisite imagination, singular insight, noble taste, masterly skill. Portfolios full of sketches, early and prime and late, were extracted from bureaux and dowry-chests. It was a most astonishing revelation of the dead painter's talented personality. And to be lost here, unknown, in this poor cottage!— This was the first intimate view which Crabbe had had of a humble Venetian dwelling, the delicious cleanliness of bareness, of embroidered sheets, of polished pewter and copper and glass and linen, the airy windows, the sweet-scented beds, the decent homely necessaries which are the luxuries of simple people. 'How did these valuable objects of art come here?' he inquired.

'Siore, I was my brother's heir, to serve you. And I thank you, Siore, for the honour of your visit.'

As they rowed away into the sunny gold of afternoon, Zildo had several things to say. If only the gondolieri of Venice knew of that picture gallery, what mountains of deniers might be gained. How? Most simply, like this. When rich English and Americans went to see the lace-makers of Burano, their gondolieri (to divert them) would say, like this, Here, also, is another little thing, and most antique. Sior Ermenegildo Novello would display his squares. The forestiers naturally would buy them, paying (let us say) three thousand franchi for the veiled picture, whereof eight hundred and fifty would go to the gondolieri for their handsel, leaving two thousand and one hundred and fifty for Sior Ermenegildo. But, what a good combination!

'But Sir Ermenegildo does not want to sell.'

'Otherwise, Sior, otherwise, I assure you. One will always sell anything for deniers in cash.'

'It's not true. There are many things of mine which I will not sell. And you, Zildo—have you nothing which you will not sell?'

'The boy, posed, rowed silently. Nicholas looked round at him. 'Speak,' he said.

'Sior, with permission, I wish first to examine my thoughts.'

'Good. Think. And, when you have finished thinking, tell me what you think. But, at this moment, tell me whether the pictures pleased you.'

'Moderately. And you, Sior?'

'They are well done.'

'Sìssior. And, Mrs Bare?'

Nicholas gave a snort of laughter. 'La Siora Ignua? Oh, she was very well done.'

'Mah! But who would be painted like that, for all to see, for ever.'

'And why not?'

'It would not please me. It would cause me much shame.'

'Now why? What have you of which to be ashamed? Are you dirty, or wicked, or hunchbacked, or distorted, or deformed, or diseased?'

'Nòssiornò! Nonòsior! No-nò! I am none of these bad things. But, nothing of me belongs to me which I could give away. And it would cause me shame, Sior, to be like that, asleep, unknowing, for all to see, at their will, for ever, taking little views of my aspect away from me. Sior, I do not wish to be observed by strangers, by persons (brutti individui) whom I do not even know, but—but only—only by whom I—trust——'

Nicholas saw the red danger-signal of the masculine pronoun; and put the brake full on. So Zildo deemed him like that grand athletic young Saint Vincent (or was it Saint Lawrence) at the church of Madonna del Orto, amiable, amiable, amiable and brave. And Zildo was saving himself—reserving himself—offering——.   O Lord!

'Well, now that you know of these pictures, tell your next Signorina Americana of them; and gain your mound of deniers,' said Nicholas, hurriedly and bleakly.

'Nòssior.   I am not as other gondolieri.   Also, with permission, I belong to my Paron.'   And not another word would he say, even when they touched Venice in a marvellous sunset of streaks of lilac edged with silver on fawn colour about a disk of boiling blood.

This indeed was desire.   But, what whole was he pursuing? Priesthood?   Or marriage?   Neither: till able to choose.

XVIII

THE blubber-lipped professor of Greek had the blazing face to write: 'Dear Crabbe, I must congratulate you on *Terribile la Femmina*, Yours Richard Macpawkins'; and set him rearing in two tantrums. How dared that unutterable one congratulate him? What in the world did the screed mean?

Crabbe was frightfully worried that morning: his mask of serenity cost an effort to bear: his conscience had been giving him beans on the score of yesterday's idiotic (and almost criminal) dalliance; and he cursed himself anew for his crab-like habit of sidling and for his unconquerable predilection for larking on verges of giddy precipices. It was sinful, too, to play with temptation, specially when another's peace was concerned. After Mass, he came across the square of the little porphyry lions in front of the patriarchal palace to drink his coffee, case-hardened anew, freshly resolved not to let himself go any more in regard to Zildo—till his way was clear. Even then, a problem would confront him—the question of continued celibacy as proof of priestly vocation: twenty years had been the measure of his vow which was to lapse at Easter —it was not an ungenerous slice of mortal life to sacrifice: it was a rather huge pearl to cast before three totally stolid archbishops one after another. He had inward warnings of the exhaustibility of human patience.

And, at this point, came the Macpawkins note, or gibe. He took it with him when he went to the club; and racked his brains for its signification. Looking over the balcony, he saw Zildo below, in the Rio, bare-legged, bare-armed, with the bark half-full of water, and its floor-boards out to be scrubbed. Active happiness was this boy's portion when he had plenty of polishing to do.

Yes: of course! *Terribile la Femmina* was the title of one of that bundle of manuscripts sent to Lord Arthur Baliol Kingsbury, the editor of *The Lykeion*, at the beginning of the year, by request of the incredible Bobugo. Ha-ha! Here, then was some money. And Crabbe instantly wrote his news to Caliban, telling to collect and send the sum due. He added something else. As the Lieutenant had forbidden personal communication with Bobugo, Crabbe

185

wished that priest to know that refusal of the Rite of Benediction had barred him from the Sacraments for three months: Easter was at hand, and it must be clearly understood that he considered himself prevented from his Easter duties as things were. It was a trick of intimidation which had been tried before, by another sacerdotal bully whom resistance had brought crashing to the ground. So he now gave Bobugo warning. No law of God or Man empowered a priest to sin in this hole-and-corner way. Formal excommunication would be welcomed, and instantly and unconditionally submitted to. But, excommunication required a bishop and a trial; and a furtive little priest, who dared to deprive of Sacraments by refusing a Rite, couldn't find a tame bishop on every bush to assist his nefarious prostitution of spiritualities for purely temporal coercive purposes. Labels are more lethal than libels.

Satisfaction, at this neat presentment of a dilemma, mitigated annoyance at Parrucchiero's uneasiness which took concrete form when he went back to the hotel for luncheon. The usual spring visitors were flocking to Venice: Crabbe occupied a desirable room: would he either change it, or pay his bill? He moved his things to the room which Zildo had occupied, No. 27, two steps across the landing, a tiny closet with a couple of windows over a narrow alley pervaded (all night long) by raucous night-birds and tipsy songsters.

Here, the final touches were put to *Sebastian Archer*; and the fair copy of it went through Cook to Messieurs Ferrer Senior in England. Maintaining his plan of secrecy, Crabbe gave the Bucintoro Club as his address; and instructed the marangon, who mended oars all day by the letter-box, to look after communications which might come for him.

Next, he nerved himself anew to make a clean sweep of the Warden's book. He returned a batch of revised proof-sheets, one evening, when the worthy man and his Wardeness came back from La Pash's weekly reception.

They had the mean little sidelong air and the solicitous feeble but attempting gait of peachicks afflicted with gapes.

The pair, toothy, pregnant, and gleaming, perched themselves by him in the hall, with the evident intention of talking with tedious concentration. The long cardboard-tipped cigarettes were lighted; and the lady began. 'We bring you,' she said, 'a message from Lady Pash——'

'And,' the Thiasarkh burst to interrupt, 'we do so sincerely hope——'

'No, Exeter,' she patted him, 'let me. Lady Pash,' she continued to Crabbe, 'has been speaking about you all the evening; and she wants us to ask you to consent—wait—let her put you on the infirmary committee—listen—because, she says, you're the only Englishman who has ever been of any real practical service to it!'

'Of course I can't do anything of the kind,' Crabbe promptly snapped.

'Oh! But why?'

'My good people—I'm not addressing Lady Pash, I'm addressing you—will you try to give your serious attention to the following considerations. I'm almost certain that I'm ruined. I'm next door to certain that I am ruined for this year at least. I really am, now. Consequently, I'm not fit to associate with comfortable people; and I'm certainly not fit to take an official position in the infirmary. I'm an undesirable, and I know it. And I have the decency, or the devilry (which you please), to take the wind out of everyone else's sails by proclaiming the damaging fact first myself.'

'But, dear person, are you so certain? Don't you think that, if you'd take us just a little bit into your confidence, we might—is it quite sure that we couldn't perhaps hit on some——'

'It's not a matter of confidence. Anyone can know everything. I only kept quiet because I do so detest a bore——'

'Oh, do then tell us what the difficulty really is.'

On this invitation, and in the sure and certain hope of a joyful riddance of rotters, he briefly and concisely told his tale, making it as black and unprepossessing and hopeless as possible, of Bobugo's treacherous breach of agreement and his attempt to get a book for next to nothing, of Morlaix and Sartor's breach of agreement in stopping allowances and refusing an account of five years' management of his property, of Caliban's authoritative assumption of responsibility for rectification and his neglect of the two books entrusted to him. 'The point is that my own hands,' he concluded, 'are tied, by command of my Lieutenant, and by want of about two hundred sterling to work with apart from him. I'm convinced that Peary-Buthlaw is a pompous palavering turncoat, that Morlaix and Sartor are stupid old fools who've omitted their duty and are ashamed to confess it, that Bonsen has adroitly used my agents and my friend for his own questionable ends, and that I'm quite comfortably embroiled with all three of 'em.'

'But do you think that a priest would——'

'Yes: a banausic one like Bobugo certainly would. You "other sheep" don't know half about the lovely lot of baa-lambs who caper inside the fold.'

'And yet, you remain——'

'Inside? Rather. And for jolly good reason. Run away and read Boccaccio's tale of the Jew. A church, which continues to flourish with criminals for its ministers, must be divine, don't you know? Beside, wasn't there a Judas among the apostles?'

'Oh! How you pain me! But—I also had just a little something to say to you. Would you mind if I made a suggestion? May I? Thank you so much. I have such a dear friend, a member of my congregation (a communicant), living at the Grand Hotel. He's a retired financier, who used to do Rothschild's most intimate and confidential work. I can tell you, from personal experience, that he's simply a magician in unravelling money-tangles. Indeed I don't know what we should do without him. We certainly shan't possibly be able to go to England unless——'

'Then you are going? When?'

'At the end of May. But we leave the hotel after Easter.'

'For your own palace?'

'Oh no! We shall be packing up there: so we're going to be the guest of dear Mrs——'

'But, you see, I don't know your financier.'

'A word from me——'

'Thank you: no.'

'I assure you—may I speak quite plainly? Thank you so much. I wanted to say that, if you'd let me speak to Mr Sappytower, you'd place him under such an obligation to you. He does so enjoy arranging money difficulties. It's his art, you see; and he takes quite an artist's joy in it. Our own case seemed absolutely hopeless; and now—dear person, do let me just name——'

'No: I can't. I detest the notion of talking to strangers about money affairs. It gives one a kind of name. And, after all, there's the bare chance that I'm exciting myself unnecessarily.'

'Do promise me—I shall be so unhappy—promise me to think it over.'

'Very well: I'll bear it in mind.'

'But—if you'd only let me speak now, I could guarantee that your worries would be ended in a week. Ours were.'

'No: I'll think it over.'

Crabbe did think it over, with tingling talons; and worried himself properly, I promise you.

What did this man really mean? Why couldn't people spit it all out straight at once? Why, with triumphant and kindly and inter-ested demonstrations, bring these two particular propositions simultaneously? What was the connection between La Pash's command to join her infirmary committee, and the assurance that money difficulties could be solved in a week by the magic of this financier of Rothschild's—if there was a connection? And, could anything be more distracting than the dropping of Rothschild's name, of all other names, among his present circumstances?

Crabbe knew that he was (as they said) the only Englishman who had ever been of any real practical service to the infirmary. He wasn't inclined to complacency about it: because the job really amused him and made him happy, and his virtue was its own (and his only) reward. But he knew, too—oh, jolly well he knew— that he could and would be infinitely more useful to the institution in an official capacity. He would have an English medical man on the premises all the time, for one thing. And, now that the new English law forbade the shipping of pneumonic and phthisical sailors at English ports for shedding in Italy and the marine patients were consequently much reduced in number, it would be well to develop the nursing-home department to provide the private treatment for which Venetian doctors howled. Also, nurses (and directresses too), who invoked La Pash against doctors whenever they felt a little hysterical, should be sacked on the spot for insubordination and unprofessional conduct, instead of compelling medical resignations and aiding the invasion of Venice by German hospitallers. Efficiency and discipline should be introduced, and rigorously maintained. Accounts should be rendered weekly, and not laboriously cooked by gas and guess for annual reports issued eight months late. And, there should be a resident steward, with charge of servants and stores, instead of the sloppy venal huggermuggery which bought through the cook from such of his friends as would tip him. Yes: Crabbe well knew how to organize the Universal Infirmary, redeeming it from its reputation in the city as an amateurish hen-roost, and from its reputation on the Island of Spinalonga as an English sort of maniacal café-chantant or casino rivalling the Sailors' Institute by the Papadopoli Gardens. And, if La Pash liked to pay the bill, she could continue to absorb the credit: but one does not take credit for charity; and, as public begging for funds went on, and, as patients paid a printed tariff, the infirmary should not sail under false pretences any longer as a charity. He had plenty of views on the place, and willingly would sacrifice time and money to carry them into effect. And, was it really a fact— for he had openly expounded these views, drumming them into the ears of the Wardens and the Portingall Jew and the bibbling directress and donnish Mactavish, scores of times—that La Pash, the supreme proprietress, actually did wish him to carry them into effect? If so, he had been doing that curvetting equine-faced female a gross injustice. If not, why did she want him on her committee? He was a nobody, possessed of no name embellishing to a prospectus; he was known to be hard-up; and he had given unmistakable tokens that he was not at all the sort of marionette whose wires can be moved by anybody. So much for La Pash's command. Next, why this sudden cut and dried offer of Sappytower to straighten his pecuniary tangles within a week? What could Rothschild's most confidential agent do—what could Rothschild (magical colossal name) himself do—which Crabbe himself could not do, were he free to move—free, from the fetters of obedience to the Lieutenant of his Order, from the shackles of his empty pockets, from the gyves of his exhausted overdraft? Was this proposal (he whispered) meant to herald the advent of a new Mæcenas? No doubt Mæcenas could do much. Even a common friend, if such a commodity appertained, could do all which was necessary, could see him through a trouble which (after all) was but of trumpery magnitude and quite temporary. Touching the matter of Mæcenas, however (he suddenly sat up and told himself out loud), it would be essential to regard the creature with great caution. Mæcenas was apt to presume: had to be taught his place and kept there, to prevent him from becoming a most infernal nuisance; and, as an axiom of purely ordinary sagacity, it was just as well not to have anything to do with him, at least till he had made a very humble access on his knees licking a substantial length of pavement in token of abjection and subjection. Yes: on the whole, Crabbe fancied that he had met the Wardens and their propositions very appropriately.

'Maaah! You dear thing!' the directress mouthed at him, when he went on Palm Sunday to the infirmary, 'so you've heard from Lady Pash that you're to come on our committee! Isn't it sweet of her?'

'I came to say that you mustn't expect me this week, because I want to go to church,' he answered, touching his cap; and rowed away.

It was Holy Week; and he promised his soul a debauch of attention. 'Si uis felicitas, terram excede' is a very good rule on these occasions. At such times, he was generally happy, away from this world, embosomed so deep and obscure in stately immemorial symbol that he approached quite close to the other. They were the times when he suspended his soul in far diviner air, to be winnowed and purged of chaff and husk—times of purification, invigoration, fortification, which he took, as he took sun-baths, and light-baths and his daily swim from Sanzorzi to La Grazia and back for the health of his body. But, this year, the result was faint. Undoubtedly the prince of darkness had leave to torment him for a season. Mass left him cold. Stations of the Cross were the most inartistically dismal of all dull dronings. The tedium of Tenebrae dried and tired him to extinction. And his meditations failed to carry him out of his valley to the higher peak and view of the city celestial. Once, indeed, he thought to have won there. It was the night of the exposition of great relics in Saint Mark's. He stood, in the thick of the crowd; and watched the procession of seven canons, in crimson copes, go, through the gloom, as of caverns, with a galaxy of torches and a wonderful song, to the treasury. Wedged in the crowd, a head above all, he watched the return of that starry throng, turning, as they turned. He watched, in the twinkling host, the seven crimson canons carrying marvellous reliquaries, shrine-shaped, cross-shaped, frames of gold and silver with cylinders or slabs of rock-crystal incrusted with gems, and the great basilican reliquary held in two hands. He watched the seven canons ascending the enormous pulpit, violet and crimson and orange and silver and yellow and scarlet and gold in the rich brown gloom as of caverns, while a forest of lofty tapers and torches held by white-robed singers amassed in a ring below, silver and primrose and mauve and lemon and daffodil yellow and snow, pale vivid pointed flamelets flickering on snow, swaying like catenas of myriads of fire-flies in the cavernous gloom. He watched the mystic circle of seven crimson canons moving round and round aloft in the pulpit, nimbused with glory, when the greatest there, stripped of his glory, simple in rochet and stole, emerging alone from the ring, to the sound of the wonderful long-drawn song, took the greatest relic of all, holding it high above the starry blaze below, and blessed the world with The Sign. He felt the lilt and the lift of soul-ascension, then, from the world of brown gloom—felt his soul gently soaring away, from heaving crowd, clustered flames, long-drawn wonderful song, splendour of crimson and primrose and silver and gold and snow—through the high golden haze splashed with golden slabs of light among the mosaics of the domes, beyond—beyond all these, up to a realm of darkness, empty, imperscutable, where he waited, waited to soar higher, or to see his way to soar. There he stayed, stayed, in a place of no joy and no pain, a place of nothingness, just out of reach of trouble, not in sight of bliss. There, with effort, he held himself, till he should have word to come up higher. On Holy Saturday, at the first Mass of Easter, again his form stood in the crowd beneath the golden domes, acutely sensible, while his soul aloft waited dryly in a dark void. Came the liturgical moment when grief is banished by joy. The deacon intoned the first Alleluias of Easter. The Easter-candle flamed. Lanthorns and lamps and tapers and torches on all sides blossomed with light. Violet veils fell from images and pictures. Violet vestments were changed for tissues of silver and gold. Violet curtains swept aside, disclosing golden altar and pala d'oro blazing with enamels and precious stones. And all the bells and organs in basilica and city rang and sounded at the chaunt of the Gloria Angelical. Now, if ever, his soul would be summoned ad audiendum verbum, would have leave to rise with its Lord in newness of perfect joy. But, under his eyes, in the crowd, just within reach of his fist, a self-unpriested oratorian—Scotch, of course—smartly and fashionably dressed as a layman by Bond Street and Savile Row, giggled, decorously flirting with an aged Erastian gossip nodding, nodding in a flower-bed of a hat. And down came Crabbe's soul, crashing, Ikaros-like, on the crags of this world of ugly horror and gloom. 'Nor knowest thou what argument Thy life to thy neighbour's creed hath lent.' The only consolation which he got was from his ruthless immitigable faith, his defiant unconquerable trust. Etiam si occiderit me, in Ipso sperabo: ueruntamen uias meas in Conspectu Eius arguam, expressed his mind. He spent his Easter in picking up the little pieces of his soul and putting them miserably but undauntedly together. 'God, Who, to enlighten the darkness of the world, didst deign to mount upon the holy cross, grant that, in my darkness, I may see Thy light, and, by it, mount upon whatever cross Thou deignst to me, and, having mounted, rise from it triumphantly to Thee, Who, with The Father and The Spirit, livest and reignest, ever, one God: Amen.' Thus, he prayed, or tried to pray, among the fierce bitter moanings of his soul. But he saw no light, tasted no Easter joy.

Zildo, clean, fed with Bread of angels, radiant in happiness un-alloyed, met him after Mass on Easter day. 'Sior,' he said, 'I augur for you a good Easter.'

'And I for you.'

'Sior, you are not quite content. Tell me why. For, with permission, that does me harm.'

'You wouldn't understand.'

'Sior, with excuses and the greatest possible respect to your blessed and valorous face, I should understand everything perfectly.'

'I am content with you. What more do you want? Che cossa vuol de più de Domeniddio?'

'Va ben. Sior, you are master: I am servant. I say no more now. But the pupparin is polished and ready, with the two banners of England and the Vexillo of the Bucintoro in honour of the festival.'

On flood-tide, the bark glided along the canal of Zuecca without effort. All the ships anchored in the Basin of Saint Mark, and the Istrian firewood trabaccoli at the Zattere, with the coal-tramps and cotton-ships and grain-ships, were bright with bunting as Nicholas went by, sitting in his cane arm-chair to read a neglected letter of Holy Week. Caliban wrote: "I sent a copy of your last to Bobugo; and he commissions me to confer upon you his New Year's Benediction: which I now do by these presents. I hope this will solve your religious difficulty. As for what is to happen, I am at a loss. Why don't you get a job of some kind? I can't make anything of Morlaix and Sartor, though I have had letters from and four interviews with them of which you know nothing. They don't seem to want to treat with me. Bobugo says that you haven't been hammered enough yet by Olympos, and hammered you will be till you give in. I've applied to *The Lykeion*: your story appeared in the issue of Jan. 23rd; and they'll send me your cheque at the end of the month. You know you really are most unjust about Wallace. Although he is a Quaker, he's incapable of rooting and snouting in any lovely catholic garden. He has only made certain suggestions, which I think it wise to adopt. Don't you understand that Wallace is a successful novelist, whose novels sell ten thousand to a thousand of yours? Surely you ought to be glad of his help, wanting money as we do. We have decided that generals of the Order and their provinces are to be called priors and priories in future, like the Templars. And We have done the Latin office for Our incoronation next June Ourself as you don't seem willing to oblige Us. Do try to get a job. I.T.SS.S."

A job? Yes. Why not make a job, a picric job, a violently dynamic job, for example? Crabbe wrote: "Kindly convey this message from me to your blessed Bobugo—Received, through a Freemason, one New Year's Benediction, three months and more after date, and too late, and not regarded as valid.—Kindly answer the following questions: 1. As *Terribile la Femmina* was printed in *The Lykeion* in Jan., the cheque was due at end of Jan.: Why have you not got it for me in Apr., with author's copies of that journal and an explanation of its surreptitious publication of my story? 2. Why don't you tell me what you've been doing with *The Weird* these nine months? 3. What have you done with *Sieur René*; and where is the remittance promised (as you alleged) by Morlaix and Sartor on condition of my sending you its proofs? 4. What are you going to do about Morlaix and Sartor, and about Bobugo, after keeping me from writing to them during four months while you have been embroiling me further with them? 5. What of your oath that no harm should touch me in my honour or my person or my property? 6. Mark this well: I refuse any of Wallace's intervention in *De Burgh's Delusion*; and I want to know what you're going to do about it? 7. Will you let me see the proper Form of Defiance, to be used by a knight of the Order wishing (on account of treachery) to withdraw his faith pledged to the Lieutenant of the Grandmagistracy of the Order? 8. Are you my friend, or my enemy? Illuminet te Sanctissima Sapientia."

In the days ensuing, Crabbe nourished himself in patience, hardening his carapax, closing the joints of his mail for defence, sharpening his awful pincers, for dreadfully offensive operations on a large scale.

Caliban wrote: "Strictly private. As you seem to wish to leave the Order, We hereby return you your faith and release you from all oaths and obligations: but, in view of your past most eminent services, We, in Our Own name and in the name of the curial council and indeed of the whole Order, hereby stablish your right to resume your rank and precedence in the said Order when it shall seem good to you so to do. Please burn Rule and return your Badge, as (in case you are in danger of publicity) it will be well to have removed all traces of your connection with the Order beforehand. Of course I am your friend though you do seem to think me your enemy. Don't be a fool. I have been again to *The Lykeion*, and they say that the manager who is absent will go into the question of remuneration on his return at the end of next week. I can't make out why Morlaix and Sartor haven't sent you what I swear they promised on receipt of *Sieur René*. You'd better write to them yourself. They are not quite so evil as you think— they repeated to me that they won't touch the profits of *Sieur René*, which should go to your credit entirely. About *The Weird* and *De Burgh's Delusion*, if you won't be mixed up with Wallace's revisions, I'll get both books published at once, either under my own name alone or 'by C. H. C. Peary-Buthlaw and Another,' of course sending you your half of the profits, but you must assign me the right of altering titles and contents of both books in any way I consider desirable at my own discretion. I enclose duplicate bonds to this effect. You will see that I have signed them with father as my witness. All you have to do is to sign them, getting someone to witness your signature, and send me one copy while you keep the other. I really have done my best to help you though I suppose you won't believe it. Here is a coupon which you can change at the post-office for a stamp worth twopence-halfpenny, as I am most anxious to have your Badge and acknowledgments of what I say about the Order. I.T.SS.S."

Crabbe wrote: "The headlong eager precipitancy with which Your Splendour has been pleased to abuse my request for the Form of Defiance shews me that my dismissal from the Order (at a time when I am in trouble through Your grievous fault) is precisely what is most greedily desired. But I will not submit to the secret dismissal, which Y.S. so timorously has sent me, with twopence-halfpenny: such hole-and-corner work being contrary to the spirit of chivalry. Therefore, I myself (in accordance with apostolic precept, which directs that all things should be done decently and in order) do here renounce my allegiance to Y.S., and defy You, for the reasons following: First, because Y.S. secretly entered into alliance with two externs, Bonsen and Macpawkins, both my declared enemies, and the former notoriously guilty of treachery against me, submitting Y.S. to their conditions in my despite, which conditions were dishonouring to me, Your faithful knight: Second, because I utterly abhor from Y.S.'s interpretation of the law of chivalry regarding the treatment due to a knight fallen on evil times. Further, I reject the secret encomiums sent by Y.S. (in the name of the curial council and indeed of the whole Order) in Your secret breve, seeing that the said encomiums are not counter-signed by the chancellor or by any curial officer or by any knight. Furthermore, I refuse and spit upon Y.S.'s secret stablishment of my right to resume my rank and precedence in the Order, seeing that (in the words of the Sage) 'It is not I who have lost the Athenians, but it is the Athenians who have lost me.' And my rentrance into the Order forms the subject of a question which could only be discussed when the Order and Y.S. very humbly have made amends for the treachery and injustice with which You have afflicted me. And I will not burn the Rule of the Order, but will hold it (with my other documents) at the disposition of the Quæstor of Venice in case of necessity. And I cannot return my Badge, which is (with

many of my other valuables) at the Mount of Piety of Venice.
And regarding other evidences of my connection with the Order,
I refuse to incur any further suffering by destroying them so that
the imbecility and infidelity and cowardice of Your Splendour
might (if possible) be concealed. And I denounce Y.S. as a craven
braggart and perjured traitor, false to your oath of defending my
honour and my person and my property. This is the Defiance of
me, Nicholas, Knight-Founder and Knight-Magnate and sometime
Provost of the Order of Sanctissima Sophia, hurled at the face of
Harricus, Lieutenant of the Grandmagistracy of the same Order,
and written with my own hand in the Sexter of Saint Mark at
Venice, and sealed with my own seal of Herakles and the Hydra
in the octave of The Lord's Resurrection, m c m viiii.—My dear
Enemy: no friend could behave as you (and your people) behave,
in spasms, in sulky silence, always and exactly contrary to my expressed will. So I say, My dear Enemy: please do nothing further
with *The Lykeion*. You only complicate a very simple matter.
I myself have written to the editor. I will not consent to the revision
of my *De Burgh's Delusion* on the lines of your Quaker, or to the
alteration of a single word, at least till after my manuscript has
been submitted to and rejected by Shortmans, Ferrer, Macmartin,
Albemarle, Dr Wright, and perhaps some others. As for your
beastly bonds, I have no intention of helping you (and your father)
to commit villainy in your rages. So I refuse to sign the enclosed:
the other copy, bearing your and your father's signatures, I shall
keep. Please understand that I decline to be the 'Ghost' of a Fool,
as you and your father have tried to make me. I'm shocked at
you both. You ought to be ashamed of yourselves. I hope this is
plain. The notion of your intermittent playing with the magnum
opus of a man in peril is more than I can stand. It is positively
awful to see you treating my pearl as animals with a preference
for acorns generally treat such gems. How (in Heaven's Name)
does your Quaker make a successful book? By writing a book
different from anybody else's book? And do you, Caliban, think
that you, tyro, can make a successful book by assimilating my already-
unique book to Wallace's books? Tush! Your only sensible and
practical and honourable course—if you lied to me in Jan., when
you said that Shortmans had promised to take *The Weird* and
De Burgh's Delusion on sight—is to send my manuscripts of both
books round the publishers, beginning with my own publishers,
until they are accepted, and (meanwhile) not to cease for an instant
from collaborating further works either to follow them or to replace

them—that is, if Life and Death and Honour and Truth and Justice mean anything to you. Apparently they don't. So I say, My dear Enemy: please do nothing further about *Sieur René*. It was bad enough to get the proofs from me on the false pretence that my retention of them was the only thing which prevented my agents from paying my usual income. And, even now, you won't tell me what you have done with my proofs. For Goodness' Sake, if you're going to belie your sovereign oath, if you won't straighten or help me to straighten my affairs, do have the decency at least not to muck them any more. For four months you have capered goatishly, entirely disregarding me. You will neither get my dues for me, nor let me get them for myself. O Friend! Please leave me alone. And don't blame me if I disown your shatterpated muddleheaded fatwitted anile inept bœotian actions now. O Enemy."

Three thunderclaps followed these fulgurations. One, to Lord Arthur Baliol Kingsbury, stated that Crabbe had no representative in England; and asked for the four-months' overdue fee for *Terribile la Femmina*. Another, to Morlaix and Sartor, repudiated Caliban; and requested them to resume direct communication with their principal. And a third went to the publisher of *Sieur René* forbidding the issue of that work before its author had seen (and passed) not only proofs of text but also proofs of illustrations and binding.

The fact is that Crabbe was very much amazed indeed at being so studiously kept in ignorance of the whereabouts of *Sieur René*. The whole of Caliban's behaviour, however, was so staggering that Crabbe (on reviewing it) debated with himself whether to use his old magic arts, or the simple sortes, for obtaining hints on the appropriate method of dealing with it. He was always a great one for concentrating every possible sidelight with the central illumination of knowledge and instinct on problems which bothered him. He got out his *Tempest* and tried, as a beginning, the sortes. And he went no further. The book opened and the blind finger indicated instantly this astounding passage:

> "*Caliban (loq.)* . . . Remember
> First to possess his books, for without them
> He's but a sot as I am."

It chimed in so accurately with the instinct which was leading him to suspect that Caliban (nerved by the example of Bobugo's persistent efforts to acquire a book for a benediction) was trying similar cantrips with the three entrusted to him, and even apeing Bobugo's appetite for witnessed bonds, that Crabbe saw that he would have to make up his mind to face another disgusting disillusionment.   The sovereign of the Order of Sanctissima Sophia was a false scoundrel.   Crabbe thought that enough had been done for the protection of *Sieur René* for the moment.   He had a half-matured plan at the back of his brain for guarding his rights in *The Weird* and *De Burgh's Delusion*: but a state of penurious uncertainty as to the attitude of his agents after Caliban's capering among them forced him to move deliberately, without weakness, and without undue precipitancy.   This does not mean that he was meek and mild; on the contrary, it signified the steady stoking of the fiery furnace of devouring and dangerous and utterly ruthless anger.

Fierce the ordeal of the One who fares forth to fight with the Many: how should he ride, and array, who is Half and not One?

WHILE collecting ideas as to the grounds of future action, Crabbe passed his time at the infirmary, comforting a convalescent, a handsome intelligent uncultivated Lancashire lad of twenty-five who, bursting provincial shackles, had come abroad to see as much of Venice and Milan and Florence as fifty hard-earned sterlings and a month of time would shew him. But measles floored Anthony Garnett at the very beginning of his tour; and he passed (in the *Blue Cross* bark) from a Venetian hotel to the infirmary on Spinalonga. Crabbe had to allay in him the awful disappointment of wasted time and money. His holiday was so short: expense of illness prevented long-looked-for pleasures. Unable to do what heart desired—to help the lad to health and then to keep him, as a guest, while he bathed in the beauty of Venice enjoying a holiday after all—Crabbe did what he could. As long as contagion lasted, he sat in the garden daily for hours, chatting with Garnett at the window. It was brilliant spring weather, and warm. When the patient was let out, he was with him, unreservedly displaying the stores of mind and memory, so that the visit to Venice (though enclosed) should mark the provincial personality. He rather liked his disciple's character. Garnett had taken his balk not unphilosophically. His hopes of seeing the opal city set in the sapphire lagoon being blighted, he made the best of the substitute provided— the would-be-friendly soul brimming with amusing instruction, the very distinct individuality laying itself out to serve and entertain. His own education was ordinary, his breeding provincially constructed: but he had (with singular personal formosity) an extraordinary faculty of appreciation and an enchanting sense of obligation. Thus Crabbe contrived (in the stress of his own embarrassments) to benefit the fussy bibbling superficial directress by relieving her of her charge, the lad of Lancashire by opening to him new vistas, and himself by sinking himself in operation for others.

The Warden set out (one night in the hall) to offer pretty thankful speeches for the careful and painstaking revision of his proofs; and asked leave to repeat the same publicly in the preface of *Social Life among the Early Christians*. Crabbe replied that he would like it immensely: advertisement of that kind is not beneath a writer's dignity.

'But we'd like to do more, if you'd only let us—wouldn't we, Exeter. You know we're all simply worrying ourselves to death about you,' La Warden abruptly put in.

'Take my tip, and don't,' Crabbe airily answered.

'No—but really—you seem to think we're stocks, or stones——'

'On the contrary, I believe you to be people who have gone some distance out of your way to be nice to a man who doesn't like you and who doesn't matter to you in the least. And that's why I don't take you further. You might get tired—and then I should have the bother of carrying you.'

'Now do you think that quite kind to us?'

'I do. It's the very kindest way I know of treating you.'

'Well, we totally disagree with you—don't we, Exeter. Day after day we see you getting more haggard and more wretched; and here are we, under the deepest obligations to you, anxious to help you—and able—and you keep us at arms' length, and call it friendship. Well, we don't.'

The Warden couldn't prevent himself from oozing in, making a pass with the canoodling bone of a finger. 'May I suggest a thought? Thank you so much. Dear person, hasn't it ever struck you that you waste precious time and talent and energy in fighting a lonely battle? Don't you know that you would be ever so much more useful to all of us if you'd let us give you a hand just now. "Two are better than one," says the Preacher. Then won't you let me put you in relations with our dear Mr Sappytower? You've no idea how clever he is—how discreet—oh, do say yes.'

Crabbe abruptly collapsed. (I don't excuse him: I only ask you to remember, o most affable reader, that he was somewhat harassed.) 'Very well,' he said, 'do as you please: put me in relations with your Sappytower: it won't be a bit of good, all the same. You'll pardon my roughness and ungraciousness, please: for the fact is I detest this letting you have your way. You know I really am ruined for the present. And I've been pawning some odds and ends at the Monte di Pieta for stamps. The man whom I trusted in England has played the common fool. And I've got three enemies to fight there now, instead of two—I mean that Peary-Buthlaw man as well as Bonsen and my agents. I'd much prefer to sit tight, and tire the beasts out. I could, you know: because they can't make a penny out of my property without my consent. But I haven't the means to sit tight. I'm sure Sappytower can't do anything

with a case like this. I don't believe that anybody can. But—
if you know better——'

'Oh thank you so much. I'll see him the very first thing in the
morning. And I do assure you that all will be arranged within a
week. I can't tell you how much we admire you for giving way.
You're doing us the greatest possible service, if you only knew it.'

The Wardens' burblings might have been couched in Chaldaic,
for all that Crabbe understood of their inwardness at this time.
He hadn't the faintest idea of the motive—(nor have you, o most
affable reader, notwithstanding your well-known perspicacity)—
and worry and suspense had pulled him down to the stage of sick-
hearted indifference in which he could not be bothered with seeking
it. Nor did he permit these positive and explicit assurances to make
him sanguine. The fact must stand clear, that he was so very much
mixed up in the thick of a most beastly imbroglione, that he could
not view affairs in a perspective sufficiently just to teach him, precisely,
at that moment, how to treat them. Hence his fabian policy of
sitting tight. His concession to the importunate Warden—the only
act of his life, save one, of which he was at all ashamed—was purely
impulsive. Inspired and saturated, as he was, with active disgust or
passive contempt of all men and priests (including of course Scotchmen and Germans)—both contempt and disgust being temperament-
ally developed to boiling-point—he didn't even take the trouble to
believe that another man could (much less would) understand his
position, or find a method of improving it. And he gave way to the
Wardens' insistence, callously, inertly, hopelessly—more for the sake
of amusing them by giving them some of his toys to play with, than in
any sort of belief that they, or Rothschild's financier, could be saviours.

He went into the office to have a word with his landlord—a duty
which seemed no longer negligible. 'I'm sorry to tell you,' he said,
'that my news from England is worse than ever. That Mr Peary-
Buthlaw, whose assurances you've seen, has been playing the traitor.
He has done nothing with my agents, or with the manuscripts
entrusted to him to sell. So what has to be done, is for me to do,
myself.'

Barbolan naturally looked glum, and inclined to snarl. 'But,
Signore, I have trusted you for five months—I want my money.'
Crabbe shot out two bald glaring eyes at him.

'If you have ceased from trusting me, I am quite willing to explain
my circumstances to the Questura.'

'But you would not like to go to prison?'

'Like? It's not a question of what I like. But I confess to you that I should like anything better than the present state of things.'

'Surely, sir, some of your other friends——'

'I have none.'

'But this Signor Warden, whose book you have——'

'I did that, gratuitously, as a friend.'

'But wouldn't he——'

'No. But perhaps I ought to tell you this—he is going to speak to a friend of his, who (he says) '—A grin split Barbolan's genial head in half, from ear to ear. Crabbe continued: 'I don't believe that anything will come of it. I'm quite competent to manage my own affairs; and I only want time, and means to move.'

'Signor, you are too pessimistic. The most excellent Signor Warden has strong friends. I know it.'

'I don't: so I say that I hope for nothing. Of course, if you feel that you still trust me—I'm not persuading you: I'm simply saying that, if you still feel inclined to trust me, I can guarantee your payment sooner or later, Let me try to make you understand. These people in England——'

'Thieves, all thieves, Signore, as I warned you long ago!'

'——hold certain property of mine, out of which money can be made. But they can't make it by themselves or without me. They can steal my manuscripts: but they can't publish them or sell them without my consent.'

'How can you prevent——'

'By describing the manuscripts and denouncing them to the Publishers Association as stolen. No publisher would dare to publish and pay for a book known to be stolen.'

'"But, so, you prevent yourself——'

'Perhaps: but I should also prevent the thieves. Rather than let them benefit by stolen property, I'll ruin the property. No one can, or shall profit by my work, excepting through me, and only through me when I've secured my own due share—out of which I shall pay your bill.'

'I understand. And I wish to see what the friend of Signor Warden will do.'

'He will do nothing. However, do you continue to trust me?'

'But yes, Signore.'

'Continue long enough, and you will not regret it.'

Crabbe crawled, by request, across the Piazza and down Ventidue Marzo, to call on Sappytower at the Grand Hotel.

Rothschild's financier was gaunt, bony, and extremely dressed. He had the vacancies and dusty dryness of canute old age (he at once proclaimed his age as seventy-seven) but he was jerkily active, though rheumy-eyed with monocle and tinted nose; and he foamed at the mouth occasionally, champing a thin old vandyked beard. They sat together on a sunny balcony overlooking Canalazzo, with curious waiters listening through the open windows of the dining-room behind them. Conversation, therefore, was entirely on one side, and mainly testimonial and reminiscent. The Sappytower said 'clup-a-clup', and burst into a vivacious description of his penchant for copying madonnas at the Academy by the aid of full-sized photographs, an original system of squares, and a natural sense of colour-key. Without pausing, he went on to furnish the story of his life, his early perfection in the French tongue, his daily attendance (with intimate correspondence) in old Baron Rothschild's bedroom, his adventures in that sanctum, his exploits in making coups to mar (or make) nations and men. He was excessively particular and clup-a-cluppy.

Crabbe, alertly still, conceived that a phonograph and a stenographer might (in his circumstances) produce an unusually scandalous but printable volume of memoirs: but there were no straws floating in that verbal cataract which he himself cared to catch-hold-of—it was mere senile didacity. He did realise, however, the prudence of potentates who poison their confidants upon retirement instead of pensioning them.

Sappytower dashed from Paris to the East, jibbering tales (full of monstrous great names) which told how he deceived this one (and that) by buying brokers to bull (or bear), how he deceived that one (and this) by sheer bluff (and inconceivable grimaces), categorizing the sum scooped on each event for firm and self. He gave himself, his acumen, his audacity, his invariable success, testimonials tremendous in tenour, all punctuated by the clup-a-clup of withered tongue on arid palate and the periodic sucking of gums. It was quite a performance. Crabbe sat, monumental, vigilant, waiting for his cue: for he fancied that this multiloquent jibble-jabble was but a chiefly-high-financial and partly-individual overture or curtain-raiser, and that the melodrama would presently begin. And, after one hour and forty-two minutes, the Sappytower suddenly said faintly that he had derived much pleasure from the conversation, and hoped that his visitor would soon come and see him again.

The Wardens, to whom Crabbe imparted his amazement after dinner, sniggered and were vastly tickled: nothing (they giggled) could be nicer. He had evidently made an excellent impression.

Rothschild's financier always was a little voluble. And, weren't his reminiscences interesting?

Crabbe hummed: but Vincenzo, the chef of the Bellavista, had fed him with the most masterly gnocchi, beef and potatoes—a far more succulent beef than the flesh of Aberdeen Angus, peas in savoury gravy, and apricot ices, that night; and he was not in a mood to tear and rend anyone. 'But, where do I come in?' he inquired.

'Oh, you must go and see him again.'

'If he invites me—but, not unless. I fancy that he talked on a trot, just to keep me from talking.'

'Oooh, no!'

'But he gave me no chance—didn't even cast a question.'

'I think, if you'll allow me—thank you so much—that I'd better see our dear friend in the morning.'

So the Warden brought, to luncheon next day, a note from his Sappytower asking Crabbe to tea that very afternoon, and the news that the chatty old darling had expected him to state his difficulties and his needs on entrance.

'He must ask me straight,' Crabbe affirmed.

'I ventured to tell him that I thought that would be better:' purred the other.

Tea was served in the financier's bed-sitting-room, muffins on chairs, cakes commodiously posited, and the tea-equipage cornered on the bureau, the rest of the room being littered with painting materials, an oily smell, and an unfinished amateurish copy of Palma Vecchio's Holy Conversation straddling on an inadequate easel. Sappytower crackled with retrospections, as before, till half-way through the repast, when (suddenly) he jumped upon Crabbe's point with a clup-a-clup-clup-clup of distinct tone-value. The Wardens, he said, had hinted things; and he found them totally devoid of difficulty. There was property—what property? There were malfeasant agents —why not sack 'em? He said clup-a-clup-clup very loud indeed; and passed for a reply.

Crabbe spat it out in an instant—property as follows: four published books, sold outright to publishers who ought to be persuaded to push sales and to make customary "presents" on extra editions to author: item, two published books, whose royalties ought to be collected and accounted-for: item, one book printed and ready for issue: item, one accepted for publication: item, four books and a great Sforza Genealogy ready for negotiation—thirteen works in all, besides a mass of short stories and essays ready for magazines. Also, there were four half-finished books stored in England. And he didn't sack his agents, because he had no new ones (nor means of finding new ones) to supplant them.

What allowance had his wicked agents made him? He didn't know—perhaps six hundred sterling. Then it was as simple as criss-cross-row. Heaps of highly competent people would gladly take over obligations and assets and make the latter pay properly, for the usual commission. A financial partner, in short, was wanted, who knew that business is the art of making valuable what isn't. Such partners were to be found fifty times a day, and for all businesses. It should be quite easy to find one for the literary business simply by writing to some book-man—Quaritch, for instance. And the magician of money scribbled a draft of a letter to Quaritch—introduced by Mr Sappytower (late of Rothschild's) he was a literary man (see *Year Book*) desiring a financial partner; and would Mr Q. kindly furnish the necessary person. 'My dear young friend, clup, to us old financiers, clup-a, who manipulate millions without ever seeing them, clup-a-clup, the way in which you non-financial people disturb yourselves about a paltry thousand or so is most amusing, clup-a-clup-clup!'

' "Your play is our death," ' said the Frog to the Stone-thrower.'

'Clup-a-clup smart of you! But, believe me, take my word, clup-a, you've no cause for disturbance—my introduction to Quaritch will, clup-a-clup. And, if, by chance, he shouldn't have your man in his pocket at the moment, I'll put you on to someone who has, clup. Make your mind easy. Your affair is now my affair, clup-a-clup clup-clup.'

Feeling a great deal happier, Crabbe thanked the Wardens quite decently that night. But he didn't believe that the thing could be done in a week.

'Ah!' they breathed, with nodded meanings, 'now that dear Mr Sappytower—others——'

'What others? And, others what?' (like a hammer).

They were not at liberty to say: but they giggled and gouged at each other like the serest and very boniest of parrakeets. Anyhow, Crabbe admitted that Sappytower had bucked him up a bit: he was deeply grateful; and hoped soon to be able to testify tangibly. They were so sure of that. And he realized that they might safely be tipped. Lord! Well: a Steinway grand, ready in their English country cottage would do.

He gave his news to Barbolan, who chirped—all, he was certain, was going well; and, meanwhile, as he personally happened to be very much pressed, could he be obliged and greatly accommodated, as follows? The account due was (say) L.2000. If Signor Crabbe would most genteely sign a bill for L.3500, a mere hundred-and-forty sterling, on which the Co-operative Bank would lend money immediately, he would keep Signor Crabbe in his hotel, as he was, all included, free of any extra charge, till the end of the year when the bill would be presented for payment. It sounded like a fair offer. Crabbe always had suspected that he had paid through his nose in the previous summer and autumn. Eighty sterling for November and from January to April was, however, not an extravagant hotel-bill. And another eight months were offered for sixty sterling more. To have the rest of the year secured to him (as he had secured it for Zildo), while he brought the chaos of his affairs to order, would be a very politic move: for he was convinced that it would take months of work to undo Caliban's silly foolery. So he cheerfully signed Barbolan's bill, and got an agreement in writing; and settled calmly and hopefully down to plan his new campaign—or (rather) to scratch together considerations for submission to his Sappytower's Quaritch's financial partner.

That night, athletic little Peter wakened him from his first sleep with news that a Signor Inglese waited to see him below. He pitched on some clothes, and came downstairs, half-awake, noticing that the hall clock recorded ten minutes to midnight. In the smoking-room, Sappytower and Barbolan smiled upon him.

'It occurred to me,' jibbered Rothschild's financier in English, 'that a word of mine might save you from having trouble with your excellent landlord, clup.' He spoke more quickly and more thickly than in the afternoon.

Barbolan, trying not to be alarmed, looked from one to the other.

The midnight Angelus sounded four sets of twenty-two strokes each, rung on the wonderful bell of Sansalvador (lent till Sammarco hangs in the rebuilt Campanile) which gives the triple sound of E♭ C♭ B♭ at each stroke, uniquely Venetian.

'Perhaps we'd better speak clup-a-clup French, and then this good man will understand us,' jabbered Sappytower.

Crabbe agreed. He was much obliged, but he and his landlord had concluded an arrangement satisfactory to both, that very evening. The financier would like to hear its terms. Barbolan put the bill, and the agreement, into his hands. He read them aloud, and made them the text of a sermon delivered in Berlitz-French atrociously

mangled and gabbled. Crabbe and his landlord reared, simultaneously, endeavouring to follow. Words, and clup-a-clups, and
gallic gestures of the caricaturists, pattered like rain on a corrugated
roof and waved and shrugged in a growing odour of rum. From
half-awake, Crabbe went to wide-awake, and (thence) through
consternation and indignation to indifference and (finally) to somnolence. Plump Barbolan sat, stiffly staring, marvelling much at
English eccentricity. Neither of them caught the drift of the discourse, nor grasped the meaning of more than one noun or verb
in nine. They gathered, however, a dim idea of being favoured
with a slightly intempestive dissertation on the economics of a paper
currency with excursions into bimetallism. It was very dull; and
they dozed drowsily, respectfully expecting an end. It came.
Sappytower, apropos to nothing, tore bill and agreement into
fragments, and tossed them aloft over the table, emitting a clup-a-
clup-a-clup-clup of unparalleled sonority and beaming with a senile
smile which anticipated applause for his trick. The other two
shrieked, dashing to save the papers: but the deed was done.

'Don't be alarmed,' said Sappytower in English, 'leave everything
to me, clup. You mustn't sign any clup-a; and he oughtn't to
have asked you, clup-a-clup.'

'But you've frightened him——'

'Leave him to me, I say, clup.' And the orator declined and fell
into French, addressing a special oration to Mossiow Parrookyarow,
as gesticulatory and as clattering and as unintelligible as before.

The landlord interrupted after a while. 'I was quite satisfied with
Signor Crabbe's signature,' he suddenly said.

'But you mustn't be. Mossiow Crabbe ought not to sign agreements or bills,' retorted Rothschild's confidential agent.

'If you mean that Signor Crabbe is not likely to be able to meet
his obligations——'

'That's what I thought. You've shattered his confidence,' snapped
Crabbe.

'Calm yourselves, both of you, I beg you; and be tranquil, clup,
while I explain the prescribed financial measures for dealing with
this kind of clup-a question, clup-a-clup. My dear Crabbe, go
to bed. I may be some time yet, clup; and I see you're clup-
clup tired. Go, then, to bed, dear clup; and trust me to put matters
on a satisfactory footing with this most excellent fellow, clup.
You're safe in my clup-a hands, clup-a-clup, I assure you; and, as
for me, clup-a-clup-clup, I'm enjoying myself—oh—clup-a-clup-a-
clup-a-clup-clup—finely.'

Crabbe retired, making up his mind to confront something or other in the morning; and put himself to sleep heavily, in preparation. Just before his objective mind left off working, he had a mental image of Zildo's grave severe young face opposing the rummy rhapsodies of Sappytower. How dreadful old age was—of that canute type. And, how lovely was youth! He slept like a child.

White-skinned Arthur brought his coffee, when he came from Mass. An ambushed grin lurked near the waiter's mouth-corners.

'Well?' said Crabbe.

'O sir! The inebriated gentleman who came to see you last night——'

'What about him?'

'He preached so long, sir, that Mr Barbolan went to bed and left him; and Little Peter and Parisotto took him home, at 2½ o'clock, preaching imbriagally all the way, so that a vizile followed them. But they found him mild, sir, though quacking incessantly; and he regaled them with a billet of ten for their gentility.'

Crabbe snorted; and drank his coffee; and read the *Gazzettino* in the hall, till Barbolan appeared and went into his office.

'What happened?' Crabbe asked, leaning over the half-door.

'I don't know nothing about nothing' (snarling openly). 'Your friend is mad, or drunk, or both: but I see that he doesn't trust you. Nor do I, now——'

Crabbe reared, in his hugest huff, baldly grim, forceps well to the front. 'Continue. But, be careful.'

'Pay my bill before noon, or leave my hotel before sunset.'

'Listen. I wish to say this. You know that I have no money, or I would have paid your bill long ago. I shall leave your hotel this afternoon. As my pockets are empty, I shall live in my bark, till I am able to go on working for money to pay you.'

'If Signor Sappytower hadn't torn up that agreement——'

'Good morning.'

He took his portfolio of papers; and sidled down to the Bucintoro, thinking hard. It was essential to keep the very stiffest of all stiff upper lips. And one place of rest for the sole of his foot—ah, that impulsive remark to the landlord was surely a god-given idea, an inspiration—he would certainly live in the pupparin. But, if Parrucchiero should sequester—let him—let anything and everything disagreeable be done. Somebody would have to suffer for it. One would put up with it as punishment for unpunished sins. One did not, though, crave for publicity—one detested it—but, publicity which would expose the miscreances of Morlaix and Sartor, of Bobugo, of Caliban, causers of this impasse, might not be so very undesirable. Still, if possible, one would avoid publicity. But no one should sequester the pupparin. No. He sat down and made a deed of gift of it, with its apparatus all complete, to the Bucintoro Club for the benefit of the timonieri. Younger brothers of members, who are admitted as coxswains of eights and fours, have few diversions in Venice; and a bark to play with is practically their only pastime. The secretary Vivien and a vice-president, who happened to be there planning extensions of the garage, accepted the donation with effusion. Crabbe stipulated that he would like to use the pupparin occasionally. They gushed that it was as his own, always at his command. But he might want to use it for days and nights together. Every effective member of the club, they affirmed, had right to reserve such bark or barks as he pleased for personal use; first comers were first served: if Signor Crabbe reserved the pupparin, it was his for days and nights, weeks, months, years, in a gorgeous crescendo. Va benone; and so many thanks.

This machiavellian ruse delighted him. The weather was warm: summer was coming in: and, after all, something was certain to happen in a week or two. Anyhow, there was the fee to expect from *The Lykeion*. Zildo need not be worried. Days could be passed as usual. One could doze at the empty club all the morning, work for the infirmary all the afternoon, and (when the boy had gone home in the evening) one could lounge about in the pupparin snatching cat-naps now and then till daybreak. Eccentric English excite no astonishment in Venice. And Crabbe got on admirably with the Venetians, being the pal of carabinieri and of all but four gondolieri.

At luncheon, he electrified the Wardens. The more thin-lipped and angrily-frightened they became, so much the more did he mock and gibe, telling the tale of Sappytower's midnight capers and clup-a-clups as though it was purely humorous. Both his hearers writhed in discomfiture. Liability to blame made them angry. Ignorance of purport frightened them. Their lips set in hard tight faint mauve lines. Crabbe didn't feel moved to blame them, though: their attitude was so pitiable that he was rather sorry for them than otherwise.

The Warden pulled himself together. 'But what are you going to do?'

'Pawn something for grub, and live in the pupparin. I must keep my head above water as long as I can—till I hear from Quaritch anyhow. And *The Lykeion* owes me some money, which may come any day; and then I can do something decent.'

'I can't make out what our dear friend Sappytower meant.'

'Nor can I.'

'May I—would you allow me to go and see him?'

'Better not. Most likely he's forgotten about last night; and people don't like reminders of their tipsy antics. Leave him alone. When I get Quaritch's letter, I'll approach him myself.'

'I'm so sure that his intentions are the best.'

'We'll give him credit for them. He begged and prayed and commanded me to leave everything to him; and I'm going to do so.'

The sky had been darkening with one of the seasonable spring squalls; and a sudden cloud-burst drenched the city, and set all the scores of gargoyles of Saint Mark's and the Procurate roaring with the pain of pouring rain.

'How can you possibly sleep in an open bark, in weather like this?' cried the Wardeness. 'Do try to think of something, Exeter!'

'Dearest, do you know, such a beautiful thought has just occurred to me.' He turned to Crabbe. 'Dear person, may I make a suggestion? Thank you so much. You know we leave here ourselves tomorrow, to stay with dear Mrs Coxon at Palazzo Selvatico while we get our sticks packed for England. Would you accept a situation as our caretaker and sleep in our empty palace? We couldn't promise you luxury: but at least you'll have a roof over your head.'

'I accept with pleasure.'

'So good of you. And when do you leave this?'

'Now. I'm only just going upstairs to pack and lock my things. I shall take a kit-bag with me.'

'Do come round, then, about 16 o'clock—Palazzo Corfù, you know, by the Academy. I'll be there, and give you the key of our castle—it's my joke to call it a castle because it's so high, you know.'

Crabbe filled a kit-bag with a couple of flannel-suits, guernseys, handkerchiefs, slippers, razors, sponge, soap, tooth-brush, and writing-materials: his silver crop required no comb or brush. This, and a burberry, he carried to the club, sailing openly out of the hotel in silence. Beside these goods, he had the blue serge suit which he was wearing; and his club-locker contained two boat-cloaks, two pigskin satchels, towels, shorts, zephyrs, and other odds and ends. At 15½ o'clock, he put kit-bag and cloaks into the pupparin. It was raining torrentially, and seemed likely to continue.

'I go to live at Palazzo Corfù, for a time,' he said to Zildo.

'Sior, you will live nearer to me,' the boy answered, with a wonderful face of joy.

They rowed up Canalazzo and turned into Rio de Santrovaso. At the second stair on the left quay Crabbe disembarked, loading himself with his luggage. Zildo rushed with a leap from the poop to be porter.

'No,' said Nicholas: 'the palace is up the alley; and it is not safe to leave the bark unguarded—beside, the bag is too weighty for you.'

'Sior, nothing of my master's is too weighty for his servant.'

'I will not be contradicted.'

'Nòssior.'

'Tomorrow morning, at 9 o'clock, at the Bucintoro.'

'Sissior. Bonazera, Sior.'

'Bonazera, Zildo.'

A carpenter, with nods and becks and wreathed smiles, informed Crabbe that the padrone was out; and delivered certain keys and a billet: "Dear Lord Castellan, so sorry but dear Lady Pash telephoned us to come to tea on certain business which I need not designate. Do make yourself free of the castle meanwhile. The carpenter who confects our crates goes at 17 o'clock. He is a sweet fellow and a communicant and will do anything for you. We hope you will use what you find in the small aumbrey in the little chamber, whether medicinal or otherwise. And we wonder whether dear Zildo would turn up his nose at a stained (singed) sweater that is good in its way? The little gas-ring works and cooks well on application of a match. There is water galore opposite, though I fear the electric light has long been fuori di uso. Sorry the crockery is packed: but there is a basin at the Accademia end of the passage on top-floor. Your obliged Exeter and Emily Warden."

He who is Half and not One, when he fares forth to fight with the Many, naked must ride, with his rawness displayed for a sign.

XX

THE Wardens' castle in Palazzo Corfù began on the fifth storey with four enormous halls and a chapel containing a lavatory, egregiously plank- and shaving-littered, obstructed by made and unmade packing-cases. Monstrous old couches, bureaux, pianos, book-shelves, crated and uncrated, sprawled and straddled across marble floors. The first hall was mucked with rejected crockery, kitchen stuff, and furniture. A winding stair in a turret led, past a kitchen (similarly disordered), to a top storey of nine garrets (one large, four tiny, all low) lying along extended corridors. Crabbe eyed all. One of the smallest garrets seemed prepared for him. It contained a naked iron bedstead with a hearth-rug and a baby's blanket, a broken chair and table, a towel on the door-knob, and nothing else but air and dirt. In the lobby outside was a gas-ring for cooking, and a water-tap. On the wall of the opposite tiny garret hung the little medicine-cupboard of the letter: it contained five cigars, eight cigarettes, two halfpenny rolls, an orange, an apple, a stale half-litre of red wine, a handful of sodden chocolate fondants, the end of a packet of tea, and a cardboard box of dried milk to be liquefied in boiling water. Under the cupboard, on the floor, were a box of sulphur matches, a small tin saucepan, spoon, cup, and plate.

Crabbe wandered about, wondering why in the world the Wardens never occupied this apartment instead of borrowing other people's or living in hotels, as Erastian Venice tittle-tattle said was his constant habit. It was light, airy, well-sunned: from its windows were simply lovely views, of Canalazzo to beyond the Salute on the one hand, and (on the other) over the marvellous tiled roofs and chalice-like chimneys and verdant terraces and gardens and solemn byzantine bell-towers of the greater part of the city, across the blue lagoon to the snow-clad battlements of the Alps seventy miles away. It was an eyrie aloft, where one might have made oneself most snug and secret and have done no end of decent work. But the rooms hadn't been prepared for habitation for years and years. The walls and ceilings bore a wash (dating, no doubt, from remote antiquity); and the long steadily-undisturbed accumulation of filth everywhere indicated that people never could have lived a godly and righteous and sober life (though they might possibly have pigged —and, in fact, had pigged) there, upon occasion. He was wandering about, after the carpenter's departure. Dusk reminded him that he could have no light but that of the gas-ring in the messy lobby until morning. He determined to sleep and rise with the sun: but sleep was uneasy in loosened day-clothes under a boat-cloak; and the hearth-rug couldn't prevent the bare bed's wires from molesting hip-bones and shoulder-blades. If the floor had not been so un-clean, preferable would have been its honest hardness. If the weather had not been so wet, the polished floor-boards of the pupparin and the sweet salt breath of the lagoon would have been infinitely more desirable. Only beggars can be choosers.

Darkness enclosed, of the first night in that huge empty palace—darkness, rustling with shavings' mysterious whispers—darkness, scratched with the scatter of sportive rats—darkness, which squeaked or groaned with the pangs of damp green planks—darkness, shot with the clang or the thud of hapless wind-driven doors and shutters, marked Crabbe's mind to visit the Monte di Pieta and a candle-shop on the morrow. Much of his wakefulness was due to hunger. He came not over-well-fed; and, on viewing his fare, resolved to consume superfluous fat for a season; and went to his wire-bed fasting. Indeed, he spread the scant provision over nine days. The tea and the dried milk lasted even longer, because the milk was in bulk, and he boiled each tea-leaf six times for its liquor before drying it to use as tobacco. He kept himself fairly fresh and fit by taking the bark at 6 o'clock from the club, long before Zildo came to polish, and swimming with it from Sanzorzi to La Grazia, or from La Grazia to Sanzorzi, according to the way of the tide. And every morning he telephoned from the club to Albergo Bella-vista, asking, 'Are there any letters for Mr Crabbe?' Generally the answer was negative: when otherwise, he strolled round to collect his mail. Quaritch politely wrote that the business was not in his line. Crabbe sent this letter (with one of his own) to Sappytower, asking for further instruction. None came. The weather persisted in atrocity.

Having no facilities for drying wet clothes, and but a paucity of suitable changes, he avoided rain, and telephoned every day from club to infirmary for orders. When the directress was really imperative, he went to her aid: when her errands would wait, he did not brave the windy and wet canal of Zuecca. Once bibbling broken-heartedness at babble heard of his plight she congratulated him on residence in Palazzo Corfù. 'Maaah! You darling! Such a lovely quiet place all to yourself! And I'm sure you're writing the trottiest things there!'

He eyed her, first, in a rictus of indigation, for he thought that she was mocking him—then, as one inspecting the improvised up-pop of a jibbering idiot from the stokehole of a steamboat. She seemed taken aback, and her jowl dropped. 'Aren't you writing?' she whimpered.

'No.'

'Oh, but why?'

'Because I'm not eating,' he said weakly; and tried not to stumble as he stepped into his bark.

'Oh do come to tea tomorrow. We're always your friends yerno!' she yelled as he swept away from the quay.

Why not go to tea oftener? It would be a diversion to which to look forward. He went to tea every day: talked amusingly to convalescents; and cleared the bread and butter plate. To this day, no Erastian believes that that and the Wardens' pittance were his sole nutriment for a fortnight. Even La Pash, who waylaid him to ask for another sandalo-boy, amiably bridled and smirked at him as one does not smirk and bridle at a man known to be starving. Of course, what deceived the Erastians was his unruffleable demeanour, the short pipe in which he smoked the Warden's six-times-boiled tea-leaves, and his stately progresses in the pupparin rowed by the well-favoured well-groomed Zildo. The Warden ventured a remark on the latter. 'Do you mind if I ask one question. Thank you so much. We're wondering how you manage to pay your boy.'

'I don't pay him.'

'Oh, but—may I—is it wise to run up more debt?'

'No; if all is not going to be well in a week,' sullenly. Then, suddenly, 'Who, please, are your "we"?'

'Your friends,' with a toothy grin and gleaming goggles.

'Have I really any?'

'Oh, lots—if only you'd use us.'

'I don't know what you mean.'

This exchange of words caused Crabbe to use strength (about three hours of it) gained from a gorge of bread and butter for a little original thinking: with the result that he inquired of Zildo as to the progress of the bead-collar industry.

'Sìssiorsì. Also a noble fortune—for I cannot make bead-collars fast enough to satiate that my treasure—my young-lady American.

'Va benon. Go in future to the Bucintoro at nine strokes. If I want you, I will be there. If I am not there at 9½ o'clock, go home and make bead-collars all day.'

'Senti, Sior——'

'I have spoken.'

'Sìssior.'

The notion of making bead-collars for Zildo's young-lady American had to be dismissed as improper. But he could give the boy more liberty. And henceforth the two were not seen together in the pupparin. Nicholas disliked causing 'admiratio'—of some kinds.

On leaving Albergo Bellavista, the Wardeness developed shingles, which kept her scratching in Palazzo Selvatico; and Crabbe never saw her again. The Warden, therefore, had to obey orders, grinning like a dog and running about the city to claw-up charitable Venetian marchionesses as purchasers of pots and pans not deemed fit for translation to Buginthorpe. He generally lingered at Palazzo Corfù, when these customers were gone; and these were the only times when Crabbe could get a word with him.

In the beginning, the worthy man was reassuring: 'Dear person, your patience is—your exemplary patience and serenity are——. Oh, how I envy——. Oh, how we ought all to——. Rest assured that One——. Only a little while longer and your reward——' and so on, and so forth. The look of these platitudes, as Crabbe carefully wrote them in his diary every night, made him so nauseated that he was convinced that even the Warden himself (if he also could see his utterances in black and white) would spit like an unapostolic and totally irreligious wild-cat.

'Why doesn't your Sappytower say something?' Crabbe iterated and reiterated, more and more insistently, in the second week.

The Warden proffered spectacled ignorance, and began to look bonily uncomfortable: the mere mention of Rothschild's redoubtable financier seemed to produce in him symptoms of deep distress, and a fear that he would really have to be going now.

Crabbe gazed upon him with growing intensity, and conceived an academic interest in him. One day the gentleman asked whether the cheque from *The Lykeion* had arrived.

'No, it hasn't. And, to tell you the truth, this fasting on bread and butter has made me forget that we're in May, and that the cheque was promised for April.'

'Surely you might write—oh, could you lunch with me today at the Scattoletti—such a charming little place, by the Academy?'

'Ho, rather!'

They went; and Crabbe revived on beef and a mezzolitro of

Verona. He was an abnormally masculine man, of the type which eats chastely but hugely and frequently with great gusto in periods of responsibility. Then spake the other with bitten lips: 'Would you allow me to provide a stamp for *The Lykeion*?'

The stamp was a billet of five franchi. Crabbe started, as though stung on the nose-tip. 'Not for worlds,' he said hurriedly.

The bony skull beside him goggled wildly. 'But—you must let your friends help you.'

Crabbe braced himself. 'Yes. That's all I'm waiting for. Your Sappytower——'

'Hasn't he said anything yet?'

Crabbe simmered. ' "Am I a sea or a whale, that thou settest a watch over me?" I'm not concealing——'

'Oh! Do you think it reverent to cite Holy Scripture like that in ordinary conversation?'

'I firmly do. But keep to the point. You know that I'm not concealing——'

'No, no: dear person, I know, I know. But, you see, we want you to let us help you. What will you do, for instance, this day week, when I must give up the keys of the palace?'

'I haven't made plans yet.'

'Would you allow me to make an arrangement for you here? I'm well known to Scattoletti. And he only charges L. 5 a day, all complete.'

Crabbe bubbled: but he laughed. 'We're at cross-purposes, I think. You must be kind enough to believe what I think fit to tell you, or we can't get on. Don't you understand that I'm not in a position to pay any pension, however moderate?'

'Oh, there would be no difficulty—we should think it such a privilege——'

Crabbe reared, steaming. 'Now I'm certain that we're at cross-purposes! I'm afraid that I must define. You propose the utterly unacceptable. I'm only trespassing on your hospitality till you tell me that your promises about Sappytower, and his promises, have been unduly sanguine. So, please don't offer alms. I'm not that kind. I have property; and I'm ready to accept a business proposition enabling me to recover and realize it. If your Sappytower isn't sober yet——'

'But, dear Lady Pash——'

'Lady Pash?'

'Perhaps I was a little indiscreet——'

'I hope so. We'll forget it. Now, do you understand? I'm open to a business arrangement, with a man; but, at the mention of alms or females, we split brass-rags with a loud bang.'

' "Split brass rags?" I fear I don't quite follow.'

'Naval term for becoming enemies.'

'O dear person, surely that is lamentable pride?'

'Pride, I sincerely hope, but not at all to be lamented. And this talk illumines me to say that something must be done. Will you kindly get something definite from your Sappytower?'

'Would you not like to call at the Grand Hotel yourself?'

Crabbe boiled over. 'Not on any account. It's eighteen days since I sent him Quaritch's letter, which he promised to follow up. For me to call upon him, uninvited, now, would put me in an undesirable position. Yet we must get at his intentions.'

'Myiphmh, m-ym-yes. But, do-o——'

'No.'

Crabbe had an entirely sleepless night after this conversation. He worked at the infirmary all the afternoon, making talk to entertain a female convalescent who likened her heart to a caged sparrow. That would have tired him enough at ordinary times: but when (at sundown) he went to his wire-mattress, he knew that he only went (as a duty) to repose his body in absence of light. Hour after hour he lay, wooing sleep, in vain. His mind was a crowded causeway, congested by interminable huddled processions of inordinate ideas. At first, he tried to disregard them; but love of method, proclivity for system, horror of the merely sketchy or impressionistic or indefinite, passion for clarity and crystallization, compelled him at length to arraign them. I fancy, o most affable reader, that (in matters of this kind) he was not altogether unmoved by human respect. There is no doubt that he disliked disesteem and took a few pains not to deserve it. It badly hurt his sensibility, for example, when suspicacious people accused him of suspicacity. He tried very hard not to be suspicacious, and he was ware that the morning's conversation with the Warden had produced a tormenting gallimaufry of notions, which (unless sorted and pondered and arranged) was extremely likely to coagulate into a very horrible suspicion indeed—a suspicion like an actual being 'with flapping wings and hideous purring, panting to spring-on and worry' his soul. And he didn't like to have his soul worried.

So, when the close patter of feet, the near murmur of voices, the distant bellowing and squealing of syrens and calliopes, and the ubiquitous chiming of bells (the only sounds in Venice), sank (after midnight) into silence, he gave up beckoning sleep; and (wide awake) deliberately divested himself of all intense little preferences, and sharp little exclusions, and deep aversions from the vulgar, and personal views of right; and set himself to submit fluctuant ideas to the watery test of an Englishman's strong strict sense of fact.

What was the Warden's little game? Had he indeed a game of his own? Was he playing two games, his own and someone else's, and both perforce? (Ha-ha-ha!) Anyhow—what game was being played?

The very moment when Crabbe opened this inquisition, he perceived a most serious impediment blocking its progress—he had disliked Warden from the very first. He was far too sagacious to refuse recognition to an instinct of this important nature. Instinct is organized memory—not one's own memory, but the total of memories of countless anterior ancestral existences. For the isolate exiguous unsteadfast ghost or soul or subjective mind which never sleeps, sensible of instinct, is directed by the reasoning—the serried congregation of reasonings—unimaginably intricate, which is the cumulative compendium of the genetic cerebration and cognition of prior existences without number. Just as the physical cosmos is composed of the dust of innumerable milliards of corpses, so the psychical cosmos teems with the infinite shades of defunct ideas and creeds, the spirits of the tenets and fancies of extinct generations. What, then, is the good of arguing—who, but a fool, would waste time and force in arguing—with instinct, which is, simply, an extremely well-informed choice of the soul? Nicholas Crabbe never knowingly did anything so fat. Apart from his unquestionable and quite unconditional obedience to Mother Church—(the dear Old Thing takes you all the way: but, Lord, She is so slow—he used to say)—he found it convenient to employ a couple of incorporeal directors. The one was that inward monitor (sometimes denominated conscience), which he regarded as a personal protective entity, and addressed as his angel-guardian. And the other was infallible instinct. Nothing could part him from either. Sometimes, it is true, his angel-guardian's directions did not err on the side of indubitable clarity and irresistible urgency; and, then, he fell back on his instincts, which never by any chance played him false or let him down. Most of man's profounder feelings, such as sympathy or dyspathy, are superindividual—external to man. They come to him—they are not from him—these multitudinous memories massed for his use and service. And they are not disputable. Science absolutely denies the individuality of love; and, what is true of that imperious instinct which we know as love at first sight, must naturally be true of its converse, hate at first sight—both are superindividual—they are directions deigned, from a source (humanly speaking) plenarily informed—they must be followed, or neglected: there is no other way for miserable mortal man unendowed with the omniscience of divinity.

Nicholas Crabbe realized that he had detested Warden and all that was his from the very beginning.

Now, although Nicholas Crabbe was one of the twenty men alive who are aware of the radical difference between love of friends and love of enemies, practising both sorts (with a certain acceptation) in accordance with his christian duty, he had (as you should know by this time) very weakly (not to say wickedly) tried to conquer his instinct against the Warden from some stupid delusion about self-distrust. The last was not a habit of his, I hasten to affirm. He had suffered so many severe punishments for lapses into infidelity concerning himself and his proper monitors, that (as a rule) he was pretty loyal to his conscience and his instincts, for the sake of personal security and mental peace. But, through all the Warden's persistent amiability (which, sinning against light, he had forced himself to reciprocate), he was invariably sensible of a radical and incorrigible loathing of that obsequious and insinuating little man. And now, with the seeming failure of the Sappytower, the coy hints about La Pash, and that execrable offer of alms—the flame of his detestation shot up, yellow and red, blazing and roaring to the very empyrean.

When dawn came—a sweet and noble dawn of spring—he dashed out of doors and across the city to the Bucintoro, determined to swim at once for the recreation and refreshment of body and of soul. Much of his difficulty he left in the sea-canal of La Grazia. What he retained for treatment, when he climbed into his pupparin and stretched himself out in the morning sun and air to dry, amounted to an admission of an all-absorbing desire to help the Warden to play his game through, before probing it and perscrutinizing it and pronouncing a judgment upon it. Yes, instinct should be obeyed. Circumstances should be provided, for the sake of observing the fashion of Erastian gambols there-among. He would see this thing through. His academic interest in Warden was now quite fiercely excited. Morlaix and Sartor, Bobugo and Caliban should have the attention of his leisure: but, cost what it might, the designs of the Wardens, that cryptic 'We' and 'Us' who yearned to be friendly, should first be cultivated and then surveyed and pondered in minutest detail to the very end.

What Tertullian said of Cæsar Hadrian, might be said of Nicholas Crabbe: 'curiositatum omnium explorator,' he diligently explored all strange things. Ordinary incarnate absurdities, who complacently spend their lives in gazing on unredeemed contradictions, will fail to comprehend the deep audacious delight with which he flung himself upon this new experiment. He was perfectly cognizant (so he thought) of its risk, its unpleasantness, its uncertainty of achievement: but he found in these features a zest and a very spicy savour. To obtain power (as Kipling expressly demonstrates) it is necessary, not to burrow like moles or to grab like venal Jesuits but, in one's own nude force to pass through all sorts of close-packed horrors, treacheries, battles, insults, in darkness, and without knowledge as to whether the road leads upward or into a hopeless cul-de-sac through which an exit must be dynamited. Not one man in nineteen millions covets wisdom obtainable only by this method. 'Si omnes, ego non,' was Crabbe's invariable attitude to the ordinary. He would have what none other has; to have it, he would go by roads universally avoided. Nothing daunted him—nothing, on this side hell. and only hell because it was so infernally vulgar. Courage, according to Emerson, consists in having done the thing before; and, though fearfully frightened, he had done this dreadful kind of thing very many times before, quite cheerfully, at appalling sacrifice, and with unmitigated success. Surveying his situation, he saw that the job before him was far and away the biggest which he had ever attempted. To know what these Erastians actually were up to, and all about it, would bring him loss and suffering and most hideous disrepute. He would become a byword among the people to whom aforetime he was as a tabret. He would have the whole blooming show down on him. Who—who would shew an atom of trust in the integrity of his intentions? Why, lutheran cagotism doesn't even trust itself, when it wishes to form a judgment of a man's character. It has recourse to secret societies, private inquiry agents, an Inquisition more impertinent than the Holy Office (and not half so efficient), which masquerade under the euphemism of charity organization societies. No matter. Ut veniant omnes. Christians, that latebrose and light-avoiding nation (as Minucius Felix calls them), rear most hairily in resentment against investigation by an imperturbability armed with a large and dazzling lanthorn. No matter. Let 'em rear. They would run wildly about, screaming that his peculiar temper made it impossible for anyone to be kind to him. They would save their consciences handsomely, and feel themselves plenarily absolved, by fitting him with resounding soubriquets—Heautontimorymenos—Ipsesepuniens—Self-tormentor. Truly Christian cranky chewers, who practise the obsolete magic of divination by bibliomancy would find exceeding great joy in the inapplicable nickname 'Ishmael.' Very well. He would make himself a brother to dragons and a companion to owls (or ostriches). The pinnacle of the ludicrous is only attained after having won all kinds of nasty opinions of oneself. Pleasure can only be reached by the gate of pain. This amusing world is best seen from a height; and the speculative height of a truer philosopher than Plato's is the height of a cross. He, who would see as God sees, must hasten to mount upon his cross; and, there suspended, crucified in his own shrinking but unblenching flesh, raised higher even than angels, he will see and understand mysteries hidden from the worldly wise and stringently concealed from the squinting of the purely prudent. Disgrace? Disgrace is for those ninnies who accept it. Defeat? Defeat is for those nidderings who acknowledge it with howls for quarter. Life is short; art, long; opportunity, fugitive; experiment, delusive; judgment, difficult, said the sapient Hippokrates. But judgment depends upon experiment and experiment must be artfully conducted, even at the cost of life itself; and here was a most glorious opportunity. Into Crabbe's mind, the remembrance flashed of an extraordinary inscription, over a door in the neighbouring church of Sanstefano, 'Humanæ imbecillitatis memor supremam diem ne nimis perhorrescit.' Who it was who, mindful of human imbecility, didn't particularly shudder greatly at the Judgment Day, he did not exactly know. But he immensely admired a mental poise of that kind; and he adopted it as his own. Yes, the Erastians should have a very full complement of rope.

Up soared the great gold sun, gilding the angel on the bell-tower of Sanzorzi. Crabbe slowly slipped into his clothes. He was quite happy about his decision. No judgment should be formed, till these objects had been thoroughly tested.

Meanwhile, for help, for comfort, who should be invoked? To which of the saints should he turn? To whom, but to the greatest saint of all? The exquisite names by which Venetians know God's Mother floated through his mind: Santamaria del Giglio, Santamaria della Grazia, Santamaria della Consolazione, Santamaria Formosa, Santamaria della Salute, Santamaria Odorifera o dell' Orto, Santamaria Pomposa, Santamaria Gloriosa dei Frari, Santamaria Mater Domini—Saint Mary of the Lily, Saint Mary of Grace, Saint Mary of Consolation, Saint Mary the Beautiful, Saint Mary of Good Health,

Saint Mary the Fragrant or Of the Garden, Saint Mary the Processional, Glorious Saint Mary of the Friars, Saint Mary Mother of the Lord.

He shot his oar on to the forcola; and rowed finely away, back to the Bucintoro, with the lovely telling phrases of the Buddhistic Litanies of Avalokitesvara, the Maid who looketh down for ever above the sound of prayer, singing on his lips, a nosegay, and a song of strengthening orison:

> *Storms and hate give way to her name;*
> *Fire is quenched by her name;*
> *Demons vanish at the sound of her name;*
> *By her name one may stand firm as the sun in the sky.*

Scraped on the sensitive raw, he must stand, shewing signal of section; only the other half, also raw, can respond.

XXI

THE fine weather burst again into floods of tears—apparently because the Warden did nothing (as far as Crabbe knew) with his Sappy-tower, and ossified more deeply every day to the starkening visage which refused to be beslimed with alms. 'I've paid for a dinner at the Scattoletti, if ever you care to go there; and I've arranged that pension I told you of,' he whimpered once or twice.

'No,' said Crabbe.

The hour came for giving up the keys of the dismantled palace. Still the sky wept torrentially. All the furniture had been crated, addressed by Crabbe to Buginthorpe, Burghley, Inghilterra, and removed by facchini in barges for shipment in the harbour of Marittima. The valuer of the Royal Academy had appraised the antiquities, sealing them with lead, and imposing a duty of L.30 on their leaving the country; and he thankfully took a tip of two franchi for his moderation.

Strange to say, our dear weird old Warden seemed to be writhing in a perfect rictus of agony. Crabbe was too near to see the true proportions of the situation. He merely looked, with interested unconcern, in the man's tortured skull-face. Tortured? Yes, that was plain. The wretched little creature was glaring, biting his lips, mortified to death with the torture of some hideous unsuccess. What unsuccess? Crabbe got a glimpse; but it was so repulsive and nauseating that he glanced away hurriedly.

The Thiasarkh mouthed at him, while rain pelted against the windows of the first hall, where they stood. Crabbe had taken his luggage to his locker at the club at 6 o'clock that morning, unbeknown even to Zildo; and he wrapped his thickest boat-cloak round him, as he handed in the key of Warden's street-door. It was nearly 19 o'clock, and dusky with the dreadful weather.

'Oooh, my dear person, what are you going to do?'

'Leave, when you leave. I suppose you won't be long.'

'But—look at the rain. Where will you go?'

'I haven't quite made up my mind.'

The Warden emitted a noise like 'Ooooeughph,' which was a

sort of mixture of a snarl and a growl and a screech strangulated in twisted guts.

'Dear me!' said Crabbe, eyeing him fastidiously.

'Of course, you know, I'm not really bound to help you, seeing that you're not a co-religionist!' screamed the infuriated self-condemner.

'Comfort yourself, o blessed of God, with that beautiful thought,' said Crabbe—and went out.

He turned to the right (as his habit was, in difficult places) toward Calle Gambara. The other way would have taken him to the quay where Zildo lived—and that was to be meticulously avoided. He passed round the back of the Academy; and stood a little while under the portico in Campo Santagnese. The club was no refuge in the evening: crowds of showy impiegati thronged it, squealing over cards and billiards and absurdly moderate consummations to such an extent that the laws of the League Against Duelling were publicly posted on the wall. (Imagine, o most affable reader, a rowing club whose members had to be permanently warned of the duty of submitting private disputes to a jury of honour!) It was unfortunate that his pockets were empty. With threepence, he might have spent the greater part of a cold wet night in a dry warm caffè.

He walked briskly, over the Academy bridge, as far as the Public Gardens eastward. About 23 o'clock, the rain became drizzle. He turned westward, going by Santazustina and Sanzanipolo and millions of little back alleys to the long solitary quay of Santamaria Odorifera, and on through the Ghetto to the three-arched bridge of Cannarezo. There, he turned, crossing the iron-bridge by the station; went round by Santachiara and Santandrea and Sanraffael to the Marittima end of the Zattere. He had walked, so far, as though on definite business; but now he slackened to a leisured dawdle. There was only a night to get through without exciting notice. In the morning, he could arrange better for the future.

The whole quay of the Zattere extended itself before him. He set himself to pace it from end to end. The drizzle ceased, and a warm haze bloomed on the darkness. He kept moving, to dry his drenched clothes.

Midnight sounded, and the stroke of one. The last ferries left the pontoons by the church of the Gesuati. He thought it a pity that that order of Gesuati, which is three centuries older than the Gesuiti, should have become extinct. The Jesuats always had a most respectable reputation. But 'whom the gods love die young.'

Had the Jesuats survived, the world might have been spared the word 'Jesuit' as a synonym (with 'Nero' and 'Borgia' and 'Judas') for ultimate turpitude. He chuckled over the witty and very exasperating concept; and thanked the Lord for permitting him the use of his wits.

On the distant bank of the wide canal of Zuecca, the lengthy line of lights along Spinalonga fluttered like little pale daffodils in a night-mist coloured like the bloom on the fruit of the vine. Great quiet reigned. He prayed, to comfort the minutes as they fled by. Holy thoughts were his, and ardent yearnings, in his unhoused loneliness. 'That sweet welcome mine, and mine for ever—that eternal home, whereunto, when all my wandering's over, I shall surely come' (a stanza of Ter Stegen's) was perhaps the strangest. But, deep in his innermost soul was the conviction that his life was wrong—wrong, because it lacked the home and the welcome which he so successfully tried to despise, with which he so easily and recklessly dispensed—which he firmly believed that he ought to acquire and be content with, like other men. I say that he believed this now. He himself has told me so: but he added that the long long years of his provoking perseverance for the priesthood had had this very strange effect upon him—he did yearn to be wanted, to belong—if it could be plainly and unmistakably offered to and pressed upon him, on those conditions he did indeed yearn for an earthly home and for earthly human love. Priesthood, and a friend. (But there were no such things as friends.) Priesthood? Or Marriage?—Zildo.—His crab-like temperament, his habit of collecting flotsam and jetsam, made him always gather things together for the adornment of some state, of some place, all of his very own, where he was wanted and to which he belonged—or for the comfort of someone of his very own. His soft warm hungry heart, which none suspected, the merest mention of which was received with derisive chokings, was always open wide to receive the Divine Friend, the David of his Jonathan, the Patroklos of his Akhilleys, the Amys of his Amyl—or the Eva of his Adam—whom he ever and everywhere confidently expected. And yet, such was the strength of the world-renunciation, which (as proof of vocation for priesthood) his supernatural sense and instinct and vow had forced him to cultivate beyond all bounds for twenty years, that he could use (as he was using) the slightest pretext for most precipitate and careless and even eager stripping himself of all, denying himself all, looking for no home but a heavenly and none to give him welcome but the inhabitants of heavenly mansions. His gaze was there. He didn't care twopence for the jobs which he had first to finish here.

You perceive his little error, o most affable reader? It was the error of eternal and unconquerable youth, which vaults so facilely from the Here to the There, omitting all consideration of the well-nigh infinite In-between. But Nicholas Crabbe was born young, and remained young, till youth was an irradicable habit of his, by the Grace of God.

The Mactavish's palace of Incurabili on the Zattere, with an ordinary modern relief of Saint George, was dark. The blue shutters were indistinguishable. Crabbe thought himself rather a fool for neglecting to go there on the three Monday evenings when the Warden had been starving him. (Now why in the world had that pastor been starving him?) Sandwiches and biscuits sometimes circulated with drinks about 23 o'clock. He would go on the Monday ensuing. Perhaps he might hear remarks.

About 3½ o'clock, one of the signors of the night addressed him, near the Albergo Calcina. These nocturnal guards are retired carabinieri, who reinforce the ordinary vigili from dark to dawn. They carry large sticks and a red-striped cap. Everyone pays a penny a week to the private firm which enlists them; and they pervade the city by night, leaving a ticket every three hours in their clients' letter-boxes and prompt to waken would-be early risers. Did the gentleman wish to enter the closed hotel, asked the guardia notturna? Crabbe chortled, returning thanks, and saying that (on the contrary) he was out to take the air while studying the effects of night-light and white dawn upon the water. He imparted an atrocious English accent to the vernacular, which assured the watchman that he was merely an admirably mad foreigner nourishing no ugly or burglarious intentions. Dawn, misty, pink and glittering grey like salmon-flesh and scales, came. Very tired and stiff and sodden, he put the night behind him; and crossed Canalazzo, walking by Sanvidal and Sammaurizio and the Piazza to the club. The pupparin was full of rain, and could be left to Zildo. He took a douche and put on dry flannels, and dozed in an easy-chair on the sunny balcony till the boy came to do his daily work. When the bark was dry and ready he let himself be rowed round Castello, out of the way, where was privacy and space for mind-forming well-directing thought.

'Take,' he said, at length, to Zildo, 'a pair of small stakes, and have them firmly fixed in the canal by your lodging.'

'Sissior. And when?'

'Today.'

'Va ben.' -

'Here, also, are commandments. When you find the pupparin moored to your new paletti, take it to the Bucintoro and wait for me. When you do not find it at your little stakes, go on foot to the Bucintoro at 9 o'clock each day. If I am not there, nor even the bark, go home, and come again on the day following. For I shall use the pupparin, I alone, very frequently, in future.'

'Va benon.'

He dismissed the boy at the stroke of one, and paddled out on the lagoon to doze in the sun during the afternoon (for he was still stiff), returning by way of the infirmary at tea-time.

The directress began bibbling as he tied up at her steps, 'Come in, do—you mystery, you terror! Come in and give an account of your extraordinary behaviour! What do you mean by frightening us all so fearfully?'

Crabbe followed her into the nurses' room, and accepted the tea which she pressed upon him. 'I don't know what you're talking about,' he said. And 'Why such a hubbub?'

'That poor Mr Warden! How could you! You can't think how pained he was, how distressed we all were!'

'What about?'

'Why, at your disappearance!'

'What nonsense! I haven't disappeared. Surely I can have my nights to myself.'

'Oh, you know what I mean. Where did you go last night?'

'For a stroll.'

'Where did you sleep, I mean?'

'Nowhere.'

'Oh, how can you say such things! What did you do?'

'Went for a stroll along the Zattere.'

'What? In all that rain?'

'There was some rain.'

'Why, you must have got wet through!'

'Please don't paw me. I'm dry now.'

'Oh, you'll kill yourself. Of course you got something to eat?'

'How silly you are! Of course I didn't.'

'Oh, how shocking. When did you eat last?'

'Here—the day before yesterday.'

'Urghrm! Do have some more bread and butter. Why haven't you ever taken any notice of my letter. Oh, why—why don't you let us——'

'I've told you why.'

'Oh, if we had only known——'

'You've known for five months: and so has your precious friend. So try to be sensible. Now, what about tomorrow's errands?'

'Oh, I can't!'

'Well then, if there's nothing to do, I may as well take myself away.'

'If you could manage to go and explain to Scarabellin, the printer in Sanluca,' she hiccoughed; and went on with details of the form of a new price-list of the infirmary's charges. 'Could you see him tomorrow and come over to tea in the afternoon with the proofs? So trotty of you—you—— Now mind you come.'

He rowed to the club for cloaks. The evening promised to be fair; and a second night of tramping might very well be postponed. He drifted about the Grand Canal, nonchalantly, till dusk came down; and then moored at the solitary pile by the English Garden on Spinalonga, sitting at ease, well wrapped up, as one who meditates —till midnight, when all was still. Then he lay down on the floor of the pupparin and slept. Now and again he wakened as some solitary fisher glided by in a two-oared buranello; for, being without either lanthorn or means of tipping, it was necessary to be alert both against thieves and the inquisitions of the water-police. The morning found him unrested. He took a dip before returning to the club for letters—there were two—and came out again to read them on the blue lagoon. It was just as well, he thought, to practise his yesterday's precepts to Zildo. So he read one of his letters— it was from the Warden—out in the open; and not until 11 o'clock, when Zildo had come and gone, did he leave the bark at the club, to free himself for the infirmary's business with the printer.

The Warden's note set him rearing in a paroxysm of amusement: "Do be sensible and go back to England. It is utterly useless for you to stay here; and if you need money to carry you respectably and with your clothes washed I am sure I can find it or Mr Sappytower can. If you had been less mysterious and reserved, the issue might well have been more pleasant. As it is, everyone is deeply wounded. So do be sensible and communicate with one or other of us if you are prepared to return to England. It is not mine to lecture or preach to you, yet I suggest that even our common allegiance to Christ seems to demand a pocketing of pride and resentment sometimes, however justifiable we may think them. Now do do as you would be done by.—E. W."

His great ferocious pincers clashed out an instant retort: "I'm infinitely obliged: but I have already been done by you as much as I can stand. As for your letter, let me congratulate you (from a literary point of view) on having produced a masterpiece of miserable hypocrisy. Thank you very much, but I firmly refuse to oblige by going and dying on someone else's doorstep, even with my clothes washed. You don't seem to understand that I take a fierce (but purely academic) interest in you, for I really did not believe that such dreadful people existed outside Ouida's *Friendship* and *In a Winter City*. Erastians one knows, metoikoi one has heard of, but what the devil you are will be my pleasing pastime to determine. And, as perhaps it will suit you (as well as me) if I make the breach between us as inviable as possible, kindly note that you are prohibited from mentioning my name or work in the preface of your book. I'm going to choose my company, for future; and I don't choose to appear in connection with a character like yours.—N. C."

He spat this caramel at Palazzo Selvatico, and spent the rest of the morning for the infirmary. While dawdling at the printers (who turned out to be Ferrari in the Calle Delle Acque and not Scarabellin of Sanluca) waiting for proofs, he remembered his second letter. It contained a guinea cheque for one of his pseudonymic storiettes. Yoicks! Could anything be a plainer mark of Heaven's Favour? Cook and Son gave him L. 25.60 for it; and he blithefully sauntered across the Piazzetta, feeling as some mediæval johnny in a secret mail-shirt pervading the Calle degli Assassini at Sanbenedetto must have felt—invulnerable, and ready for any of 'em.

With sedateness without and hilarity within, he took its price-list proofs to the infirmary in the afternoon. The directress bibble-babbled rather more incoherently than usual, and sent him to tea with two nurses while she dashed hither and thither, entertaining tub-hatted long-pursed visitors in the blue room, gabbling at gondolieri, cackling at the cook who cursed her back, and harrying patients on exhibition in the wards. There was talk of a tombola and lottery for putting in a heating apparatus.

Crabbe lingered, as long as decency dictated, for commands. When tedium took him out into the hall, he found the lady fumbling to stick a notice on the door by which one leaves. 'Let me,' he said.

'Oh! Ah! Thank you so much,' she babbled with a nervous gasp.

As he stuck the pins in, he read, "Afternoon Tea, 6d.;" and a cold silver smile irradiated his visage. He took out sixty schei and made to confer them.

'Oh, no no!' she bubbled. 'That's not meant for you!'

'Nonsense, my good creature, you know perfectly, and I perfectly know, whom it's meant for and what it means. You've added a tea-shop to this casino; and you charge a tanner for tea. Well, here are sixty centesimi for my tannin; and I shan't want any more, thank you.'

'Oh, I can't take it from you!'

'Then let me put it in your contribution-box,' he said with finality.

That, of course, ended his connection with La Pash's infirmary, which (a few weeks earlier) had been on its knees to him, imploring him to join its committee. The incident furnished further data for his judgment. These Erastians only wanted him while they believed him to be (despite his numerous explicit denials) an acquisition pecuniarily worth consideration. It was impossible that they could have believed his previsions of impending ruin; and it needed the Warden's personal inspection of his three weeks' semi-starvation and bedlessness to convince them that he had told the exact truth all along. But what, then, had signified the insistent proposals of help, the Sappytower, and all the confidently-made subsequently-belied promises and assurances which had delayed his action against that gang in England at this very important time? And, what was the precise signification of the rather rancorous element present in the Warden and the infirmary now? Of course, news of his frightful pinching of the Warden had been passed by gondola up Canalazzo and telephoned by 10.04 (with instructions) to the infirmary. Hence the tea notice. The back so ready to cringe, the abject unctuous obsequious squirming of body and soul to mammon, had their due reward. The tuft-hunting Warden was (under La Pash) dictator of the Erastian aliens resident in Venice. Toad-eating paid. Such a nice man could do no wrong, and the nonentities whose toads he swallowed would rally round him. Crabbe was frightfully bucked at his luck in having that totally unlooked-for sixpence to spit out so promptly; and he chortled for hours at the notion of mystifying (to the verge of vertigo) these dastards, who, believing him penniless, knowing him homeless and starving, had had the cheek to deal him so cowardly a blow. Oh yes: inquisition into their moral code, experiments with the excellences of their ethics, promised to be more than diverting. And he set about attending to them immediately, nel modo che 'l seguente canto canta.

He spread out his guinea wonderfully, in toilet niceties, paper, washing, and a daily debauch of three cioppe—little hard Venetian rolls of the populace at ten centesimi for three.   On dry nights, he slept in the pupparin moored south of Spinalonga.   When it rained, he walked the streets, and dozed at the club the next day.   The pupparin, being an open bark with a floor of movable planks, was not a comfortable couch on wet nights; it had to be baled so frequently; and damage done by mud and water to clothes would have betrayed secrets to the profane vulgar.   Yet he dare not to spend money, even if he had enough, in fitting an impermeable canvas shelter from prow to poop; nor might he set up the infinitely cheaper one of matting which fishermen use.   Both would have excited inaccurate or undesirable opinions.   He did not wish the mob to know that he had come down in the world, even to sleeping under matting; nor did he intend a decent canvas awning to delude Warden with the comforting notion that Fortune had turned her wheel.   He didn't, in fact, intend it to be turned till he had finished his experiment.   When persons of principle are put in contact with truth, their principles perfect their practice: with unprincipled persons, or with perjurers of Pecksniffian principles, the case is otherwise.

He went to Mactavish's Monday at $21\frac{1}{2}$ o'clock, in a clean lavender-coloured flannel suit and white guernsey.   The butler placed him alone in the great gallery where receptions always took place, saying that the Paron was still at dinner.   In a minute or two, Mactavish entered, supporting a wonderful tottering dame of ninety in black satin and lace and diamonds.   'Talk to my mother, will you?' he stammered.   'I've got a few friends here: but we won't be long.'

Crabbe got out his chat.   It wasn't easy work.   The old lady was hard of hearing, and preferred to mew monologues.   He set himself to win fame as a listener to interminable incomprehensible reminiscences about her youthful exploits in swimming—evidently she had been coached as to his notorious wet-bobbishness—and he so far succeeded that she bridled and giggled without a single offer to lash him across the face with her ebony crutch.   And, presently, half a dozen gorgeous diners entered in procession.   Some Crabbe already knew, others Mactavish presented: [1] 'Lord Hippis—the Honble. Noel——'

Crabbe literally shrieked with laughter all to himself, at this inconceivably comic encounter; but his grave brown face remained stark,

[1] Here again, in this meeting with the late Lord Rosebery and his son in Horatio Brown's apartments, Rolfe is relating an actual occurrence.

alert, recondite, neither forbidding nor inviting advances. For the
Earl of Hippis, an ex-prime-minister of England, a Knight of the
Garter, and an intellect of high reputation, was a personage far (oh,
far) above the worlds through which Crabbe's pilgrimage hitherto
had led him; and, moreover, this peer happened to be chairman of
those very Rhodon Trustees allied with that very Constitutional
Company of British South Libya, whose expert adviser's agricultural
and pastoral book Crabbe had written at the cost of his own former
ruin. How much Lord Hippis knew—whether Lord Hippis ever had
heard of him, excepting as a rather precise small writer of history and
Italian folk-lore, Crabbe had not the remotest idea: nor did he propose
to inquire—o Lord, no: let the gods (who, for once, had thrown
two together on equal terms) go farther or not, as they pleased.
Enough for him to observe this earl.

Most of the guests surrounded Mrs Mactavish, listening. Nelson
came to court his latest. 'Have you, hum, been rowing much lately?'
he said to Crabbe.

'Rather, in this fine weather,' that crustacean replied; 'and I
can't imagine anything more entrancing than these white dawns of
spring.

'Are you, hum, out so, hum, early?' Mactavish laughed. The
Honble. Noel drifted near, and took a chair near the head of Crabbe's
double couch. He and his father had come from Naples in their
yacht.

'The one which flies the R.Y.S. White Ensign, moored by the
torpedo-catchers at the mouth of the Zuecca Canal?' Crabbe asked.

Mrs Mactavish withdrew, slowly, statelily, even sacramentally.
Cigarettes and liqueurs became apparent. Nelson brought up his
principal guest. 'You're just the very man we wanted,' he said to
Crabbe: 'if anyone knows anything about Venetian barks and the
lagoon, you do. Do tell Lord Hippis all about them. He sleeps in
his pupparin,' he added, to the earl.

Lord Hippis took the other seat on the couch. For the instant,
Crabbe's heart stood still. How much did Mactavish, treasurer of
the infirmary, know—or want to know? What did Lord Hippis
know and want to hear personally from him?

'Do you really sleep out of doors as early in the year as this?'
asked the most exquisite and most enchanting man in the world, firm,
grave, sleek, plump as a church cat (the cat of Sampolo, for example),
marvellously clean and clear and straight of eye, the very finest
flower and quintessence of the last and best which mighty unconquerable England can make of a man.

'I'm as hard as nails, as you see; and the lagoon is delicious,' Crabbe replied.

If Mactavish knew why and how he was sleeping out of doors, and if (by any chance) the chairman of the Rhodon Trustees wished to shew attention to the writer of *Agricultural and Pastoral Prospects in British South Libya*—in short, if the present was a tardy epiphany of the mystic 'we' who did so yearn to be friendly—(do, o most affable reader, mark the piteous eagerness to believe in the goodness of man which these workings of Crabbe's mind exhibit)—very well, then— only, it would be necessary to be as flat-footed as a butler—every i would have to be dotted, and crossed each t. After the variegated games which had been played with him, Crabbe was not for making easy any path but the path of straight and open talk. Rather would he make impediments, and sow them on all roads, as a test of good faith. So he sat tight, in the citadel of his hardened carapax, and shoved the conversation away from his individuality. He described pupparini and the smaller sandoli called buranelli which one rower drives with a beautiful generous action of two crossed oars or one; he treated of the joyful possibilities of a trabaccolo fitted as a house-boat moored at the Doganale; he mentioned bliss tasted in a six-ton sailing topo; and he dwelled upon the notion of a smaller topo, say of three tons at most, with appropriate fitments, wherein (he fearlessly affirmed) one might live one's life and do one's job with a peace and a freedom and a salubrity unattainable elsewhere.

'You have a cabin, or at least an awning of some sort, in your bark?' Lord Hippis inquired.

'No ; I just roll up in a cloak, and use my satchel of papers and grub for a pillow.'

'You must be as hard as nails, undoubtedly,' with a quick glance sideways and a tinge of envy.

Crabbe grinned. Mactavish was bringing someone else to present to him—a terrified-looking painter with a twisted face. A hoary chatterer with an axe to grind obsequiated the earl. Crabbe said a few nothings, and glided away, satisfied. He had spoken. But there had been no sandwiches, and he was so frightfully hungry. Never mind. His reception had been cordial, and he had not made a fool of himself. His flannel suit had been quite as decorative in its way as the dinner-dress of the others; and in physique, of course, he could give them all points. Oh, yes: he was as good a man, if not better, than those others. They recognized that. He would go to Palazzo dei Incurabili again. The Warden, playing some damnable double game yet to be defined, had cast him out because he wasn't an

Erastian: the infirmary (following its leader) had sheepishly warned him off by trying (in the belief that he was stony) to stump him with a charge for tea. He thanked the Lord for that gift of consolation, his keen sense of the ridiculous. What a lark it all was, really! The motive of it, though, remained to be discovered. And, for the rest, he wouldn't change his habits—he wouldn't avoid anyone—till he was avoided. And then——.

More than a signal for juncture, more than a touchstone of traitors: rawness (exposed) enables a juncture to be.

XXII

THE brilliant Bobugo, who had been preaching the Lent in Rome, diverged to Venice on his way to England. Imagining (in his singularly optimistic simplicity) that this piqued prig, repentant, wished to look him up and make an honourable amend, Crabbe confined himself to public thoroughfares and the vicinity of the club, holding himself ready and willing for a meeting. But few assassins there be who are ever able to refrain themselves from the corpse of their victim; and Bobugo housed at the Tolenti in the palace of a resident alien, one Losel, a magazine-laudator of eccentric countesses, that identical dyspathetic featureless old-youngster whom Crabbe most felicitously had snubbed on sight at Mactavish's. Bonsen shewed no sign of penitence: he was apparently horribly alarmed by the monster which his turpilucricupidity and lust for power had created. So extraordinarily reckless and ruthless a di-gladiator as Crabbe required watching—by someone on the spot. Crabbe grinned baldly and sardonically; and laid traps for the self-deception of Bobugo's small spy. Losel's reports would be very amusing, and misleading.

More rain followed. Crabbe, in his dirtiest clothes, tramped, night after night, avoiding populous places like the station and the arcades of the Piazza. Long deserted quays beyond the Misericordia supplied parallel stretches: the labyrinthine alleys of Sancassian and Sancancian afforded entertainment in connection with what Zildo scornfully designated 'certi brutti individui.' A hobbledehoy (whose fist was armed with a razor) had to be dug in the diaphragm with rigid finger-tips and left to gasp in the kennel. A pair of black-mailers, on the Riva dei Schiavoni (near the House of God), found themselves so frightfully chopped on the neck-side with a hard hard hand-edge that they suddenly sat by the water's edge vomiting. An extremely tipsy Welsh apprentice had to be kindly conducted from celebrations at the house with a chancel by the Fondamenta Rosmarin to his ship in the harbour of Marittima at 3 o'clock in the morning.

Caliban, cavorting about England for new pageants where he might swagger as a skewbald harlequin, appeared to have no time for writing but in the third person. Most people—(and Carlyle has told us what most people are)—fall back into the third person when they have quarrelled and are not on terms. It never occurs to them that a quarrel makes the other party much more interesting: they haven't the faintest notion of the fact that a new enemy has infinitely more attractive features (and possibilities) than an old friend. And they avoid, just because they have neither the brains nor the pluck to face, the change of relations. Than which nothing can be more fat. Sulks amount to stagnation: stagnation is septic. "By conflict, fresh experience is always being gained," said Alkibiades. Selah. Caliban wrote in the third person, trying to bluff and frighten Crabbe: he asked for an address to which to send the manuscripts of *The Weird* and *De Burgh's Delusion* and all Crabbe's property stored at Uskvale, clothes galore, books, tools of trade, material and work of a lifetime. Crabbe replied that, being homeless, through the treachery and pusillanimity of the Lieutenant of the Grand-magistracy of the Order of Sanctissima Sophia, he had no place in which to receive his goods.

Crabbe also demanded of Morlaix and Sartor an account of their five years' administration of his assets, with his overdue publisher's account of the last three half-years and a statement of their intentions. They refused anything of the sort, saying that they were acting in the interests of Mr Peary-Buthlaw. Having forced this declaration, Crabbe put these people at the back of his mind to consider what he should do with them. Meanwhile, it occurred to him that he might as well have the manuscripts of his two last books with him. Caliban possessed typed copies of both *Weird* and *Delusion*; and Crabbe conceived that his own holographs of these works would serve to identify and characterize him, if found on his body in the event of its collapse under hardship and semi-starvation. The profane vulgar always attributes final unsuccess to drink or idleness; and Crabbe had no intention of accepting credit for vices which he didn't practise. So he demanded his manuscripts. Caliban promptly replied that he was now going to stick to them till their author had gratuitously tipped him L. 625, and to Crabbe's goods and work and tools till he had received a full discharge and cost of carriage. Crabbe thought him over.

The rain continued. 'Lord Hippis left yesterday, hum,' said merry magenta Mactavish, the next time when he saw Crabbe; 'and he asked if you slept in your pupparin in this beastly weather.'

'No, I don't,' the crustacean spirted: 'the bark gets water-logged and messy. I really must see about a tarpaulin, or something.'

So these people were ignorant of all, excepting of a certain hardy man who slept for choice in the open. But no sandwiches appeared with the whisky at the Palazzo dei Incurabili's Mondays.

The Queen-Empress of England and the Empress-Mother of Russia came, in the *Victoria and Albert*, pervaded the Piazza and the Merceria, shopped, glided in ordinary gondole, and rushed all over the show with childlike glee. Of course the sun blazed out; Venice displayed herself serenely; and the Venetians went stark mad with admiration. The agility of Their Majesties was simply astounding. They went everywhere (even to La Pash's infirmary), and saw everything (excepting the Sailors' Institute), without turning a hair. They were followed by panting and perspiring suites, who, instantly, whenever their Majesties deigned to sit, seized and sank into the nearest unoccupied seats, the English breathing stertorously, the Russians lolling out their tongues in desperation. So Mactavish reported. Crabbe watched it all from the club balcony: he observed the obsequious Warden, in a borrowed gondola full of tabid Erastian tabbies, creeping down Canalazzo to the royal yacht and its attendant destroyer anchored in the Basin of Saint Mark, not by any means unready to crawl aboard upon the slightest word of invitation. But he saw no more of the thin-lipped Wardeness, who continued to shingle in Palazzo Selvatico.

His guinea melted away: four days and nights without food tried his temper. And then *The Lykeion* shot forth two guineas and a copy of its January number containing *Terribile la Femmina*. He counted the words—three and a half thousand. Now Bobugo, who introduced him, knew his price to be five guineas a thousand; and he had named that sum to the editor, both in submitting manuscripts and in his recent requests for long-delayed payment. What, then, was the meaning of this two guineas? And, what about the other manuscripts of his which *The Lykeion* still held? He felt that he must feed, that he might think. Playing about the streets was all very nice and instructive, but business must be attended to. Of course the present cheque was merely an instalment—rather odd of Lord Arthur Baliol Kingsbury and a respectable paper like *The Lykeion*.

He went down to the Accademia and lunched at Scattoletti's. This eating-house with lodgings had a humble air, and the merit of being almost midway between Zildo in Santrovaso and the club in the Giardinetto Reale. The obese and smutty innkeeper cringed in recognition, making melting play with rounded eyes, and cooing alluring inquiries 'Va bene cosi-i-i' in a baby-voice at every dish.

Crabbe ate a beef-steak and cheese, and drank a mezzolitro of very unremarkable Verona; for which refection Scattoletti refused to charge him, affirming that the most observable and most worthy Signor Warden already had paid.

'This does not please me,' Crabbe declared. 'Return his deniers to your Warden, and give me a bill. I wish to lodge myself here for a little while, but not unless I pay my own charges.'

Scattoletti—(it goes without saying that his Christian name was Arcanzolo)—slavered submissive objection. There was a decent little chamber above, with plain old nut-wood furniture. It looked clean. And there was a backyard covered with young vines, where one could feed. Crabbe didn't think of coming to a combination without terms: the Warden had named L. 5 a day as the customary pension: and The Lykeion's cheque worth L. 52.80 could see him through a clear week anyhow. He brought kit-bag, clothes, and papers from the club; and slept in a decent bed for the first time in seven weeks. His first act was to acknowledge receipt of two guineas on account from The Lykeion, pointing out that sixteen sterling odd remained due to him; and he asked for the return of his half-dozen unused manuscripts.

Now that a little vista of peace seemed opening, a curious reversion took place in his mind. Years ago, he had read, with pleasure and admiration mingled with disgust and detestation, Edward Carpenter's Towards Democracy. The splendid language of the poem pleased him: its doctrine set him rearing in revolt. Alkibiades' condemnation to the Lakedaimonians as reported by Thucydides was as forceful as ever, 'there were demagogues, as there always have been, who led the people into evil ways,' and 'the follies of democracy are universally admitted; and there is nothing new to be said about them.' And Crabbe had written, on the tablets of his mind, as something to be done on a fitting occasion, a big book of verses as a counterblast, magnificent hexameters, bright iambics, melodious hendecasyllabics—a new whole duty of man, from the gardener's boy and the scullery-maid, and the chauffeur and the typist, and the shopman and the factory-girl, and the man and the woman up to the King and the Pope, in their progress Towards Aristocracy on the road which leads to The Best. Thoughts and images clothed themselves with measure in his brain, and cried to be set down, at this time. The idea seemed feasible. Honour forbade him to cease from being an eyesore to the Erastians; and to move from Venice would prevent a conclusion of his experiment. He had lost his world, and was alone. Zildo must not be counted. He would begin again, living very simply on occasional guineas from his caches till *Sebastian Archer* hit the gold. He could keep himself in evidence in the city at morn and eve, and spend the lovely summer days in versifying, in the pupparin, on the blue lagoon. Lord, how delicious! As for the Warden and his wife, inquisition could best be pursued by letting them disclose themselves. Occasions and sets of circumstances should be provided for the sake of noting the fashion of their gambols thereamong. And, if anyone temerariously chose to assume the offensive, he must be very prompt to punch hard each head as it raised itself against him.

The more he pondered this plan, the better he liked it. As for Caliban, he must be left squatting, dog-in-the-manger-like, on stolen property, for the present, till a stable habitation was secured with means of forcing him to disgorge. When Crabbe had those, and when he had scratched up some competent and trustworthy agent in England, then he would go tooth and talon for Caliban. But, meanwhile, desirous of ending enforced idleness, much could be done with the material sequestered by Parrucchiero. It was necessary to make some sort of a proposition to him.

He had a weariful interview with the well-meaning little man. It was impossible to conceal from himself that his landlord had a good deal of reason for distrusting him after the way in which his intimate friends had been treating him. Most landlords would have packed him off to prison long ago; but he knew that Barbolan had the sense to see that that course would prevent all chances of payment. And Crabbe hoped to get the man to realize that to help him to work would be the quickest and surest way to settlement. Parrucchiero was increasing his hotel by the addition of twenty rooms in the adjoining Clock Tower. The place was full of workmen, and Crabbe and his landlord talked as they walked from room to room. It certainly had finer views, more unique views, than any other house in the world. The rooms were not large: but, from their lovely balconies and terraces, the Square of Saint Mark, the gold and porphyry front of the basilica, the Piazzetta, Ducal Palace, Columns, Grand Canal, with the distant islet of Sanzorzi Mazore, were seen from a point of view which has no equal anywhere. It is exactly right. There isn't a single hotel on the Grand Canal itself which has anything approaching a view like this. Crabbe fed his eyes with the exquisite life and beauty of it whenever the conversation touched on tedium.

Barbolan was immensely tickled by Crabbe's answer to an inquiry

as to why he had broken from Warden. 'I let him interfere with
my affairs when I thought him a friend,' said Crabbe. 'When I
found that he wasn't——'

Barbolan tittered: 'What simplicity! Why, he was my friend—
not yours. Don't you know that he owed me L. 500 when he left
my hotel?'

'No,' Crabbe snapped, restively; 'he told me little or nothing
of his private affairs, and extracted all about mine.'

'That was his case, in fact. He acted for me—not for you. He
was penniless, like you—a bill to me, his lady's frocks from the best
modiste of Milano, bills everywhere. Never could he live in his
own house—always in hotels, with my cousin of the Vapore, with
a baroness whom he caught at the Victoria, at the Calcina, or in
his friends' palaces which he cried them to lend, Lady Contessa di Pas,
the Signora Curzia——'

'I don't want to hear.'

'And he wrestled to borrow two hundred sterling, to clear himself
and take a fresh start in England——'

Crabbe reared, and lashed out. 'I won't hear another word—
excepting this: tell me what you mean by saying that he was not
my friend, but yours.'

Barbolan giggled. 'He said that it was incredible that a gentleman
so clever and so bold as you, Signore, could be really without friends
or money. And he said that he believed you to be concealing something, which he thought he could force you to reveal.'

'Force? Force me?'

'Sissignore—force you to reveal the true state of your affairs, and
shew some disposition to work to pay me.'

Crabbe roared. 'This is ineffably comic—I mean the notion that
anyone could force me to anything. But please continue.'

Barbolan twittered nervously. 'So he kept you in his palace, doing
nothing, without food, without bed, alone, in the dark——'

'Oh, but this is superb! Here is the twentieth century, and you
Venetians haven't got the notion of your pozzi and your piombi
and your tormentors out of your heads yet. Here is the twentieth
century, and all ecclesiastical parties fly when balked to physical
torture quite naturally. Excellent Christians! Excellent friend!
And you—you believed this pious ruffian; and connived at his
attempt to kill me? Bless my soul, what geese there are in this
world!'

'Geese?'

'Yes, geese. All three of us. Perhaps I'm the greatest of these.

I persuaded myself to believe that pimp to be honest and a friend. He thought me false and timid, a liar and a coward. And you, for the sake of the L. 500 which you say he owed you, let him try to kill me who owe you L. 2000—kill the only goose at all likely to lay golden eggs. Understand? Well: you've lost me three most valuable months, piled an addition to my load of obligations (for of course I shall have a severe account to settle with your Warden), and you've made my difficulties infinitely worse than they ever were——'

'I offer excuses——'

Crabbe waved them aside. 'I don't quite know for the moment what to do with you. You don't deserve that I should consider you specially, as a matter of fact. And I won't, unless you renounce this bestial plotting behind my back, and trust me.'

'What, Signore, would you propose?'

'It seems that, between you and your abominable Warden and my fatuous Peary-Buthlaw, I have been carefully kept from doing anything myself. And I am the only person who can do anything. Understand? But I must have time, and means. With time and means to act, I'll undo all the harm done by my stupid agents and my false friends. It will take three months, perhaps. Remember, I am master of the situation. No one can make sixpence out of my books, excepting with my consent. And I'll consent to nothing unless my proper share is secured to me. My agents and my friends can steal my property: but they shan't profit from it. Rather than that, I'll damn my own books and stop their sales; and I'll warn the Publishers' Association against my own manuscripts. On the other hand, if you're willing to help me to recover my own property——'

'Yes, Signore.'

'I'll make you a proposition. Let me use the papers and the clothes which you've sequestered: renew my bill, and increase it to L. 4000, and let me have the balance to use. Do this, and I'll have my goods sent from England and give you a lien on all I possess. I'll find new agents to sell the books which are ready, and you shall supervise all my correspondence. And I'll instantly go on writing, to make up for lost time.

Barbolan hesitated.

'You warned me, months ago, that I was being robbed; and I didn't believe you. I believe you now; and I offer to put myself absolutely in your hands.

Barbolan was lost. The man who addressed him was wan and

frightfully shabby: Warden still lingered in Venice, and had very influential connections. 'You ought to have said this before,' he at length pronounced.

'Yes: I'm sorry that I didn't. But I'm saying it now. Think it over; and telephone to me any day at the Bucintoro,' Crabbe concluded.

He went away enlightened and delighted. One mystery was solved—the mystery of one of the motives of the Wardens. He, quite unconsciously, had been their rival. They wanted hospitality, while they cringed and squirmed to scratch up a little money: they couldn't avail themselves of the chance of a permanent establishment, unless they could borrow two hundred sterling—the very sum which he had once innocently named as essential to the untying of his own hands. Naturally, it was out of the question that pawky professional parasites—for it was plain that the Wardens were pre-hensile—should plead with their patrons (on whom they were sponging for loans, hospitality, interest), to enter into business relations with a haughty disdainer of alms.

But, how was it that the Wardens were in such a bestial position? Both were clever in Horace's golden mediocre way: both wrote books, but not books which pay for the paper. They wasted what they had of knowledge and force over the production of tracts, theological treatises, biographies of unimportant Italians. They were feckless sciolistic unbusiness-like rushers-about in society (her frocks and furs and feathers and fetters cost money), devoid of physical stamina, salient mental superiority, or dominant power. They were just poor specimens. Oh, if they had only been frank with him from the beginning. He might have passed over their ugliness and their Erastianism; and he would very gladly have helped their helplessness by leaguing with them. As you know, o most affable reader, his ever-present sense of incompleteness rendered him always ready to join forces with anyone who shewed real need of him. They never had done that, really. They had pushed and pried and pursued him (with false pretences) for his society, never hinting that they wanted him to help them. If they had trusted him, if they had used influence for him, if they had caused anyone simply to instruct some reputable solicitor to take over his affairs from his defaulting agents, he would have been on firm footing—and they with him. Instead, they had played a private game. To recommend themselves, they had used force—force—to make him an object of charity to propitiate their benefactors. And he realized the disappointment and humiliation and exasperation of their little souls at being prevented from offering him up to the lust for advertisement of the professional philanthropists on whom they depended. That— and the odium theologicum 'I'm not really bound to help you, seeing that you're not a co-religionist,' when flattery and fiction and even force had failed—were the torches which enlightened the mysterious motive of the Wardens. The exhibition of what he had fondly believed to be obsolescent sectarian bigotry shocked him to the core—shocked him even more than the destruction of his illusion. The best thing to do would be to wipe these people as a man, wiping a dish, wipes it, and turns it upside down. He was done with them. They would not dare to interfere with him again.

There remained, though, the lark of testing the rest, an experiment which promised to be fascinating. La Pash and her infirmary might be taken as tried. For the rest of the Erastians—and I have not mentioned, in these pages, half of those who sought Crabbe's society while he was thought to be warm—for these, dummies of the infirmary committee, married and single old maids of both genders, it remained to provide spectacles for them to comment upon. Caps should be hung up for whoever might choose to snatch and don them. Traps should be laid for the snaring of vermin.

The Scattoletti's first weekly bill amounted to L. 47.50. 'This displeases me,' Crabbe told the greasy innkeeper as he paid; 'your customary pension is L. 5 a day: if you combine for that, well—if not, I go away.'

'I combine, I combine, o Treasure!' cooed the smutty-faced melting-eyed archangel.

Oh but the process is slow of reaching perfection of rawness: every flinching atom of flesh must be flayed.

XXIII

ANOTHER unspeakable Scotchman sat up and wrote hectically from *The Lykeion*. The two guineas were payment in full: to expect more was impertinence: and he didn't admire Crabbe's morals. Crabbe promptly pinched him with a Who-are-you, and a recitation of facts. The manuscripts had been sent, priced, on the Reverend Bobugo's introduction and at Lord Arthur Baliol Kingsbury's request. *Terribile la Femmina* had been printed without consultation of author, who found out the liberty by accident. He was corresponding solely with the editor; and renewed request for balance due and return of unused manuscripts.

If this failed, there would be difficulty about Scattoletti's next bill. Of course fruit might appear from his secret sowings; but it was risky to count on that. And glorious summer made him yearn and burn for sunlit seas. No word had come from Barbolan. Crabbe rang him up on the telephone 'Have you pondered my proposition?' 'I want deeds, not words.' Crabbe reared. 'Don't you understand that I offer you deeds?' 'Yes, but I want no words, only deeds.' 'In short, you reject my proposition. Va ben. Now listen. You prevent me from working to pay you; so I must work for bare life. Will you let me have a blue linen-suit which is in my luggage?' 'What for?' 'I shall earn my living as a barcariol.' Barbolan guffawed, and rang off.

Crabbe was quite serious about undertaking menial work. He liked it. And he knew not shame. For the sake of his health he was determined to spend the summer out of doors, and gladly would have rowed a bark of beer-barrels: but menial employment is denied to brains which do not dress the part. Failing the blue linen of a workman, he applied by letter to six of the Warden's male fellow-Erastians for a job as second gondoliere, in which capacity a blouse and a uniform would be provided for him. Five refused— some with sneers, others with jeers—and the lay-living oratorian (who danced and went to plays and was the ladies' darling) maintained religious silence. They thought it the hugest joke; and passed it to their females, who jibble-jabbled about it at tea-tables. No one had the wit to see that misbehaviour was beginning to be publicly exemplified. No one dreamed of consequences. No one suspected that the work of weeding and testing was relentlessly initiated.

Crabbe expatiated much in the Piazza and other public places at this time, pacing with bald and lofty fastidiousness where sleeve-rubbing was likely to occur, or rowing aloof in Canalazzo with the tranquil and worthy allure of a burgher about to breakfast. He excited feverish interest. 'Whatever is he going to do?' was a question festered in bosoms and foamed from frail lips. The infirmary directress couldn't stop herself in time from sweeping him a brazen bow on the Piazzetta; and was blasted by the Cut Straight. Thereafter the kallipygs of the Erastian colony held off him a little, rolling and waddling with majestuous rotundity, presenting an indecent visage and most hideous rear in respectful perspective. Somehow their males kept out of his way. He was content to wait for manifestations of dangerously comic reservations in Erastianism, which (he was certain) would occur; and he spent his time in preparing pinches to make even rhinoceroses caper, or in jotting down rhythmic and splendid hexameters.

A curiosity occurred one evening at the club. Crabbe chained his bark as usual, and was about to pass out through the somewhat crowded atrium when two or three naval lieutenants rushed at him—please, for gentility's sake, would he speak to an English, a member of the Naples Rowing Club, who wished to join the Bucintoro.

It was a stumpy little clean-faced ruddy one, with a calm voice, and the benevolently pug-doggy manner of stubby curates who vespertinally teach boxing to hooligans. Crabbe was civil. Excited Italians (amazed at absence of kisses) posed on all sides, admiring the phlegm of the Englishmen's mutual sniffing and summings-up. The new-comer gave his name as Butler. He looked all right: his clothes were nothing much, but not bad. He said that he was an artist from Naples, intending to put in a year at Venice: mentioned his banker Jesurum, his agent Cook, and letters introducing to consuls and wife's relations. Crabbe continued civility, and spoke of putting his name down for election, but encouraged no intimacy. The other, however, beamed a good deal, and effected so many encounters on the ensuing days, that Crabbe felt a little chastened. The man had plenty to say, not uninteresting, not ill-said. He at once minimized his means and position: a small income (paid through a reputable English firm) formed a skeleton, which prices of pictures clothed for a wife and a girl of seven who were content with humble living at a trattoria not unlike the Scattoletti. In short, Crabbe found him a decent paste of man and by no means upsetting; but, having rather a fastidy of taking any more people into his own life, he said that temporary disorder of his affairs prevented him from being social, and he hoped that he would be let alone. The Butler, however, persisted in amiability: it was impossible to refuse a homely luncheon, which could be paid for by rowing about the city prospecting sites for pictures. These excursions were shared by his daughter, a veritable gamin, with cropped hair, a bad knee, and a squint, who chattered and gesticulated Neapolitan, demanding a little beaker of Marsala at every pub. Her father expounded his plans. The great point about him was that he was totally devoid of swagger and of shame. He evidently had no intention, though, of remaining in shadow. On his own account, he discovered and visited La Pash's infirmary; and laid himself out for the acquaintance of casual Erastians, on the ground of nationality, not of faith, he being Catholic by conversion on marriage, in Egypt, with a Dalmatian of Venetian extraction born in England. Crabbe, consequently, had to be explicit on his personal relations with Warden and his kind: which he did, to the sound of sympathy (of a sort) tinctured with counsel as to prudence, rashness, and the common vices. And, after a few days, he sheered off on a plea of prior engagements. The home-life of this family, at their fifth-rate trattoria in Campo de Sanfélipezaccomo, was not decorative or enticing. Butler's incessant 'Lin-der gimme glass o' wine,' or 'Lin-der gimme cigarette,' and the wife's grave silent almost-oriental obedience (accompanied by absence of a wedding-ring) at first amusing, became a little monotonous. There was talk of taking an apartment, and beginning seriously to paint, on arrival of goods from Naples. It might be wise to let these people settle themselves in a milieu of their own before criticizing them. So Crabbe kept clear, at the Scattoletti during the heat of the long days, or on the lagoon at dawn and until after sunset.

He gave himself this monition—Zildo must be kept from the Butlers, for innumerable reasons. He altered the boy's hours again, giving him the whole day to himself and requiring service only from 17 o'clock till dusk. The idea of weaning was coming to the front of his mind.

Some artfulness was needed to escape notice in the long light evenings. All Venice is abroad at this time of day and year. Eights and fours and pairs and skiffs of the rowing-clubs swing swaggering round the city. Gondole swarm. 'Divieto di nuoto,' on the street corners, is a dead letter: water-babies (pudic, though incredibly tattered) wallow in every canal. You even may see respectable mothers of families blissfully seated, up to the necks in water, on their backdoor-steps. 'If "Swimming is Prohibited" by the police, what must one do when run down by a motor-launch—pay a fine, or drown?' Nicholas once asked laughingly of Zildo.

'As for me, I should swim: but, Sior, keep (as I do) one special lira always prompt and apart in the pocket, for evitating disputes with the vizili.'

'What, bribe the police?'

'Sior, with permission, I said no such ugly word: but—a little beaker of wine—what is it? All the same, Sior, offer nothing but an infrequent cigar of Tuscany to the carabinieri, unless you wish to go incarcerated instantly for corruption.'

Nicholas used to pick up his boy in Rio de Santrovaso, and swoop across the canal of Zuecca, through narrow Santeufemia, and along Canale Nuovo to the shallows where it joins large-looping Canale Fasiol. Here was sumptuous solitude on the wide wide wide lagoon, mirroring pageants of sunsets behind the violet Euganean Hills. Zildo rowed his master, along the meanderings of Fasiol, as far as the new maize-marked channel by the piroga of the finance. Nicholas rested his soul and body in this hour, saying little, sometimes looking at the boy's amazingly clever patterns for bead-collars, or hearing gentle chatter about a biadajuolo anxious to supply comestibles on credit. 'And, Sior, I said to him, like this: "Thus do improvident gondolieri, taking food from you all the winter without paying; and, in the summer, when much money is earned from forestiers, you make them pay you double." '

Nicholas chuckled: 'And what did he say?'

'Sior, he said, like this: "One must live; but who are you?" And I said to him, like this, "I am the servant of a very powerful English; and, if your chandlery is cheap and of good quality, I will buy it for deniers down; but if not, favour me with your absence, o son of the priest and the countess! Sa!" '

It is true that, during long silences in these evenings, Nicholas was aware of being gravely eyed; but he never was pricked with an anxious or inquisitive or even an inconvenient question. Zildo was a stay and a refuge. And, at twilight, Nicholas landed him on Spinalonga to return home by ferry; and himself resought the lonely lagoon for a long evening swim.

One morning, when he was in the act of shooting away from

the club to bathe, he had an entirely delicious astonishment. Zildo, in a new bark, came darting down the Grand Canal, across his course—a new Zildo, more wonderful than ever. Nicholas stayed firm, to let him come alongside the pupparin. It was before 5 o'clock: the sun, just up, turned everything into clean aquamarine set in newly minted gold. The boy was all in white duck of sailor fashion, nobly worn, exquisitely fitting; and he had a straw hat with vermilion riband tilted over his laughing eyes. His bark was a tiny moscherata, about three metres long, rowed with a slender pair of crossed oars; it was painted black, and contained a little mat, a clean towel, and a blue linen blouse neatly folded, and nothing else. Nicholas looked him over, from the honey-hued triangle of generous bare breast to the toes of the quickening feet tinted with the native carnation of amaranth.

'Sior, with permission, do you esteem me like this?'

'But, tremendously.'

'Tante grazie, Sior: I knew that you would be pleased to permit me a diversion of this type. Sa!'

'And whence came these splendours?'

'Sior, I shall tell everything. And I bought the vestment in Campo Sanbortolmio at the shop of Barbaro; but, after, in my house, I cut pieces from the giubba and sewed the seams again, also pantaloons, to accommodate them more justly to me so that I cannot feel them. And the bark, I bought it at Ognissanti for twenty-seven franchi all complete, oars, forks, everything. Isn't it beautiful, subtile, most light? For I had a reason, don't you know?'

'What reason?'

'Sior, for health and for pleasure, at this season, to plunge myself and swim to polish myself——'

'And where?'

'Sior, is there not a deepish canal without pali, which leads from Canale La Grazia to that of Orfanello; and none pass that way. No one shall see ins and outs—only a boy's head in the sea. And what is that? Sior, let me accompany you to the parting of the way, I pray.'

They rowed on. Zildo's tiny bark flickered round and about the heavier pupparin like a gleeful midge. His beautifully dexterous action with the crossed oars was a sight to see. The charm of the lagoon, at that hour of the morning is that one easily can enshroud oneself in immense empty open spaces for privacy. When they came to the cross-canal, the boy went to the left. Nicholas swept onward to the islet and moored at the second palo short of it. As he bounded on the poop to dive, a slim pink strip slipped from a mite of dark strip dancing on the ripples far away. The boy was in the water first. He was enormously content with the initiative, the nice clean delicate healthy instinct and the audacious modesty of Zildo. 'Se 'l corpo che amo xe servo e vijano, la bejezza che m' innamora xe jibera e zentil,' he sang to the sunbeams. And gorgeous forebodings of the pudibundery of Erastian peeping toms and other types of tartufes simply made him squeal with joy as he fled headlong in a great curve through the air to the sea.

They met again at the parted way, and rowed back across the Basin of Saint Mark together. The Austrian *S.S. Metcovich* was toppling Teutonic tourists into a shoal of grabbing gondole. At the club Zildo chained both barks, and donned a long blue working-smock, rolling up his trousers, and began to repolish the pupparin for the day. Nicholas inspected him from the balcony for a few minutes before going in for his letters. 'Wasn't it good?' he said presently.

'Good, Sior, and fresh as a kiss.'

'There's better swimming in the wide Canale Orfano, where the sea is nine—ten—metres in depth. Sometimes a marine bastiment passes, sometimes a torpedo-destroyer: but one can take opportunities; and, as you say, a head in the water offends nobody. It is far, though.'

'Sior, if we might go, together, like this, with two oars in the pupparin, and my moschereta towed behind, then we could go and return with the greatest celerity. Vuol?'

'Va ben. Let us try. I will moor at one palo; and you shall distance your bark four—five—pali away.'

'Sior, and why?'

Nicholas didn't answer. He looked. The greenish-blue eyes scintillated in a vermeil flush, the rosy lips thought of the tiniest frank and open smile, and then set gravely. 'Sìssior: as you will. Lei xe Paron. I will distance myself of four hundred metres from my—master—for obedience.'

A singular and horrid letter came from the hectic tartar of *The Lykeion*, stating that Lord Arthur Baliol Kingsbury knew nothing of Bobugo Bonsen, never asked for anybody's work, had not asked for Crabbe's, nor seen it nor read letters addressed to him on the subject: no more money would be sent for *Terribile la Femmina*; and the unused manuscripts would not be returned.

Bobugo, invited to explain, snarled a refusal. Crabbe faced loss of his pay and of half a dozen manuscripts, uttering sundry lurid comments on the trick to reduce him to such straits as to force him to write the priest's book about Saint Thomas of Canterbury.

Scattoletti (for reasons known only to himself) refrained from presenting bills, and Crabbe abstained from demanding them. He was getting on finely with his verses—

'Forms immortal of flaming whiteness, the splendour of ray'd hair,
Lighten that land of a dream, where candour and cleanness and vim rule'

—were picturesque and hexametrical; and, with the notion that something would turn up sooner or later, he let bills slide. But he reduced his meals to morning coffee and a plate of risotto in the evening, on the ground that the weather was too hot for gross feeding.

Mactavish, on a Monday, again chaffed him about sleeping out of doors.

'Mi stanca,' snapped Crabbe: 'don't you know that I'm ruined, and that I did it out of sheer necessity.'

'That's, hum, dreadful! Would, hum, you allow——' a billet of ten lire offered with a squeezed face.

'Not for your life.'

'I, hum, understand—and quite approve—but a, hum, full belly you know—do lunch with, hum, me at the Bellavenezia tomorrow, and tell me all about your, hum, teroubles.'

They lunched; and Crabbe answered quantities of questions, while Mactavish poured white wine down. The Scotchman was touched-up by the respectable prices paid for his guest's work: 'I don't make thirty, hum, shillings a thousand words, myself,' he complained, with a little envy.

'We, to whom literature is a sole crutch, look upon you, to whom it is a mere walking-stick, as criminals. You cut prices by presenting Barabbas with four-fifths of the value of your stuff. As a matter of public decency, you rich men ought to be prohibited from writing at all, specially when you write well. If I were dictator, I'd decapitate the lot of you, beginning with Sir Gilbert Parker,' was Crabbe's smack on the smack-red cheek beside him.

Mactavish offered the other: 'Let, hum, me help you. Why not send for your things, and sell, hum, some of your finished, hum, manuscripts.'

'That's precisely what I'm panting to do. But I haven't the

means. If you want to help, lend me three hundred sterling, or guarantee my bill to Barbolan; and I'll give you a lien on everything I have.'

'Oh, hum, but—I couldn't entertain either of those proposals.'

'Then you waste my time,' concluded Crabbe, who never could ask for anything except with his horrible and menacing pincers.

He went home, rearing, and lashing out for all he was worth. Somebody would have to suffer. He denounced his defaulting agents, formally, to the Law Society, as stolid stupids who refused to render accounts. He warned the Publishers' Association against negotiating with anyone but himself for *The Weird* and *De Burgh's Delusion*, giving Caliban's name as being in possession of them. And he renewed his monition to the publisher of *Sieur René* against issuing that work without his expressed permission. Thus, having comfortably hung up his books, so that thieves could not profit by them, he felt relieved in mind and replenished with a deep and hilarious peace.

The effect of this offensive sally soon made itself felt by the grand-magistracial Caliban. That popinjay wrote again for an address to which he might forward the two manuscripts thus (at a blow) rendered useless to him. And Crabbe, immovable (excepting at his own will and pleasure), replied that he had no sure address, and left the things to fester rancorously on Caliban's dirty hands. They were no good to him till he had secured proper management for them, and they might as well be at Uskvale as elsewhere. To be additionally exasperating, he said, further: 'I refuse to receive anything from you, excepting on the following terms: (*a*) carriage and duty paid; (*b*) your written guarantee that I shall receive everything in the same condition as when entrusted to your care; (*c*) a written expression of regret for your unwarrantable detention of my property signed by you and your mother and your father.' And then deep silence reigned.

Scattoletti asked for money. 'Wait a week,' said Crabbe.

Scattoletti demanded money. 'Wait another week,' said Crabbe; and went six days without food, which stopped his work. The melting-eyed smutty-face presented a bill for L. 193.40, cooing 'Va bene cosi?' Crabbe said something indignant about the overcharge of L. 57.40. The extortioner gave him truculence, flung a flask of white wine over a clean suit of flannels, and retired to beat his wife and babies in the kitchen. And that day's post brought

a cheque (for a story sown in England) which Cook changed into
L. 524.

Rather breathed at the pace of this race, and wondering whether
the authorities couldn't be persuaded to a little more liberality in
the matter of margins and handicaps, Crabbe went about for a
day or two with the cash in his pocket, feeling fine.

Butler turned up again at the club, saying that he was ready to
be elected right away. He had moved to a little apartment in the
Alley of the Angel, and was for being visited. It was a queer show:
furniture (of incredible skimpiness and cheapness) hired from the
landlord, mixed with the vaunted goods from Naples, which last
consisted of a trunk of books worth perhaps ninepence and another
of ramshackle paints with a score of amateurish dauby sketches.
The funny thing about Butler, as I say, was that he shewed neither
bumptiousness nor shame. He neither bragged of nor excused
shortcomings. His sangfroid, or obtuseness, or insensibility was
about the most densely stolid British thing that Crabbe had ever
encountered. He stuck up his daubs with modest satisfaction,
punctuated with 'Lin-der gimme glass o' wine,' and explained that
little things satisfied him, adding the inevitable 'Lin-der gimme
cigarette.' His monumental wife tacked old photographs and
picture post-cards and fans on walls, in the intervals of producing celestially-odoured soups from inconsiderable pans; and
the baby of seven skipped among the medley, cackling and
squinting.

All sorts of things had been happening, and the painter had
loads to say to Crabbe's address. He began by proposing a partnership point-blank. 'We're both rather pushed, and might as well
stand by each other. My quarterly L. 800 is due next month, and
then we shall be all right. Lin-der gimme glass o' wine. I can get
you an attic top of this house for L. 25 a month; and, if our grub's
good enough for you, you're welcome. Then we can have each
other's company, and get to work, and share and share alike. You
leave it all to me. Lin-der gimme cigarette.'

'Out of the question,' said Crabbe; 'you don't suppose that I'll
take something for nothing?'

'No, no—gimme a chance: I want your bark to take me painting.
And, if you'll be my gondoliere, I'll gladly give you board and
lodging. Lin-der gimme glass o' wine.'

That perhaps might do. Why not versify on the poop while
Butler painted at the prow? The spectacle thus provided would

be famishingly exciting for the resident aliens, giving them food for frantic gossip, and weaving webs about their clumsy hoofs. Crabbe chuckled at the notion of the tosses which the Erastians were sure to take.

'Tell me something,' he said: 'you won't mind—but, are things at all tight with you?'

'Well, the cost of our move from Naples——'

'Yes: would a tenner on account be of any service?'

'O, my God! If I could get a loan of a tenner——'

Crabbe pulled out notes for L. 250 and passed them over.

'Oh, I say! Lin-der, Lin-der, here's our saviour. Gim glass-o' wine. Gimme glass too!'

Explanations. Exultations. 'Well, you are a godsend! Sure you can spare it! Lin-der gimme cigarette. Gim one too.'

Crabbe expounded his plans, unfolding his own situation, with special reference to the nefariousness of the archangel Scattoletti. 'I propose,' he said, 'to offer this brigand of Warden's L. 150 in full discharge. And, if he won't take it, I'll go to the Questura.'

'Better leave it to me. I know how to deal with Italians. If he refuses L. 150, pay L. 100 on account; and I'll guarantee the rest out of this money you've lent me. It'll be all right next month when I get my cheque. You leave everything to me.'

They crossed to the Accademia together. Arcanzolo was glum, and posed as a deeply injured idiot, fat, smutty, and past the prime of life. He refused L. 150; took L. 100 and Butler's signature for L. 93.40; and Crabbe cleared to the Calle del Anzolo.

'New commandments for you, Zildo mio,' he said, when the boy joined him after swimming in the deep-water canal between the islets of Sanclemente and Sanservolo, the following morning.

'Sior, command me.'

'The bark must be polished and ready every morning at 5½ o'clock. After then you are free. I have found a friend, an English, whom I shall row all day——'

'It pleases me that my Paròn has found a friend, an English——'

'And Zildo—if you encounter me, you do not know me. Understand?'

'Sior, I understand well. But I will not encounter you after the morning swimming: for I have my house and my beads to occupy me, don't you know. Sior, hear that I have gained a mound of deniers——'

'I don't wish to hear of them: but I am glad.'

'Also I am glad: but I don't wish to have them, Sior.'

'Nonsense!'

'Nonòsior.'

'——!'

'Sìssior.'

Every sensitive nerve must be severed and tortured to wincing: every sinew be snatched from its mooring, and torn.

XXIIII

Butler arranged a plain garret under the roof for his gondoliere. It had no outlook; but things might be stored, and work done, there on wet days. Cash in hand made the painter festive. When his quarterly allowance came, sorrow and sighing would flee away. But the ready enabled the teaching of the banker Jesurum and one or two other banausic persons their places, who (not being impressed by letters of introduction) had shied at obvious impecuniosity. His wife, grateful apart, exhibited marriage-lines with certificates of birth, baptism, husband's conversion and what not—she didn't know what they would have done but for her little brooch (presented by an Egyptian princess whose dame de compagnie she had been) and her wedding-ring. Crabbe demanded the tickets, and cut off to the Monte di Pietà to redeem them. The baby, seeing things pleasant, yelped for regalements. Her father (quite the genial hail-fellow) cried: 'Do take her out—Lin-der gimme glass o' wine—and buy her something, Crabbe, there's a good chap, and I'll pay you later—Lin-der gimme cigarette.' A giant doll and pram and sewing-machine appeared an hour later; and packets of cigarettes, dotted all over the apartment, confirmed Crabbe's reputation as a saviour.

The painter's news, delivered at leisure in the pupparin, was most juicy. He had been snouting privately, on his own account, among the Erastians, collecting commentaries. He was quite naïve about it, fairly impersonal (though naturally biased toward his tangible benefactor), and he certainly wasn't clever enough to invent. The Warden and his Sappytower, it appeared, had regretfully offered the ingeniously damaging surmise that Crabbe's refusal to be shunted to England (first-class and with his clothes washed) was due to the fact that he was wanted there by the police.

Crabbe reared. No reputation can stand poverty and calumny (*i.e.* slander which is false) at the same time. He at first was flabbergasted by these resident aliens, not having believed (as he told the woozy Warden) that such specimens actually survived outside Ouida's *Friendship* and *In a Winter City*. He had Tauchnitz Editions of both books in his club locker; and he got them out and read them over again. Yes: here they all were, tuft-hunters, sycophants, pickthanks, prôneurs, puffers, backbiters, and physidoyls or born slaves. Having done evil, they could imagine nothing but evil. And, of all injured vanities, we all know that that of the reproved buffoon, of the histrionic self-deceived, is far and away more savage than that of the brat-robbed gorilla. It was no more than natural, then, that, having chased him, imploring his society, begging and commanding him to connect officially with them, as long as they thought him wealthy —and having been baldly and grimly and bleakly rebuffed—and then having failed to drive him away, or to kill him, or to bring one trace of appeal to that dreadful disdainful face, which suffered so horribly and would make others suffer for his sufferings—that strange strong awful face (not a wicked one)—which struck no fear (oh no!) to the heart of Zildo—that strange strong awful face whose features presented downward lines of wistful melancholy intersected with upward lines of bitter resolute withering derision—yes, it was no more than natural that they should snatch up the dirty dagger used for Julius Cæsar, and Michelangelo, and Shakespeare—the dirty dagger of calumny and spite, and stab his scorn in the back. Very well. Of course, he would have to sacrifice his reputation, such as it was. But he was prompt and very apt fartum facere ex hostibus, as Plautus says. They wanted war? Bloody war, grim-visaged war, horrida bella, à la mort, à l'outrance—the real thing—they should have. 'To kill him.'—Wouldn't all sorts of respectable people say that he was mad to think so extravagantly. No doubt they would. But he did them the justice of remembering, 'They know not what they do.' It's the very rarest thing in the world to find a man or woman able, or willing, to let themselves foresee the effects of the causes which they so gaily set in motion. And, when you do find such a man or woman, he or she is generally a deliberate bad 'un, or a selfish self-seeker desiring relief from incumbrance. 'What a blessing it would be if he would make a good confession and communion, and then die suddenly!' said Bobugo once to Crabbe, when their mutual friend (the original of Chris in 'The Sensibilist') had been knocked down by new and unmerited misfortune. Oh yes, whether they knew it or not, whether they meant it or not, plenty of people had the will and the power and the desire to cause his removal. Crabbe was quite aware of it. He sharpened his portentous pincers.

He wrote twice to Warden, safely stewing (at some adorer's expense) in the Baths of Aix, demanding categorical contradiction. Obtaining no replies, he used a severe post-card. Meanwhile, he confronted the Sappytower with a similar ultimatum.

Rothschild's cluppy financier temporized. It wasn't exactly a question of being wanted by the police, but rather of being kept in exile by financial embarrassments. He thought that he might contradict the former: he feared that he suspected the latter.

"The latter is precisely the case—pecuniary embarrassments exaggerated by your tipsy meddling: but not such as to prevent me from returning to England when I choose. I do not choose, till I have tidied up Venice; and, meanwhile, my comment on your splenetic attempt at defamation is the Word of the Vine. Down to the root though thou nibblest me, goat, yet my branches shall yield thee wine to besprinkle thee when thou on the altar dost bleed," Crabbe fulminated, with much private delectament, in Greek.

For further amusement, he thought (with his usual tardy mistrust of established reputations) that a little inquisition concerning the Sappytower might be worth time. And a note to Rothschild's in Paris brought a pleasing testimonial that the tipsy old totterer had really once been in the employ of that firm, which had since lost sight of him—only a mere matter of more than forty years ago. Now I ask you, o most affable reader, how many years' hard labour in the third division would a false pretender, too poor to paint at a Grand Hotel, too proud and too brave to cringe to a Pash, too Christian to pervert (for protection and profit) to Erastianism—get, as a general rule, for messing a financial matter on a reputation based on repetitions of adventures in Baron Rothschild's bedroom, tabid with more than forty years' putrescence? Crabbe, however, saw nothing in this exposure of the Sappytower but food for inextinguishable laughter, at the venally credulous gullibility of the abject tuft-hunting Warden, and at his own ridiculous persistence in trusting apparent piety. He never was quick to detect rascality—but foolishness, stupidity, vulgarity, always, at first sight; and not without reason.

The Festival of The Redentore passed. Zildo gave an account of the vigil when he met his master at the club in the morning— the long bridge of barges across the wide canal of Zuecca—the long long summer night, with all Venice on the water feasting in illuminated barks—specially a boy of the Benedetto Marcello School, in yellow, who sounded a gravicembalo in a peata hung with lanterns like gigantic oranges. Zildo was appassionated for music, he confessed: but even his lovely archaic words for playing the pianoforte could not lift the frown from his master's brow that day. Were these Erastians hypocrites? Or grotesques?

The post-card to the Warden touched the button, eliciting a meekly acid purr: "Your kind card has just reached me at this rather dismal Bain. I of course give the categorical contradiction you expect, and I wish you had not denied me completely all opportunities of helping you." Crabbe instantly circulated calumny and "kind card" contradiction among the resident aliens, as a gibe, and as a warning. And then, all of a sudden, the shingly Wardeness leaped (with a yelp) from the Baths.

She—she—wrote to Crabbe, in the astonishing but hackneyed pose of the Devoted Wife, sheltering her man behind her petticoat while she said 'Shoo' to mendicants, extortioners, blackmailers, merely casual hotel acquaintances, and so on, and so forth. Could anything, o most affable reader, be juster than that 'merely casual acquaintance,' addressed to Crabbe by the woman whose persistent hunting and courting of him, in his cane arm-chair in the hall, even to this day sets Albergo Bellavista sniggering and guffawing at its brazen memory? Her said man, she shrieked, was but a poor weak thing; and she would steal his letters, and go all lengths and some others, rather than let his earning power (such as it was) be interfered with. Incidentally, she let out the delicious news that the Warden's pusillanimous timidity had made him destroy (unread) Crabbe's reply to the prayer that he would let himself be paid to go and die on any doorstep but that of Erastian Venice. Now, as the destroyed letter contained a certain prohibition, Crabbe foresaw an extremely dainty complication ahead. At this point, therefore, he held his peace: none of these vermin, who had scuffled to infest him when he was believed to be worth blooding, should be aided in escaping the earthly sequels of very vile idiocy. But, as it offended his fastidious taste to see a churchman's lady bestemmiating like a minuscular baggage, he took a private copy of her balderdash and returned the original, telling her that she'd better burn it. He also held out to her a very gentle olive-branch; which, of course, was liable to translation as an admission of weakening.

Here he began a practice as terrible as that of Saint Uriel Archangel, the Prefect of Divine Archives. He initiated a full and exhaustive record. Hitherto, he had made drafts of all correspondence, more for the pleasure of working literary flavour into his letters than for prudence's sake; and, by the mercy of some god, he had kept all his rough drafts. Now he procured a ream of quarto paper and a blank book: in the latter he codified previous and drafted future letters; on the former he did the same, sending the filled sheets (and each future sheet as he filled it) under seal to a literary man (name obvious) with whom he then had a slight acquaintance, in

America. But the book of correspondence, with all originals, he kept as his constant companion, for the information of the Quæstor of Venice in the event of his collapse. La vita ze 'na cosa molto pericolosa: pochi sono quei che oltrepassarono viventi.

For it was borne in upon him, not that his absence was desired, but that it was to be procured (without actual collision with the law) by lying words, grieved hints, sad suggestions, pained persecutions, ostracism, calumny, tricks fit for peddlers, and a show of legality and humble Erastianism as varnish over all. He clearly saw that the experiment on which he was embarked was a huge and a hugely dangerous one. It was another awful example of the One and the Many, a new Athanasius contra Mundum. Erastian Venice, scarlet with shame, mortified to the core, at being caught in the flagrant delict of making such a disgustingly knavish and mercenary fool of itself about him, would go to all lengths (in the words of the Warden's estimable lady) to obliterate the standing and hideously articulate monument of its own dishonour. Would he consent to be obliterated? Would he be sensible and take pay to go away with his clothes washed? No. He would stay, and do his work, as long as he could. And then? Charity? Brrr! Or Death? Death, with pleasure. But, before death, an interval of observed horrors? Even that, if needs must. There could be no going back. The fight must be pressed, till it ended in victory—or in death, as the victim of friendly treachery and Erastian exasperation. A martyr's suicide is the reward of a nonconformist conscience. Good. Thank the Lord he was unconnected with anything of the nature of an Establishment, Erastian or dissenting. He girded his loins again for the fray.

The Wardeness tossed back his olive-branch, unopened. He sent it to her man. Again the vicious female returned it, unstamped and unopened. He sent it to the Sappytower, who returned it, saying that it didn't interest him as he was leaving Venice. Crabbe hoped that Rothschild's financier would make himself less ridiculous elsewhere; and sent the olive-branch to the infirmary directress, telling her (as the Warden's dear friend) that he wished in fairness to say things privately to them before saying them publicly. She burned it, unread, at the Warden's request. So she said, that incomparable touch of feminility.

Messieurs Paddington sent the Warden's book, *Social Life of the Early Gnostics*, whose preface (of course) contained his name, with an expression of thanks for gratuitous revising and editing. He promptly requested the publishers to remove his name from future editions, in accordance with the prohibition which the Warden had funked in May. He gave clear and severe reasons for not desiring association with a creature of the Warden's character. Messieurs Paddington, not being animated by spite or bad manners, at once gave proper assurances. This brought the woozy Warden to the fore, cringingly grieved. Crabbe demanded and received from him a humble apology for his incontinent helpmeet's use of the terms 'mendicant,' 'extortion,' 'blackmail,' as unjustified reproaches; and said good-bye to him; and circulated his apology; and sat down to wait for the next ebullition.

He didn't tell Butler all details of his doings, not having assured himself yet that that connection would improve with close acquaintance. They were a comic family. What their past had been was an Oriental mystery. They brimmed with Egyptian tales of the very weirdest kind; and the things which the wife didn't know of Ismail Pasha's harem, poisoned coffee, and other Eastern amenities, were not worth knowing. Husband and wife were always writing letters to Egyptian princesses, exhibiting the addressed envelopes, and telling disconnected tales about the addresses. The wife never by any chance went out of doors, excepting once or twice at night to visit (and borrow money from) mysterious relations at Santa-zustina and Palazzo Stampalia Zuerini. But she was always gravely happy, occupied with her cigarettes and incessant housework; and her cooking was miraculous. Her husband was a problem. Beginning each day as an apparition in a covert-coat and fat hairy legs, chanting 'Lin-der gimme glass o' wine', he spent it in wandering about, making pals of all the active artists he could catch, or in admiring the Modern Art at Palazzo Pesaro, or in being rowed hither and thither by Crabbe to paint or to find paintable points. He was an easy dog. His favourite station was the point by the Doganale where the Istrian firewood-barks lie; here he made sketches day after day—sketches of some merit and a little promise; —and he used to declaim, in the evenings, as to how he would finish them, as to the instantly-saleable pictures which he would make of them. Crabbe kept a rigid pair of expressionless eyes shot out at him, heard him, thought him comical, and wrapped himself up in letters and verses.

The resident aliens got up and coughed in defence of their Warden, rushing about the city enlarging on the vindictiveness of Crabbe. "Among the bushes they brayed, and under the nettles they were gathered together." Pots always do call the kettle smutty. Such was their mental twist that their conception of le mot juste was to call Crabbe 'vindictive.' Their poor friend, said some, had perhaps been indiscreet in not opening the letter which forbade him to use Crabbe's name; but an indiscretion didn't deserve personal description to one's publishers. The punishment was too great for the crime. But others—of the infirmary class—hit back. Mactavish cut him and the painter on the canal of Zuecca. Crabbe's preliminary condition of service, that he was not to be thanked or acknowledged in any way, was disregarded. The infirmary issued its annual report, naming Mr Crabbe as the donor of one oar. He shrieked with laughter, and set to pinching. What's a mere breach of faith to a pair of scorned women? Foolishness, o most affable reader, this counter-stroke of La Pash and the bibbling directress, most certainly was. But foolishness can do quite as much harm as knavery; and is equally devoid of excuse or justification. After all, wherein does your fool really differ from my knave in capability of evil-doing? The voice of the snake and the voice of the goose are one and the same—both hiss. Don't they? Very well, then.

He formally addressed the bibbler, La Pash the honorary secretary, Mactavish the treasurer, with a Portingall Jew (chiefly probosis and trousers) and a farmer too tired to do any more in life, who composed the obsequious committee. He complained that the report breached his preliminary condition of service, and was an infringement of an author's trade-mark, viz. his name; and he suggested imitation of the publishers' courteous action regarding the Warden's book. The directress incontinently bibbled that she'd only made courteous acknowledgment. Crabbe replied that acknowledgments of every kind had been prohibited from the very first, and that to gibbet him—him—as the giver of a single oar was a suppression of truth and a suggestion of falsehood which was rather more than he could stand. The farmer and the treasurer said that the report had been issued without their knowledge. The Jew boomed 'Avaunt' with several solemn pompous inexactitudes. And the honorary secretary held her tongue, and pen. Very good. The infirmary hit him on the Warden's behalf: he would return the blow straight, with interest. Chi xemina spine no vadi descalzo.

He informed Messieurs Paddington that their Warden's behaviour was continuing to annoy him, and necessitated reprinting of the whole preface with elision of his name, and insertion of such reprint in all unsold copies of *Social Life of the Early Gnostics*. This, of course, was most exacerbating, not to say costly, to the author: publishers can't be expected to pay for their hack's idiotic pusillanimity

—if the Warden really hadn't the courage to open and read the prohibition of May. Then the infirmary people tore madly round and round, shaking aprons and beating knees, piteously bibble-babbling that that dreadful Mr Crabbe was trying to pick quarrels with everybody in revenge for having been courteously requested to discontinue the scandal of his too frequent visits to the nurses. The directress suggested an anonymous letter in reference to Crabbe's misfortunes; alleging (as justification) that Venice was a great place for anonymous letters. As for Crabbe, he simply published his letter to Messieurs Paddington, giving precise reasons for shaking off the dust of his feet at the author of *Social Life of the Early Gnostics*; and there he left the woozy Warden to welter.

There didn't seem anything particular to be done to La Pash's hobby. Crabbe wasn't such a diorthotic beast as to wage war willingly on women, witless or wicked. When they became obstreperous, all he did was just firmly to bunt and hustle them back again behind their proper lattices; though he fancied a smack in the face, on faces poked into improper positions, to be rather meritorious than otherwise. Convalescents of the infirmary, whom he had served, sometimes wrote to him. As there were none whose acquaintance he cared to retain, he replied that he wasn't on terms with the infirmary, that details were obtainable not from him but from it, and that choice must be made between it and him. That generally sufficed to suffocate: when it didn't, when weak fools suggested the pact (between comfort and cowardice) which, under the delusion of expediency, is called compromise (and is far worse than death)—he freely used the opportunity of giving the infirmary a character (fairly concise and exhaustive in details) which made Erastian Venice look like an epic hero caught suddenly with his epithet off. What is Akhates without his "faithful"? What even Odysseus, without his "long-enduring much-contriving"? The fact is—and his uncurbed reckless ruthless proclamation of blind and naked and very shocking truth proves it—he had only just reached that stage of enlightenment (which your motor-maniac reaches in a week) when he understood and realized the wickedness as well as the futility of applying the brake against the power. It was said that Crabbe's power was invective. It wasn't really: but lazy people found it easier to think so. He actually had only spat out the gag of his tormentors and was giving God's law of gravitation a chance. Fact is more frightful than fiction—candour than caricature. And, after all, o most affable reader, was he following any less noble example than the Scriptural example of Samson, betrayed, a prisoner, execrated, decorticated, using the remnant of his force to bury himself in the ruins of Philistines?

Butler's cheque didn't arrive to date. Other things did, though. First, there came the certainty that this man never did anything. He said Lin-der gimme glass o' wine in the morning, and went out to paint after saying Lin-der gimme cigarette. He dropped into pubs. He returned to lunch, saying Lin-der gimme glass o' wine; and went out to paint again, after saying Lin-der gimme cigarette. He returned at dusk, and parroted in intervals of eating till he went to bed. But he never finished anything. His sketches remained dauby. One day, Crabbe's curiosity took him to Palazzo Pesaro to see what excited this man's unbounded admiration—a collection of eccentric young artists' mistakes of the large for the great, of the weird for the wonderful, of wildness for wisdom, of the How for the What, of technique for type. Butler was striving to imitate these. 'Here's another Physidoyl, another born slave afraid of original thinking, able only to ape instead of using his gifts and striking out a line of his own,' Crabbe said sickly to himself. But the second thing to arrive was even more upsetting—hungry creditors arrived from Naples, aware of the quarterly remittance, and prepared to sit gossiping on the door-step to anticipate a share of it. This news reached Crabbe in the shape of a scribbled screech from his patron. "Urgent—I wish to consult you about gross breach of confidence on the part of my agents who have given my address to a Person— please come down."

The baby of seven brought this billet to Crabbe, who was writing in his garret, the day being wet. He found an altogether new Butler sitting on a table saying Lin-der gimme glass o' wine, with meek but immovable creditors camped around him. His wife, graver than any judge, looked from the kitchen: she had the noble unspeaking air of a Niobe. The baby, frightened to death, darted hither and thither, squinting appallingly. Crabbe was wanted to draw up a severe letter to Cook's head office denouncing the Venice manager for breach of confidence. 'Nonsense,' he said: 'they take in letters for you; and naturally they'll give your address to anyone who asks for it, unless you've fishily given them a prohibition. Why not attend to the more immediate matter?' Up the stair and into the apartment tore a tornado—the Venetian landlord and his wife. Neapolitan nosing in the neighbourhood had done its work. 'O Dio mio, Di-o mi-o,' squalled the new-comers: 'pay me rent—I want a necklace for the Assumption—pay my furniture bill—how shall I live—oh pay my money!' 'Lin-der gimme cigarette,' was Butler's perspiring whimper. People's heads peered out of windows all round the courtyard. 'What are you going to do?' Crabbe stonily asked. They'd all been drawing the thing rather close; and there wasn't a penny in the show. 'God only knows,' whined the painter.

Crabbe inspected him; and saw what he had never seen before— an alcoolizato. Incessant sippings had undermined Butler: he was alcoholized, never drunk, but never quite sober—at ordinary times, calm, obtuse, insensible, because he was a thoroughly sodden and saturated sot. And, in a time of stress, he completely lost head, nerve, decency, everything which enables man to stand trial. It was very interesting.

Of course it was out of the question that Crabbe should desert these people now. He supposed that his own money—the L. 250 and other sums subscribed to the partnership—might be taken as gone for the present And he observed that the wife was in a state of pregnant petrifaction, as one who knew all and couldn't use her knowledge: while the man was simply incapable. His seemed the only head able to think, the only force capable of resolute action; and he noticed also that his bald imperturbability and the quick grim tone of his English interrogation of their debtor had some- what calmed the observant Italians. So, without moving a muscle, he plainly asked the painter when his allowance really was coming.

'Do you, too, doubt my bona-fides? O my God!'

'Don't be silly. Of course I don't. But, tell me straight how much is coming, and when; and I'll make up some sort of a tale to pitch at these people.'

Sheaves of shoved papers answered him. They looked all right— past letters, of regular dates, from a London solicitor, advising enclosure of quarterly allowance of L. 800. And an instalment was due that very day.

'Siori e siore,' he said to the creditors, 'your presence is an un- warrantable intrusion——'

'O oysters! O Christ God! O Maryvirgin! Why doesn't she pay his debts instead of smoking cigarettes all day?' the Venetian landlord's wife yelled, with an eye on the Niobe. The women's eyes flashed.

'Tasi!' snapped Crabbe. 'If this lady is going to be hysterical, ler het husband slap her. If she's tipsy, let's call the vizili.' He glared ferociously, and went on. 'Leave your bills on the table. Siore e siore. Deniers are due from England. They may come tonight, or they may come tomorrow. God, and the government-post, are responsible. And, when they come, you will have your share. Understand? Then, for gentility's sake, favour me with your absence, o timid little persons of excellent breeding!'

'As for you,' he said to the alcoolizato, when the place was clear, 'come out; and I'll row you round a bit to freshen you up.'

Niobe said nothing: her silence was clearer than words. The two men went downstairs together, the painter sweating and quaking fatly. Crabbe never knew why he hadn't detested the man's side-whiskers and air of a groom before. At the water-gate, where he began to put oar and forcola into the pupparin, Butler leaned against the wall and became a solemn and impressive injured party. 'Crabbe, old man,' he quivered, 'you've stood by me nobly, like a true pal. What I've suffered from that woman, God only knows. I ain't got much—what's thirty-two pound a quarter?—but thirty pound of that I give her regularly to keep us; and what she does with it I swear that I bloody well donò. Every quarter there's this same row; and it's enough to make a man cut his throat—damn, and blast, and——'

'Here! Hi! Whom are you talking about?' Crabbe roughly stumped him.

'That woman whom I was fool enough to marry——'

'Oh rot! Don't you try to come that sort of piffle over me. Just pull yourself together, and behave like a man. She's yours—you've got a perfect slave who keeps you admirably; and, if that thirty's all she has to do it on, she's a marvel. You just buck up, and stop tippling; and finish some pictures to sell,' Crabbe said, shoving under Ponte Anzolo and rowing past the palace of the Cardinal-Patriarch, under the Bridge of Sighs and out into the open.

He kept the poor thing in the fresh air, bullying him, bathing him in good advice, till he thought that he had stung the creature into a condition sufficiently plastic to be worked (in time) into some respectable shape. The other took it all, at first complaining that he was ill-used and misunderstood, then whimpering with an inter-position of filthy obscenity which brought his gondoliere down from the poop to chuck him overboard, then sulkily apologizing and rigescing into the deeply pained hauteur of a deserver denied sympathy. At which Crabbe took him home and left him for the night, intending to proceed with his cure in the morning. There

was a song being yelled all over Venice just then, which was purely
maddening:

Lai - de, la - i - de	por	—	ta	pa - zi — en - za e senti
Questi no xe mo — men	—	ti	d'a - bando-nor l'a — mor
O bando - na - to'l	pri	—	mo,	bando - ne - to'l se — condo
O bando - na - to'l	mon	—	do,	no mi ma - ri - to piú

The lagoon was the only place where its monotony did not bite
and smite the ear. Crabbe thought that he could preach with more
acceptance at a distance from these incessant admonitions to 'Adelaide.'

But matters moved otherwise. The cheque came by the morning's
mail; and Butler, calm, equable, with the exhausted but pardoning
air of the martyr who has passed through his rackings, nose-wringings,
and thumb-screwing with some distinction, made a stately progress
satisfying creditors. On the day following, he was delivered of a
reserved and dignified statement. After the scene made by his
landlord, he was for quitting that same day. He would go to an
apartment-agency at the Veneta Marina end of the city—would
Crabbe kindly take two lire for his grub and search the vicinity of
Sanstefano for a suitable apartment—they could meet where they
were, in the afternoon, to compare their findings. After luncheon,
when Crabbe returned, he found everything settled. The painter
had found an admirable furnished apartment for self and family
(with garden for the baby) on Via Garibaldi. They were moving
there at once. Crabbe would retain his garret, which was paid for
till the month-end: spend his days rowing the pupparin, as usual;
and take his meals with his patron in the Via Garibaldi. Meanwhile,
here were another two lire for grub; and his room was preferred to
his company, till 8 a.m.—at the new abode.

Crabbe brought the pupparin, at the hour appointed, from the
club to Veneta Marina at the far end of the Bacino di Sammarco,
and tied up in the Rio della Tana. Butler, half-shaved, half-lathered,
in shirt and calico trousers, sent his gondoliere for a tot of brandy—
he had been much upset; and things were in confusion; but he
would be better presently, and was really going to paint in earnest.
If Crabbe could have the decency to give a chap a chance, he—should
—see how mistaken his clearly-perceived judgments were. Things
were indeed in abnormal confusion. The apartment was a crimson
plush bedroom in a common noisy lodging-house with use of kitchen.

Gad, what a kitchen! And the 'garden' was a stagnant backyard about four metres by three. Happenings might be expected.

Crabbe took his patron and painting-gear on board at 9 o'clock, and rowed him about till 19 o'clock. They had a paper-bag of luncheon, two rolls and two hard eggs and a flask of wine. Butler dozed. No point of view seemed paintable to him. Crabbe rowed him across to Sanzorzi Mazzore: thence to the fishing-barks and baskets in Rio del Pontejungo on Spinalonga: up and down all the little canals of that island, as far as the piroga beyond Sacca Sambiazo: thence across the lagoon between the harbour of Marittima and the mainland, right under the two-mile viaduct which carries the railway and past the public slaughter-house at the end of Cannarezo: in and out of the long parallel canals of Sanzerolamo and Senza and Santalvise to find the House of the Camel: round the open lagoon on the north, by the jealously-guarded American garden and the Sacca della Misericordia: all along the Fondamente Nuove and the Arsenal: twice round the islet of Olivolo (whose church was the cathedral of Venice till only a century ago), with its lovely campanile, and its most picturesque fishing fleet at anchor: through the Canale di Santelena and along the front of the Public Gardens, to the pub of the Belgedere by the pontoon of Veneta Marina—the whole circuit of the city, with several considerable indentations. The tide was adversely strong on the last stretch; and Crabbe didn't refuse a proffered glass of wine. His tympanum and temper had been tried all day by the ungracious discontent and flatulent somnolence of his excessively inferior passenger. He held the bark, by muscular force, at the water-gate of the pub. while his patron entered. It was hard work, for the evening was windy and the water here is always agitated by the steam-ferries at the near pontoon. Besides, he was tired, as well as bored. A glass of thin white wine was handed down to him.

'I'll just run into the house, and see if dinner's ready,' said his patron.

'Look sharp, then, for I'm starving,' Crabbe answered: 'but it isn't safe for me to leave the bark unguarded here, so I'll just row round into the Rio della Tana. Come and fetch me when you're ready. The water's not so rough there; and I can shelter under the bridge, as it's going to rain.'

He waited one hour, till it was nearly dark. No one came. It began to rain, just after sunset. As he had no lamp, he rowed as fast as he could against wind and current to chain the bark at the club for the night; and walked back to Via Garibaldi for his grub, furious at neglect, and faint with hunger and the long day's operose toil. The dirty house was dark, though it was only 21½ o'clock. Butler staggered down, in night-shirt and trousers, fuddled to the miserable stage. 'Allo,' he wheezed: 'we put your dinner out, but you didn't come; and then I forgot. This windy day's made me dam drowsy.' He led the way into the dark kitchen, which Crabbe had but glanced at in the morning. 'There you are,' he added. 'I expect it's cold by now.'

Crabbe struck a match and looked round. The kitchen was about three metres square and unspeakably more obscene than an English sty. On the table was a plate of coagulate risotto undergoing the attentions of a cloud of blue-bottles and mosquitoes. In the corner was the water-closet of the house. 'Is that common to all the lodgers?' he asked.

'Of course.'

'Is this my dinner? You expect me to eat this flyblown muck in this filthy hole?'

'Oh, well——'

'You're going to lose your gondoliere, my dear; but first I'll take the pleasure of expressing my opinion of you.'

'Here! I don't want any lip——'

'You're going to have hands, not lip.' Crabbe plastered a double-handful of the glutinous rice, firmly and prolongedly, over the sot's face, stuffing up his mouth and eyes and nose and ears, and rubbing the clammy mass well into his hair and whiskerettes. Then he smashed the plate on the sputtering head. 'I think you'll do nicely so; and you can go to the devil and your own way,' he quietly concluded.

He strolled back to the club, and cancelled his nomination of Butler for membership. 'I needn't give you a formal reason,' he said to the secretary, 'but I can tell you privately that I've discovered the man to be a lazy-bones, chased by creditors—he's had L. 300 odd of me—and never quite sober. For my part, I've done with him.'

Every bone must be smashed till it spurts out ikhor and marrow: every artery gush with the blood and the life.

XXV

NICHOLAS wondered when the gods would have done with sending him such detestable samples, mocking his desire and impeding his pursuit of alliance. He didn't go one centimetre out of his way to seek them. They flopped on him, or barged up against him; and he was afraid to refuse the job of testing them. Cowardice of that refusing kind he abominated. No one knew how he outraged his tastes and senses and ambitions over these testings: but they seemed to be his duty, and he did it. This last experiment, however, brimmed his chalice of endurance. He never would touch any of his past subjects any more, unless they voluntarily came and began at once with a full and spontaneous apology for their stupidity. That was all he wanted: but he insisted on it. And he would contract no new relations, unless one came and began with a business-like proposition for putting him in working order. He believed these conditions to be sufficiently prohibitive. 'So much the better,' he told God: 'I'm sick of this life, which is just one damned thing after another.'

There was a week of his tenure of the garret in the Calle del Anzolo yet to run. He spent most of it in bed, storing up a good provision of sleep against the time when he might want it. As for food—qui dort dine—he kept the forty centesimi, which remained in his pocket, for some desperate emergency. But, of course, on the sixth day, a matter of four guineas came from his secret sowing: so that he was able to leave the Alley of the Angel, fed, and with a bold carriage deceptive to all observers. This money—his last— he set out to economize. Life in the pupparin was clearly indicated for the two remaining summer months. Only alone, on the lagoon, could he avoid fighting with beasts. Only on the lagoon could sun and sea keep him in life: little there was really needed for eating and drinking when one took one's time about it; and cash could be spun out; and there would be peace for really poetic work.

Life on the lagoon was good for his soul as well. It crystallized determination: it sifted out the urgencies of desires. Little by little his system of meditation by incantation renewed its efficacy, carrying him once more to the heights where the spirit breathes in Conspectu. The festival of Marymas in August filled him with joy. There was an Armenian Mass in Saint Mark's. The byzantine Madonna of Nikopoieia was exposed at the high altar, on an antependium and dossal of gold brocade veiling the Pala d'Oro. The extreme dignity of the bearded celebrant in a high-collared cope of filmy tissue, and of the two Armenian children who served him, made a deep impression upon Crabbe: here was catholicity untainted by influences of the nonsensical modern fetish of uniformity. He treated himself to a regular debauch of religious observances that day, going from church to church between dawn and noon. At Sansalvador, high over the great silver altar, he found the very latest modern ideal of Mary Virgin, a glorified handmaiden, humbly and pathetically and triumphantly emerging from a background all of shadowy gold with distance in it, coming from a distant world of gold, crowned with a most marvellous nimbus of electricity, through an archway of ivory, down into this world of a myriad stars on a forest of tapers. In every church, The Lord's Table was spread with snowy napery—not the skimpy Erastian communion-rail, where your ingenious inquisitor may always find crumbs of the broken bread beneath the exiguous kneeling-mat: but row after row of generous boards in concentric semicircles extending half-way down the churches, where whole parishes could (and did) make communion simultaneously. When Nicholas, victor of people, perceived the uncountable crowds, of males of all ages and ranks communicating from 5 to 8 o'clock, of females from 8 o'clock to noon, he understood why polemical acatholic swashbucklers, like the lying prophet of Ca' Struan, fought against fact, sinned against light, by alleging that Italy has lost Her faith—that, of Her thirty millions, not more than two ever cross a church's threshold, and those only of lowest intelligence and simply contemptible position in society. They snored—these controversialists, who were so jolly fond of shouting "Nunc dii tanquan mures" with the author of the *Satyricon*—they stertorously snored in their feather-beds—while Italy worshipped the Bright and Morning Star! He roared. The wild cats which they saw were nothing but the lice on their own eyelids. The nests, teeming with bad eggs, which they made such a devil of a fuss about, were only the productions of their own bat nightmares. He reared. No one is so blind as the blind leaders of the blind, who shut their eyes to all which it doesn't pay them (in pelf or preferment or polite society) to see. And his ire arose when he remembered sanctimonious Pecksniffs, "forgers of lies and physicians of no value," who parade in private houses, with earsplitting screeches, or brag and conviction of sin, "covering their faces with fatness and making collops of fat on their flanks," and practise all the time a skin-deep sentimentality (with a careless cynical cruelty reaching down to the core) which invents devices of every conceivable kind for keeping alive the unfit and insane who wanted to die, while according only neglect and insult to the fit and the sane who want to live—which maintained hospitals for the incapable and hopeless, and refused to the capable and ambitious even bread. Questo xe un mestier che guadagna. It's a trade which pays, nowadays. But yet, "Sol omnibus lucet. Luna innumerabilis comitata sideribus etiam feras ducit ad pabulum—The sun shines on all: the moon, accompanied by innumerable constellations, leads even wild beasts to their provender." Even wild beasts!—Here his rage sent him rushing away to his open lair on the Canale Fasiol, where he was safe from the bestialities of entirely estimable Erastians.

About the middle of the last month of summer, he found to his horror that his physical fitness was diminishing. He had been into the city to buy his weekly provision of seven rolls, costing twenty-three centesimi: for he had got himself down to the dull and strait diet of one hard roll a day. And, just out of the defiant devilry which invariably stiffened him when his back was against the wall, he must needs row up and down Canalazzo, with the aspect of one merely taking pleasure of his leisure. At the great curve of the canal by the Rio di Ca' Foscari, he was caught between two steam-boats: there is always a disconcerting wash set up by these nuisances, specially at that point where the swirlings of cross-currents also have to be considered. He was sufficiently master of his mystery to preserve his poise on the lofty poop, easing the long light bark with dexterous oar as it jumped with sounding slaps from billow to billow; and passengers on the steamers looked with amusement at the Englishman's grim insuperability amid perturbations which made Venetians bellow for Mariavergine. All was happening as usual, and Crabbe was holding his own, when (from behind him) came swooping two motor-launches—the heavy omnibus of a Lido hotel, and the vicious cigar-shaped racer of Palazzo Contarini, adding their waves to the wash of the Vaporetti. An instant of vertigo took him; and, to save himself from cascading into the canal, he stepped down. It was the kind of thing which every gondoliere has to do occasionally: but that was the very reason why the action of leaving the poop for the floor of the bark upset Crabbe's equanimity. He had lost confidence in his physique; and, for the sake of appearances, he ceased to risk himself publicly where

difficulties were likely to occur. In fact, he confined his rowing
hereafter to the daily journey between the club (where he shewed
himself, while Zildo polished the pupparin) and the canals of Fasiol
and Scoazze on the lagoon south of Spinalonga.

By the first week of October, not only his nerve but his strength
had waned to such an extent that he gave up his life on the water.
The pupparin was not actually his own; and he no longer felt
secure about returning it in decent condition to the club. Its bottom
was weed-clogged after the summer's warmth of water; and it was
very much heavier to row, as Zildo repeatedly warned him. He
had no objection to being found dead in a club bark: but no one
should find his gift to the club damaged, or oar-robbed, with him
moribund on the floor of it.

He made out a duplicate list of the four hundred and sixty-one
bridges of the city; and instructed his servant. 'Listen, Zildo,'
he said. 'You are to understand, o toso mio, that I now know all
the waterways of Venice. And it becomes necessary for my writing
that I should affright myself to study the streets. Sa?'

'Mi lo so ben.'

Nicholas looked sharply at him. Was there a second intention
in that lovely unruffleable voice? How much knowledge was there,
actually, in the brain behind those translucent innocent ignorant
wistful eyes? 'What do you know so well?' he demanded.

'That my Paròn knows the rii, and wants to study the alleys.'

'Va benòn. Take, then, this list of bridges. See, I have its companion. Tomorrow, at 8 o'clock, you will bring the pupparin to
the first bridge. Wait there five minutes. If you see me, I shall
give you certain commandments. If not, take the pupparin to your
house. At 16 o'clock, bring the pupparin to the second bridge.
Wait there five minutes. If you see me, I shall give you certain
commandments. If not, take the pupparin to the Bucintoro; and
chain it for the night. You have your key: I have mine. I can
take the bark if I want it: you can take it at the hours appointed.
Have you understood?'

'Go ben capiò, Sior.'

'And, on the next day, you will go to the next two bridges at
the same hours, observing the same rules. And, on the day after,
to the next two. And so on, till the list is exhausted. And, remember,
when I desire service I shall speak: but, when I am silent, favour
me with a touch of tranquillity for my studies.'

'Sìssior—con permesso, one little word of my own. Sior, be
pleased to consider certain things. I am a faithful servant, and

I speak only of the well-being of the pupparin—though I could, and I would, speak of other——'

'And what about the pupparin?'

'This, Sior. The Bucintoro moorings are at the entrance of Rio Palazzo Reale. Within one stroke of an oar is the open Basin of Saint Mark. Within two—three—strokes is the steamboat pontoon of Calle Vallaresco. Autumn is here. There will occur winds, storms, and always the wash of those quintuply accursed and ill-created steamboats. Va ben. Also, the pali of the Bucintoro are rotten, badly fixed with rusty wire to broken nails in a rotting wall. Wherefore I demand whether my Paron would not rather command his pupparin to be chained, at night, under his faithful servant's eye, at my house in Rio Santrovaso?'

'Benissimo. Moor at your pali at night. In the morning, after you have visited the bridge, moor at the Bucintoro for the day. But tell the barcariol of the club that I still reserve the bark: otherwise members may seize it for their diversions——'

'Nòssior. They shall not. That is my affair. And, regarding other matters——'

'Basta, basta: go caplo.'

'Sìssior.'

It remained to manœuvre a private life on land. He spent much time on the islet of Santelena—or rather on the new islet, the grass-clad Field of Mars used for football and military drill, which has been built on the lagoon mud between the islet of Santelena and the Public Gardens. The adding of fresh islets to the hundred and eighteen which compose Venice goes on slowly though surely. Recent mud-banks are staked off with double rows of massive wooden piles well rammed down: the space between is filled with concrete, and a stone wall built on the sea-face: the enclosed mud-bank is then pumped dry, and filled with rubbish stamped to a certain degree of solidity. In course of time houses spring up for the increasing population, which necessitates fresh pile-driving as foundations for the walls. But the Campo di Marte has not yet reached this stage: it is only a huge uneven plot of rough grass raised about a metre and a half above high-water mark so far. Crabbe very much wanted to get on the actual island of Santelena. The modern iron-foundry there, which was made of the old church and monastery, seems to have failed financially; and the place is deserted, but for a caretaker. But the bridge, which connects it with the new Campo de Marte, is gated; and attempts to pass, with or without permission, might have aroused undesirable curiosity. The life of the homeless half-starving man, whose one aim is to evade attention, is a very singular one in Venice. Venice, serenely walled-in by her lagoon, is not a city where Lazarus can hide his sores without the exercise of masterly and continuous ingenuity. Refuges there are, such as the Asili dei Senza Tetto: but he had no use for them. To apply for shelter at any of the Asylums for the Without-Roofs would be to accept charity, which was out of the question; and, further, it would have proclaimed his nationality and procured his instant deportation beyond the frontier under military escort, foreigners not being permitted to be homeless and starving in Italy. It pleased him to remember that he was not the first, however. There is a dreadful little shrine under a dilapidated archway leading into an incredibly squalid alley in the parish of Santaponal, which has this inscription on its lintel, in the mixture of miscellaneously spelled Latin and Italian which was the mode in Venice seven hundred and thirty-three years ago:

Alexander the Third, Supreme Pontiff, flying from the armies of Frederick the Emperor, coming to Venice, here reposed the first night; and then conceded a perpetual plenary indulgence to whoever shall say The Lord's Prayer and the Angelic Salutation in this place. Let it not be heavy for thee to say Hail Mother. The year 1177. And by the charity of the devout it is lighted day and night as is seen.[1]

The disguised Pope, uncertain whether the Serene Republic of Venice was His friend or His enemy, and having the splendid magnificent character of His predecessor Pope Hadrian the Fourth (Nicholas Breakspeare the Englishman) fresh in His memory, took service as scullion the next day at the abbey of La Carità (now the Academy), where He worked unknown and unknowing during six months, until recognized by the French ambassador to the Serene Republic. Then came the Serene Prince the Doge, with the Greater Council and the patricians, to escort God's Vicegerent here on earth to set His foot on the neck of the conquered and penitent German Emperor Frederick Redbeard, offering homage on the spot marked by the slab of porphyry in the porch of the basilica of Saint Mark.

Many many times, Nicholas Crabbe said Pater and Ave on this historic site. It was in his mind, also, to have slept there in the place which was good enough for Pope Alexander the Third. But

[1] ALESSANDRO TERZO SOMMO PONTEFICE FVGIENDO L'ARMI DI FEDRICO VENENDO AVENETIA QVI RIPOSSO LA PRIMA NOTTE ET POI CONCESSE IN-DVGIENZA PERRPETVA IN QVESTO LOCCHO DICENDO VN PATER NOSTER ET VNA AVE MARIA TBI NON SIT GRAVE DICERE MATER AVE LANO MCLXXVII ET CON LA CARITA DI DEVOTI SILVMINA GIORNO E NOTE COME SI VEDE.

the shrine has been left to decay: the lamp shines no longer by day or by night, though the mark of its heat can still be plainly seen; and the arch is the entrance to a section of a densely populated slum of indescribable squalor. He said the prayers prescribed for gaining the plenary indulgence. So much I know. As to his vow to restore archway and shrine and court to pristine dignity on reaching a happy issue out of all his affliction, I shall have important things to say in a subsequent volume.

Crabbe began his last wanderings by walking and walking (with one of his leathern satchels slung on his shoulder and a sketch-book in his hand) about the new Campo di Marte, till there was no nook or recess or inequality of its sea-wall unknown to him: he tested them all by daylight, day after day, apparently jotting down sketches of skies and clouds above the wide lagoon for the benefit of chance observers, but really sampling their qualities of wind- or rain-shelter for use as a couch at night. This was his main retreat. It was the loneliest place accessible to him. And, because of its value, he used it only in cases of necessity when rain made the quays a sodden horror, or when he felt that he must either sleep or rave. Most of the time he spent in the streets. From the moment when the churches opened at dawn, he heard Mass after Mass, the roof of God's House being his for three—five—hours each day. Often he strolled about the harbour of Marittima, watching loading and un-loading, and the long line of lusty grain-sack-laden dancers daintily dancing lithely barefoot down long planks from ship to shore. This excited him: he knew himself capable of carrying those sacks on his shoulders, but doubted the steadiness of his head for the passage along swaying planks slight as slack-wire—a slip, a failure, would have attracted notice to an English curiously circumstanced, which was above all to be meticulously avoided. The last stretch of the Fondamente Nuove also was a favourite haunt of his. The wide quay ends abruptly on the Sacca della Misericordia, that great square bay of the northern lagoon where the floats of timber are stored. There is no cross-alley within thirty metres of the quay-end. Those thirty metres are almost always empty: no one howls the horrible ditty here about 'Adelaide': the view of the cemetery-island, and the Island-City of Murano, and all the lagoon to the mainland twenty miles away and to the ridge of the Alps seventy miles away, is broken only by the outjutting ghost-haunted Casa dei Spiriti which an American artist uses for a studio and occasional lugubrious carnivals. Here, and in similar seclusions, he dawdled by day, waiting for fruits of his sure but secret sowing, or (of course) for

that which he never ceased to hope for in the depth of his heart—
the repentance of those who had wronged and robbed him, Morlaix
and Sartor, Bobugo, Caliban. Work for a living? Try to get a
job? No. He could not dig: he would not beg: six months'
exposure and starvation had brought him low: and was it likely
that for a mere matter of keeping himself in life he should consult
the convenience of Erastians? He mocked the bare idea. 'Where
is the injustice if I, or anyone who feels himself superior to another,
refuse to be on a level with him?' he said, in the words of splendid
Alkibiades. Beside, he had worked, he had done far more than
his share of work, and he confidently left the fruition of it to The
Authorities. 'Vi dicho in uerita che il cillicio risplendera chome il
solle, he ogni pidochio che per ammore di dio hauera lomo sopportato
si conuertira in margarita,' according to the Mahommedan Gospel
of Saint Barnabus.

At dusk, he began brisk walking through populous alleys.

One night, about 22 o'clock, he met the white-faced Arthur
snatching a stroll on the Academy Bridge. The waiter was solicitous,
sympathetic, had wondered what had happened, would know (if
he might) what Mr Crabbe was doing—where he lived now. 'Nowhere,' said Crabbe, so utterly uninterestedly that he wasn't taken
at the foot of the letter. Arthur understood that privacy was desired,
and shewed himself as the courteous and most worthy gentleman
which Nature made him. He had drawn his lot for military service
in the following year, most likely in the cavalry.

Crabbe had a comical experience at Treponti, so called (I suppose)
because there are not three bridges, but six. He had been walking
all night, and found himself in that neighbourhood at dawn. A
couple of individuals were sleeping on the steps of the second bridge,
one here, one there. As Crabbe came near, the first (who looked
like a stone-cutter) woke, with limbs benumbed—enlarged his
frame with a crocodile's yawn, rubbed his eyes and brow, and
exclaimed to himself, 'Xelo 'no pisolo che go fato! (I've been
having a good nap!)' Then he felt for his watch, a pure-blooded
Roskopf worth two francs ninety-five centesimi—but, alas, it was
absent. 'I say, you, Nigger,' he cried to the other individual, who
had distanced himself a few steps farther up the bridge, 'you gimme
my watch!' (There's only one word in the Venetian dialect for
'watch' and 'clock'—'el relozo' (i.e. ''l orologio') which simply
means 'time-teller.') 'Time-teller?' said the other napper, sleepily;
'why don't you go and look at Saint Mark's?' 'Nonò: I mean my
time-teller which you've stolen.' The other became wide-awake

at this charge. 'Either you joke, or you want me to go and see the time for you.' The hard-hearted stone-cutter seized him by the head. 'For my part, I arrest you.' Said: done. He called two guards, and made them conduct the unknown to the police-barracks of Malcanton—'On my responsibility,' he said. 'Va ben,' subjoined the guards: 'but, meanwhile, be pleased to come in also you.' And they conducted the accuser with the accused. By great good luck, Crabbe happened to know these guards; and his interrogating lift of eyebrows obtained permission to follow. The time-teller wasn't found; the individual indicated as the author of a theft proved his innocence, and was let go. 'And now I will go away also me,' said the stone-cutter, making a bow. 'Softly, softly,' the guards replied; 'but first let's see if your watch isn't still in your pocket.' The stone-cutter was looked through. No time-teller was there. And a sickle-shaped knife, such as one uses for massacres, was. 'But, for this little plaything, dear Fair Male, we can no more let you go away,' said the guards. And the stone-cutter was declared under arrest, and denounced for carrying a weapon of violence. Crabbe was pleased and tickled at this incident, lightening the end of a long miserable night. The clear thinking, the plain speaking, the perfect politeness, pleased his sense of decency. And, as he wet his parched lips at the fountain by the Carmini, the memory of the naïve and picturesque diction, and the farcical character of the whole business, made him smile. He never, at any time (thank Heaven), let go of his sense of humour.

On a wet Thursday afternoon, on the Fondamenta Rosmarin, a group of lads were waiting for the gymnasium of the Palestra Marziale to open its doors as Crabbe passed. One detached himself with a respectful salutation. It was Beltramio, the Ghezzo, much taller, slim, with small round head and blue-black hair and eyes. And how was the Signor Inglese, whom he had failed to meet all the summer? Very well? He himself had gone into commerce, to earn a few lire weekly for the pocket, as clerk to De Paoli the carriers on the Riva del Carbon. If he did well there, his uncle (a merchant of leather at Sancancian) was going to take him into the business at Christmas. He looked at Crabbe again. Had the Signor Inglese been ill? He did not carry the fierce svelte air of those days of the Beneficenza-joke? Crabbe instantly felt rather bored: the lad was going to be a nuisance. 'I find myself ruined, and without a single friend,' he said, with the intention of throttling further intimacies. 'Nonòssignore,' replied the Ghezzo; 'you gave me a ring, and I swore to be your friend for Always. Permit me to offer you a cigarette.' Crabbe took the little offering kindly, and said farewell as the gymnasium doors opened. This was his last taste of tobacco.

After two nights on the open shore of the Lido, where a mere hour's rest on the sand soaked him with frost—thick white frost— and so stiffened him that he could have cried like a baby with the fearful aching, he noticed that his shabby clothes were notably conspicuous from exposure to rain and sun: specially his cap had changed colour from indigo to the odious violet worn by knights of the Order of Sanctissima Sophia. His visits to the club had been fewer and shorter: but now he knew that he must relinquish them altogether. Shabbiness might pass: but clothes obviously rotting might not be exhibited by England to young Venice. He went to the Bucintoro at mid-morning, when no one was there, and substituted the greenish-grey boat-cloak of Harris Mixture for the blue one which he had been carrying; it would not shew stains so easily. He put his Wilkinson razors and some washing-gear with a towel into his largest pigskin satchel; and filled it up with manuscripts. Then he put all his other belongings into his locker and snapped the padlock for good and all. If fortune turned, he could come back for them. He promised himself employment for the next fine day, sitting on the grass of the sea-wall of the Campo di Marte, sorting his papers—the incomplete manuscript of *Toward Aristocracy*, his draft-letter book, diary, and all the letters received since his return from Calabria—keeping only those which accounted for and described his agony, for me, for the Quæstor or for the Giudice Istruttore of Venice—letters of Bobugo and Caliban, of Warden and Wardendom.

Among the last he made an appalling discovery.

He was carefully reading the letters bibbled at him by the infirmary-directress during the months of his almost daily service of bark and two strong and intelligent barcaiuoli, himself and Zildo. These scrawls chiefly consisted of orders for errands, or appointments to give detailed instructions for particular or difficult or diplomatic jobs. But he found one in which this sentence occurred: "In generous sympathy and practical help you are a larger subscriber to the infirmary than anyone else has ever been."

This made him think violently. These were the very words with which (as coming from La Pash) she used to torment him. And what was it which the Wardens had reported also, as being La Pash's opinion: "wants us to ask you to consent to let her put you on the infirmary-committee, because she says you're the only Englishman who has ever been of any real practical service to it." Curious coincidence!

And then he found, in another letter from the directress—written in one of her absences (even then she needs must bibble)—a flash of blinding light—"I owe you boundless debts of gratitude for all you do for the infirmary. I am always hearing of your kind deeds; and your constant interest in it means so much. Nobody, except Lady Pash, has ever taken any real or helpful interest in the infirmary before. So glad you're coming on the committee—'tis going to energize a publisher into sending a thousand sterling on account immediately for *De Burgh's Delusion*."

It was worse than a stab in the eye to him—this revelation. It set him physically sick and retching. What an innumerable multitude of sorts of a fool he had been! Contempt and nausea for the woman always had made him habitually skip the complimentary parts of her excited and illegible scribbles, and confine his attention solely to her beastly business. And here, here, was the very key to the mystery, which he had sought at such awful cost—the mystery of why he was chased, nor ever left (as he had asked) alone—the mystery of the Warden's "we" and "us" who yearned to be friendly, who would settle all difficulties within a week, upon condition. ("So glad you're coming on the committee——") Alfred Albemarle (the artist-brother of James Albemarle the publisher), who married a niece of La Pash, actually was La Pash's guest. Crabbe had met him with Lord Hippis at Mactavish's ("—'tis going to energize a publisher into sending a thousand sterlings on account immediately for *De Burgh's Delusion*"). Is it necessary for me to dot another i, to cross another t, o most affable reader? I will be as flat-footed as a butler. Crabbe was invited—wheedled—commanded—intimidated—attempted to be forced (the word is not mine) by the toad-eating Warden and Wardendom to swallow his "Leave me alone" addressed to La Pash on Twelfth Night by joining her infirmary-committee of her creatures and henchmen, as satisfaction to "spretæ inuria formæ." La Pash had "never been refused by anyone before"—"she was never so snubbed in her life"—"She won't take no for an answer." Invitation, wheedling, command, force, bribe—she, a sanctimonious Tarnowska of Erastianism, could attract and suggestionize minions to work her will—and to wreak her revenge. Terrible is the Female.

But, she had failed, she had failed, she had failed.

Nononò! His instincts had never led him astray. He praised The Lord, Who had kept his feet out of the snare: Who mercifully had let him keep his hands clean.   Spero cis moriar, at mortuus non erubescam.

What should be done with such evil ones?   They were past everything but praying.   He, indeed, had prayed every day, "Libera nos a malo."   And he still would pray, every day, "Deliver me from evil."

When that the victim of spite has all but accomplished his passion, life he has given must give him love's balm for his wounds.

XXVI

No fruit came from his sowing. Nothing was left in him, or of him, but an unconquerable capacity for endurance till sweet white Death should have leave to touch him, with an insuperable determination to keep his crisis from the hideous eyes of all men. Terrible as was his bodily emaciation, languid as was his mind, aching and stiff and feeble as were his weary weary limbs, he contrived to preserve his leisured imperscrutable carriage, and to present to the world a face offensive, disdainful, slightly sardonic, utterly unapproachable. The short pipe, which he always sported, was long empty but not (as he believed) noticeably empty; and it added that tinge of casual insolence which freed him from suspicion of dying fast of privation and exposure.

He went, every evening, to the sermon and benediction at the church of the Gesuati on the Zattere: first, to pay the prodigious debt of the present to the past—the duty of love and piety to the dead; and, second, for the sake of an hour in quiet sheltered obscurity. The grand palladian temple, prepared for the Month of the Dead, draped in silver and black, with its forest of slim soaring tapers crowned with primrose stars in mid-air half-way up the vault, and the huge glittering constellation aloft in the apse where God in His Sacrament was enthroned, replenished his beauty-worshipping soul with peace and bliss. The patter of the preacher passed him unheard. His wordless prayer, for eternal rest in the meanest crevice of purgatory, poured forth unceasingly with the prayers of the dark crowd kneeling with him in the dimness below.

On the Day of All Saints he strolled carelessly (one would have said) —he successfully accomplished the giddy feat of not staggering (if one must speak accurately)—across the long wooden bridge of barks to the cemetery on the islet of Sammichele. It was a last pious pilgrimage, with the holy and wholesome thought of praying for the dead, that they (in turn) might pray for him who had none living to spit him a suffrage. The place was a garden. On all sides thronged the quick, to deck the graves of their dead with tapers and lamps and flowers. The place was a garden, hallowed by prayer, hallowed by human love. In the place where God deigned to mount upon The Cross, and to be crucified for love, also, there was a garden.

He slowly paced along cypress-avenues, between the graves of little children with blue or white standards and the graves of adults marked be more sombre memorials. All around him were patricians bringing sheaves of painted candles and gorgeous garlands of orchids and ever-lastings, or plebeians on their knees grubbing up weeds and tracing pathetic designs with cheap chrysanthemums and farthing night-lights. Here, were a baker's boy and a telegraph-messenger, repainting their father's grave-post with a tin of black and a bottle of gold. There, were half a dozen ribald venal dishonest licentious young gondo-lieri, quiet and alone on their wicked knees round the grave of a comrade. And there went Zildo, creeping swiftly somewhere, with an armful of dark red roses hiding his face. Nicholas turned away to the open gates of private chapels, revealing byzantine interiors, with gold-winged suns in turquoise vaults, over altars of porphyry and violet marble and alabaster inlaid with mother-o'-pearl in dull silver, and triptycks of hammered silver set with lapis lazuli and ivory, blazing with slender tapers, starred with lanthorns of beaten bronze, carpeted with dewy-fresh flowers. Even the loculi, the tombs in the cemetery-walls, each had its bordure of brilliant bloom with tapers to burn on the pavement before it. All the morning, masses were offered in the church of Saint Michael and in the chapel of Saint Christopher. From time to time a minor friar, in surplice and stole, went, with some black-robed family, to bless the new memorial on a recent grave.

He found himself in the field where Venice buries strangers, and looked for the grave of the engineer who died at the Universal Infirmary nine months before. He remembered its site, but it was unmarked, totally neglected, unrecognizable. Evidently the grave had not been bought in perpetuity; and the bones had gone (or would go) to the common ossuary, with none to care or make memorial. He went on, praying, and entered the columbarium. Here was the plain marble urn of an English baby, Lawrence, burned and forgotten. Here was the plain marble urn of that other Englishman who died at the Universal Infirmary in March: one had remembered him, then, with red roses and a card of love: but flowers fade, and love—Love can move the sun and the other stars. O loyal love! Zildo had not forgotten his father.

It was the eighth day since Nicholas had tasted any food at all. He had a bit of bread in his pocket—a half of one of those biscuit-like rings of the poor, hard as stone, which are so satiating. He had two lire and sixty centesimi also. But he could not eat. The last morsel had naus-eated him so cataclysmically. He had tried milk, but it had made him reel. Water, a handful of it, surreptitiously taken, at night, from the fountain in some campo, satisfied him now.

It was the eleventh day since he had caught a glimpse of Zildo's face, at the Ponte dei Pugni in Sambarnaba. He dared not submit to the scrutiny of those lovely wistful pellucid eyes, which, somehow, seemed to be beginning to know all things hidden since the world began. Of course he avoided Santrovaso by daylight; and, at night, when he walked swiftly by, closed window-shutters veiled the gleam of candles. He would have liked to have seen that wonderful exquisite dear child again. He would have liked many other indecorous things: but nothing could justify invasion or confusion of a young life like Zildo's. Never—never. Alone he had lived: he would at least pluck up enough sense of propriety to do his dying by himself. He sauntered on.

Late at night he came to the gated bridge of the islet of Santelena. The torrential rain of Sunday had not made his favourite nook impracticable; and, though his long-soaked clothes clung heavily and stickily to him, he rather glowed than felt their chill. But Sleep had deserted him; for five days and nights he had been wide-awake. Oh that the suave twin-brothers might come very soon—first, kind Sleep—then, gentle Death.

But, "Not my will——"

And, "Though He slay me, yet I will trust in Him: but I will maintain mine own ways before Him."

Stars spangled the blackness of heaven. Over the distant lagoon the Bear prowled away from the Lido, and Orion the Huntsman rushed across the sky between the islands of Burano and Santerasmo. Later, the waning moon made shift to rise. The deadly cold and damp struck and unnerved him. 'God, do give me a home,' he sighed, shivering, too stiff to move without crying, all night long.

At $5\frac{1}{2}$ o'clock the black horizon beyond the Lido channel seemed to develop a monstrous interminable blacker wall, with a paler black light behind it, which shewed above it. At $6\frac{1}{2}$ o'clock an orange-coloured stripe unrolled itself along the base of the wall which shimmered in deepest greys; and a pink sun peered out of the sea with a certain air of urgency. Another day in this world! Surely he had untied all the strings which bound him here? Had he? Had he? No: not quite all.

He rose, moving delicately to ease his stiffness, till he felt fit and able to ramble, in freedom from remark, on an errand which his angel-guardian indicated for him. Something more seemed to be expected from him. "Nothing in my hand I bring," but his hand was not yet empty.

Once more he went toward the cemetery. In Campo Sanzancristomo he bought an armful of white crysanthemums and a handful of white rose-buds with his last coins. Let the forgotten Dead remember him, as he remembered them. Let them.

There were many people, also bearing flowers: but not the close-packed mob of yesterday. This was the Day of the Dead. Later, all Venice would throng the bridge of barks. He must do his errand swiftly.

In the columbarium he placed rose-buds at the urn containing the ashes of the unremembered baby, and a nosegay in place of the faded roses at the urn of the Englishman. No one was about, yet. He went to the forgotten grave of the engineer, and marked out a great white cross of chrysanthemums on the level grass. And he prayed long for the repose of their Protestant souls, that they also might pray for him in his great loneliness. Even now he was alone, faint, yet pursuing.

From those secluded enclosures he went into the crowded church of Saint Michael Archangel and Soul-Weigher, to hear a mass and commemorate his own dear dead whose remains lay far away. In those ancestral memories, fragrant, most beloved, he offered what merit there was in his remembrance of forgotten dead whom (in life) he had never even seen. Thence he travelled to the chapel of Saint Christopher Giant and God-bearer. The Cardinal-Patriarch was saying mass, a gentle courtly white-haired elder, with the delicate hands and ordered manner of reticent but pregnant gesture and utterance of the hierarchy. Nicholas prayed near the door till the prelate emerged to the open to bless and absolve all those whose remains awaited resurrection in the earth around him. The grey and orange of dawn had lightened, and a clear sky of pink and silver and pale violet shot with paler gold hung like a canopy above.

To escape the observation (and exhalation) of the mob he returned to the city, now nearly deserted, and wandered all day through quieter alleys between the Ghetto and Santalvise in the sexter of Cannarezo. A brace of sandy-haired black-shawled wenches gave him a scratch of annoyance by glancing from his boots to his face and back to his boots, as he paced the long quay of La Senza near the Abbey of Pity. They grinned. He wondered how haggard he really was. His boots, he knew, were purely frightful. But how ghastly was unintelligent note and criticism. He thanked God for that crowning mercy which is called blind night.

By dusk he had strayed southward over the station-bridge into Santacroxe and Sampolo. The magnificent bells, and the splendid sweetly-rolling diapason of the organ, in the huge dim church of the Frari, enormously revived him at an early Benediction. He rested there awhile, after, between the shades of Titian and Canova, till intonation of the Vespers of The Dead began. Then, on again— he must not fail to finish his sequence of nine-days' prayer at the church of the Gesuati.

The sermon was nearly over when he entered. A great white hearse reared its pyramid aloft (crowned with a winged orb) in the middle of the crowded fane, where an army of lance-like tapers sprang fearlessly trustful to the height tipped as with auspicious stars. Great was the company of mourners softly illumined below. The voice of the friar in the pulpit ceased. Gentle sad hopeful music poured from the loft, the insisting patience of violins, the throb of 'cellos, the resolute concord of organs, weaving intricate networks of harmony round the faithful voices of men chanting the dirge. Then, the silent asperging and censing of the mighty bier, and the last prayer for all the dead, "Requiem aeternam dona eis, Domine; et lux perpetua luceat eis."

Eternal rest. . . . Everlasting light. . . . It was dark. Where should he find rest? He could not get to Santelena now. There was no way but through the most flaring and crowded parts of the city, and the glances of a mob would send him raving mad. He ought to have economized his forces, to get there before he became so dead-tired—tired, but not yet dead. The time was here when he would cry God mercy—man, never—Kyrie eleèson.

When they closed the church he went up the Zattere, as far as the gated bridge of the Doganale over Rio della Salute. He rested here by the wood-store, pretending to admire the view across the Canal of Zuecca. But no one approached. Venice itself was tired, and refrained from dissipation on the night of the Day of The Dead. He crept down the dark little alley by Ca' Struan, and crossed the bridge to the great quay and stairs of the Salute. Just by the bridge, the empty bark of old Bastian Vianello was moored to its pali, littered and dirty with the fragments of faggots. He wondered whether the firewood merchant would let him sleep there. No. There were darker nooks high up on the steps of the church.

After an hour or so he moved back, through the Rio Terrà dei dei Catecumeni, where Ottoman infidels used to be confined till they knew their catechism. One of his old gondolieri kennelled here, a bluff plausible faithless little dog. The wide long stretch of the Zattere invited him. He hesitated; and presently went toward Marittima, very slowly, and with frequent pauses, for he seemed to have lost all sense of his limbs, and walked but automatically. Kyrie eleèson. At every post he stopped, to lean against it with the cultivated air of leisured pensive meditation which cost no effort, having been made habitual. Time tore on. Passers-by became fewer and very far between. He had whole sections of the quay entirely to himself. The last lights went out in the wine-shop by the ferry-pontoons. Sometimes he lost consciousness for several minutes. Kyrie eleèson, he murmured all the while.

He turned, apathetically, under the arcade at the corner of Rio di Santrovaso to take one more look at Zildo's window. All was dark.

An instantaneous coruscation burst in his brain, and something broke—breast—heart—Kyrie eleèson.

He found himself on his hands and knees on the pavement, with a sound of rushing water surging. He must move. He must move very far away from there, at once. It could not be a flood, for he remembered no sirocco. No: it was only a sudden squall— but how sudden, how violent! Kyrie eleèson. He picked himself up and tottered to the parapet of the quay for support, just while he satisfied himself as to the state of the tide in the canal.

Right beneath him was the pupparin, chained to its pali. The pupparin! The very thing! And his own key of its padlock was in his trousers-pocket. What luck! He would paddle it, with a floor-board, out on the great canal of Zuecca, and let the flood— for undoubtedly there was a terrible sudden flood—carry him where it would. If he could but get as far as the friendly solitary sea! Kyrie eleèson.

At last he was in the bark again. How the water roared in his ears! He must be very calm. Kyrie eleèson. Perhaps it would be as well to lie down, satchel for pillow, and rest—only for a few minutes. How very dark the night was! Or, had the wind blown out the lamps? Yes: he would lie down, and recollect a little strength before doing anything. Then he would fumble for the padlock; set the bark free. Kyrie eleèson.

This was not suicide. On the contrary, it was a precaution of safety. Moored barks were often swamped, or hung up on their own moorings and battered to bits, in storms like this. Whereas, if he let her go, nothing could upset her: she would ride bravely on any swell: and one could rest more securely in her than on inundated quays—and in perfect privacy too. Kyrie eleèson. Yes: he would count up to a hundred. Then he would take the key from his pocket, and count fifty. Then he would find the padlock, in this dense rocking din, and count another fifty—fifty Kyries, a hundred Kyries, counted on his fingers, understood. Then he would paddle under the bridge to the open. Kyrie eleèson.

He was lying on his back in the bark. Why? Where was she now?—The rushing and the rocking of the water in the dark. No one could see.—He had unlocked the chain? Had he? He couldn't remember. Kyrie eleèson.—The long strong booming of the wind in the dark. What did that matter? He was all alone.—Now it was imperatively necessary to be extremely artful. He must make quite sure about the bark. Kyrie eleèson.—Key—pocket . . . Hand . . . Where? . . . The crashing of great stormy streams in the dark. . . . Deus, in adiutorium meum intende. . . .

XXVII

THERE was a soft clear light flickering from somewhere behind him, by which he dimly could distinguish things not understood at all. There was a most delicious suggestion, all about him, of an odour of warmth and freshness and cleanliness and strength of life. There was the saltish tang of rich health on his tongue. He was lying, at mellow ease, in an immensity of comfortable peace, straight, his arms by his sides, something hard but loose under one hand, something flat and slightly crepitant under the other. He could feel himself, though he did not even try to move himself. And, somewhere very near, a gentle voice, low and potent and unspeakably pure, like the quiet vibrance of some distant bell, crooned little snatches of song, quaintly full of melody, with promising intonations and solemn meditations and long long luxuriantly-cadenced terminations, all so clear, all so dear, all so brimful of love:

> Sospira, cuor, che ragion tu ne hai
> Aver 'l amante e no vederlo mai:
>   el sospirar vien dal ben volere,
>   desiderar, e no poder avere.[1]

> Se quel che passa fusse 'l amor mio,
>   certo che a la finestra me traria
> so fosse un zovenoto che ma amasse,
>   dal caminar mi lo conossarìa.[2]

> In dove xestù stà che ti xe sta tanto,
>   o delicato fior del paradiso?
> dopo chei ti xe stà via go sempre pianto:
>   da la mia boca no s' ha visto 'n riso.
> Adesso che ti xe venìo io rido e canto,
>   me par che s' abbia verto el paradiso.[3]

[1] Sigh, heart, for thou hast cause, having thy love but never seeing him, Sighing comes from loving—from desiring what cannot be had.

[2] If this passer-by were my lover, surely I would drag myself to the window : if he were a youth who loves me, I should know him by his gait.

[3] Where hast thou been, that thou hast been so long, o gentle flower of paradise? Since thou hast been away, I have always wept: on my mouth not one smile has been seen. Now thou art come, I laugh and sing: for paradise has turned to me.

He opened his eyes again. A little way away, low and level at his arm's length, he could just distinguish the shape of a head, a fair bright head which was a cluster of waving hair, turned to him with the glitter of thoughtful eyes, marvellous eyes, in the soft dimness. He would have moved his shoulders a little, to lift himself up. A kind hand restrained him, and thrilled him. 'Sior, do a favour and stay firm,' said the tranquil wonderful voice of Zildo.

'Where am I?' he contrived to whisper.

'Excuse me. His Sioria is in his bed of his chamber of his little house at Santrovaso.'

The boy turned away, for an instant, to take something from near-by. Nicholas felt a warm young arm slide under his shoulders, raising him, and pillowing his head on a firm flexible breast. A little aluminium mug of something aromatic came to his lips.

'Sior, do the pleasure of sipping—wine, old, red, heated with an egg and a touch of sugar.'

He could discriminate three ambrosial fragrances—from the mug, from the sumptuous flesh, and another rich and most strange but fresh as the high sea. He perceived also that Zildo—a new Zildo again—wore a long blue linen house-smock, belted at the waist, with the sleeves rolled above glorious honey-hued shoulders. And, on the lower third of the muscular forearm, he observed a tightly-twisted handkerchief with a dark spot on it. 'I pray you,' he murmured, 'to make me know what has occurred to me?'

'Sior, with permission, you being dead in the bark, I brought you here—also your largest envelope of leather.'

'Did anyone see?'

'Nonòssiornò. But no. Only the Lord God and I the servant of both of you.'

'I wish to use my thoughts, please. But don't leave me.'

'Think, Sior, with confidence. I, your Zildo, stand always between you and all annoyance. And I will never leave you.'

His head was lowered, and the supporting arm gently withdrew. He seemed to be floating into heaven.

When he woke, Zildo again offered hot sweet wine and egg—a liquid red 'zabajon.' He sipped it deliberately, regaining strength every moment. After, he lay a little while, without moving though he felt that he could move, surmising, thinking.

'Sior, how do you feel yourself?' said Zildo, watching him.

'Better.'

He remained dozing. Then, 'How long have I been here?'

'Sior, it has sounded 5 o'clock of the morning; and I have had you during twenty-nine hours.'

He pondered that. Then, 'Why did you find me? Make me to know everything, I pray,' he said, at length.

'Sissior. And, in the first beginning, I demand pardon. For I have never left you—excepting during a certain six days—having sworn that I never would leave you. But, seeing that you wished to go alone—and so you commanded—I have followed you in such a fashion that neither you nor any other living has known it. I demand pardon for that. And specially I demand pardon for this—that when, on the other yesterday night, I saw you cascade from the wall into the pupparin, and—(with excuses—for well thou knowest, o Paron, that I would have thee live six hundred and seventy-eight years)—and die there, then, Sior my Paron, I butted myself after you; and fretted myself to bring the bark to the steps, quickly, most quickly; and carried you here, at least for respectable funerals——'

'You carried me up all these stairs?'

'Sior, you (with a million obsequiousnesses) are most meagre, most gracile, and (though long) of very small weight. Beside——'

'You carried me——'

'Sior, I demand pardon; but you, one time, carried me—farther than a mere matter of up these stairs.'

Nicholas was dumb. But, of course you always get back exactly what you give. How artistically accurate God's golden meteyard is!

'And next, Sior, because of a reason, I said that you should not be dead, any more than I was really dead when (having looked upon me) you took me from La Tasca. Else, why did you take me? Wherefore, having your locality ready, as it has been from the first beginning—behold, you are not dead, don't you know.'

As he lay listening, his fingers fiddled weakly with what lay under his hands in the bed. One he felt to be a sealed letter—he distinctly could feel the seal. The other two bothered him—flurried him—discs, in bags—money? His head began to whirl.

'Sior,' said the vigilant Zildo, 'I pray you to drink a thing which I shall give you, a little beverage of two mouthfuls, saying nothing; and then to repose yourself more fully.'

The boy disappeared, but returned in a few moments and offered a mug of broth, rich in flavour, rather salt, and very warm. The tang was familiar: it had been on his tongue when first he awakened. Its effect was like that of an elixir. Following it, Zildo gave another draught of the red zabajon.

'No,' Nicholas protested, afterward: 'I will not rest till you have finished speaking. You shall begin at the very beginning, tell all, and make an end. But, first, I will not remain in this bed.'

'Sior, command me. Your vestments are here, dried, clean, by the fireplace. The room is your own.'

'Favour me with your absence, I pray.'

'Va ben.'

'Now.'

'Sìssior.'

When the door was shut, Nicholas struggled out of bed and gazed about him.

So this was Zildo's nest—this clean warm fragrant room with low rafters shining in the firelight, and the gleaming furniture reflected in the polished floor. What neatness! What exquisite order! What thought!

The bed jutted out from the inner wall, with its head backed to windows and fireplace, so that all light reached him who reposed on it from behind, just as Nicholas had arranged his own bed at the Albergo Bellavista. On the shelf of the bed-foot was a crucifix and sprig of olive, a byzantine Virgin-Mother of Nikopoieia, the Seat of Wisdom, and a night-light in a clear glass. By the bedside was a cane table, with a clean handkerchief, his keys, his empty pipe and pouch, his letter-case, his locked satchel. Behind the bed-head, facing the fire, was a cane arm-chair. By the north wall was a wardrobe, the mirrored door of which stood a little open. Nicholas peeped in. It was empty, unused. By the south wall was a marble-topped chest of drawers, with jug and basin on a mat, a pair of new candles, new soap, clean towel. A square mirror looked down from the wall above it. There was a fire of logs burning cheerfully under the chimney; near it, a couple of fat-cheeked cooking-pots sat with their hats on to keep themselves warm. The shelf round the chimney-hood carried a small collection of aluminium pots and pans and plates and basins, which shone like silver. From rafter to rafter across the room, in front of the fire, a stout cord festooned itself. On it Nicholas found his clothes, dark-blue guernsey, serge trousers and jacket and cap, and the old greyish-green boat-cloak of Harris Mixture, no longer sodden and mud-stained, but cleaned and dried and neatly folded. He had had no socks or underclothes for five months. At the foot of the fireplace were his dreadful old boots, dry, shaped on crumpled newspapers. The walls were bare, and brown. The curtains and counterpane

were dark-blue linen, such as Zildo's smock was made of—the
regular sensible useful (and most amazingly artistic) yoked smock
of thirteenth-century pattern used by ordinary gondolieri for housework. The stone floor looked as though made of petrified sausage-
meat polished to the speckless brilliancy of a mirror. With the
exception of the cooking apparatus and the disordered bed and his
clothes, there was no sign that the room had ever been used; it
resembled a room prepared for one expected. Yes. Nicholas
wondered what had become of the oaken chests which had been
brought here from the topo in January: he had recognized most
of the other things.

When he had dressed himself, he went to open the door. Zildo
came in, with eyes of most lovely refulgence, bringing clean mugs
and spoons, washed and shining.

'Sior, you stand well?'

'Very well. I owe you much, my Zildo.'

'Sior, excuse me; it is I who pay my debt. You save me; I save
you. Now we are equal. Sa? And it remains—— But, Sior, you
esteem me? That contents me. And your chamber contents you?'

'Where, then, is your chamber?'

'By here, Sior; behold it there.'

The boy lightly led him along the corridor, past a lavabo with
towels and cloths and soap-dish and sand-sprinkler above its tap,
and into the back-room. Here were the two oaken chests, with
a couple of mattresses and blankets on them, arranged and used as
a bed. On the glassy floor was a blue cushion on a strip of blue
carpet, and a big shaded lamp brilliantly burning. Near it were
half a dozen newspapers heaped with beads and tools of bead-work,
with a few of the cheap books which young Venice reads: *The Errant
Hebrew, The Baker's Boy of Venice, The Evisceration of Ladies in Berlin,
Cialoch Olmes the Detective, The Duty to the Neighbour,* and some
numbers of the *Ricamo* and the *Disegnatore,* open at instructions
about needlework. But all most methodically arranged. A cord
crossed the room, carrying spare clothes folded on it. The window
was wide open, shewing heaven above Sanzorzi Mazore sown with
ever vigilant constellations.

Nicholas went humbly back, and sat in the chair before the fire.

Zildo brought fresh logs. 'Sior, with permission,' he said, per-
suasively, 'I will now declare the whole truth. For you shall well
understand, Sior, that when you did not speak to me at the bridges
for so long a time, then I could not help saying to myself, like this,
Zildo, that treasure, the Paron, is ill, and most unhappy, as thou has

observed during many months, and more so since the festival of
The Redeemer, being a prey of traitors of whom I say no more
than damn them with an irremovable anathema. Moreover, he
does not change his vestments; and they have become threadbare,
shabby, vile, and ugly, which grieves him much, because he loves
neat splendour. And, as for his beautiful white guernseys of English
wool, they are no more; for he wears always the guernsey of a
mariner, which (being of obscure tincture) no one can call clean or
dirty, unless one looks intensely to observe whether the neck is
newly washed and tight, or unwashed and stretched loose by neck
movements. And, furthermore, he never uses a match; and, as
for his pipe, one might wear one's thumb in it, neither burning nor
fouling the thumb-nail. Lastly, he does not enter shops, excepting
the shops of bakers, and most rarely. Where, then, can a Sior go,
without a change of clothes, without (as I believe) the price of a
Gazzettino in his pocket, very sick in his body, and very very sad
in his mind because of religious ruffians now damned? So, with
excuses on account of fidelity, Sior, I set myself to play the pietose
polizotto, being at the same time fearfully fearful lest the just and
proper prepotence of my Paron (who is very prepotent) should do
me some harm. Therefore, I said to myself, like this, Courage,
Zildo! And, Sior, I discovered that the pupparin was moved sometimes by night. For, one day, having had a special commandment
at the Bridge of the Honest Woman, to chain the bark at the Bucintoro, by there I chained it; but, in the morning, it was chained here.
And chaining it by here, always by commandment, four times I
have found it in the morning chained at the Bucintoro. Yet, of its
champion four-lever padlock, no one has the key, save me and my
Paron. I was disturbed. My heart made me a pain. See, Sior,
between what a type of Mark and what a type of Theodore I stood.
I am a faithful servant. My faith constringed me to make secret
observations, not for disobedience—nonò—but that I might not be
false to my oath to stand between my Paron and all trouble. And
how could I be leal to my oath to my Paron when I did not know
precisely what trouble troubled him? For, Sior, I understood that
very grave trouble was troubling you. I understand, also I, that you
were "fra un Marcogne un Todaro" of your own——'

'Have I given you permission to inquire about my troubles?'

'Nòssior. But the troubles of my Paron are mine—I wish to say
that his troubles must not be next to him, but next to me and on the
other side of me, according to the agreement——'

'Oh!'

'Sior! You esteem me?'

'Yes. Go on.'

'Sissior. Wherefore I did inquire. For there was not any commandment like this: It is prohibited to observe the Paron. I obeyed all existing commandments. Isn't it true? Every day I rowed the bark to the bridge and at the hour written on the list which you gave me, as you have seen. Isn't it true? I did not know what kind of studies carried you to those little bridges of those little canals, by here, by there, by everywhere: or why you rejected rowing for walking: or why you sometimes came, and sometimes came not, and (lately) never came near. I had a commandment. I obeyed it. It was too easy. But, after I had done my duty, polishing the pupparin on returning, then, Sior, I freely jetted myself about the city, coursing after you, so that I might be faithful to my oath. I would have spoken to you, to tell you: but I daren't.'

'Why?'

'Sior—with excuses—I was afraid that you would scold me prepotentially. And also, Sior, there were secrets, your secrets, not mine—no—ohime!—not mine——'

'What secrets?'

'Sior, you no longer lived at the Albergo Bellavista, for I watched the door all night from the tailor's window at the angle of the Spaderia; and you neither went in nor came out. And you no longer lived at Palazzo Corfù, for I watched all night from the angle of Calle Gambara; and you neither went in nor came out. And you no longer lived at the osteria by the Academy, for I watched all night from the little basin on Canalazzo behind the pontoon, sitting in the pupparin; and you neither went in nor came out. Then, you took the bark to row the fat painter with the calico trousers and the squinting girl-child. Then, you brought back the pupparin; and you no longer lived in the Celle del Anzolo, for I watched all night at the Trattoria of the Angel; and you neither went in nor came out. I didn't know why you left the Albergo Bellavista—why you lived a week by there, a week by there, a fifteen days elsewhere. It was your secret. I divined that, as I am telling you, you were a companion of those unhappy ones undergoing their death-agony between the Columns of the Piazzetta in antique times, poverty being your Column of Saint Mark, honour being your Column of Saint Theodore: but these were your secrets. And, Sior, it gave me such a pain when I continually lost you. But that also was your secret—not mine.'

Nicholas sat, still as stone, shading his eyes with his hand from the light of the fire. This lealty, this reverence, this affection, were more than he could confront.

Zildo watched him for a moment, then he quietly shifted a little behind the chair, relieving his master's tender face from the sting of anxious regard. 'Sior,' he set out to say, with most dulcet persuasion, 'do not sadden yourself any more. Misfortune is finished.'

'It is only just begun.'

'Nòssior. Nòssiornò. You are not alone now. We face it together.'

'Finish your story, I pray.'

'Sior, to serve you. And then, I demanded of myself whether any saint had been offended. I found none. I said then, like this, Let these blessed ones intervene, specially those of my Paron—it is an opportunity, and a duty—plainly it is for them to attend to it. As for myself, and for my own part, I went into the church of Santrovaso; and harangued my own saint most seriously——'

'Whom?'

'My saint, Sior.'

'Santermenegildo?'

'Sìssior.'

'What did you say to him?'

'Sir, with permission, that is my secret.'

'Excuse me.'

'But he told me quite plainly, breaking silence at last, what I must do to gain the response from my prayer. And I did it.'

'And then?'

'Sior, it is done.'

'What is done?'

'What Santermenegildo told me to do.'

'God bless this boy! What did he tell you to do?'

'Sior, don't you know what he told me to do?'

'No.'

Nicholas couldn't see Zildo's movements; but he heard a light step back, a quick approach to the bed, the disturbance of bed-clothes—then, silence.

Then, 'Nòssior: you do not know.'

'No: I do not know.'

Zildo came back to the dark side of the chair, a little behind it. 'Sior, he told me to do this,' said the tiniest thin thread of a whisper.

Something came into Nicholas's lap—a registered letter, which he tore open and looked at, but could not see—and two heavy little bags—o God—bags of money!

'What,' he cried terribly, 'is this?'

Zildo was trembling and deathly pale, and his voice quivered. 'Sior,' he said, 'the carpenter of the Bucintoro said to me the other yesterday, like this, Have you seen your Paron? Of course I lied to him instantly, saying, like this, that I always saw you. He said to me, like this, Here is a letter for that blessed of God your Paron which came this morning, meaning Monday, and I have signed the receipt of it. I said to him, like this, Give it to me and I shall carry it forthwith to the palace of my Paron whom even the good marangon of the Bucintoro loves. Which I have now done and you have your letter, Sior. Moreover' (he licked his lovely lips), 'Sior, for love of God—at least pity me—know, Sior,—this—also,—that the large bag is my portion of a hundred and twenty-three gold sterling, which, having made a little voyage by train last week to Calabria, all in secret, I took from Santermenegildo himself, who had guarded it for me in that hollow olive-tree in the olivet of La Tasca, now a wilderness. And the small bag, Sior, is my economies of sixty-nine sterling and half a sterling, which I have collected in this way— thirty-six sterling gained from the making of bead-collars for my young-lady American, and nineteen sterling and half a sterling economized from the weekly deniers of Sior Caloprin, and fourteen sterling economized from the monthly deniers of the same, Sior, with permission.'

When Zildo began to speak, Nicholas sank a little forward in his chair; and his glance fell on the letter and enclosure in his hand. The light of the fire glared upon it. As the exquisite voice went quivering on, at first hesitant, then with bravest nudity—that wistful persuasive voice which would have won a favour from the prince of the archangels—the sense of the written words stamped itself, simultaneously with the spoken words, upon his understanding:

". . . given our most careful consideration—manuscript romance entitled *Sebastian Archer*—good enough to let us see—unanimous advice of our readers—privilege of issuing at an early date—endeavour to meet your wishes—suggest a Royalty Agreement for 22½ per cent. up to 10,000 copies and 25 per cent. thereafter—further inquire— certain manuscripts—formerly offered—are still—think it desirable to issue them in conjunction with *Sebastian Archer*—consider the same terms—success—issuing four or even five works from the same brain together—transfer to us the right of republishing *Peter*

of England and *Don Superbo*—not seem to have met with the enter-
prizing handling which they merit; and we could guarantee—forward duplicate forms of Agreement for your—beg to enclose cheque
—Coutts—Seven Hundred Guineas (£735 stg.) in advance of—
obedient humble servants, Ferrer Senior and Company."

Nicholas violently snatched his wits and his strength. All mists,
all paralysis, all doubt and hesitation, went as by magic from his
mind. 'L'amor xe fato per chi lo sa fare.' Love is for him who
knows how to make it.

'O my dear Zildo,' he said, without looking round with his
streaming eyes, 'you have been more than faithful. And I am much
more than grateful. I can never thank you enough—but I am going
to try. First, though, you must keep your deniers. I do not want
them. This letter——'

There was the sudden quiet thud of a collapse by the side of the
bed.

Nicholas bounded up.

The faithful one was beginning to swoon.

Nicholas brought him round to the firelight. His magnificent
left arm was bleeding dreadfully, soaking the twisted handkerchief.
In an instant Nicholas had the linen off and tourniqueted with a
seized spoon above the elbow. He laid the boy flat, and burst
open the window-shutters to let in the air of pearly dawn. Then he
looked about for wine.

What were those two nasty little punctures. They were not
fresh. Who would stab Zildo?

'Servo suo,' said the boy, stirring to sit up.

'Who stabbed your arm?' Nicholas demanded.

'Sior, it is nothing.'

A perfectly atrocious thought flashed.

Zildo was on his feet, staggering, and trying not to sob hopelessly.

Nicholas seized him in his arms. 'With what did you stab your
arm?' he said, using the prepotent tone of which Zildo seemed to
be so hideously afraid.

'Scusi, Sior, scissors; but indeed it is nothing.'

'You gave me your blood?'

'You were dead, Sior.'

'Oh my dear, my dear, my dear, I have been hunting for you
all my life.'

'Sior?'

'Gilda!'

She looked straight into his eyes. What she saw sent her right arm shyly round him.

'Oh, you Primitive! Oh, you Mediæval! How I have wanted you! But why did you?' he asked her.

'It was yours.'

'Then you are me, and I am you.'

'Sìssior. My beloved is mine and I am his.'

'When did you know that?'

'Sior, when but as soon as I knew that you had seen me.'

'At La Tasca? You dear delight!'

'Sìssior.'

'Nòssiora. Niccolo, I pray.'

'Nikè!'

'O Victory!'

Lips clung to lips, and eyes looked into eyes, long. Breast pressed breast and heart beat unto heart. Halves, which had found each other, were joined and dissolved in each other as one.

'Mio, why Victory?'

'Have I not won Mia?'

'And those people, who are already damned?'

'We will attend to them together.'

'Mio—excuse me—you will not hide again?'

'How can I hide from Mia?'

She laughed. 'I shall help. For I also know some things of certain brutal individuals——'

He closed her lips.

'Tell me, Gilda, what was your secret about Santermenegildo?'

'This.'

'What?'

'Give all, gain all.'

'Oh my goodness! What time is it? Where's my cap? Light me downstairs. There's a doctor at the corner of the rio. And then I'm going to see the parroco.'

'Sior, command me. Nikè, excuse me——'

'Little she-urchin! What new crime——?'

'The parroco knows. He was here yesterday. I brought him when I had fear. He is a good priest, antique, sage, discreet; and I insigned him with all secrets. Of course he scolded me—such notions—me—but he patted my head. And—he has settled with the municipality—also. If—if you desire—we can go to him now. Vuol? Vuol? The doctor afterward. Vuol?

'Do I desire? Lord! Scolded you—oh, let us go! Let us go!'

She rolled her smock-sleeves down carefully over the spoon.
'Aspetta momento.'

A moment—whence did she snatch the miraculous shawl to cover
her fair bright head.

'Pronti!'

So the Desire and Pursuit of the Whole was crowned and rewarded
by Love.